ECOSYSTEM SERVICES A POVERTY ALLEVIATION

Understanding how to sustain the services that ecosystems provide in support of human wellbeing is an active and growing research area. This book provides a state-of-the-art review of current thinking on the links between ecosystem services and poverty alleviation. In part it showcases the key findings of the Ecosystem Services for Poverty Alleviation (ESPA) programme, which has funded over 120 research projects in more than 50 countries since 2010. ESPA's goal is to ensure that ecosystems are being sustainably managed in a way that contributes to poverty alleviation as well as to inclusive and sustainable growth. As governments across the world map how they will achieve the 17 ambitious Sustainable Development Goals, most of which have poverty alleviation, wellbeing and sustainable environmental management at their heart, ESPA's findings have never been more timely and relevant.

The book synthesises the headline messages and compelling evidence to address the questions at the heart of ecosystems and wellbeing research. The authors, all leading specialists, address the evolving framings and contexts for the work; review the impacts of ongoing drivers of change; present new ways to achieve sustainable wellbeing, equity, diversity and resilience; and evaluate the potential contributions from conservation projects, payment schemes and novel governance approaches across scales from local to national and international.

The cross-cutting, thematic chapters challenge conventional wisdom in some areas, and validate new methods and approaches for sustainable development in others. The book will provide a rich and important reference source for advanced students, researchers and policy-makers in ecology, environmental studies, ecological economics and sustainable development.

Kate Schreckenberg is a Reader in Development Geography at King's College London, UK and Director of the Ecosystem Services for Poverty Alleviation (ESPA) programme. Her research focuses on equity in natural resource governance.

Georgina Mace is Professor of Biodiversity and Ecosystems and Director of the Centre for Biodiversity and Environment Research, University College London, UK and scientific adviser to the ESPA research programme. Her research focuses on the causes and consequence of biodiversity loss and ecosystem change.

Mahesh Poudyal is a Postdoctoral Fellow at the Ecosystem Services for Poverty Alleviation (ESPA) Programme Directorate. He is an environmental social scientist with research focusing on the poverty–environment nexus.

Routledge Studies in Ecosystem Services

Ecosystem Services and Poverty Alleviation

Trade-offs and Governance

Edited by Kate Schreckenberg, Georgina Mace and Mahesh Poudyal

ECOSYSTEM SERVICES AND POVERTY ALLEVIATION

Trade-offs and Governance

Edited by
Kate Schreckenberg,
Georgina Mace and
Mahesh Poudyal

LONDON AND NEW YORK

First published 2018
by Routledge
2 Park Square, Milton Park, Abingdon, Oxon OX14 4RN

and by Routledge
711 Third Avenue, New York, NY 10017

Routledge is an imprint of the Taylor & Francis Group, an informa business

© 2018 selection and editorial matter, Kate Schreckenberg, Georgina Mace and Mahesh Poudyal; individual chapters, the contributors

The right of Kate Schreckenberg, Georgina Mace and Mahesh Poudyal to be identified as the authors of the editorial material, and of the authors for their individual chapters, has been asserted in accordance with sections 77 and 78 of the Copyright, Designs and Patents Act 1988.

The Open Access version of this book, available at www.taylorfrancis.com, has been made available under a Creative Commons Attribution-Non Commercial-No Derivatives 3.0 license.

Trademark notice: Product or corporate names may be trademarks or registered trademarks, and are used only for identification and explanation without intent to infringe.

British Library Cataloguing-in-Publication Data
A catalogue record for this book is available from the British Library

Library of Congress Cataloging-in-Publication Data
A catalog record for this book has been requested

ISBN: 978-1-138-58083-1 (hbk)
ISBN: 978-1-138-58084-8 (pbk)
ISBN: 978-0-429-50709-0 (ebk)

Typeset in Bembo and Stone Sans
by Florence Production Ltd, Stoodleigh, Devon, UK

'This document has been produced by the Ecosystem Services for Poverty Alleviation (ESPA) Programme. ESPA is a programme funded by the Department for International Development (DFID), Economic and Social Research Council (ESRC) and Natural Environment Research Council (NERC). The ESPA Directorate is hosted by Research into Results Limited, a wholly-owned subsidiary company of the University of Edinburgh, responsible for the delivery of research and project management services in the area of international development. The views expressed here are those of the authors and do not necessarily represent those of the ESPA programme, Research into Results, The University of Edinburgh, other partners in the ESPA Directorate, NERC, ESRC or DFID.'

CONTENTS

Contributors   *x*
Preface   *xvii*
Acknowledgements   *xxiii*
List of acronyms and abbreviations   *xxv*

PART I
Evolving framings and contexts   1

1 Seeing the wood for the trees: exploring the evolution of frameworks of ecosystem services for human wellbeing   3
 Unai Pascual and Caroline Howe

2 Justice and equity: emerging research and policy approaches to address ecosystem service trade-offs   22
 Neil Dawson, Brendan Coolsaet and Adrian Martin

3 Social-ecological systems approaches: revealing and navigating the complex trade-offs of sustainable development   39
 Belinda Reyers and Odirilwe Selomane

4 Limits and thresholds: setting global, local and regional safe operating spaces   55
 John Dearing

PART II
Ongoing and rapid system changes   75

5   Interactions of migration and population dynamics with ecosystem services   77
W Neil Adger and Matt Fortnam

6   Land use intensification: the promise of sustainability and the reality of trade-offs   94
Adrian Martin, Brendan Coolsaet, Esteve Corbera, Neil Dawson, Janet Fisher, Phil Franks, Ole Mertz, Unai Pascual, Laura Vang Rasmussen and Casey Ryan

7   Ecosystem services and poverty alleviation in urbanising contexts   111
Fiona Marshall, Jonathan Dolley, Ramila Bisht, Ritu Priya, Linda Waldman, Priyanie Amerasinghe and Pritpal Randhawa

8   Reciprocal commitments for addressing forest–water relationships   126
Lana Whittaker, Eszter K Kovacs and Bhaskar Vira

9   Restoration of ecosystems and ecosystem services   142
Alison Cameron

PART III
Improving governance   157

10   Governing for ecosystem health and human wellbeing   159
Fiona Nunan, Mary Menton, Constance McDermott and Kate Schreckenberg

11   Co-generating knowledge on ecosystem services and the role of new technologies   174
Wouter Buytaert, Boris F Ochoa-Tocachi, David M Hannah, Julian Clark and Art Dewulf

12   PES: payments for ecosystem services and poverty alleviation?   189
Mary Menton and Aoife Bennett

13	Scaling-up conditional transfers for environmental protection and poverty alleviation *Ina Porras and Nigel Asquith*	204
14	Social impacts of protected areas: exploring evidence of trade-offs and synergies *Emily Woodhouse, Claire Bedelian, Neil Dawson and Paul Barnes*	222

PART IV
Achieving sustainable wellbeing — 241

15	Multiple dimensions of wellbeing in practice *Sarah Coulthard, J Allister McGregor and Carole White*	243
16	Gender and ecosystem services: a blind spot *Katrina Brown and Matt Fortnam*	257
17	Resilience and wellbeing for sustainability *Lucy Szaboova, Katrina Brown, Tomas Chaigneau, Sarah Coulthard, Tim M Daw and Thomas James*	273
18	Insights for sustainable small-scale fisheries *Daniela Diz and Elisa Morgera*	288

PART V
Concluding thoughts — 303

19	Ecosystem services for human wellbeing: trade-offs and governance *Georgina Mace, Kate Schreckenberg and Mahesh Poudyal*	305

Index — 317

CONTRIBUTORS

W Neil Adger is Professor of Human Geography at the University of Exeter, with research focusing on environmental change, ecosystem services, health and demographic and social dynamics.

Priyanie Amerasinghe is a Senior Researcher at the International Water Management Institute, Colombo, Sri Lanka. Her research focuses on environmental and human health, natural resources utilisation by marginalised communities, multi-sector governance and policy formulation.

Nigel Asquith is Director of Strategy and Policy at Fundación Natura Bolivia, where he helped design the Andean Watershared programme. He was Principal Investigator on two ESPA projects that assessed the feasibility of using Randomised Controlled Trial methodologies for evaluating the socioeconomic and environmental impacts of conservation interventions.

Paul Barnes is a PhD student in the Anthropology Department at University College London and the Institute of Zoology at the Zoological Society London. His research focuses on relationships between people and nature and the political ecology of conservation in Southeast Asia and Melanesia.

Steve Bass is Senior Associate at the International Institute for Environment and Development (IIED). He researches sustainable development policy and institution-building. He served as Chair of ESPA's Programme Executive Board throughout the programme.

Claire Bedelian is a Postdoctoral Research Associate in the Anthropology Department at University College London. Her research investigates the links between conservation and human wellbeing, with a focus on conservation and development interventions and pastoral livelihoods in East Africa.

Aoife Bennett is a doctoral candidate at the School of Geography, University of Oxford. Her research focuses on the political ecology of deforestation and oil palm in the Peruvian Amazon.

Ramila Bisht is Professor and Chairperson at the Centre for Social Medicine & Community Health (CSMCH), Jawaharlal Nehru University, New Delhi. Her research covers issues related to health disparities, women's health, environment and health, and health policy and administration.

Katrina Brown is Professor of Social Science at University of Exeter in the UK, and works on interdisciplinary analysis of environmental and social change.

Wouter Buytaert is a Reader in Hydrology and Water Resources at Imperial College London. His research focuses on the interface between hydrological process understanding, water resources management and sustainable development.

Alison Cameron is a Lecturer in Conservation at Bangor University in the UK, specialising in spatio-temporal modelling and optimisation algorithms for conservation planning, and is now adapting her experience to reforestation planning.

Tomas Chaigneau is a Lecturer at the University of Exeter, and is interested in coastal resource management and the relationship between ecosystem services and wellbeing.

Julian Clark is an Associate Professor in the School of Geography, Earth and Environmental Sciences at the University of Birmingham. A political geographer, his research focuses on natural resource governance, the governance of emerging technologies and the spatialities of the state.

Brendan Coolsaet is an Assistant Professor of environment and development at Lille Catholic University (France) and a Senior Research Associate at the University of East Anglia (UK). He works on environmental justice, biodiversity governance and food politics.

Esteve Corbera is a Senior Researcher at the Institute of Environmental Science and Technology, Universitat Autònoma de Barcelona, interested in the effects of land-use climate change mitigation policies on rural livelihoods, institutions and people's behaviour.

Sarah Coulthard is a Senior Lecturer at Northumbria University, and focuses on natural resource governance, social responses to environmental change and the relationship between poverty alleviation and conservation agendas.

Tim M Daw is a Researcher at the Stockholm Resilience Centre, and studies interconnections between people and coastal ecosystems.

Neil Dawson is a Research Fellow at the Universities of East Anglia and Aberdeen, and Steering Committee Member of the IUCN Commission on Economic, Environmental and Social Policy. His research explores poverty, wellbeing and environmental justice from the often-overlooked perspective of rural inhabitants in developing countries.

John Dearing is Professor in Physical Geography at the University of Southampton, and has researched the dynamics of social-ecological systems for over 20 years, specialising in reconstructing complex biophysical responses to human activities.

Art Dewulf is an Associate Professor at the Public Administration and Policy group at Wageningen University. He studies complex problems of natural resource governance, with a focus on interactive processes of sense making and decision making in water and climate governance.

Daniela Diz is a Research Fellow in international environmental law at the University of Strathclyde, Law School, and works on international processes related to marine biodiversity and fisheries.

Jonathan Dolley is a Research Fellow at the Science Policy Research Unity (SPRU), University of Sussex. He researches the links between urban development policy, peri-urban food systems and potential transformations towards sustainable urbanisation in rapidly urbanising countries.

Yvonne Erasmus is a Senior Researcher and specialist in evidence-informed decision making and evidence synthesis at the University of Johannesburg's Africa Centre for Evidence, with a broad research interest spanning the social sciences.

Janet Fisher is a Chancellor's Fellow in environmental social science at Edinburgh University (GeoSciences), and is interested in the links between conservation, climate change and human livelihoods and wellbeing.

Matt Fortnam is a Research Fellow at the University of Exeter, specialising in resilience, ecosystem services and development.

Phil Franks is a Senior Researcher at the International Institute for Environment and Development, with expertise on the social dimension of natural resource management and conservation.

David M Hannah is Professor of Hydrology and UNESCO Chair in Water Sciences at the University of Birmingham, UK. His research focuses on hydroclimatological processes, climate and river flow regimes and river energy budget and thermal dynamics.

Caroline Howe is a Lecturer in Ecosystem Science at Imperial College London. She was a member of the ESPA Directorate and is a Contributing Author to the IPBES Global Assessment on Biodiversity and Ecosystem Services.

Thomas James is a Research Fellow, and Impact and Partnership Development Manager at the University of Exeter. His work focuses on resilience, transformation and learning.

Eszter K Kovacs is a Postdoctoral Research Associate in the Department of Geography, University of Cambridge and a Research Fellow at Corvinus University of Budapest. She has been engaged with ESPA research in the Himalayas since 2014, and will hold a Leverhulme Early Career Research Fellowship at Cambridge from 2018.

Laurenz Langer is an Evidence Synthesis Specialist at the University of Johannesburg's Africa Centre for Evidence, and works on supporting national government decision makers to integrate evidence from research synthesis in the formulation and design of public policies and programmes.

Georgina Mace is Professor of Biodiversity and Ecosystems and Director of the Centre for Biodiversity and Environment Research, University College London, UK. Her research focuses on the causes and consequence of biodiversity loss and ecosystem change.

Fiona Marshall is Professor of Environment and Development at the Science Policy Research Unit (SPRU), University of Sussex. She undertakes trans-disciplinary research on environmental change and food systems; science and technology policy; the water–energy–food environment nexus; and sustainable urban development in the Global South.

Adrian Martin is Professor of Environment and Development in the School of International Development, University of East Anglia, and Director of the Global Environmental Justice research group.

Constance McDermott is a Senior Fellow and Leader of the Ecosystem Governance Group at the Environmental Change Institute, University of Oxford. Her research covers the multi-scale governance of natural resources and land use change.

J Allister McGregor holds a chair in political economy at Sheffield University.

Mary Menton is a Research Fellow at the International Development Department, University of Birmingham and co-founder of SEED, a partnership that focuses on the evidence-base for policies and practices that empower local people and balance conservation and development objectives. Her research focuses on governance, livelihoods and rights in the Amazon.

Ole Mertz is Professor of Human Geography and head of the Section for Geography, Department of Geosciences and Natural Resource Management, University of Copenhagen.

Elisa Morgera is Professor of Global Environmental Law and Co-director of Strathclyde Centre for Environmental Law and Governance (SCELG). Her research focuses on the intersection of biodiversity conservation, human rights and integrated ocean management.

Fiona Nunan is a Senior Lecturer in Environment and Development and Head of the International Development Department at the University of Birmingham. Her research is concerned with renewable natural resource governance and livelihoods in developing countries, particularly related to inland fisheries and coastal ecosystems.

Boris F Ochoa-Tocachi holds a President's PhD Scholarship at Imperial College London. His research focuses on participatory approaches to hydrological monitoring to support sustainable development.

Unai Pascual is Ikerbasque Research Professor at the Basque Centre for Climate Change (BC3). He is elected member of the IPBES Multidisciplinary Expert Panel 2015–2018, as well as of various scientific committees related to ecosystem services and biodiversity conservation, such as ecoSERVICES and the Global Land Programme of Future Earth.

Ina Porras is a Senior Economist at the International Institute for Environment and Development, and works in the design, implementation and/or assessment of payment for ecosystem services in multiple countries.

Mahesh Poudyal is a Postdoctoral Fellow at the Ecosystem Services for Poverty Alleviation (ESPA) Programme Directorate. He is an environmental social scientist with research focusing on the poverty–environment nexus.

Ritu Priya is a Professor at the Centre of Social Medicine & Community Health, Jawaharlal Nehru University (JNU), New Delhi. Her research focuses on urban health and the health and wellbeing of marginalised groups.

Pritpal Randhawa is based in New Delhi, and carries out research on policy processes, governance, informality, local knowledge, environmental health and everyday environmentalism in the urban and peri-urban contexts.

Laura Vang Rasmussen is a Postdoctoral Fellow investigating links between agricultural intensification and food security at the Landscapes and Livelihoods Lab at the University of British Columbia and at the department of Geosciences and Natural Resource Management, University of Copenhagen.

Belinda Reyers is Professor of Sustainability Science and Programme Director at the Stockholm Resilience Centre, Sweden and Stellenbosch University, South Africa, where she works to develop understanding of complex social-ecological systems and resilience.

Casey Ryan is a Senior Lecturer in ecosystem services and global change at the University of Edinburgh, School of GeoSciences, with research interests in tropical land use change science and ecosystem ecology.

Kate Schreckenberg is a Reader in Development Geography at King's College London and Director of the Ecosystem Services for Poverty Alleviation (ESPA) programme. Her research focuses on equity in natural resource governance.

Odirilwe Selomane is a Postdoctoral candidate at Stockholm Resilience Centre, Sweden researching complex systems approaches to measuring and tracking changes in social-ecological systems for sustainability.

Lucy Szaboova is a Research Fellow at the University of Exeter, and works on the wellbeing and ecosystem services relationship, the capability approach and access analysis.

Natalie Tannous is based at the University of Johannesburg's Africa Centre for Evidence, and has worked in evidence synthesis on different development reviews since 2012. Her interests lie specifically in environmental issues and how these relate to various aspects of society and development.

Carina van Rooyen is a Senior Researcher and Co-Director of the Centre for Environmental Evidence Johannesburg based at the University of Johannesburg's Africa Centre for Evidence.

Bhaskar Vira is Professor of Political Economy and Director of the University of Cambridge Conservation Research Institute. He has been closely involved with the ESPA research programme, bringing a political economy dimension to work at the interdisciplinary interface of environment and development.

Linda Waldman is a Research Fellow in the Health and Nutrition Cluster, and Director of Teaching and Learning at the Institute of Development Studies, University of Sussex. Her research focuses on the intersections between health, poverty, gender, sustainability and policy.

Carole White is a Senior Research Associate in the Global Environmental Justice Group at the School for International Development, University of East Anglia. Her research has focused on coastal communities and explored the implications of responding to change for wellbeing and resilience.

Lana Whittaker is a Research Assistant at the Department of Geography, University of Cambridge.

Emily Woodhouse is a Lecturer in Environmental Anthropology in the Anthropology Department of University College London. Her research focuses on the social dimensions of nature conservation and the governance of pastoral rangelands.

PREFACE

It has long been known that poverty reduction and environmental conservation are connected endeavours, even if many who work in one field do so unaware of the other. Two major advances, one in each field, now assert these close connections, each reflecting the new millennium in their titles as if to stress that a brand new era is upon us:

- For poverty reduction, the 2000 Millennium Development Goals included one goal on achieving environmental sustainability, although the dependence of the seven other goals on environment was unexplored.
- For environment, the 2005 Millennium Ecosystem Assessment found that global development gains had been achieved at the cost of 15 of the 24 ecosystem services it examined becoming degraded or used unsustainably, this creating deep burdens on poor people for whom the environment is a principal means of livelihood.

If ecosystems were beginning to be recognised as foundations for producing the food, fibre, clean water and air needed for everyone's wellbeing, how these benefits are secured was weakly conceptualised at the time. The evidence base on what works for poor people was especially patchy. This has been a severe constraint to turning around environment and development decisions.

Introducing ESPA

The principal UK Government response to the MA was an ambitious research programme: Ecosystem Services for Poverty Alleviation (ESPA). Planned between 2006 and 2009, and concluding in 2018, ESPA has attempted to fill the evidence gap on how ecosystems can contribute sustainably to poverty reduction. It was the first partnership between the Department for International Development (DFID) and two research councils, the Natural Environment Research Council (NERC) and the Economic and Social Research Council (ESRC). It has been able to realise synergies between mandates – DFID's for development impact and the research councils' for research excellence: ESPA's interdisciplinary science has engaged with poor groups and policy-makers in nearly 50 countries in the Global South.

A meeting in South Africa in June 2008 proved critical. We sketched an initial 'ESPA framework' of the components we determined to research (Figure 0.1): a central focus on people's wellbeing; their close dependence on the ecosystem (the surrounding circle); and the many external conditions that affect this relationship (the outer circle). What our diagram missed was how the layers interact – this being the overall research question. My notes of the meeting recorded that

> We agreed the need was to achieve clarity on the circumstances where delivery of ecosystem services offers a safeguard, where it opens up a route out of poverty, or indeed where it creates a poverty trap. What makes it so, and what can improve the situation, is often a matter of governance and political economy, and so our research must involve both policy-makers and poor groups – and improve the capacity of developing country scientists to do this.

ESPA was subsequently launched in 2009, with four objectives:

1. To create a strong evidence base on the connections between ecosystem services, their dynamics and management, their human use and pathways to sustainable poverty reduction.
2. To develop innovative, interdisciplinary research methodologies, delivering tools and approaches that support decision makers.
3. To engage and communicate effectively with policy makers and practitioners, so that research is well understood and used.
4. To enhance the capacity of Southern researchers to conduct, lead, use and communicate high-quality, interdisciplinary research.

ESPA operated through several public research calls seeking proposals for diverse regions and themes. By 2018, 125 research projects in 53 countries, involving nearly 1000 scientists in over 100 institutions, had identified the dependencies of human wellbeing on the environment, the drivers of environmental loss and replenishment, the human consequences of these dynamics and the governance that shapes them. Nearly 350 papers had been published by the end of 2017, 60% with developing-country authors and 72% of them interdisciplinary. Annual Science Conferences enabled researchers to meet, and share methodologies and findings. The 2017 Conference looked beyond individual projects to discuss and validate the draft chapters in this volume – some produced in response to a call for synthesis research, others from gap-filling synthesis contracts, and one on fisheries through a dedicated working group. Each is an exciting contribution, exploring the large new ESPA body of knowledge alongside other relevant evidence.

The world has changed, and ESPA has been part of it:

Mainstream players are becoming concerned about 'ES-PA' issues

The 2005 MA asserted that development in the last half century has exploited both nature and poor people, and this message is now getting through to the 'mainstream'. Where once environment interests had to push such concerns, increasingly it is development and finance authorities, poor groups and markets that demand environment action – and that are becoming open to distributional questions. The World Economic Forum has cited poverty, inequality, environmental degradation and climate change in its top ten global risks in each of the last six years.

A new, universal policy space has opened

Our dilemma in 2008 was how to hook ESPA to a big policy process that would demand the breadth of ESPA science. Some research projects were able to do this locally. Today, the Sustainable Development Goals provide an agreed, comprehensive and integrated agenda for poverty reduction and environmental conservation in every country. The SDGs have engaged businesses as well, many shifting their concern from simple environmental impact to their dependence on natural assets, and some seeing poor groups as legitimate stakeholders in value chains. The current search for 'SDG implementation' has unleashed demand for integrated information and decision support tools of the type ESPA has pioneered. In some countries, inclusive green economy and circular economy plans have similar integrated environment-development aspirations.

The ecosystem services approach has improved in its utility

Before ESPA, 'ecosystem services' was essentially a biophysical concept, assuming deterministic and linear flows of material benefits. Today, a social-ecological framing links ecosystems to human needs and interventions; it elucidates many feedback loops, plural values, power relations and governance. The 'planetary boundaries' concept has been introduced, pointing to limits to ecosystem use, and demanding better evidence of thresholds and irreversibility. ESPA has both influenced the evolution of many post-MA frameworks that serve particular purposes, and has been influenced in return.

Poverty is better understood as multiple deprivations

When ESPA started, poverty was defined narrowly and externally in financial terms, e.g. as a $1.25/day threshold, which naturally favoured market-based solutions and missed the poorest who operate in informal economies. ESPA, among others, has promoted multi-dimensional measures of wellbeing, wealth, capabilities, freedoms and security – and the notion of poor people defining poverty themselves. With

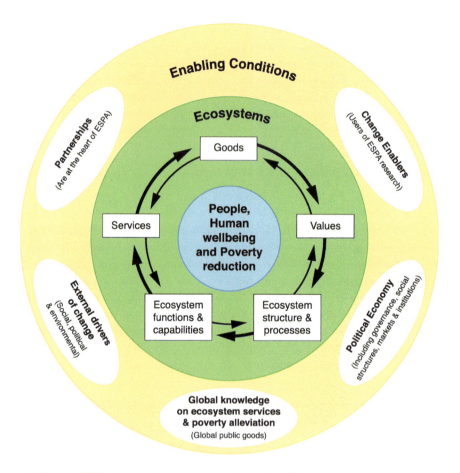

FIGURE 0.1 ESPA framework at programme launch, 2009

rising concern for both inequality and justice, multi-level governance solutions are being framed to achieve multiple values.

Diverse knowledge systems are being embraced

Western science's utilitarian and linear notions of relations between environment and people may have constrained both imagination and method when ESPA was launched. Today, there is growing openness to traditional knowledge systems, citizen science and plural and deliberative approaches, as is evident in the 2006 International Assessment of Agricultural Knowledge, Science and Technology for Development (IAASTD) and the Intergovernmental Science-Policy Platform on Biodiversity and Ecosystem Services (IPBES). Advances in ICT and data visualisation offer new potentials for rethinking environment–poverty relations.

There is increasing realisation that better-informed trade-offs need to be made

Decision makers either did not act on complex environment–poverty problems (being perhaps paralysed by their complexity) or pinned hopes on 'magic bullets' such as payments for ecosystem services (PES), land-use intensification, protected area establishment or other 'win-wins' without good evidence of their wider impacts. It is now clear that trade-offs are more likely than 'win-wins' within and between poverty reduction and environmental management. Some ESPA research and decision support tools have helped decision makers even in low-data contexts, identifying nuanced solutions that suit local contexts and better distribute costs and benefits.

ESPA-like science is consequently growing

Before ESPA, any such research was rare, in obscure silos, not interacting or narrowly technical. It was certainly tough initially for ESPA's funders and scientists to focus ESPA's research questions and methods. Since then, diverse ESPA projects have pointed to the value of interdisciplinary, cross-scale, cross-ecosystem service research that engages both policy and poor groups. To date this has lacked a global stock-take and validation of the diverse frameworks, findings and lessons. The current volume now does this: it is a timely academic reflection, which we hope will give further impetus to future research and its use.

Looking to the future

The findings in this volume can help us address three important future challenges:

Achieving the SDGs

The complexity of our world is its blessing and its curse. The SDGs are a hard-won attempt to manage complexity. But action on the SDGs is challenging everyone:

the SDGs are 'indivisible', yet the first thing that governments do is divide them mong institutions, which merely mirrors the *status quo*. ESPA has improved understanding of complex interactions between environment and poverty, and of how to assess and plan for the trade-offs needed.

Bridging science, policy and people

It is worth recalling how, in April 2017, ordinary people in more than 600 cities marched to strengthen science's role in policymaking, protesting against 'post-truth', anti-expert sentiments. While keeping political and scientific agendas separate can prevent unhealthy contamination, the future of people and planet depends on finding ways to integrate research into policy decisions without compromising the integrity of either endeavour. Wherever people are being 'left behind' (in the SDGs language) it is perhaps the duty of scientists to examine how this can be turned around, and the ESPA community has been diligent in this respect. As one Member of the Ugandan Parliament implored at the 2016 ESPA Science Conference, 'We politicians need to hear from scientists more than ever'.

Institutional reform

Linked poverty and environment problems are misunderstood and mishandled by their fragmented treatment in government, business and academia. There is a real imperative to better integrate currently siloed institutional machinery: making existing institutions with integrated mandates work better, e.g. land use planning and community-based natural resource management; shaping economic institutions to reflect social and ecological systems; mobilising the intermediaries that can draw players closer together; and providing the information they need to tackle underlying causes of intractable problems. ESPA certainly offers some of the necessary institutional 'DNA'.

For their intelligent, robust and instructive synthesis of eight years of ESPA work and more, many thanks are due to Kate Schreckenberg, Georgina Mace, Mahesh Poudyal, and all chapter authors. Thanks are due equally to all ESPA researchers, policy partners and local organisations who conducted the 125 research projects on which this volume draws. In so many cases, the ESPA community has already brought the results into promising new policy and practice for joint poverty reduction and environmental conservation.

Steve Bass
Chair, ESPA Programme Executive Board
26 January 2018

ACKNOWLEDGEMENTS

This book has been funded by the Ecosystem Services for Poverty Alleviation (ESPA) Programme. The ESPA programme is funded by the Department for International Development (DFID), the Economic and Social Research Council (ESRC) and the Natural Environment Research Council (NERC). The views expressed in the book are those of the authors and do not necessarily represent those of NERC, ESRC and DFID.

The idea for the book was first mooted in early 2017, and we are grateful to the members of ESPA's Programme Executive Board (Alessandro Moscuzza, Sophie Martin, Simon Kerley and Steve Bass) for agreeing to fund it. We would also like to thank members of the PEB, their colleagues Ken de Souza, Beth Taylor and Dominique Butt, as well as ESPA's International Programme Advisory Committee (Atiq Rahman, Katrina Brown, Virgílio Viana, Janet Ranganathan, John Adeoti and Christo Fabricius) for their feedback on the structure and content of the book as it developed. Sincere thanks also to Liz Carlile, IIED, and to Charles Hill (Research into Results Ltd., University of Edinburgh) for their support and advice throughout.

It would not have been possible to turn our ideas into reality had it not been for the incredibly efficient support of the ESPA Directorate staff (Eliane Reid, Rebecca Murray, Bouchra Chakroune, Dave Bell, Sam Mwangi, Raj Patra, Mairi Dupar, Eeli Lee, Valeria Izzi, James Gigg and Lucie Kelleher), who managed multiple contracts, arranged webinars with authors and organised an excellent Annual Science Conference in November 2017 at which the chapters were discussed with a wider audience. We thank the Conference participants for their intensive discussion, which helped shape the final versions of the chapters. To the chapter authors we owe a major debt of gratitude for working with us to incredibly tight deadlines, always with good humour and a common enthusiasm for the project in hand. Thanks also to Tim Hardwick and colleagues at Routledge for their efficient collaboration on the production of this book.

Finally, we must thank our respective families for their interest and support, and apologise for the many missed dinners!

Kate Schreckenberg, Georgina Mace
and Mahesh Poudyal

ACRONYMS AND ABBREVIATIONS

CAZ	Corridor Ankeniheny Zahamena (Madagascar)
CBD	Convention on Biological Diversity
CT	Conditional Transfer
DFID	Department for International Development (UK)
EDSS	Environmental Decision Support Systems
ESPA	Ecosystem Services for Poverty Alleviation (Programme)
FAO	Food and Agriculture Organization of the UN
FPIC	Free, Prior and Informed Consent
ICT	Information and Communication Technology
IPBES	The Intergovernmental Science-Policy Platform on Biodiversity and Ecosystem Services
IUCN	International Union for Conservation of Nature
MA	Millennium Ecosystem Assessment
MPA	Marine Protected Area
MSY	Maximum Sustainable Yield
NGO	Non-governmental Organisation
PES	Payment for Ecosystem Services
PGIS	Participatory Geographic Information Systems
REDD+	Reducing Emissions from Deforestation and Forest Degradation and the role of conservation, sustainable management of forests and enhancement of forest carbon stocks
RWA	Reciprocal Watershed Agreement
SDG	Sustainable Development Goal
SES	Social-Ecological Systems
SLCP	Sloping Land Conversion Programme (China)

TEEB	The Economics of Ecosystems and Biodiversity
UNFCCC	United Nations Framework Convention on Climate Change
USAID	United States Agency for International Development
WMA	Wildlife Management Area (Tanzania)

PART I
Evolving framings and contexts

The four chapters in this section trace the evolution of thinking in science and policy through the life of the ESPA programme (2009–2018) and illustrate emerging trends. Pascual and Howe (Chapter 1) trace the trends in conceptual frameworks linking environment and development over recent decades, showing how key ideas from both socio-political and ecological perspectives have coalesced and developed. They emphasise the important role played by the knowledge communities involved, that have learned from one another and in turn shaped new thinking. Key trends are towards systems approaches – recognising the interactive framework where both ecological and social factors feed back and influence each other, and away from the more deterministic flow of ecosystem goods and services that characterised earlier thinking.

At the same time, there has been a very strong emerging set of questions about how the benefits from ecosystems end up being distributed; particularly concerning who wins and who loses, but most importantly who is involved in determining which actions, based on whose knowledge, where, when and how? One of the strongest shifts has been to a much more sophisticated integration of issues of justice and equity, described by Dawson and colleagues (Chapter 2). The principles relating to justice and equity are well developed in theory but putting them into practice, especially alongside sophisticated and highly technical ecosystem management science, is a significant challenge that both Chapters 1 and 2 highlight. Methods and metrics for greater equity and sustainability are much sought after by policy and decision makers, and Dawson and colleagues describe recent progress in both developing and testing them in real-world development settings.

The complex nature of social-ecological systems, and the multiple interacting scales and dimensions, were other features of post Millennium Ecosystem Assessment findings. Systems approaches pioneered by both physical and social sciences recognise that simple analytical approaches cannot be used to predict the behaviour of such systems. Limits and thresholds, feedbacks, non-linearities and phase shifts are all features of many social-ecological systems relevant to ESPA which researchers have pioneered new ways to investigate and work with. Reyers and Selomane (Chapter 3) provide an overview of systems approaches in the context of ecosystem services and poverty alleviation. They show the importance of recognising and working with this complexity, and emphasise the significance of cross-scale interactions, especially for cross-sector development objectives such as those included in the UN Sustainable Development Goals. Siloed approaches within sectors often lead to unanticipated and undesirable consequences displaced in space and/or time. New approaches are needed and Dearing (Chapter 4) describes the progress that has derived from concepts such as planetary boundaries and safe operating spaces. Some ESPA projects have led the way in making these approaches relevant in practice and at local to regional scales where decisions can be taken, and using methods that are both inclusive and deliberative. They allow exploration of management alternatives to identify actions to maintain systems within a safe and just operating space.

1
SEEING THE WOOD FOR THE TREES

Exploring the evolution of frameworks of ecosystem services for human wellbeing

Unai Pascual and Caroline Howe

Introduction

The concept of 'ecosystem services' provides a particular lens for framing social-ecological relationships. Since its emergence about 20 years ago it has provided valuable common ground for different disciplines to discuss broadly interdependent environmental and development goals. The concept does however, sometimes mask different and divergent ideologies and priorities with respect to ecosystem management and development planning. These differing principles are shaped by, and in turn shape, different epistemic communities, or 'networks of professionals (e.g. in academia and policy) with recognised expertise and competence in a particular domain and an authoritative claim to policy relevant knowledge within that domain or issue' (Haas, 1992).

The decade since the publication of the Millennium Ecosystem Assessment (MA) (2005) has seen a remarkable evolution in conceptual frameworks of ecosystem services for human wellbeing, reflecting the way different epistemic communities, including those in the science–policy interface, have embraced the approach. The relevant actors in research and policy development are a large, although not cohesive, group. They share debates about how to achieve 'win-win' solutions by managing ecosystems sustainably and reducing poverty with some common rationales, narratives and expected/desired outcomes. However, there are significant contrasts in values and positions. These differences are characterised by a variety of normative positions that reflect different mixes of concern, and interpretations about the linkages between ecosystem condition and economic development, creating a series of epistemic communities (Howe et al., 2018). These normative positions have evolved from earlier, narrower debates concerning poverty alleviation and biodiversity conservation (e.g. Adams et al., 2004), and have deepened as ecosystem services for human wellbeing frameworks emerged and developed. In turn, such changes in normative positions influence how the epistemic communities themselves connect to policy and so the frameworks co-evolve with epistemic communities, continually influencing one another. However, these interactions between epistemic communities and emerging concepts are seldom recognised in the literature, even while the ecosystem services concept has become a boundary object that enables integration across diverse bodies of knowledge (Abson et al., 2014).

Conceptual frameworks are tools by which complex systems can be clarified. They facilitate the deliberation of, and agreement on, essential components and interactions of the system being studied, as well as highlighting uncertainties and gaps in understanding (Tomich et al., 2010). The process of developing a conceptual framework is inherently value-laden, involving balance and contention among and between different epistemic communities and their underlying ideologies, principles and interests (Díaz et al., 2015). Where conceptual frameworks are used by a research programme – for example, the UK-led Ecosystem Services for Poverty Alleviation (ESPA) programme – they provide a basis for research design and fertile interactions among different epistemic communities involved (for example, researchers, policy makers and practitioners).

The MA (2005) was the first comprehensive attempt with global influence to unify thinking around ecosystem services. Its framing evolved from conceptualisations of natural capital (e.g. Daily, 1997; Jansson et al., 1994), and associated (weak vs. strong) sustainability schools of thought (Ekins et al., 2003), with an emphasis on the supply of 'ecological goods and services'. The MA gave birth to many initiatives; from sub-global ecosystem assessments at both national, e.g. the United Kingdom National Ecosystem Assessment (UKNEA, 2011), and regional scale, e.g. the European Commission Mapping and Assessment of Ecosystem Services (MAES, 2013); economic assessments, e.g. The Economics of Ecosystems and Biodiversity (TEEB) (Kumar, 2010); and, perhaps the most politically important from a global standpoint, the UN-based Intergovernmental Science-Policy Platform on Biodiversity and Ecosystem Services (IPBES) (Díaz et al., 2018).

The last decade has also seen the emergence of social-ecological systems (SES) thinking (e.g. Ostrom, 2009; Reyers and Selomane, this volume). This was pioneered by work undertaken by, for instance, the Programme on Ecosystem Change and Society of Future Earth, the Stockholm Resilience Centre, the Ecosystem Services Partnership and academic societies such as the International Society for Ecological Economics. These interdisciplinary research communities interact among themselves, and with the wider research and practice communities. They are, therefore, in an ideal position to broaden the boundary space and connect to other knowledge systems, including those of indigenous people, which generally do not match with the western scientific approach to systematising and generalising knowledge (Tengö et al., 2014). This thinking has coalesced within IPBES, where an evolution has occurred towards interpreting ecosystem services more broadly as Nature's Contributions to People (NCP) (Díaz et al., 2018). NCP emphasises the effects of nature as perceived and valued by individuals and social groups across different cultural, environmental and socio-economic contexts, allowing for both generalising (i.e. scientific) as well as more context-specific (e.g. indigenous and local knowledge) perspectives (Pascual et al., 2017a).

ESPA was developed in response to the findings of the MA and has been significant in the evolution of conceptual framings, with an explicit emphasis on ecosystem management for poverty alleviation. It has contributed to ideas such as the co-production of ecosystem services (Lele et al., 2013; Reyers et al., 2013), ecosystem service trade-offs (e.g. Bennett et al., 2015; Howe et al., 2014) and multiple human values for ecosystem services (e.g. Pascual et al., 2017a) within governance contexts in the Global South (see Nunan et al., this volume). ESPA has been nourished by and branched out to tackle innovative views about social-ecological interdependencies (Ostrom, 2009), justice and equity (Sikor, 2013), disaggregated approaches to human wellbeing (Daw et al., 2011; Fisher et al., 2013; Coulthard et al., this volume) and tele-coupling, e.g. in environmental assessments (Pascual et al., 2017b).

This chapter explores the development of ecosystem services framings over the last decade. It also reflects on the potential direct implications for the design of ecosystem service-related policy instruments, such as payments for ecosystem services (PES), and takes a brief look at the future, by identifying emergent challenges associated with future framings.

Historical background to ecosystem service frameworks

Evolution of core and satellite ecosystem service frameworks

This section explores the emergence of 'core' and 'satellite' frameworks for connections between ecosystem services and human wellbeing, associated with different epistemic communities. We define 'core' frameworks as those which have become a fundamental part of the mainstream approach to addressing ecosystem services for human wellbeing. In contrast, 'satellite' frameworks have either significantly influenced the evolution of core frameworks, or have drawn on elements of 'core' frameworks to tackle more nuanced aspects like cultural perceptions and the social co-production of ecosystem services.

The MA framework is the first of several core frameworks born out of the integration of thinking by different influential epistemic communities (Reid and Mooney, 2016), including those working in ecology, economics (Jansson et al., 1994) and interdisciplinary scientists that embraced the idea of natural capital (Farley, 2012). Gretchen Daily (1997) defined ecosystem services as the 'conditions and processes through which natural ecosystems, and the species that make them up, sustain and fulfil human life', while Costanza et al. (1997) further promoted the concept through estimating the economic value of global ecosystem services.

These ideas developed into various global scientific programmes such as DIVERSITAS (the international programme on biodiversity science, established in 1991 by the International Council for Science Unions), with its focus on the impacts of biodiversity changes on ecosystem functioning and thereby the provision of ecological goods and services of relevance to human societies (Larigauderie et al., 2012). At the same time, they built on satellite frameworks such as that of the Drivers-Pressures-States-Impacts-Responses (DPSIR) (Smeets and Weterings, 1999) and the Sustainable Livelihoods Framework (Scoones, 1998), as well as the core MA (2005) framework. This in turn created opportunities for the development of other core frameworks such as those associated with global assessments, including TEEB (Kumar, 2010) and IPBES (Díaz et al., 2015), sub-global ecosystem assessments, including the UK NEA (UKNEA, 2011), as well as programme frameworks including ESPA (ESPA, 2013; also see Preface to this volume) and ecoSERVICES (Bennett et al., 2015) currently under the Future Earth Programme (previously under DIVERSITAS).

From the biophysical perspective, a significant difference between earlier and later conceptualisations is in the categorisation of ecosystem services. The MA defined four main categories: provisioning, regulating, supporting and cultural services. However, by 2009 efforts to formalise social-ecological systems for analysis had led to supporting services being incorporated as ecosystem functions and properties (Carpenter et al., 2009) now reflected in the IPBES conceptual framework (Díaz et al., 2015). In addition, in IPBES the NCP approach embraces the different perceptions and understandings of people about material, non-material and regulating NCP (Díaz et al., 2018), and thus the multiple ways that NCP values are conceptualised (Pascual et al., 2017a). The emphasis about the role of culture is one of the main contributions of the NCP approach, and this goes beyond the ways the ecosystem services approach embraces cultural services in the MA sense, including within ESPA projects.

Figure 1.1 provides a timeline of the evolution of core frameworks, both assessment- and research programme-based. It also includes significant satellite frameworks that have been influential regarding the ideas behind the development of core frameworks. Conceptual framings have evolved from the earlier, more linear 'natural capital as stock, ecosystem services as flow' metaphor, to more system-based thinking which allows for feedbacks, and with governance (as the key indirect driver) having more centrality. Likewise, it shows an emerging emphasis on the multi-dimensionality of human wellbeing, with ESPA being a clear example of trying to capture both the biophysical dimension of ecosystem services and the multi-dimensionality of human wellbeing, and poverty specifically. This can be compared for instance with TEEB, which by being primarily interested in economic valuation of ecosystem services, has not addressed multi-dimensional wellbeing. Fisher et al. (2013) provides a useful summary of some of the frameworks discussed here, as well as several other satellite frameworks.

The Sustainable Livelihoods Framework (Scoones, 1998) was an early contribution to articulating the contributions of natural capital to livelihoods, especially in the Global South. In a complementary approach to the weak vs strong sustainability debate in ecological economics, the development community brought natural capital to the fore as a fundamental asset that determines people's livelihood options and outcomes. The framework was developed alongside more advanced analysis on, for example, the concept of 'investment poverty' whereby degradation of natural capital is seen as a key determinant of asset-based poverty status (Reardon and Vosti, 1995) which can ultimately lead to 'poverty traps' (Barrett et al., 2011).

The *Drivers–Pressures–States–Impacts–Response* (DPSIR) framework (Smeets and Weterings, 1999) was also articulated as a more linear framework that examines how changes in pressures via drivers affect environmental systems, but is weaker on how changes in the system then feed back to affect social drivers and thus pressures (Tomich et al., 2010). Early applications of the framework were as a tool in adaptive management, particularly in marine and coastal sectors (Vugteveen et al., 2015).

The MA introduced feedback loops and drivers of change as well as considering multiple spatial and temporal scales. Its central idea is that human wellbeing is tightly linked to the condition of ecosystems and the provision of different broad types of ecosystem services (MA, 2005). Therefore, it is assumed that their loss or degradation will have negative consequences for human wellbeing, offering the potential for ecosystem management and restoration to play a part in development strategies aimed at poverty alleviation. Another legacy of the MA has been the assumption of the trickle-down effect whereby improvements in ecosystem services should automatically increase wellbeing. This has led to consideration, especially within ESPA, of the differential impacts of changes in ecosystem service flows, and the trade-offs among different social groups, especially on those who depend most directly on ecosystem services (Daw et al., 2011; Fisher et al., 2013).

TEEB was launched as an economic complement to the MA. It took a more systematic approach to economic valuation as a contribution to biodiversity and ecosystems, giving them a more central role in decision making (Kumar, 2010) and helped to enrich economic conceptualisation of ecosystem service values (e.g. Pascual et al., 2010). Interestingly, while the TEEB approach has been heralded in many national and international policy fora, it has fallen short of being taken up in practice by governments or industry, partly because it did not fully connect to the realities of decision-making processes and also because the aggregate economic valuations it produced were difficult to put into practice (Wegner and Pascual, 2011).

More recently, the IPBES conceptual framework (Díaz et al., 2015) recognised strong feedbacks among 'nature' (i.e. biodiversity and ecosystems), NCP (including ecosystem services) and people's 'good quality of life' (including wellbeing) via the centrality of institutions and governance systems. The IPBES framework aims to represent different epistemic communities and knowledge systems, including, prominently, those of indigenous peoples and local communities. This is also reflected in the diverse conceptualisations of values of NCP (Pascual et al., 2017a). It is

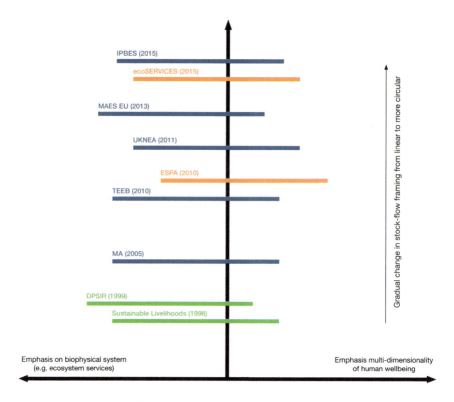

FIGURE 1.1 Timeline illustrating the evolution of 'core' frameworks and their relationship to significant 'satellite' frameworks (blue lines illustrate 'core' assessment frameworks, orange lines 'core' research programme frameworks and green lines key 'satellite' frameworks). The timeline illustrates the general shift from a linear stock-flow framing towards a more circular stock-flow framing approach (note: this shift is gradual and does not always coincide completely with the chronological development of frameworks). The emphasis each framework places on either the biophysical system (e.g. ecosystem services) or the multi-dimensionality of human wellbeing is illustrated by their position relative to the timeline. The ESPA framework referred to in this figure is illustrated within the ESPA Knowledge Strategy (ESPA, 2013), and reproduced in the Preface to this volume (Figure 0.1).

important to note that while the MA was not part of an intergovernmental process, its frameworks and findings were recognised by the Parties to the Convention on Biological Diversity (CBD). The IPBES framework, on the other hand, is officially endorsed by all 129 governments who are members of this intergovernmental body.

Stemming from the MA and, more directly, the UK NEA, the ESPA programme framework aims at researching the general vision that ecosystems, when sustainably managed, can contribute to poverty alleviation as well as to inclusive and sustainable economic growth (ESPA, 2013). Various reviews highlighted key dimensions for understanding and assessing the impact of ecosystem changes on human wellbeing (Fisher et al., 2013; Agarwala et al., 2014). These include, *inter alia*, the importance of multidisciplinary consideration of wellbeing (Suich, 2012), the need for frameworks that integrate subjective and objective aspects of wellbeing, the central importance of context and relational aspects of wellbeing, the constraints of access and of aggregate availability of ecosystem services, and the differences between ecosystem services, their pathways of co-production, distribution across social groups, and contributions to improving the livelihood of the poor and vulnerable people, most often in rural settings (Keane, 2016).

In general, the ecosystem services approach has not explicitly considered either the relationship between biotic (e.g. biodiversity and ecosystem service flows) and abiotic components (e.g. fossil fuels and minerals) associated with development pathways, or the relationships between different biotic elements and different constituents of wellbeing. Interestingly, the role of abiotic resources in development pathways has remained out of focus of ESPA, and this may perhaps have limited some of its potential policy uptake in relation to poverty alleviation. By contrast the focus on multi-dimensional aspects of human wellbeing, as well as how differentiated access to ecosystem services plays a role in poverty alleviation, has been a key contribution compared with other programmes.

Throughout the evolution of these frameworks, key concepts like the co-production of ecosystem services, systems thinking and the centrality of governance at the ecosystem service–wellbeing nexus, have come to the fore, drawn from emerging research. Each of the frameworks discussed has embraced these concepts to differing degrees depending on when they first appeared and the interests of associated epistemic communities. Figure 1.2 illustrates the emphasis that different frameworks place on biophysical, human wellbeing and governance concepts. We observe a gradual increase in depth of colour from left to right illustrating a greater inclusion of key concepts within newer ecosystem service frameworks.

Figure 1.3 illustrates how these concepts are connected to different epistemic communities (as grouped by Howe et al., 2018) and, in turn, influence core frameworks. The epistemic communities have evolved over time from integrated conservation and development projects (ICDPs), through a drive to address environmental conservation and poverty eradication (Adams et al., 2004), to attempts to achieve the holy grail of win-wins for both environmental conservation and poverty alleviation. Inevitably, the key concepts have been championed and/or embraced to differing extents. Together Figures 1.2 and 1.3 illustrate the interplay between epistemic communities and the various core frameworks, and provide an overview of how frameworks, emerging concepts and associated epistemic communities have co-evolved over the last decade.

Biodiversity and poverty nexus in ecosystem service framings

Generally, the frameworks consider biodiversity as an underlying driver, a regulator of the processes and flows providing ecosystem services, and/or as a final benefit

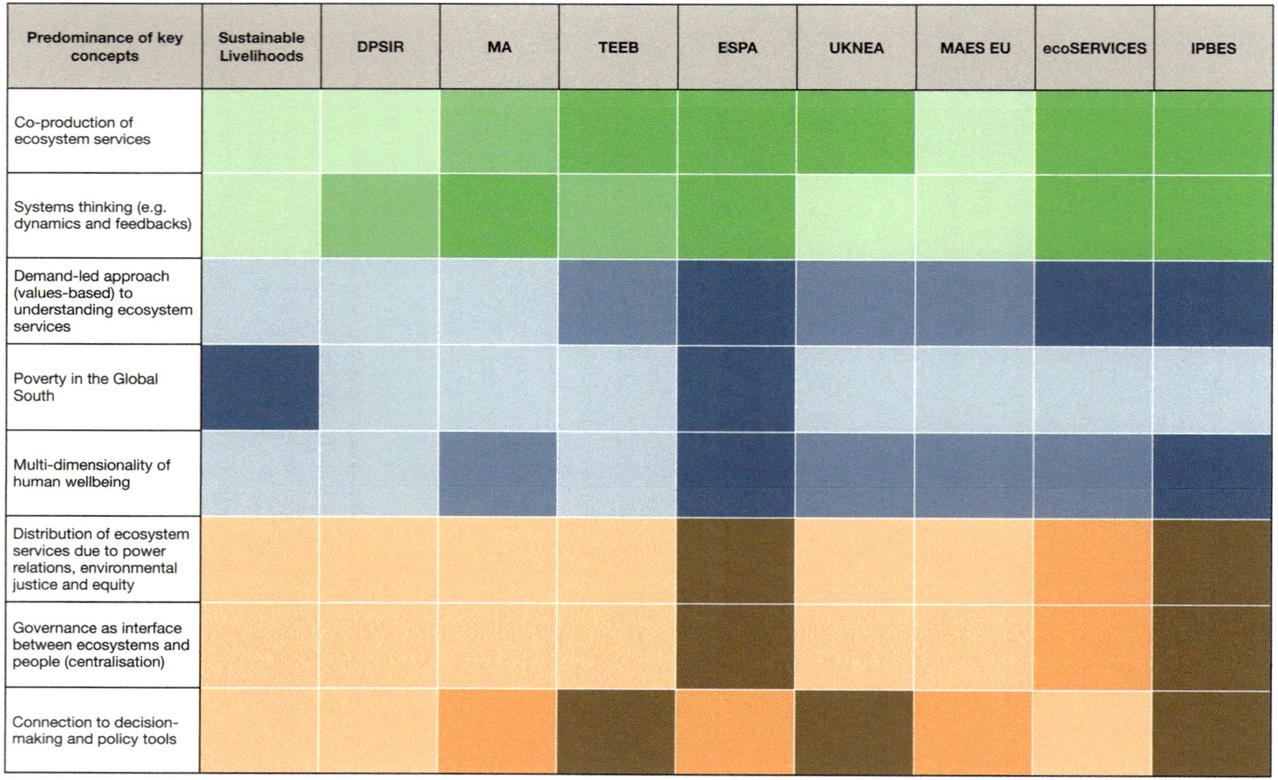

Predominance of key concepts	Sustainable Livelihoods	DPSIR	MA	TEEB	ESPA	UKNEA	MAES EU	ecoSERVICES	IPBES
Co-production of ecosystem services									
Systems thinking (e.g. dynamics and feedbacks)									
Demand-led approach (values-based) to understanding ecosystem services									
Poverty in the Global South									
Multi-dimensionality of human wellbeing									
Distribution of ecosystem services due to power relations, environmental justice and equity									
Governance as interface between ecosystems and people (centralisation)									
Connection to decision-making and policy tools									

FIGURE 1.2 Predominance of key conceptual attributes within the 'core' and 'satellite' frameworks discussed in Figure 1.1. The intensity of the colour indicates whether a framework interacts lightly or heavily with the attribute. Green concepts relate to the biophysical, blue to human wellbeing and yellow to governance elements of the conceptual framings.

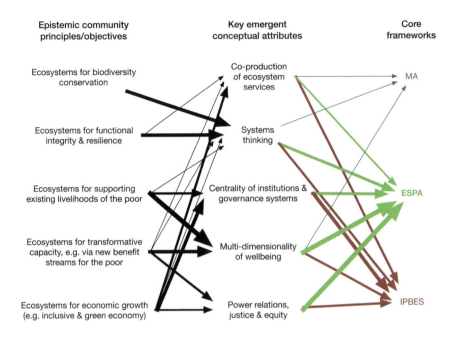

FIGURE 1.3 Relationship between key emergent conceptual attributes, epistemic communities and core frameworks. Epistemic community principles (as grouped by Howe et al., 2018) are linked to key concepts and core frameworks, in order to illustrate the interaction within and between epistemic communities and examples of core framings for ecosystem services (MA, ESPA and IPBES). The thickness of the arrows represents the level of association.

or good in itself (Mace et al., 2012). In earlier core and satellite frameworks, assumptions made about the relationships between biodiversity and ecosystem services were unclear and often confused by different uses of the terms (e.g. biodiversity, supporting ecosystem services, ecosystem benefits). In addition, in some later frameworks, such as the UK NEA (Bateman et al., 2011) and IPBES (Díaz et al., 2015), ecosystem services were specifically separated from benefits. The reasoning for this is that for robust valuation, the change in benefits perceived or realised by people needs to be attributable to changes in ecosystem contributions as well as non-ecosystem/anthropogenic contributions (Fisher and Turner, 2008).

Most commonly, only direct (often consumptive) uses of biodiversity and their positive links to limited dimensions of poverty (income, assets and food security) are studied (Roe et al., 2012). However, the realities concerning the linkages between biodiversity conservation and the provision of ecosystem services for the poor are significantly more complex. For example, many geographical areas of high biodiversity are located in countries that are relatively poor, and the favoured conservation approach of protected areas has often disadvantaged local residents and neighbours (Martin et al., 2013). At larger spatial scales and over much longer time frames, loss of functional and phylogenetic biodiversity may pose more significant obstacles to ecosystem services and associated benefit flows (Mace et al., 2014). Over the short term, however, local loss of biodiversity may not always be an obstacle to poverty alleviation and is often associated with increased income.

Different frameworks deal with human wellbeing in different ways. The MA drew on the *Voices of the Poor* exercise for the five elements of wellbeing used (MA, 2005; Narayan et al., 2000), and while many more dimensions have been identified in the literature (Alkire, 2007), relatively few (easier to measure) dimensions (e.g. income, employment, health) have been the main focus of research. Generally, the MA framework did not make explicit the poverty aspects associated with wellbeing and took for granted that ecosystem services help the poor through an undefined trickle-down effect. ESPA has maintained a stronger focus on the wellbeing of the poor (as opposed to people more generally) and the impact of ecosystem services management on alleviating poverty, including via additional conceptualisations and complex pathways, e.g. capabilities, freedoms and security (Keane, 2016).

Ecosystem services are more likely to be associated with poverty prevention, rather than reduction, or with mitigation of some impacts of poverty (Dewees et al., 2010), as they act as a safety net rather than a route out of poverty (Fisher et al., 2013). However, many other aspects of the relationship between ecosystem services and poverty remain unresolved. This is in part due to the lack of empirical evidence on multi-causal pathways and time lags, as well as the complexity of conceptualising poverty in its different dimensions (Suich et al., 2015; Martin et al., this volume). The core conceptual frameworks do not fully address the direction of causality, i.e. whether poverty creates or is a result of environmental degradation (Sandker et al., 2012), whether ecosystem services can actually alleviate poverty (Suich et al., 2015) or whether a reliance on ecosystem services might in fact contribute to continuing poverty (Fisher et al., 2013).

Recent ecosystem service framings are moving towards acknowledging interconnected social-ecological systems (Reyers and Selomane; Dearing, both this volume). In both ESPA and IPBES, there has been a shift from an ecological framing of ecosystem services to a more balanced social-ecological construct between biophysical dynamics, people's perceptions, needs and values for ecosystem services, and governance systems. This is clearly exemplified in Díaz et al. (2018), where the notion of NCP is highly dependent on the cultural lens and thus the perceptions of the relationships between ecosystem flows and human wellbeing, beyond a linear and somewhat deterministic stock-flow view. Alongside this shift in framing, there has been an increase in conceptual developments on e.g. plurality of values (Pascual et al., 2017a), co-production of ecosystem services (Reyers et al., 2013), power and justice (Sikor, 2013), social-ecological trade-offs (Bennett et al., 2015) and disaggregation of poverty analyses (Daw et al., 2011).

Emergent conceptual attributes from the evolution of ecosystem service frameworks

Several significant conceptual attributes have emerged over the last decade.

On co-production of ecosystem services

The benefits or contributions from ecosystems arise through a combination of ecosystem entities and anthropogenic assets (including human and social capital, financial and man-made capital) as well as human labour. For example, the production of food as provisioning service requires different inputs such as regulating soil services, farmers' labour and knowledge. This process is understood as ecosystem service co-production (Reyers et al., 2013). It is important for understanding not only how ecosystem services are supplied, but also how service flows are distributed, since intermediary services and anthropogenic inputs are unequally distributed across ecosystems and accessible by different actors in society (Lele et al., 2013; Reyers et al., 2013). Palomo et al. (2016) differentiate two main types of co-production: the *physical* processes which affect final ecosystem service flows via ecosystem management using anthropogenic assets; and the *cognitive* processes, which are shaped, for example culturally by social norms, leading to changes in ways that ecosystem services are demanded and/or enjoyed.

A focus on ecosystem service co-production is key to understanding their delivery and distribution across social groups. Thus, we can understand the differentiated impacts on wellbeing among different people given different levels of access, control and use of anthropogenic assets and labour (Berbés-Blázquez et al., 2016). The MA acknowledged the role of different capital types in the co-production of ecosystem services, and the NCP approach of IPBES has (physical and cognitive) co-production as a central focus. However, the potential effects of different ecosystem service co-production pathways for poverty alleviation remain under-studied and under-conceptualised, and the nested nature of co-produced ecosystem service bundles via ecological and social factors is not yet well understood. For example, it is not the same to allocate young girls' time vis-à-vis adults' time to fuelwood collection, as this may impact on the young girls' time for investing in human capital (e.g. formal education), which in turn may affect the co-production of other ecosystem services that may require certain levels of education and in particular, the increased education of girls/women.

On power and justice

Framing ecosystem services for poverty alleviation should help understand how social power relations shape ecosystem service governance systems that regulate entitlements to ecosystem resources. Focusing on power dynamics can help to better identify social trade-offs in terms of winners and losers (Berbés-Blázquez et al., 2016). The use of an ecosystem service framework, without acknowledging the role of power relations, risks reifying the *status quo* at the expense of already disenfranchised social groups. In general, ecosystem assessments do not yet capture, nor question, the role that power relations play in the co-production of ecosystem services and the associated distribution of benefits and burdens across social groups.

Ecosystem service 'cascades' have been proposed to identify intermediary steps between biophysical functions of ecosystems and changes in human well-being (Haines-Young and Potschin, 2010). They have not yet been applied to identify social factors determining the operation of critical intermediate steps in the cascade. For example, this could involve identifying who may have power at any one of these stages in order to determine who has access to an ecosystem service, at the expense of others, thereby determining who wins and who loses. Likewise, the cascade approach could be adapted to help to identify whether, and to what extent, political and economic elites capture a disproportionate share of benefits from ecosystem services, as well as the systematic displacements of ecosystem service burdens onto disadvantaged actors as a result of power differentials (Berbés-Blázquez et al., 2016).

Including social power relations in ecosystem service frameworks is vital to understand the institutional context of differentiated social groups (Brown and Fortnam, this volume). For instance, land allocation and associated ecosystem service flows in many African societies respond less to productivity and more to cultural considerations via gender roles, allowing certain social elites to maintain control (Berbés-Blázquez et al., 2016). It follows that justice must become more central in ecosystem service framings, considering socially differentiated groups of people with respect to wealth, power, gender and identities (Sikor, 2013; Dawson et al., this volume).

On ecosystem service valuation

The MA, and subsequent core frameworks, emanate from understanding ecosystems or nature as a capital asset. In this context, the flow of ecosystem services can be viewed as the return or interest that society receives from natural capital, thus implying that the level of the interest (ecosystem service quality or quantity) changes as the level/quality of the asset changes (ecosystems are altered). The MA recognised that economic valuation was hard to achieve consistently and with confidence, as peoples' preferences for ecosystem services are hard to express, and many, especially those associated with intangible benefits (e.g. cultural ecosystem services), do not easily lend themselves to economic valuation (Carpenter et al., 2009).

Framings for the economic valuation of ecosystem services have led to three important conceptual anchoring points: (i) ecosystem services are as dependent on ecological functions and processes as they are on social constructs connected to benefits and thus are experienced or perceived by people (Wegner and Pascual, 2011); (ii) separating intermediate (e.g. crop pollination as regulating service) from final ecosystem services (e.g. crop production) and benefits to people (e.g. food contributing to health) is key to avoiding double counting in economic valuation of ecosystem services (Fisher and Turner, 2008); and (iii) an ecosystem property such as resilience ought to be seen as an intermediate ecosystem service in as much it provides stability to the flow of benefits via final services, and can be connected to the idea of the insurance value of biodiversity (Pascual et al., 2010).

Efforts to conceptualise ecosystem service values using an economic logic have resulted in frameworks downplaying non-instrumental values and the significance of ethical or other held-values/principles that people associate with nature (Jax et al., 2013). As a reaction to the dominant utilitarian approach of the ecosystem service framing, new ways of conceptualising ecosystem service values are being proposed, e.g. via the idea of 'relational values' (Chan et al., 2016). This is impacting the way IPBES, among others, is embracing the idea of wellbeing outcomes from ecosystem services beyond utilitarian benefits, and extending it to aspects of agency, place identity, empathy, caring for nature and other-regarding actions (Pascual et al., 2017a). Opening up the valuation space beyond a restricted utilitarian approach can create a more integrated social-ecological perspective where ecosystem service flows are associated with broader notions of sustainability and justice. It is important to recognise that valuation is itself a value-laden process and that power relations through which such different types of values are expressed ought to be a central component of valuation exercises and assessments.

Application and implications of ecosystem service framings for policy instruments

Ecosystem service-wellbeing framings have had some impact on the way certain policies are formulated and designed, as well as being influenced in their turn by policy-making processes.

Perhaps the key policy instrument that has been most greatly influenced by epistemic communities and their preferred ecosystem service framings, is centred on Payments for Ecosystem Services (PES). PES emerged in the early 2000s as a direct response to strict biodiversity conservation approaches based on 'command and control' or 'fences and fines' (mostly in the form of protected areas of high ecological and biodiversity value). These approaches were criticised for the lack of voluntary engagement of ecosystem service providers (Menton and Bennett; Porras and Asquith, both this volume), as well as a neglect of social concerns on the impacts on local communities (Adams et al., 2004). Different epistemic communities, each with their own value framings and interests, have influenced the various framings behind PES, understood as payments, compensations or rewards, and therefore their design (Menton and Bennett, this volume).

In areas with high poverty levels, the general logic behind pro-poor PES schemes is that providers of ecosystem services are poor landholders or disadvantaged communities, and that direct and conditional payments can contribute to poverty alleviation of people voluntarily participating in the schemes, resulting in the alluring possibilities of 'win-win' outcomes (Muradian et al., 2013). Furthermore, for some scholars PES is thought to play a role in development in the Global South, as the cost-effectiveness of the schemes cannot be achieved without integrating complementary social objectives, especially with regards to social equity (e.g. Pascual et al., 2014). In practice, PES cannot be decoupled from political aspects of social legitimacy, and perceptions of social equity and fairness. Conceptual framings of the ecosystem service–poverty nexus, and experience in the implementation of PES schemes suggests that PES requires contextually customised design features, in terms of *inter alia* payment vehicles and contract flexibility, as well as understanding of impacts of payment differentiation, spatial targeting and enforced conditionality that prove highly sensitive to the social and poverty contexts (Engel, 2016).

The evolution of ecosystem service framings for human wellbeing, along with ideas of co-production, power relations, equity and justice, nourished by knowledge generated from programmes such as ESPA, is having a discernible impact on how PES is being reframed. There seems to be less emphasis on monetisation and a greater focus on the transfer of resources at the complex interplay between conservation and rural development, though still with a discernible conditionality component (Menton and Bennett; Porras and Asquith, both this volume).

Conclusions

Since the twin milestones of the Sustainable Livelihoods Framework (Scoones, 1998) and the MA (2005), epistemic communities and their associated core and satellite ecosystem service frameworks have attempted to refine and improve ways to frame human-nature relations. There have been many routes for this, for instance by enlightening an economic dimension beyond commodification, stressing social-ecological co-production processes, linking institutions and governance systems with power relations and environmental justice frames as filters through which we can better understand the way management of ecosystems creates winners and losers, and opening the space of valuation of ecosystem services. The ESPA programme has influenced and has been influenced by this kaleidoscopic evolution of conceptual frameworks.

There is an ethical mandate and responsibility for the research and decision-making communities to broaden the Western utilitarian ecosystem service framing, derived from the legacy of a linear stock-flow type of human relationship with nature. It is necessary to re-politicise how, why, by whom and for whom ecosystems are managed and how concepts such as wellbeing and poverty are articulated (Fisher et al., 2013). The design and implementation of policy instruments do not occur in an intellectual vacuum. They are affected by, and in turn affect, the way ecosystem service–poverty frameworks are devised given the interplay of epistemic communities and communities of practice. Policy instruments, such as PES, appear to be preferred by policy makers to connect the conservation of ecosystem service flows and developmental objectives in the Global South; however, as conceptual framings and epistemic communities continue to evolve, so will PES programmes.

Since the MA, investment in the scientific evidence base through programmes such as ESPA and other connected institutions and programmes (especially those connected to social-ecological system thinking) have influenced the lens through which the links between ecosystem services and wellbeing are seen in more inclusive ways. This evolution is also having an impact on the interpretation of human–nature relations at the science–policy interface, and can potentially influence the ways in which different epistemic communities work in the context of the Sustainable Development Goals. Allowing different knowledge systems to engage in dialogue and more inclusive (and culturally legitimate) co-construction of knowledge about the ecosystem service–wellbeing nexus is vital. But at the same time, we face accelerated global environmental change, including dramatic biodiversity loss and the ethical imperative to raise millions of people out of poverty, many of whom, directly or indirectly, rely on protecting and enhancing ecosystem service flows now and in the future. In this context, we point to two future challenges for research in ecosystem service framings.

First, we need to avoid thinking that a single framework, whether narrow or complex, can be the solution. While simple frameworks may help different epistemic communities to agree on common concepts and linkages, they may also promote the idea that win-win outcomes are easily attainable. Complex frameworks on the other hand, while recognising the intricacy of social-ecological systems, may still fall short of some key elements (such as power imbalances and associated political economy) and be too intricate for decision makers or researchers to use. At this stage, it may be that we have yet to find a way of describing the ecosystem service for human wellbeing relationships in a way that really speaks to all people, and this must continue to be one focal point of future efforts.

Second, given the exponential increase in the capability of information systems, there may be a strong temptation to develop ecosystem service approaches that are fixated in data-hungry technological developments, e.g. creating overly detailed typologies of ecosystem services, unduly enhancing the resolution of ecosystem service maps, etc. Such an approach can compete with alternative ways of mobilising funding and effort into more transdisciplinary collaborations among different epistemic communities in order to co-construct knowledge that can empower those often without a voice in debates and decision making, such as the landless and marginalised indigenous peoples. Of course, there is also an ideal position which implies devising and applying new technology that can foster data acquisition, processing and interpretation to help foster trans-disciplinary approaches with the active participation of stakeholders, including those who most need it in terms of poverty alleviation. Such involvement should also ideally help identify technological development that better favours more informed decision making across sectors, from poor households, development and conservation NGOs, business and governments.

We recommend that future frameworks reflect basic relationships between ecosystem services and human wellbeing but are adapted for the specific purpose they seek to address. In this manner, they can find a way of describing our relationship with nature that speaks to all people and thus can offer the potential to achieve social-ecological transformations required for environmental sustainability and poverty alleviation.

References

(ESPA outputs marked with '★')

Abson DJ, von Wehrden H, Baumgärtner S, et al. (2014) Ecosystem services as a boundary object for sustainability. *Ecological Economics* 103: 29–37.

Adams WM, Aveling R, Brockington D, et al. (2004) Biodiversity conservation and the eradication of poverty. *Science* 306: 1146–1149.

Agarwala M, Atkinson G, Fry B, et al. (2014) Assessing the relationship between human well-being and ecosystem services: a review of frameworks. *Conservation and Society* 12: 437–449.

Alkire S (2007) *Choosing Dimensions: The Capability Approach and Multidimensional Poverty*. Oxford: Chronic Poverty Research Centre.

Barrett CB, Travis AJ and Dasgupta P. (2011) On biodiversity conservation and poverty traps. *Proceedings of the National Academy of Sciences* 108: 13907–13912.

Bateman IJ, Mace GM, Fezzi C, et al. (2011) Economic analysis for ecosystem service assessments. *Environmental and Resource Economics* 48: 177–218.

Bennett EM, Cramer W, Begossi A, et al. (2015) Linking biodiversity, ecosystem services, and human well-being: three challenges for designing research for sustainability. *Current Opinion in Environmental Sustainability* 14: 76–85.

Berbés-Blázquez M, González JA and Pascual U. (2016) Towards an ecosystem services approach that addresses social power relations. *Current Opinion in Environmental Sustainability* 19: 134–143.

Carpenter SR, Mooney HA, Agard J, et al. (2009) Science for managing ecosystem services: beyond the Millennium Ecosystem Assessment. *Proceedings of the National Academy of Sciences* 106: 1305–1312.

Chan KMA, Balvanera P, Benessaiah K, et al. (2016) Why protect nature? Rethinking values and the environment. *Proceedings of the National Academy of Sciences* 113: 1462–1465.

Costanza R, d'Arge R, de Groot R, et al. (1997) The value of the world's ecosystem services and natural capital. *Nature* 387: 253.

Daily G (1997) Introduction: What Are Ecosystem Services? In: Daily G (ed.) *Nature's Services: Societal Dependence on Natural Ecosystems*. Washington, DC: Island Press.

★Daw T, Brown K, Rosendo S, et al. (2011) Applying the ecosystem services concept to poverty alleviation: the need to disaggregate human well-being. *Environmental Conservation* 38: 370–379.

★Daw TM, Coulthard S, Cheung WWL, et al. (2015) Evaluating taboo trade-offs in ecosystems services and human well-being. *Proceedings of the National Academy of Sciences* 112: 6949–6954.

Dewees PA, Campbell BM, Katerere Y, et al. (2010) Managing the Miombo woodlands of Southern Africa: policies, incentives and options for the rural poor. *Journal of Natural Resources Policy Research* 2: 57–73.

*Díaz S, Demissew S, Carabias J, et al. (2015) The IPBES conceptual framework – connecting nature and people. *Current Opinion in Environmental Sustainability* 14: 1–16.

Díaz S, Pascual U, Stenseke M, et al. (2018) Assessing nature's contributions to people. *Science* 359: 270–272.

Ekins P, Simon S, Deutsch L, et al. (2003) A framework for the practical application of the concepts of critical natural capital and strong sustainability. *Ecological Economics* 44: 165–185.

Engel S (2016) The Devil in the detail: a practical guide on designing payments for environmental services. *International Review of Environmental and Resource Economics* 9: 131–177.

*ESPA. (2013) *ESPA Knowledge Strategy*. Available at: http://bit.ly/ESPAFramework

Farley J. (2012) Natural Capital. In: Craig RK, Nagle JC, Pardy B, et al. (eds) *Berkshire Encyclopedia of Sustainability: Ecosystem Management and Sustainability*. Gt Barrington, MA: Berkshire Publishing.

Fisher B and Turner RK. (2008) Ecosystem services: classification for valuation. *Biological Conservation* 141: 1167–1169.

*Fisher JA, Patenaude G, Meir P, et al. (2013) Strengthening conceptual foundations: analysing frameworks for ecosystem services and poverty alleviation research. *Global Environmental Change* 23: 1098–1111.

Haas PM. (1992) Introduction: epistemic communities and international policy coordination. *International Organization* 46: 1–35.

Haines-Young R and Potschin M. (2010) The links between biodiversity, ecosystem services and human well-being. In: Frid CLJ and Raffaelli DG (eds) *Ecosystem Ecology: A New Synthesis*. Cambridge, UK: Cambridge University Press, 110–139.

*Howe, C, Corbera., E, Vira. B, et al. (2018) Distinct positions underpin ecosystem services for poverty alleviation. *Oryx* [in press].

*Howe C, Suich H, Vira B, et al. (2014) Creating win-wins from trade-offs? Ecosystem services for human well-being: a meta-analysis of ecosystem service trade-offs and synergies in the real world. *Global Environmental Change* 28: 263–275.

Jansson AM, Hammer M, Folke C, et al., eds. (1994) *Investing in Natural Capital: The Ecological Economics Approach to Sustainability*. Washington, DC: Island Press.

Jax K, Barton DN, Chan KMA, et al. (2013) Ecosystem services and ethics. *Ecological Economics* 93: 260–268.

*Keane A. (2016) A review of conceptual frameworks arising from the ESPA programme. Edinburgh, UK: Ecosystem Services for Poverty Alleviation (ESPA) Programme.

Kumar P, ed. (2010) *The Economics of Ecosystems and Biodiversity: Ecological and Economic Foundations*. London: Earthscan.

Larigauderie A, Prieur-Richard A-H, Mace GM, et al. (2012) Biodiversity and ecosystem services science for a sustainable planet: the DIVERSITAS vision for 2012–20. *Current Opinion in Environmental Sustainability* 4: 101–105.

*Lele S, Springate-Baginski O, Lakerveld R, et al. (2013) Ecosystem services: origins, contributions, pitfalls, and alternatives. *Conservation and Society* 11: 343.

MA. (2005) *Millennium Ecosystem Assessment, 2005. Ecosystems and Human Well-Being: Synthesis*. Washington, DC: Island Press.

*Mace GM, Norris K and Fitter AH (2012) Biodiversity and ecosystem services: a multilayered relationship. *Trends in Ecology and Evolution* 27: 19–26.

Mace GM, Reyers B, Alkemade R, et al. (2014) Approaches to defining a planetary boundary for biodiversity. *Global Environmental Change* 28: 289–297.

MAES. (2013) Mapping and assessment of ecosystems and their services: technical report. European Commission.

★Martin A, Akol A and Phillips J. (2013) Just conservation? On the fairness of sharing benefits. In: Sikor T (ed.) *The Justices and Injustices of Ecosystem Services.* Abingdon, UK: Routledge.

★Muradian R, Arsel M, Pellegrini L, et al. (2013) Payments for ecosystem services and the fatal attraction of win-win solutions. *Conservation Letters* 6: 274–279.

Narayan D, Patel R, Schafft K, et al. (2000) *Voices of the Poor: Can Anyone Hear Us?* New York: Oxford University Press (for the World Bank).

Ostrom E. (2009) A general framework for analyzing sustainability of social-ecological systems. *Science* 325: 419–422.

Palomo I, Felipe-Lucia MR, Bennett EM, et al. (2016) Disentangling the pathways and effects of ecosystem service co-production. *Advances in Ecological Research* 54: 245–283.

Pascual U, Balvanera P, Díaz S, et al. (2017a) Valuing nature's contributions to people: the IPBES approach. *Current Opinion in Environmental Sustainability* 26–27: 7–16.

Pascual U, Muradian R, Brander L, et al. (2010) The economics of valuing ecosystem services and biodiversity. In: Kumar P (ed.) *The Economics of Ecosystems and Biodiversity: Ecological and Economic Foundations.* London: Earthscan, 183–256.

★Pascual U, Palomo I, Adams WM, et al. (2017b) Off-stage ecosystem service burdens: a blind spot for global sustainability. *Environmental Research Letters* 12: 075001.

Pascual U, Phelps J, Garmendia E, et al. (2014) Social equity matters in payments for ecosystem services. *BioScience* 64: 1027–1036.

Reardon T and Vosti SA. (1995) Links between rural poverty and the environment in developing countries: asset categories and investment poverty. *World Development* 23: 1495–1506.

Reid WV and Mooney HA. (2016) The Millennium Ecosystem Assessment: testing the limits of interdisciplinary and multi-scale science. *Current Opinion in Environmental Sustainability* 19: 40–46.

Reyers B, Biggs R, Cumming GS, et al. (2013) Getting the measure of ecosystem services: a social-ecological approach. *Frontiers in Ecology and the Environment* 11: 268–273.

★Roe D, Elliott J, Sandbrook C, et al. (2012) *Biodiversity conservation and poverty alleviation: exploring the evidence for a link.* Chichester, UK: Wiley.

Sandker M, Ruiz-Perez M and Campbell BM. (2012) Trade-offs between biodiversity conservation and economic development in five tropical forest landscapes. *Environmental Management* 50: 633–644.

Scoones I (1998) Sustainable rural livelihoods: a framework for analysis. Sussex, UK: Institute of Development Studies.

★Sikor T, ed. (2013) *The Justices and Injustices of Ecosystem Services.* Abingdon, UK: Routledge.

Smeets E and Weterings R. (1999) Environmental indicators: typology and overview. Technical Report 25. Copenhagen, Denmark: European Environment Agency.

★Suich H (2012) *Conceptual Framework: Poverty.* Available at: http://bit.ly/ESPAPoverty

★Suich H, Howe C and Mace G. (2015) Ecosystem services and poverty alleviation: a review of the empirical links. *Ecosystem Services* 12: 137–147.

Tengö M, Brondizio ES, Elmqvist T, et al. (2014) Connecting diverse knowledge systems for enhanced ecosystem governance: the multiple evidence base approach. *Ambio* 43: 579–591.

Tomich TP, Argumedo A, Baste I, et al. (2010) Conceptual frameworks for ecosystem assessment: their development, ownership, and use. In: Ash N, Blanco H, Brown C, et al. (eds) *Ecosystems and Human Well-Being: A Manual for Assessment Practitioners.* Washington, DC: Island Press, 71–114.

UKNEA. (2011) *The UK National Ecosystem Assessment: Synthesis of Key Findings.* Cambridge, UK: UNEP-WCMC.

Vugteveen P, van Katwijk MM, Rouwette E, et al. (2015) Developing an effective adaptive monitoring network to support integrated coastal management in a multiuser nature reserve. *Ecology and Society* 20: 59.

Wegner G and Pascual U. (2011) Cost-benefit analysis in the context of ecosystem services for human well-being: a multidisciplinary critique. *Global Environmental Change* 21: 492–504.

2

JUSTICE AND EQUITY

Emerging research and policy approaches to address ecosystem service trade-offs

Neil Dawson, Brendan Coolsaet and Adrian Martin

Introduction

Since the Millennium Ecosystem Assessment (MA, 2005) cemented the popularity of the concept of ecosystem services, ecosystem services studies have increased awareness of the extent to which ecosystems support, and have capacity to continue to support, the wellbeing of humans at multiple scales (Steffen et al., 2015). However, ecosystem service frameworks have been criticised for targeting improvements in aggregate human wellbeing, a utilitarian perspective overlooking precisely which people benefit, where, in what ways, and who may be made worse off and how (Chan et al., 2012; Lele et al., 2013). Specifically, it is important to consider how ecosystem governance driven by objectives of producing regulating ecosystem services, or protecting specific forms of biodiversity for distant stakeholders (both spatially and temporally), may affect the poor or social and cultural minorities locally, particularly in developing countries (Suich et al., 2015). Epistemic communities have thus emerged to address the complex interrelations between social and ecological systems, revealing the diverse ways in which people are affected by ecosystem services (and disservices) and the importance of political factors in mediating whether and how different groups benefit (Fisher et al., 2014). This enhanced picture of the ways in which governance affects different people's wellbeing, and the types of trade-offs which result, reveals the need to approach ecosystem governance as a matter of justice. At a conceptual level, the overarching goal of environmental or ecosystem governance has therefore been articulated as the pursuit of a safe *and just* operating space (Dearing et al., 2014), while acknowledging that ecosystem service-based interventions simultaneously create justices and injustices for different groups of people, including impacts on the rights and basic needs of some of the poorest and most vulnerable people on the planet (Sikor, 2013a).

The growing body of research exploring the social elements of ecosystem service trade-offs has endorsed the relevance of three broad areas of concern that dominate theories of social justice: distribution, procedure and recognition. Regarding distribution, environmental governance determines the distribution of costs and benefits, opportunities and risks between different social groups, influencing who can access ecosystem services and who suffers from disservices. Decisions determining the distribution of access to ecosystem services involve social-ecological trade-offs, such that provision of ecosystem services to one group of stakeholders is often at the expense of other groups, while the poor and vulnerable are disproportionately dependent on access to ecosystem services (Daw et al., 2011). For example, increased forest protection to provide global climate regulation services, to ensure provision of water to downstream users, or to protect species with high potential for tourism, commonly leads to short-term losses of provisioning services for food, fuel and other basic needs to local populations, or increased prevalence of disservices such as to local farmers through crop-raiding animals (Howe et al., 2014).

While most studies have focused on the distributional elements of trade-offs, a small number have also focused on the procedures by which decisions about ecosystem services are made, including the influence of power and the politics of who wins and who loses. Those studies highlight the importance of what information goes into decision making, whose perspectives are represented, and whose and which values influence decision-making processes at various scales (Rival, 2012; Vira et al., 2012). In coastal Kenya, around the Mombasa Marine National Park, multi-stakeholder workshops generated the collaborative understanding necessary to underpin decisions regulating fishing activities, as plans to support at-sea capture methods at the expense of land-based fishing were revealed to affect groups beyond the fishers themselves, including female fish traders, who depended upon the income to support their families yet had no voice in decision making (Galafassi et al., 2017). Research into community-based forest management in Tanzania further reinforces the importance of procedural factors relative to distribution – enhanced local decision making is sufficient motivation to participate in and support forest management, even in the absence of significant material benefits (Gross-Camp, 2017). At higher scales of governance, powerful stakeholders are shown to shape the way social issues are framed in policies, for example leading to contrasting interpretations of Free, Prior and Informed Consent (FPIC) between mining and forestry sectors (Mahanty and McDermott, 2013).

A further area of justice concern is the extent to which those holding different worldviews, often deeply connected to nature, ecosystems and places, are recognised. This line of concern has involved critical scrutiny of the ecosystem services framework itself, asking whether the rudimentary conceptualisation of cultural values and 'siloing' of them from other types of services (inadvertently) promotes a worldview that precludes alternative, possibly more just, ways of knowing nature-society relations (Chan et al., 2016; Martin et al., 2013; Pascual and Howe, this volume). A compromise response to such a critique, staying within the ecosystem

BOX 2.1 THE THREE DIMENSIONS OF ENVIRONMENTAL JUSTICE

Early or 'first generation' environmental justice studies focused on the maldistribution of environmental externalities from industry in the United States (Walker, 2012). A second approach to environmental justice emerged as an analytical frame in the early 2000s, focusing on three interrelated dimensions: distribution, procedure and recognition, and has since gained global renown and application. This builds on work by Nancy Fraser (Fraser, 1995) and others who initially put forward the same three dimensions to comprise theories of social justice, which were subsequently developed as a theory of environmental justice, notably by David Schlosberg, who further notes the importance of future generations and non-human nature as groups affected by environmental governance (Schlosberg, 2004).

- **Distribution** concerns the different subjects who realise benefits or incur costs and risks, whether material or non-material, objective or subjective (Walker, 2012).
- **Procedure** refers to how decisions are made and by whom, whether formal rules and processes or informal interactions, necessitating attention to unequal power relations and differential ability to assert or oppose different claims (Dawson et al., 2017b).
- **Recognition** revolves around the status afforded to different social and cultural values or identities and to the social groups who hold them (Martin et al., 2016).

Although there is debate over which dimension may be most central, and how they interact, there is wide acknowledgement in ecosystem services scholarship that all three matter, are interrelated and should be given broad, simultaneous consideration when addressing empirically the perspectives of different people on environmental governance and change. Claims about justices and injustices may pertain to any and most likely to all of those dimensions.

The convergence of equity with environmental justice

The idea of 'environmental equity' has taken a similar trajectory to that of 'environmental justice'. In ecosystem service research, recent work has aligned the two concepts such that there is no longer a clear lexical distinction (Schreckenberg et al., 2016). Historically, however, the concepts find their origin in rather different settings. 'Environmental equity' mainly gained prominence in policy circles, and was originally formulated exclusively as a matter of inter- and intra-generational distribution (Pearce et al., 1989). In 1992, the US Environmental Protection Agency established the 'Environmental Equity Workgroup' and published the 'Environmental Equity report', anchoring the concept in policy-circles. However, the preference for equity within policy-circles has been criticised for ignoring underlying issues of social exclusion, power, race and class in the context of the environment (Gauna, 1995).

'Environmental justice', however, appears to have much more of a grass-roots origin. It emerged through struggles of African-American communities denouncing the inequitable distribution of environmental harm, and its origin is often traced back to the 1978 pollution scandal in Love Canal, New York. The concept gained nationwide attention in 1991, with the adoption of the 'seventeen principles of environmental justice' during the First National People of Colour Environmental Leadership Summit in Washington, DC and led to the adoption of the Environmental Justice Executive Order 12898 in 1994.

Despite the repeated articulation of environmental justice and equity definitions encompassing these three dimensions, the vast majority of studies referring to equity or environmental justice focus very narrowly on issues of material distribution and equality of outcomes, downplaying the importance of decision-making processes and of cultural difference. These narrow definitions are poorly supported by theories of equity and justice (going back as far as Aristotle) and overlook key factors shaping people's experiences of ecosystem governance, or ecosystem service trade-offs.

services framing, is to ensure that research disaggregates social groups and their values (Daw et al., 2011; Díaz et al., 2015). For example, Dawson and Martin (2015) show through analysis of the wellbeing of rural Rwandans, that differences in values and practices relating to land and natural resources, food production and income generation, and the social and political dynamics which marginalise certain groups, are crucial to the way poverty and trade-offs are experienced. In Rwanda, strict regulation over agriculture and forestry practices combine to override the rights and interests of cultural minorities, including the indigenous Twa and others who depend on the use of traditional knowledge, customary land tenure and embedded social practices around sharing and trade of crops.

These three critical concerns of ecosystem governance or management of ecosystem services trade-offs – distribution, procedure and recognition – have been elaborated as three interrelated dimensions of environmental justice (Box 2.1, Figure 2.1). Justice or equity framings essentially focus attention on all three dimensions simultaneously and so offer a holistic exploration, revealing differences between stakeholder perspectives, across multiple values and also scales of space and time (Sikor et al., 2014). For example, one of the more common ways to resolve ecosystem service trade-offs is to employ financial mechanisms such as payments for ecosystem services or compensation. While such distribution-oriented mechanisms are often (though not always) considered legitimate by local communities, they only deal with one dimension of injustice and therefore are often not sufficient to

Interrelated Dimensions	Distribution ←------→	Recognition ←------→	Procedure
Definition	Distribution of costs and benefits, risks and opportunities, material or non-material, objective or subjective, for & between stakeholders/generations	Recognition of different worldviews, identities, values and practices and respect for the dignity of those holding them	Procedures through which decisions are made (both formal or informal rules, institutions, interactions), inclusiveness and effectiveness of participation and power relations
Value for Exploring Ecosystem Services Trade-offs	Extends beyond material trade-offs to explore perceptions of different stakeholders Multidimensional, subject-driven understandings of poverty & wellbeing	Recognises plural worldviews, values & conceptions of justice revealing trade-offs, including environmental values Disaggregation according to locally meaningful social categories	Beyond outcomes, considers decision-making (formal & informal), extent & quality of participation, informing ecosystem services governance Explores underlying societal structures, political dynamics and norms creating trade-offs

Elicits 'social feedbacks' - how people perceive & respond to decision-making processes

FIGURE 2.1 Dimensions of environmental justice or equity and their contribution to the elaboration of ecosystem service trade-offs.

promote justice for all, as they neglect other aspects of justice which may be more important to people, such as having a voice in land-use decisions or gaining recognition of their particular identities and practices (Martin et al., 2013).

The application of equity and justice approaches to ecosystem governance research, and increasingly as policy objectives, is a frontier with great potential impact on the practice of ecosystem governance. However, it is important to note that supporting knowledge of socio-economic status, livelihoods, social difference, cultural values, knowledge systems and impacts of change on people's lives is a necessary foundation for environmental justice research, and can be provided by complementary wellbeing research (Dawson et al., 2017a; Schlosberg and Carruthers, 2010; Coulthard et al., this volume).

In the remainder of this chapter, we first describe the emergence of equity and justice as goals in policy and, through an environmental justice lens, critically assess the framings of justice employed and mechanisms or strategies set out to attain them. Second, we draw on recent studies that have taken a holistic equity or justice framing to explore ecosystem service trade-offs to consider: how to define, assess and operationalise equity or justice for ecosystem governance; the normative barriers and opportunities that exist for promoting equity as a policy goal; and some of the characteristics of equitable or just governance in different contexts and sectors.

Equity and justice in environmental policy

Following the first Earth Summit in 1992, social objectives have gained increasing prominence in global environmental policy. In the context of conservation and ecosystem services, this has led to a shift from a focus on nature preservation alone to solutions that target simultaneous and synergistic social and ecological gains, through integrating sectors and land uses to produce more holistic, long-term solutions for development and the environment (Rival, 2012). The interrelation between social and ecological systems, policies and outcomes has been intensified through accelerating environmental change, increasing populations, infrastructure proliferation and globalisation processes (Adger and Winkels, 2014). But 'win-win' solutions do not come easily (Howe et al., 2014), and experiences have revealed negative impacts of governance interventions upon local populations, even as a consequence of supposedly 'people-friendly' approaches. Consideration of ecosystem services has been used to support market-based solutions such as payments for ecosystem services, whereby local people cease use of certain provisioning and/or cultural ecosystem services to maintain ecosystem structure and functions, and are compensated by the remote stakeholders who benefit. Such schemes can in principle resolve trade-offs in pro-poor and equitable ways because they involve financial transfers from wealthier to more marginal groups, and in principle do so on the basis of free and informed exchange (Pagiola et al., 2005). Yet such projects have been highly controversial and frequently shown to be inequitable because they are procedurally coercive (Fisher, 2013; McAfee, 2012); fail to distribute benefits to those who suffer the costs (Poudyal et al., 2016), or to marginalised groups (Corbera et al., 2007); and impose a solution framework that fails to recognise alternative values (Martin et al., 2013). Effective and equitable ecosystem services policy therefore requires a more explicit deliberation over justice framings and objectives against which to assess performance. Equity (and to a lesser extent justice) concerns have therefore landed and recently proliferated as terms in policy documents (Table 2.1).

Policy norms related to justice and equity reflect all three dimensions introduced above: distribution (mostly in the form of benefit-sharing arrangements); procedure (norms related to the improvement in participation of local stakeholders, e.g. free prior informed consent); and recognition (often in the form of respect for rights and knowledge of indigenous peoples and local communities). For example, environmental justice has gained global attention in the water sector. Since the 1980s, activists have voiced demands for universal access to water, inspiring global declarations such as the 1992 Dublin Statement on Water and Sustainable Development. This statement highlights the need to involve the full range of affected stakeholders, including women, in management (Principles 2 and 3), and eventual recognition by the United Nations in 2010 of access to clean water and sanitation as a human right (Principle 4) (ICWE, 1992). Some, such as the CBD Aichi Target 11, provide for a wide scope covering multiple dimensions, stating that 'communities should be fully engaged in governing and managing protected areas according to their rights, knowledge, capacities and institutions, should equitably share in the benefits arising from protected areas and should not bear inequitable costs' (CBD, 2010). Most however, do not include a working definition of equity or justice or describe the terms and principles by which justice is framed across different spatial scales, leaving it to states (and other stakeholders where processes allow) to interpret and assess these concepts and whether and how to develop strategies to pursue them. This ambiguity runs the risk of creating inconsistencies between policy initiatives and of enabling weak interpretations which support the *status quo* and preclude transformative change.

While the inclusion of justice references in policy came about through the proliferation of justice-related claim-making emanating from social movements,

TABLE 2.1 Examples of equity and justice measures and concepts used in selected policy documents (post-2000), and related theoretical concepts

Year	Policy document	Concepts	Environmental justice aspects
2016	IUCN Green List for Protected Areas	Free, prior and informed consent; Rights-holders effectively involved in decision making	Procedure
		Recognise the legitimate rights of Indigenous Peoples and Local Communities (IPLCs)	Recognition
2013	IUCN Instruments for Governance of Protected Areas	Appropriate compensation for the cost of protected areas	Distribution
		Full and effective participation	Procedure
		Respect substantive rights	Recognition
2013	IPBES Conceptual framework	Multidimensional value systems and 'alternative' knowledge systems	Recognition
2012	Sustainable Development Goal 15 (life on land)	Access and Benefit-sharing	Distribution
2012	Sustainable Development Goal 14 (life below water)	Recognizing [. . .] differential treatment for developing and least developed countries	Distribution
2010	CBD Nagoya Protocol	Access and Benefit-sharing	Distribution
		Prior Informed Consent	Procedure
2010	Aichi Biodiversity Targets 11 and 16	Equitable management of protected areas	Distribution Procedure Recognition
2010	UNFCCC REDD+ safeguards (Cancun Agreement)	Respect for the knowledge and rights of IPLCs	Recognition
		The full and effective participation of relevant stakeholders, in particular IPLCs	Procedure
2009	Conservation Initiative on Human Rights	Respect and promote human rights	Recognition
2001	FAO Treaty on Plant Genetic Resources for Food and Agriculture	Access and Benefit-sharing	Distribution

it is unclear how much overlap exists with the principles appearing in the documents. Indeed, indigenous, land rights, smallholder and other justice movements perceive that environmental policies, in tandem with development and agricultural policies, often override customary practices and tenure systems that underpin fair land allocation, food production and social relations, framing them as reasons for biodiversity loss rather than part of possible solutions. In other words, a 'justice gap' exists between the pathways to conservation and development outcomes envisioned in global (and national) policies and the perspectives of many indigenous peoples and local communities about how these outcomes should be achieved (Martin et al., 2016). Bridging this justice gap is not only important for moral reasons, to avoid adverse impacts and uphold human rights, but there is also increasing acknowledgement and evidence to suggest that equitable governance is instrumental in achieving ecological policy goals, rather than contrary to them (Coolsaet, 2015; Martin, 2017; Oldekop et al., 2016; Schreckenberg et al., 2016). More explicit framings of justice or equity and transparency around negotiation of terms and definitions between different interest groups are required to move beyond ambiguous and inconsistent references in policy. Greater attention to and consensus about equity and justice definitions could, in turn, inform development of guidelines and tools for how to assess and pursue more just, equitable and sustainable governance at various scales (Lele et al., 2013).

Defining, assessing and operationalising equity or justice for ecosystem services research and governance

Environmental justice frameworks, with a focus on the three interrelated dimensions of distribution, procedure and recognition, offer minimal guidance as to what justice issues may exist and how to observe and analyse them. This brevity is both a strength and a weakness. The breadth of the three dimensions demands attention to a set of inter-twined issues rather than focusing on a single aspect such as material distributional outcomes. The absence of a universal definition also enables research that explores plural justice perspectives, including inquiry into what people consider to be just or unjust in various contexts, at various spatial and temporal scales of analysis and through the lens of widely differing worldviews (Schlosberg and Carruthers, 2010; Box 2.2). On the other hand, the emergence of equity and justice as policy goals inevitably leads to calls for elaboration of operational principles of justice, along with suitable, replicable approaches to describe justice outcomes in various contexts and even standardised and quantifiable indicators and measures of justice that can be used to assess progress towards achieving the goal (Zafra-Calvo et al., 2017). Yet, there is limited guidance even for what should be considered within each dimension and how to elicit understanding about them. Here we synthesise contemporary scientific literature about how equity and environmental justice may be defined, assessed and operationalised to take issues of poverty, rights and trade-offs into account, with or without compromising attention to pluralism.

BOX 2.2 VALUE OF ENVIRONMENTAL JUSTICE OR EQUITY RESEARCH FOR EXPLORING ECOSYSTEM SERVICES TRADE-OFFS

Research into environmental justice or equity:

- Goes beyond identification of material and economic trade-offs to explore how different individuals and stakeholder groups perceive and feel about these trade-offs.

- Explores not only outcomes, but also the decision-making processes (both formal and informal), the extent and quality of participation for different stakeholders and how they shape perceptions of decisions and their outcomes.

- Recognises plural worldviews, values and conceptions of justice, including those that may be incompatible with an ecosystem services framing, thereby revealing a wider array of trade-offs experienced by different social groups. The absence of detailed, universal definition and conception maintains this flexibility.

- Addresses power relations among different perspectives in the conceptualisation and production of knowledge about ecosystem services and their valuation, to better represent worldviews and knowledge systems of marginalised groups.

- Disaggregates the outcomes of trade-offs for human wellbeing according to social categories that are locally relevant and meaningful (e.g. age, indigeneity, gender).

- Attends to major international social justice referents, including human rights declarations, basic needs thresholds and FPIC.

- Adopts a multi-dimensional understanding of poverty and wellbeing beyond standard measures of poverty or material wellbeing, which for example neglect issues recurrently central to local justice concerns such as land tenure security. Such approaches therefore more aligned with relatively holistic approaches to sustainable development such as SDGs.

- Captures how people perceive changes affecting them and respond behaviourally to them – eliciting 'social feedbacks' affecting ecosystems and uncovering implications for governance, looking beyond 'eudaimonic' methodologies focused on trajectories in people's wellbeing.

- Looks beyond the immediate manifestation of inequitable outcomes to explore the underlying societal structures that give rise to these and their drivers across different spatial and temporal scales.

Several studies have proposed options for enhancing the ability of empirical justice research to elicit plural perspectives and explore trade-offs. Sikor et al. (2014) put forward a framework for empirical studies which distinguishes, in addition to the three dimensions, who the various subjects of justice are (e.g. current people, future people, non-human animals) and the criteria which guide their notions of justice, or principles guiding what the various subjects consider to be fair (e.g. individual human rights, aggregate happiness). Others have differentiated between social norms, principles or 'notions' of justice and specific claims made by individuals or groups in response to certain impacts (Dawson et al., 2017a). Martin et al. (2016), in addition to considering the dimensions and subjects of justice, extend their analysis to consider the different types of harms which may constitute injustices (to include psychological harms such as loss of esteem and dignity), the mechanisms through which they are experienced (including unequal status conferred to different social groups) and the types of responses which may be considered to mitigate or counter those harms (such as recognition of difference).

Schreckenberg et al. (2016) go further and propose, in response to Aichi Target 11 of the CBD, a generalised set of principles for equitable ecosystem governance in the context of protected areas, drawing on inputs from existing international policy and law, from academics and practitioner stakeholders and informed by site-level case studies in East Africa. They identify 17 universal principles cutting across the three dimensions. Far from presenting prescriptive or limited approaches to understanding equity, the principles represent widely held norms supporting inclusive multi-stakeholder governance. For recognition, these include respect for human rights, land and resource tenure, both customary and statutory systems, identities, knowledge systems and institutions, and powers to influence. For procedure, the principles cover full and effective participation, clear responsibilities, accountability, access to justice, transparency, and FPIC. Distributional principles include identification of costs, risks and trade-offs, with attempts to mitigate costs and attention to the distributional outcomes for future generations. These principles elaborate important criteria for attaining or moving towards more equitable governance without promoting prescriptive approaches or a single governance form for doing so. Agreement between nation states and civil society representatives on justice-related norms and principles is evident, perhaps most notably through the UN Declaration on Human Rights. Such clear consensus on sets of principles suggests a more universal definition of environmental justice is possible for ecosystem services-related governance or the environment sector more widely. However, persistent political barriers to the adoption and implementation of human rights principles at national and subnational scales illustrate the enormity of the task.

Field studies focused on the perspectives of local inhabitants most affected by ecosystem governance have reiterated the importance of open, exploratory and plural approaches to equity and justice, which may complement the more deductive application of general principles. For example, Dawson et al. (2017b) find, through empirical research at Nam Et-Phou Louey National Protected Area in Laos, that aspects of governance important to local stakeholders' perceptions of equity include the informal interactions through which land and resource access is negotiated or customary access maintained in the face of formal rules, social and economic changes leading to re-evaluation of costs incurred through protected area management, and place attachments connecting people to locations inside protected area boundaries. Through exploring local priorities and perspectives, these studies highlighted that degazetting part of the protected area for local agricultural use was not seen to be an equitable solution to local claims. Rather, potential synergies between equity and conservation effectiveness were uncovered through more consistent and transparent enforcement of rules, acknowledgement of and reparation for broken promises of livelihood support, provision of development assistance more appropriate to local aspirations, and re-targeting of benefits towards those suffering the greatest costs of conservation restrictions.

ESPA research on justice and water management particularly revolves around the issue of involvement of affected people. Through questions like 'who decides who gets water, when, how and why' or 'who should be involved in the water catchment management', and 'whose knowledge on wastewater counts?' authors try making sense of the inevitable trade-offs, characterised by complex interdependencies between biophysical processes, uses and users, at local or at international level (Karpouzoglou and Zimmer, 2016; Wei et al., 2012; Zeitoun et al., 2014). Interestingly, while these studies have a common interest in the mechanisms of justice – i.e. the 'design features of governance interventions' (Sikor, 2013a: 14) – they focus on different aspects and different scales of the problem, hence highlighting different possible outcomes of more inclusive water management processes. For example, drawing on an experimental social learning platform in Lake Baiyangdian, China, Wei and colleagues (2012) show how the development of a reflexive governance process helps to improve the water catchment system by better apprehending its complexity.

Such features, though crucial for assessing equity and guiding responses, may not be easily captured in cursory top-down assessments or standardised indicators. Rather, the importance of these complex, non-material, procedural and evolving facets to perceptions of equity (and their centrality to the effective conservation of ecosystems) means that attempts to identify and address complex trade-offs must include trust-building and dialogue with all stakeholders, but particularly local communities, including the poor and marginalised among them, and collaborative, adaptive governance processes to respond to evolving issues and opportunities (Galafassi et al., 2017).

Normative boundaries to enhancing equity and addressing injustice

Enduring differences exist regarding the equitability of ecosystem governance, particularly between implementing institutions (at international and national levels) and the indigenous and local communities most affected. The 'justice gap' arises partly due to difficulties in implementing policies negotiated at the global or state level, but crucially is also caused by normative differences in how ecosystems should be equitably governed (Figure 2.2). In other words, addressing diverse equity concerns from multiple perspectives requires not only financial and human resources to implement equity principles but perhaps, more importantly, a change of thinking allowing dominant discourses to be challenged to the extent that persistent, entrenched injustices may be addressed. Indeed, advances in environmental justice research focus on radical counter-hegemony, including the recognition of different knowledge systems (Pellow, 2016), to better represent worldviews of marginalised groups and the political and social dynamics which cause and perpetuate injustices, particularly in the face of increasing global economic and political influences.

Unequal power between interest groups is a common and persistent feature of environmental management in developing countries (Sikor, 2013a). For example, research into the equity of forest certification schemes has revealed how power inequalities between international companies, timber producers, land owners and local communities tend to reproduce the same social and environmental injustices (McDermott, 2013; Pinto and McDermott, 2013). Zeitoun et al. (2014) consider how a focus on justice can mitigate power asymmetries between states in transboundary water arrangements, by providing counter-hegemonic alternatives. By showing how the exposure of poorer urban citizens to untreated wastewater is the result of particular framings of the problems, Karpouzoglou and Zimmer (2016) also look at strategies of counter-hegemony. In each case, the proposed pathway to enhanced justice lies in legitimising 'alternative' knowledge systems by ensuring poorer citizens have greater voice in defining the political agenda of wastewater management.

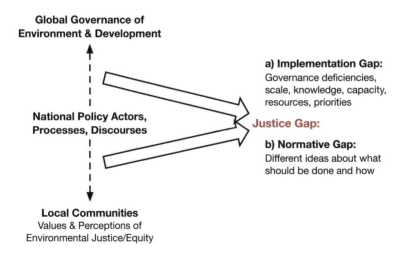

FIGURE 2.2 The justice gap between global and national ecosystem service governance and local communities comprises normative differences and implementation deficiencies.

Research into the framing and implementation of equity in ecosystem governance reveals an emphasis on access restrictions and financial compensation as central elements of governance, while complex issues relating to rights, tenure, cultural practices and participation are compartmentalised and deprioritised as safeguards or principles to be addressed through technocratic exercises comprising minimal monitoring and evaluation or accountability (Sikor, 2013b). Although the policies may refer to aspects of all three dimensions of justice, they commonly fail to deliver processes or outcomes perceived as equitable by local people or significant progress towards ecological goals. Such watering-down of justice issues has been demonstrated for PES projects (Fisher, 2013), Reduced Emissions from Deforestation and Forest Degradation schemes (REDD+) (Ituarte-Lima et al., 2014; Poudyal et al., 2016), biodiversity offsetting (Bidaud et al., 2017), water governance (Lele, 2017) and ecotourism projects (Martin et al., 2013). This cursory attention to, or lack of regard for, local justice framings fails to bring into negotiation the norms and discourses which support exclusionary, centralised approaches and reproduce entrenched injustices. Indeed, in many circumstances those who suffer injustices continue to be viewed as an obstacle to effective management, engaging in backward or even criminal activities (Dawson et al., 2016; Martin, 2017). Research has increasingly shown that granting autonomy to Indigenous Peoples to manage their lands and resources, particularly in the Amazon, leads to enhanced equity and a win-win for forest conservation and wellbeing (Iwamura et al., 2016). However, it remains poorly understood in more complex contexts in other regions, such as Africa and South Asia, what forms of governance achieve conservation goals while also conforming to local values and the wellbeing of local communities, including cultural minorities and the poor (Díaz et al., 2015).

Conclusions

Environmental justice provides an important research approach for detailing social and ecological aspects of ecosystem service trade-offs. The broad focus on procedure and recognition, in addition to distribution, is well suited to: explore multivalency and plural perspectives of diverse stakeholders; consider the political dynamics, which may promote or impede justice; and look across different land uses, sectors and policy arenas to uncover possible adaptations in governance to manage trade-offs. Studies of equity and environmental justice in the context of ecosystem service trade-offs have revealed the persistent gap between policies, programmes and local perspectives, across water, protected area, forest governance and other sectors. They have also uncovered opportunities for moving towards safe and just scenarios in challenging, complex contexts. Most notably, studies consistently reveal hegemony to be the enemy of equitable governance in situations with diverse interest groups and multiple value systems. Embracing broader definitions and framings of equity to support enhanced information, deliberation and mutual understanding of other stakeholders' motivations and experiences tends to reveal potential opportunities for innovative and synergistic solutions as well as highlighting emerging threats and trade-offs.

Research has a key role in elaborating why local experiences may diverge from policy, and in characterising best practice from countries, stakeholders and sites implementing innovative and progressive governance to inform practice at local to global scales. Areas that have been relatively neglected in environmental justice and equity research in the context of ecosystem services include: analysis of gender-related issues (Brown and Fortnam, this volume); spaces for participation and how they are perceived by different actors (Nunan et al., this volume); analyses comparing the perceived rights and responsibilities of stakeholders across scales ('tele-coupling'); and greater attention to the politics through which equity is framed at different policy scales, and responses designed and implemented. An increasing body of qualitative, quantitative and interdisciplinary evidence is required detailing the mechanisms through which equitable or inequitable circumstances influence people's behaviour and impact ecological outcomes. Studies building on this evidence to further elaborate guidelines and tools for how to assess and operationalise equity can feed into a number of important ongoing debates in various policy arenas. These include negotiations over how to assess ecosystem services at local and national scales, the means to implement increasingly popular landscape approaches, the definition of non-carbon benefits and equity in climate policy, approaches to assess and implement SDGs, and approaches to define, assess and pursue equity in the CBD.

The current political climate represents a crossroads for equity, the term favoured in policy, and justice, that favoured by social movements. Recent global environmental governance and targets for SDGs, climate policy and biodiversity conservation are under negotiation and are soon to be implemented across regions of high poverty and cultural diversity. Where attempts are made to enhance the prioritisation of equity in policy, through a deeper consideration of diverse values, disaggregated social impacts, more inclusive and accountable decision making at all scales and to substantive, accessible procedures to protect the rights of the most vulnerable, we may see those terms converge and a narrowing of the justice gap in practice as in research.

References

(ESPA outputs marked with '★')

Adger WN and Winkels A (2014) Vulnerability, Poverty and Sustaining Wellbeing. In: Atkinson G, Dietz S, Neumayer E, et al. (eds) *Handbook of Sustainable Development*. 2nd edn. Cheltenham, UK: Edward Elgar, 206–216.

★Bidaud C, Schreckenberg K, Rabeharison M, et al. (2017) The sweet and the bitter: intertwined positive and negative social impacts of a biodiversity offset. *Conservation and Society* 15: 1–13.

CBD. (2010) Convention on Biological Diversity (CBD) Decision X/2. The Strategic Plan for Biodiversity 2011–2020 and the Aichi Biodiversity Targets. Nagoya, Japan: Convention on Biological Diversity.

Chan KMA, Balvanera P, Benessaiah K, et al. (2016) Why protect nature? Rethinking values and the environment. *Proceedings of the National Academy of Sciences* 113: 1462–1465.

Chan KMA, Guerry AD, Balvanera P, et al. (2012) Where are cultural and social in ecosystem services? A framework for constructive engagement. *Bioscience* 62: 744–756.

Coolsaet B. (2015) Transformative participation in agrobiodiversity governance: making the case for an environmental justice approach. *Journal of Agricultural and Environmental Ethics* 28: 1089–1104.

Corbera E, Brown K and Adger WN. (2007) The equity and legitimacy of markets for ecosystem services. *Development and Change* 38: 587–613.

*Daw T, Brown K, Rosendo S, et al. (2011) Applying the ecosystem services concept to poverty alleviation: the need to disaggregate human well-being. *Environmental Conservation* 38: 370–379.

*Dawson N, Grogan K, Martin A, et al. (2017a) Environmental justice research shows the importance of social feedbacks in ecosystem service trade-offs. *Ecology and Society* 22: 12.

*Dawson N and Martin A. (2015) Assessing the contribution of ecosystem services to human wellbeing: a disaggregated study in western Rwanda. *Ecological Economics* 117: 62–72.

*Dawson N, Martin A and Danielsen F. (2017b) Assessing equity in protected area governance: approaches to promote just and effective conservation. *Conservation Letters*.

*Dawson N, Martin A and Sikor T. (2016) Green revolution in sub-Saharan Africa: implications of imposed innovation for the wellbeing of rural smallholders. *World Development* 78: 204–218.

*Dearing JA, Wang R, Zhang K, et al. (2014) Safe and just operating spaces for regional social-ecological systems. *Global Environmental Change* 28: 227–238.

*Díaz S, Demissew S, Carabias J, et al. (2015) The IPBES conceptual framework – connecting nature and people. *Current Opinion in Environmental Sustainability* 14: 1–16.

*Fisher JA. (2013) Justice implications of conditionality in payments for ecosystem services: a case study from Uganda. In: Sikor T (ed.) *The Justices and Injustices of Ecosystem Services*. Abingdon, UK: Routledge, 21–45.

*Fisher JA, Patenaude G, Giri K, et al. (2014) Understanding the relationships between ecosystem services and poverty alleviation: a conceptual framework. *Ecosystem Services* 7: 34–45.

Fraser N. (1995) From redistribution to recognition? Dilemmas of justice in a 'post-socialist' age. *New Left Review 1995*: 68–68.

*Galafassi D, Daw TM, Munyi L, et al. (2017) Learning about social-ecological trade-offs. *Ecology and Society* 22: 2.

Gauna E. (1995) Federal environmental citizen provisions: obstacles and incentives on the road to environmental justice. *Ecology Law Quarterly* 22: 1–87.

*Gross-Camp N. (2017) Tanzania's community forests: their impact on human well-being and persistence in spite of the lack of benefit. *Ecology and Society* 22: 37.

*Howe C, Suich H, Vira B, et al. (2014) Creating win-wins from trade-offs? Ecosystem services for human well-being: a meta-analysis of ecosystem service trade-offs and synergies in the real world. *Global Environmental Change* 28: 263–275.

ICWE. (1992) The Dublin Statement on Water and Sustainable Development. Dublin, Ireland: International Conference on Water and the Environment (ICWE).

*Ituarte-Lima C, McDermott CL and Mulyani M. (2014) Assessing equity in national legal frameworks for REDD plus: the case of Indonesia. *Environmental Science and Policy* 44: 291–300.

Iwamura T, Lambin EF, Silvius KM, et al. (2016) Socio–environmental sustainability of indigenous lands: simulating coupled human–natural systems in the Amazon. *Frontiers in Ecology and the Environment* 14: 77–83.

*Karpouzoglou T and Zimmer A. (2016) Ways of knowing the wastewaterscape: urban political ecology and the politics of wastewater in Delhi, India. *Habitat International* 54: 150–160.

Lele S. (2017) Sustainable Development Goal 6: watering down justice concerns. *Wiley Interdisciplinary Reviews: Water* 4.

*Lele S, Springate-Baginski O, Lakerveld R, et al. (2013) Ecosystem services: origins, contributions, pitfalls, and alternatives. *Conservation and Society* 11: 343.

MA. (2005) *Millennium Ecosystem Assessment, 2005. Ecosystems and Human Well-Being: Synthesis*. Washington, DC: Island Press.

McAfee K. (2012) The contradictory logic of global ecosystem services markets. *Development and Change* 43: 105–131.

*McDermott CL. (2013) Certification and equity: applying an 'equity framework' to compare certification schemes across product sectors and scales. *Environmental Science and Policy* 33: 428–437.

*Mahanty S and McDermott CL. (2013) How does Free, Prior and Informed Consent (FPIC) impact social equity? Lessons from mining and forestry and their implications for REDD+. *Land Use Policy* 35: 406–416.

*Martin A. (2017) *Just Conservation: Biodiversity, Wellbeing and Sustainability*. Abingdon, UK: Routledge.

*Martin A, Akol A and Phillips J. (2013) Just conservation? On the fairness of sharing benefits. In: Sikor T (ed.) *The Justices and Injustices of Ecosystem Services*. Abingdon, UK: Routledge.

*Martin A, Coolsaet B, Corbera E, et al. (2016) Justice and conservation: the need to incorporate recognition. *Biological Conservation* 197: 254–261.

Oldekop JA, Holmes G, Harris WE, et al. (2016) A global assessment of the social and conservation outcomes of protected areas. *Conservation Biology* 30: 133–141.

Pagiola S, Arcenas A and Platais G. (2005) Can payments for environmental services help reduce poverty? An exploration of the issues and the evidence to date from Latin America. *World Development* 33: 237–253.

Pearce DW, Markandya A and Barbier E. (1989) *Blueprint for a green economy*. London: Earthscan.

Pellow DN. (2016) Toward a Critical Environmental Justice Studies: Black Lives Matter as an Environmental Justice Challenge. *Du Bois Review: Social Science Research on Race* 13: 221–236.

Pinto LFG and McDermott C. (2013) Equity and forest certification – a case study in Brazil. *Forest Policy and Economics* 30: 23–29.

*Poudyal M, Ramamonjisoa B, Hockley N, et al. (2016) Can REDD+ social safeguards reach the 'right' people? Lessons from Madagascar. *Global Environmental Change* 37: 31–42.

*Rival L. (2012) Sustainable development through policy integration in Latin America: a comparative approach. *Development* 55: 63–70.

Schlosberg D. (2004) Reconceiving environmental justice: global movements and political theories. *Environmental Politics* 13: 517–540.

Schlosberg D and Carruthers D. (2010) Indigenous struggles, environmental justice, and community capabilities. *Global Environmental Politics* 10: 12–35.

*Schreckenberg K, Franks P, Martin A, et al. (2016) Unpacking equity for protected area conservation. *Parks* 22: 11–26.

*Sikor T, ed. (2013a) *The Justices and Injustices of Ecosystem Services*. Abingdon, UK: Routledge.

*Sikor T. (2013b) REDD+: justice effects of technical design. In: Sikor T (ed.) *The Justices and Injustices of Ecosystem Services*. Abingdon, UK: Routledge, 46–68.

*Sikor T, Martin A, Fisher J, et al. (2014) Toward an empirical analysis of justice in ecosystem governance. *Conservation Letters* 7: 524–532.

*Steffen W, Richardson K, Rockström J, et al. (2015) Planetary boundaries: guiding human development on a changing planet. *Science* 347: 1259855.

*Suich H, Howe C and Mace G. (2015) Ecosystem services and poverty alleviation: a review of the empirical links. *Ecosystem Services* 12: 137–147.

*Vira B, Adams B, Agarwal C, et al. (2012) Negotiating trade-offs: choices about ecosystem services for poverty alleviation. *Economic and Political Weekly* 47: 67–75.

Walker G. (2012) Environmental Justice: Concepts, Evidence and Politics. Abingdon, UK: Routledge.

*Wei Y, Ison R, Colvin J, et al. (2012) Reframing water governance: a multi-perspective study of an over-engineered catchment in China. *Journal of Environmental Planning and Management* 55: 297–318.

Zafra-Calvo N, Pascual U, Brockington D, et al. (2017) Towards an indicator system to assess equitable management in protected areas. *Biological Conservation* 211: 134–141.

*Zeitoun M, Warner J, Mirumachi N, et al. (2014) Transboundary water justice: a combined reading of literature on critical transboundary water interaction and justice, for analysis and diplomacy. *Water Policy* 16: 174–193.

3
SOCIAL-ECOLOGICAL SYSTEMS APPROACHES

Revealing and navigating the complex trade-offs of sustainable development

Belinda Reyers and Odirilwe Selomane

Introduction

Recent reviews on the relationships between ecosystem services, human wellbeing and poverty alleviation have highlighted the challenges caused by limited evidence of empirical links, and even less evidence and understanding of mechanisms (Raudsepp-Hearne et al., 2010; Suich et al., 2015). These reviews have shown that most empirical studies have adopted a reductionist approach focusing on single services, resources or measures of wellbeing. Similarly, reviews of the conceptual frameworks in use in ecosystem service and poverty alleviation research and practice also highlight the predominance of linear conceptual models of the relationships between the biophysical supply of ecosystem services, the social end points of human wellbeing or values, and diverse social or biophysical inputs into these flows (Fisher et al., 2013; Pascual and Howe, this volume). While useful in calculating the values of some ecosystem services, and raising awareness of the importance, distribution, trends and links between ecosystems and wellbeing, these studies have largely failed to demonstrate the contribution of biodiversity and ecosystem services to poverty alleviation, particularly the mechanisms or causal pathways by which this takes place (Suich et al., 2015).

At the same time, work in the field of complex social-ecological systems (Box 3.1) began to highlight the role of factors such as scale, time lags, feedbacks and thresholds in our understanding of the complex interactions between biodiversity, ecosystem services, human activities and human wellbeing (Folke, 2006; Holling, 2001). While work on ecosystem services began from a perspective of complex dynamic systems (e.g. Berkes and Folke, 1993), the challenge of collecting empirical evidence, quantifying change and developing indicators for policy targets has tended to drive more linear and reductionist approaches (Norgaard, 2010). This disconnect between the complexity of natural and human systems and their interlinkages, and the reductionist approaches dominating the empirical study of

> **BOX 3.1 SOCIAL-ECOLOGICAL SYSTEMS CONCEPTS AND DEFINITIONS**
>
> Social-ecological systems (SES) research brings together complex adaptive systems science and the intertwined approach of humans-in-nature, rejecting 'the delineation between social and natural systems [as] artificial and arbitrary' (Berkes and Folke, 1998) and emphasising the embedded and interdependent nature of society and ecosystems and the long history (and future) of the two shaping, and being shaped by, one another (Folke et al., 2016).
>
> Complex adaptive systems (CAS) comprise many individual and diverse components or actors that interact, forming a diverse network which self-organises, learns and adapts over time. These co-evolutionary processes result in emergent behaviour or properties at a macro-level which cannot be predicted from micro-level components or properties (Levin, 2002).
>
> SES and CAS move away from previous equilibrium-based models of systems, to a more dynamic view which emphasises (among others) tight couplings, non-linear relations, constant change (both fast and gradual), thresholds effects, surprises and uncertainty (Holling, 1973; Levin et al., 2012).

ecosystem services and poverty alleviation, not only thwarts efforts to improve understanding and management, it also excludes a vast body of interdisciplinary literature and knowledge available to work with this complexity (Schoon and van der Leeuw, 2015).

We begin this chapter by highlighting and expanding upon key elements of a social–ecological systems approach to ecosystem services and poverty alleviation. We then move onto a review of the conceptual and analytical advances made by projects and publications from the Ecosystem Services for Poverty Alleviation (ESPA) programme in applying these elements.

Elements of social-ecological systems frameworks and approaches

Box 3.1 provides a definition of social–ecological systems (SES) as complex adaptive systems. Exploring what this definition means for the study of ecosystem services and poverty alleviation, this section highlights some key elements that are the focus of this chapter.

First, SES emphasise the importance of *interactions and feedbacks* between social and ecological components or systems. This goes beyond the flow of materials or energy between systems often depicted in linear ecosystem service models, to a deeper co-evolutionary view in which ecosystem benefits and wellbeing are emergent outcomes co-produced by these couplings (Fischer-Kowalski and Weisz, 2016; Liu et al., 2007).

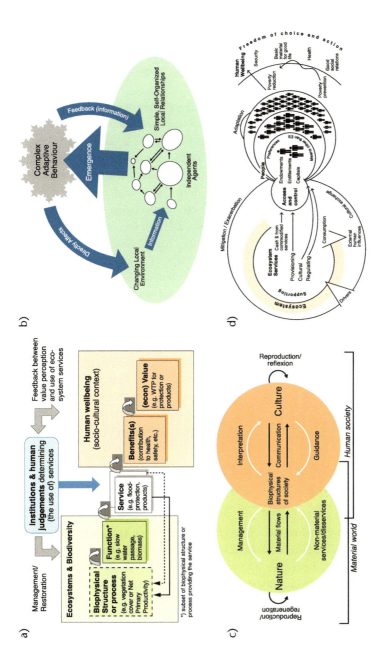

FIGURE 3.1 Conceptual frameworks for understanding and managing the links between ecosystem services and poverty alleviation: (a) linear 'cascade' approach adopted by TEEB (2010); (b) a framework of complex adaptive systems; (c) an attempt to depict complex social–ecological systems for measurement; (d) the framework developed by Fisher et al. (2014).

Sources: (a) Braat and de Groot, 2012; reproduced with permission; (b) Joe Graham, Wikimedia Commons, CC-BY-SA-3; (c) Reyers et al., 2017; CC-BY-NC-ND-4.0 license; (d) reproduced with permission.

The feedbacks and interactions in SES manifest in space and time, highlighting the *cross-scale dynamics* in these systems. Spatially, these could be characterised as social-ecological interactions over distances, including telecouplings (social and environmental connections between different places) and teleconnections (biophysical transcontinental connections). These cross-scale dynamics can also manifest temporally (e.g. through time lags and legacy effects) or as path dependencies of previous social-ecological interactions on later conditions (Scholes et al., 2013).

SES research also emphasises the importance of the *diversity* of system components and actors, their effects on system trajectories, resilience and social-ecological couplings over time and space. Diversity comprises of variety, disparity and balance (Kotschy et al., 2015). Another fundament of complex adaptive systems is their *non-linearity*, the disproportionality of inputs and outputs, linked to non-linear relationships, feedbacks, thresholds and regime shifts (Biggs et al., 2009).

Linked to these ideas of dynamics, SES research introduces the concept of *resilience*, as the capacities of an individual, household, community, institution or system to continue to develop with and through change (Szaboova et al., this volume). This includes the ability to persist, to adapt or to transform through a reconfiguration of the system and its interactions (Folke, 2016). Resilience can be viewed as a system property, but it is increasingly also used as an approach to studying and managing complex adaptive systems (Folke, 2006).

In the area of ecosystem services and poverty alleviation research, several conceptual and analytical frameworks have been developed in an attempt to clarify the complex and dynamic linkages between ecosystems and wellbeing (see Binder et al., 2013) (Figure 3.1). Fisher et al. (2014) present a conceptual framework which aims to strengthen the depiction of meaningful relationships between ecosystem service and poverty framework components, better integrate the social and natural sciences, and to align with concepts such as complex dynamics, social differentiation, non-linearity and cross-scale linkages.

ESPA analytical advances and social-ecological systems elements

Many ESPA projects aimed to tackle the challenge of more accurately capturing and representing the complex social-ecological dynamics important to improved understanding of the links between ecosystem services and human wellbeing. We begin below with a review of these projects highlighting progress made and challenges encountered in putting SES elements into practice in research projects. We focus on findings that are relevant for understanding and governing trade-offs that emerge from the complex interactions in SES. We then explore some key studies in the broader literature in order to highlight new frontiers and approaches in this arena.

Interactions and feedbacks

SES perspectives highlight the complex web of interdependencies between ecosystems and society. ESPA has had a major focus on understanding the flow of benefits from ecosystems to people, but a focus on the feedbacks from that interaction has only recently started to emerge. SES approaches employed in ESPA studies demonstrate that feedbacks between poverty and ecosystems, and the resultant trade-offs, are not simple or linear. For example, Kafumbata et al. (2014) highlight that it's not simply the overuse of provisioning services that causes negative feedbacks and ecosystem declines but rather a complex network of drivers, including population size and management regime, which determine the type and magnitude of trade-off. In fact, in some cases it was found that both declines and improvements in wellbeing had negative feedbacks on ecosystem services (Dawson and Martin, 2015). Sometimes, the impact of a feedback was negative for some groups or ecosystem services, and positive for others, if results were disaggregated across different services, ecosystems and beneficiary groups (Adams et al., 2013; Daw et al., 2015). Furthermore, cross-scale effects over space and time further complicate these analyses (see next section). Gasparatos et al. (2015) find that provisioning service trade-offs in biofuels production involves positive and negative feedbacks that manifest differently at national, local and household scales. They show that biofuel production can have negative impacts on food production at the local scale (through competition for resources), create competition for land at national scale (through large-scale land acquisitions) and positively contribute to poverty alleviation at the local scale through provision of stable salaries (Gasparatos et al., 2015). A second important area of research on feedbacks was in the area of non-linear change, where system feedbacks associated with agricultural practices and water quality changes were linked over decades with declines in system resilience and tipping points in important ecosystem services (Willcock et al., 2016; Zhang et al., 2015).

A current inability to model or collect data on these feedbacks was raised by numerous ESPA studies as a constraint to understanding the effects of external drivers and ecosystem change on human wellbeing, and then the consequences of changes in wellbeing for ecosystem services. Approaches that can take account of dynamic features such as tipping points, long-term trends, time lags and cross-scale effects are needed to properly interrogate complex trade-offs (e.g. Dearing et al., 2014). New approaches that are able to conceptualise and analyse the system in a more integrated fashion or at a macro-level scale offer some promise. Poppy et al. (2014), in their exploration of agro-ecosystems, adopt a more integrated SES approach to understand how ecosystems supporting multiple ecosystem services and food production can co-exist. This more integrated approach includes a conceptual framework which elaborates the interactions and feedbacks between multi-dimensional ecosystem services and disaggregated wellbeing.

Cross-scale dynamics

The concept of scale is frequently raised in ESPA studies as an important issue in both ecological and human systems, and in the study of the links between the two. SES approaches emphasise the need to focus on cross-scale dynamics, which looks at how multiple scales interact through system feedbacks and dynamics (see Scholes et al., 2013 for a review). Several of the ESPA studies that explored feedbacks examined the cross-scale nature of these feedbacks and resultant trade-offs in space and time. They all highlighted that seemingly unrelated events can and do have influence on local action and trade-offs through markets, policies, governance and even corruption (Hossain et al., 2015; Howe et al., 2014; Kafumbata et al., 2014; von Maltitz et al., 2014) (Figure 3.2). For example, Howe et al. (2014) find that different users of water ecosystem services at different spatial scales are interlinked and affect one another. In Bangladesh, local implementation of climate mitigation projects was often impeded by regional and global policies controlling cooperation with regional and international partners on challenges such as climate change and water resource management (Hossain et al., 2015). Similarly, achieving positive outcomes in projects can be limited by external factors and global markets, as exemplified by the hype and collapse of Jatropha in Southern Africa where local biofuel projects were influenced by many factors including the 2008 financial market collapse, leading investors to pull out, and the drop in oil prices around the same time (von Maltitz et al., 2014).

In terms of temporal scales, Wang et al. (2012) and Zhang et al. (2015) use long-term data to show that earlier activities causing nutrient loading in agricultural landscapes lead to abrupt changes in water quality and systemic shifts later on.

While data availability is a key constraint for studying SES, Suich et al. (2015) and Dearing et al. (2014) suggest that more work is needed on the topic of cross-scale dynamics to shed light on complex linkages. Suich et al. (2015) highlight that current research is constrained by a focus on micro or meso scales, while Dearing et al. (2014) point to the current limited ability of models to account for inter-regional linkages – especially social-ecological linkages across regions, biomes and geographies (Willcock et al., 2016). While many frameworks attempt to represent multiple scales, the absence of feedbacks, over time and space, in most frameworks limits ability to explore important aspects including teleconnections, surprise and cascading effects that seem to dominate in rural poverty contexts. Similarly, considering the role of history, initial conditions and path dependency that can maintain poverty, the absence of data and approaches to include these effects and their impacts on current conditions and trade-offs is a constraint (Haider et al., 2018).

Diversity

Social-ecological diversity has been highlighted as an important component of the capacity of systems to cope with and adapt to change. Systems with greater diversity of species, ecosystems, ecological functions and ecosystem services, as well

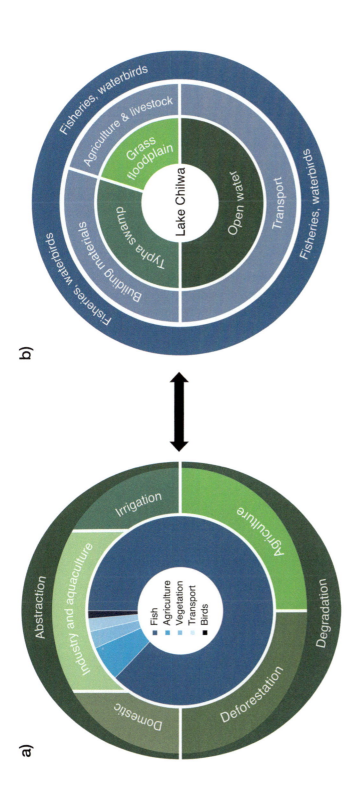

FIGURE 3.2 Cross-scale connections linking the Lake Chilwa wetland (inner circle), the practices in the catchment (intermediate circle) and threats (outer circle) to the wetland; (b) the major wetland components (inner circle) and the main livelihood activities that are practised in each of these (outer circles).

Source: Kafumbata et al., 2014; reproduced by permission of the Royal Society.

as a diversity of human actions and responses, have been linked to enhanced resilience and wellbeing. While ESPA studies did not explore the links between diversity and system resilience, several studies focused on better capturing social complexity or diversity within and between groups or wellbeing dimensions (especially non-income dimensions) (Daw et al., 2015; Dawson and Martin, 2015; Hamann et al., 2015). The motivation behind this often included an enhanced understanding of the wellbeing consequences of trade-offs that may be hidden by the 'socio-ecological reductionism' prevalent in ecosystem services and poverty alleviation studies dominated by single, aggregated or average values (Daw et al., 2015; Dawson and Martin, 2015; Hamann et al., 2015, 2016; Kent and Dorward, 2014). Cruz-Garcia et al. (2016) highlighted the importance of diversity in food security, including utilisation, access and stability, to emphasise the heterogeneity and complexity in addressing food security policy targets.

These studies used, developed and tested a variety of analytical approaches including wellbeing research, participatory workshops, the creation of a social-ecological 'toy model' (Figure 3.3) and scenario development (Daw et al., 2015), a capability approach to multi-dimensional wellbeing (Dawson and Martin, 2015), livelihood frameworks and the use of national household census data on ecosystem use and wellbeing, together with spatial cluster analyses (Hamann et al., 2015, 2016).

Overall, it appears that these approaches were useful in emphasising the complexity often hidden within apparent trade-offs and synergies. This complexity can be made clear by examining specific benefits to different resource users, groups or scales (Daw et al., 2015), and may also serve to highlight power relations, conflicts

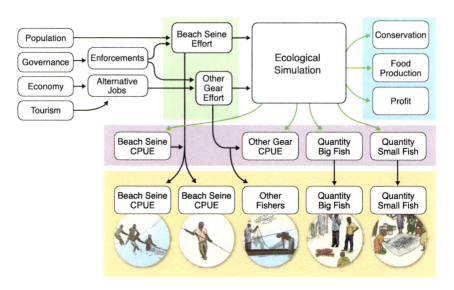

FIGURE 3.3 Toy model of social-ecological system to demonstrate disaggregated beneficiary outcomes in fisheries management. CPUE denotes catch per unit effort.

Source: Daw et al., 2015; CC-BY-NC-ND-4.0 license.

and tensions, as well as impacts that can potentially reinforce poverty (Dawson and Martin, 2015; Kent and Dorward, 2014). Zulkafli et al. (2017) propose a participatory framework for designing environmental decision support tools that emphasise a more complete understanding of decision-making structures in a polycentric management system.

Data gaps emerged as a challenge in several of these studies, including a lack of data on non-provisioning services and human wellbeing dimensions, e.g. social relations, subjective wellbeing and other metrics of wellbeing. Hamann et al. (2016) highlight the importance of approaches that can portray and analyse multi-dimensional wellbeing and ecosystem services bundles, revealing patterns that are not found by existing additive or composite indicators.

Non-linearities

The concept of tipping points, beyond which runaway change propels the system to a new state (Biggs et al., 2009), was the focus of several ESPA projects examining non-linearities. These studies, with access to long-term social and ecological data, as well as modelling, were useful in demonstrating how complexity science theory may be applied to real-world SES to help identify possible system transitions and non-linearities (Dearing et al., 2014; Wang et al., 2012; Zhang et al., 2015). The studies used the concept of ecological and social planetary boundaries (*sensu* Raworth, 2012; Steffen et al., 2015) at regional levels. They also highlighted the complex non-linear relationships between multiple drivers of long-term environmental degradation, declines in regulating services and increases in provisioning services (which may later also decline) (Zhang et al., 2015).

These approaches using long-term data to expose non-linearities revealed trade-offs around water quality (from nutrient loading associated with food production) where the environmental threshold is already exceeded, while social standards for water supply and sanitation are not being met (Dearing et al., 2014). The concept of 'flickering' whereby a system switches back and forth between alternative states in response to large impacts, variability in indicators of water quality, and increased sensitivity to drivers were proposed as early warning indicators for a system approaching thresholds (Wang et al., 2012), although these indicators were sometimes associated with no evidence of tipping points (Zhang et al., 2015).

Wang et al. (2012) also highlight how models and data complement one another, and where observed data are limited, models and proxies are useful as additional sources of understanding. Dearing et al. (2014) demonstrate how the use of national governments' stated social priorities can be translated into the setting of social boundaries, linked to environmental conditions. But they further highlight the challenges of integrating elements such as social-ecological feedbacks, time lags and interregional connections and fluxes into this work. In a conceptual overview of complex systems and sustainability, Willcock et al. (2016) explore the non-linear aspects of complex systems and point to the challenges posed by current global indicators and the lack of early warning systems. Their review finds that hybrid models are a useful way to combine models and overcome limitations associated with single approaches in order to generate understanding of system trade-offs and tipping points, as well as policy outcomes.

Resilience

Szaboova et al. (this volume) highlight that ESPA research adopts resilience as a system property shaped by and shaping the SES elements explored in this chapter, such as feedbacks, diversity, cross-scale dynamics and non-linear change. Kent and Dorward (2014) describe how resilience and responses to environmental change and shocks are linked to social and economic dynamics, as well as social differentiation across groups. Kafumbata et al. (2014) assert that climate shocks and change influence ecosystem services related to food security. However, neither study looks into the details of the structures or capacities to cope or adapt to these changes. Kent and Dorward (2014) describe livelihood diversification as a possible feature of households' capacities to adapt to loss of forest assets. Zhang et al. (2015) highlight how changes in system feedbacks are linked to declines in resilience in the systems.

Beyond these studies, little attention was paid to the study of system resilience – especially the contemporary advances in SES resilience (Folke, 2016). This may offer new directions and insights for future work on the topic of ecosystems and poverty, to which we return in the next section.

Advances in ecosystem services and poverty research from SES approaches

The general failure of previous ecosystem services and poverty research to demonstrate the contribution of ecosystem services to poverty alleviation, particularly the mechanisms by which this takes place, was a major impetus for the ESPA programme to develop a stronger focus on complexity and SES. At a Complexity workshop in 2014, ESPA (2014: 1) highlighted the need to 'consider the links between multiple ecosystem services and multiple dimensions of poverty, their interactions, synergies, trade-offs and tipping points, whilst also recognising that these relationships vary in space in time'.

It is evident from our review that the challenge of integrating SES concepts, frameworks, theories and approaches was embraced by many ESPA projects, across multiple elements of complex SES, in diverse yet complementary ways.

Key findings and methodological advances

All ESPA projects reviewed highlighted new findings and outcomes in sites and regions; of particular relevance were some key findings that expose shortcomings in more conventional linear or reductionist approaches to ecosystem services and poverty alleviation.

- ESPA work on including social and ecological diversity revealed invisible trade-offs and emergent outcomes which would have been hidden by the use of more widely used indicators and average/additive approaches (e.g. Daw et al., 2015; Hamann et al., 2015).
- Projects that focused on social-ecological feedbacks challenged the simple assumptions of linear trade-offs between poverty and ecosystem services declines (e.g. Dawson and Martin, 2015; Kafumbata et al., 2014).
- The use of multi-decadal time series to explore non-linearities showed the value of such data in highlighting risks for sustainability not obvious in most current ecosystem service models and datasets. It further suggested possible early warning indicators of tipping points (e.g. Dearing et al., 2014; Wang et al., 2012; Zhang et al., 2015).
- Cross-scale aspects explored in projects highlighted temporal dynamics of gradual and fast change, demonstrating trade-offs across time (and space) which would not have been evidence from current indicators. It further explored interactions between fast and slow change (e.g. Howe et al., 2014; Kafumbata et al., 2014; Wang et al., 2012).
- Resilience, as it was used in ESPA studies as an analytical approach, highlighted the power of exploring system dynamics and capacities for responding to change, suggesting new directions beyond the current focus on efforts to build resilience as a way to withstand change (e.g. Zhang et al., 2015).

Several ESPA projects also sought to develop and test new methods with which to address these elements of SES in their case studies. Some key advances include:

- The combination of long-term social and ecological data, with modelling approaches, enabled advances in understanding of non-linear dynamics and temporal connections (Dearing et al., 2014; Wang et al., 2012; Zhang et al., 2015).
- The comparison of existing model categories for use in exploring non-linearities and for better coupling of social and ecological data and models (Willcock et al., 2016).
- The combination of existing and new methods to reveal trade-offs, and share understanding among stakeholders of these trade-offs (Daw et al., 2015).
- Piloting the use of national data on wellbeing (Dearing et al., 2014; Hamann et al., 2015) and ecosystem service use (Hamann et al., 2015, 2016), as well as social priorities as thresholds, to explore relationships, system dynamics and emergent outcomes.
- The development of new frameworks for exploring the complex connections in SES (Fisher et al., 2013, 2014; Kafumbata et al., 2014; Poppy et al., 2014; Willcock et al., 2016).

New directions and frontiers

Across these projects, it also became apparent that some aspects of SES elements were more dominant or useful, and thus some concepts were adopted in a narrower sense than SES theory would suggest. This is expected in the early phases of testing theory in new domains, and suggests that further iterations between theory and application will be needed in future to provide stronger evidence that can be used in practice.

In applying diversity, much emphasis was on social differentiation and multi-dimensional wellbeing, due to the focus on these issues within the ESPA programme. There was less focus on other elements of social-ecological diversity, e.g. diversity of actors, culture and ecological systems, but also the importance of diversity in social-ecological interactions as a means to respond to shocks or ongoing change through adaptation or transformation. Diversity provides sources for novelty/innovation, knowledge, memory, practices and strategies that are critical for adapting to, or transforming with unexpected change (Haider et al., 2018; Leslie and McCabe, 2013).

In the area of non-linearities, most focus was on the concept of tipping points, strongly influenced by the planetary boundaries (Rockström et al., 2009) and 'doughnut' models (Raworth, 2012) of ecological and social tipping points. Less emphasis was placed on non-linear relationships and thresholds (although Dearing et al., 2014 explore a typology of these), and regime shifts were mentioned but not applied. The idea of systemic shifts encapsulated in SES regime shifts important to persistent poverty and traps appear to be useful to explore further for understanding ecosystem services and their links to poverty. Drivers of system feedbacks, indicators of system resilience and capacities to cope with such shifts appear relevant, as does research on the non-linear nature of poverty traps, social-ecological traps and transformations (Lade et al., 2017; Scheffer et al., 2009).

Feedbacks between social and ecological actors or components are clearly important for understanding the links between ecosystems and people, as well as the outcomes of policy and actions. However, their complexity can be overwhelming, and most ESPA studies tackled only single feedbacks. Recent work on social-ecological co-production models of ecosystem services (Reyers et al., 2013), along with advances in examining health as an emergent process (Jayasinghe, 2011) and advances in the measurement of SES (Quinlan et al., 2015), offer alternatives for navigating the complexity within feedbacks at the macro rather than the micro level. Further work on social-ecological co-evolution also offers important avenues for exploration (Gual and Norgaard, 2010).

Similarly, cross-scale dynamics, which are undeniably important for revealing trade-offs over space and time, were mostly focused on as temporal changes in key variables, or larger-scale drivers of change in local systems (Hossain et al., 2015; Kafumbata et al., 2014; von Maltitz et al., 2014). Considering the increasingly connected global context (Liu et al., 2015), there is a need for new approaches with which to capture and explore the inter-regional, cross-scale connections between social and ecological systems from global to local systems. New approaches from SES research, including SES syndromes (local recurring patterns of social and ecological outcomes) and trade, telecouplings and global systemic risk may offer innovative avenues for future research on ecosystems and poverty (Crona et al., 2015). Furthermore, approaches that account for history, such as legacy effects and path dependencies, will be key for understanding the current state and potential trajectories (Haider et al., 2018).

Resilience, as an overarching analytical approach to bringing all these elements of SES together into the study of ecosystem services and poverty in the context of change and turbulence, appears valuable. While resilience did not appear strongly in many of the studies, aspects of coping with and responding to change were present and useful. However as Folke et al. (2016) highlight in their review of SES resilience, the use of the term to mean only the ability to withstand or bounce back from shocks is a limited view on resilience. This limited view ignores both the need to adapt to shocks and longer-term changes, as well as the notion of transformability – the capacity to create a fundamentally new system when ecological, economic or social structures make the existing system untenable. Resilience as transformability is receiving increased attention in development and poverty alleviation arenas, where traps, persistent poverty and turbulence require the reconfigurations of systems to build capacity to continue to develop in the face of change (Folke, 2016; Moore et al., 2014).

Conclusions: implications for policy

SES approaches open up new directions and opportunities for policy, with clear indications for policy shifts that recognise the intersectoral, cross-scalar nature of sustainability challenges to recognise and govern social-ecological feedbacks and cross-scale dynamics. The UN Agenda 2030 and its associated Sustainable Development Goals and targets are a move in this direction, intended to direct and inform policy coordination across sectors and scales. Advances in SES research and practice give some indication of directions towards better coordination through the development of more integrated social-ecological models, indicators and analyses bringing together water, food, development and conservation sectors in their work, as well as the need to consider multiple and cross-scale dynamics for sustainable development.

Central to SES theories is the dynamic view of systems that emphasises constant change (both fast and gradual), threshold effects, surprises and uncertainty. Implementing sustainable development in a dynamic context poses substantial challenges for current policy and practice, especially in light of the more turbulent and globalised context of the Anthropocene. Bringing these insights together recognises the risks of ignoring complex social-ecological dynamics and feedbacks, the cross-scale drivers of trade and financial flows, the power asymmetries at work in the world and the rapidly approaching tipping points in the climate and earth system. SES perspectives open up new policy opportunities for development, recognising and governing dynamics from local to global scales, and embracing, rather than withstanding, change as a force for renewal, diversity and transformations.

References

(ESPA outputs marked with '★')

★Adams H, Adger WN, Huq H, et al. (2013) Wellbeing-ecosystem service links: mechanisms and dynamics in the southwest coastal zone of Bangladesh. *ESPA Deltas Working Paper #2*, 56 pp.

Berkes F and Folke C. (1993) A systems perspectives on the interrelationships between natural, human-made and cultural capital. *Ecological Economics* 5: 1–8.

Berkes F and Folke C. (1998) *Linking Social and Ecological Systems: Management Practices and Social Mechanisms for Building Resilience*. Cambridge, UK: Cambridge University Press.

Biggs R, Carpenter SR and Brock WA. (2009) Turning back from the brink: detecting an impending regime shift in time to avert it. *Proceedings of the National Academy of Sciences* 106: 826–831.

Binder CR, Hinkel J, Bots PWG, et al. (2013) Comparison of frameworks for analyzing social-ecological systems. *Ecology and Society* 18: 26.

Braat LC and de Groot R. (2012) The ecosystem services agenda: bridging the worlds of natural science and economics, conservation and development, and public and private policy. *Ecosystem Services* 1: 4–15.

Crona BI, Van Holt T, Petersson M, et al. (2015) Using social-ecological syndromes to understand impacts of international seafood trade on small-scale fisheries. *Global Environmental Change* 35: 162–175.

★Cruz-Garcia GS, Sachet E, Vanegas M, et al. (2016) Are the major imperatives of food security missing in ecosystem services research? *Ecosystem Services* 19: 19–31.

★Daw TM, Coulthard S, Cheung WWL, et al. (2015) Evaluating taboo trade-offs in ecosystems services and human well-being. *Proceedings of the National Academy of Sciences* 112: 6949–6954.

★Dawson N and Martin A. (2015) Assessing the contribution of ecosystem services to human wellbeing: a disaggregated study in western Rwanda. *Ecological Economics* 117: 62–72.

★Dearing JA, Wang R, Zhang K, et al. (2014) Safe and just operating spaces for regional social-ecological systems. *Global Environmental Change* 28: 227–238.

★ESPA. (2014) *ESPA Complexity Workshop, 8–9 July 2014, London*. Available at: http://bit.ly/ESPAComplexity

Fischer-Kowalski M and Weisz H. (2016) The Archipelago of Social Ecology and the Island of the Vienna School. In: Haberl H, Fischer-Kowalski M, Krausmann F, et al. (eds) *Social Ecology: Society–Nature Relations across Time and Space*. Cham, Switzerland: Springer, 3–28.

★Fisher JA, Patenaude G, Giri K, et al. (2014) Understanding the relationships between ecosystem services and poverty alleviation: a conceptual framework. *Ecosystem Services* 7: 34–45.

★Fisher JA, Patenaude G, Meir P, et al. (2013) Strengthening conceptual foundations: analysing frameworks for ecosystem services and poverty alleviation research. *Global Environmental Change* 23: 1098–1111.

Folke C. (2006) Resilience: the emergence of a perspective for social-ecological systems analyses. *Global Environmental Change* 16: 253–267.

Folke C. (2016) Resilience (re-published). *Ecology and Society* 21: 44.

Folke C, Biggs R, Norström AV, et al. (2016) Social-ecological resilience and biosphere-based sustainability science. *Ecology and Society* 21: 41.

★Gasparatos A, von Maltitz GP, Johnson FX, et al. (2015) Biofuels in sub-Sahara Africa: drivers, impacts and priority policy areas. *Renewable and Sustainable Energy Reviews* 45: 879–901.

Gual MA and Norgaard RB. (2010) Bridging ecological and social systems coevolution: a review and proposal. *Ecological Economics* 69: 707–717.

Haider LJ, Boonstra WJ, Peterson GD, et al. (2018) Traps and sustainable development in rural areas: a review. *World Development* 101: 311–321.

★Hamann M, Biggs R and Reyers B. (2015) Mapping social-ecological systems: identifying 'green-loop' and 'red-loop' dynamics based on characteristic bundles of ecosystem service use. *Global Environmental Change* 34: 218–226.

★Hamann M, Biggs R and Reyers B. (2016) An exploration of human well-being bundles as identifiers of ecosystem service use patterns. *PLoS ONE* 11: e0163476.

Holling CS. (1973) Resilience and stability of ecological systems. *Annual Review of Ecology and Systematics* 4: 1–23.

Holling CS. (2001) Understanding the complexity of economic, ecological, and social systems. *Ecosystems* 4: 390–405.

★Hossain MS, Johnson FA, Dearing JA, et al. (2015) Recent trends of human wellbeing in the Bangladesh delta. *Environmental Development* 17: 21–32.

★Howe C, Suich H, Vira B, et al. (2014) Creating win-wins from trade-offs? Ecosystem services for human well-being: a meta-analysis of ecosystem service trade-offs and synergies in the real world. *Global Environmental Change* 28: 263–275.

Jayasinghe S. (2011) Conceptualising population health: from mechanistic thinking to complexity science. *Emerging Themes in Epidemiology* 8: 2.

★Kafumbata D, Jamu D and Chiotha S. (2014) Riparian ecosystem resilience and livelihood strategies under test: lessons from Lake Chilwa in Malawi and other lakes in Africa. *Philosophical Transactions of the Royal Society B: Biological Sciences* 369: 20130052–20130052.

★Kent R and Dorward A. (2014) Livelihood responses to Lantana camara invasion and biodiversity change in southern India: application of an asset function framework. *Regional Environmental Change* 15: 353–364.

Kotschy K, Biggs R, Daw T, et al. (2015) Principle 1–Maintain diversity and redundancy. In: Biggs R, Schluter M and Schoon M (eds) *Principles for Building Resilience: Sustaining Ecosystem Services in Social-Ecological Systems*. Cambridge, UK: Cambridge University Press, 50–79.

Lade SJ, Haider LJ, Engström G, et al. (2017) Resilience offers escape from trapped thinking on poverty alleviation. *Science Advances* 3.

Leslie P and McCabe JT. (2013) Response diversity and resilience in social-ecological systems. *Current Anthropology* 54: 114–143.

Levin S. (2002) Complex adaptive systems: exploring the known, the unknown and the unknowable. *Bulletin of the American Mathematical Society* 40: 3–19.

Levin S, Xepapadeas T, Crépin A-S, et al. (2012) Social-ecological systems as complex adaptive systems: modeling and policy implications. *Environment and Development Economics* 18: 111–132.

Liu J, Dietz T, Carpenter SR, et al. (2007) Complexity of coupled human and natural systems. *Science* 317: 1513–1516.

Liu J, Mooney HA, Hull V, et al. (2015) Systems integration for global sustainability. *Science* 347: 1258832.

Moore ML, Tjornbo O, Enfors E, et al. (2014) Studying the complexity of change: toward an analytical framework for understanding deliberate social-ecological transformations. *Ecology and Society* 19: 54.

Norgaard RB. (2010) Ecosystem services: from eye-opening metaphor to complexity blinder. *Ecological Economics* 69: 1219–1227.

★Poppy GM, Chiotha S, Eigenbrod F, et al. (2014) Food security in a perfect storm: using the ecosystem services framework to increase understanding. *Philosophical Transactions of the Royal Society B: Biological Sciences* 369.

Quinlan AE, Berbés-Blázquez M, Haider LJ, et al. (2015) Measuring and assessing resilience: broadening understanding through multiple disciplinary perspectives. *Journal of Applied Ecology* 53: 677–687.

Raudsepp-Hearne C, Peterson GD, Tengö M, et al. (2010) Untangling the environmentalist's paradox: why is human well-being increasing as ecosystem services degrade? *BioScience* 60: 576–589.

Raworth K. (2012) A safe and just space for humanity: can we live within the doughnut? *Oxfam Policy and Practice: Climate Change and Resilience* 8: 1–26.

Reyers B, Biggs R, Cumming GS, et al. (2013) Getting the measure of ecosystem services: a social-ecological approach. *Frontiers in Ecology and the Environment* 11: 268–273.

Reyers B, Stafford-Smith M, Erb K-H, et al. (2017) Essential Variables help to focus Sustainable Development Goals monitoring. *Current Opinion in Environmental Sustainability* 26: 97–105.

Rockström J, Steffen W, Noone K, et al. (2009) A safe operating space for humanity. *Nature* 461: 472–475.

Scheffer M, Bascompte J, Brock WA, et al. (2009) Early-warning signals for critical transitions. *Nature* 461: 53–59.

Scholes RJ, Reyers B, Biggs R, et al. (2013) Multi-scale and cross-scale assessments of social-ecological systems and their ecosystem services. *Current Opinion in Environmental Sustainability* 5: 16–25.

Schoon ML and van der Leeuw S. (2015) The shift toward social-ecological systems perspectives: insights into the human-nature relationship. *Natures Sciences Societes* 23: 166–174.

★Steffen W, Richardson K, Rockström J, et al. (2015) Planetary boundaries: guiding human development on a changing planet. *Science* 347: 1259855.

★Suich H, Howe C and Mace G. (2015) Ecosystem services and poverty alleviation: a review of the empirical links. *Ecosystem Services* 12: 137–147.

TEEB. (2010) *The Economics of Ecosystems and Biodiversity Ecological and Economic Foundations.* Edited by Pushpam Kumar. London and Washington, DC: Earthscan.

★von Maltitz G, Gasparatos A and Fabricius C. (2014) The rise, fall and potential resilience benefits of Jatropha in Southern Africa. *Sustainability* 6: 3615–3643.

★Wang R, Dearing JA, Langdon PG, et al. (2012) Flickering gives early warning signals of a critical transition to a eutrophic lake state. *Nature* 492: 419–422.

★Willcock S, Hossain S and Poppy GM. (2016) Managing complex systems to enhance sustainability. In: Solan M and Whiteley NM (eds) *Stressors in the Marine Environment.* Oxford: Oxford University Press, 301–312.

★Zhang K, Dearing JA, Dawson TP, et al. (2015) Poverty alleviation strategies in eastern China lead to critical ecological dynamics. *Science of the Total Environment* 506–507: 164–181.

★Zulkafli Z, Perez K, Vitolo C, et al. (2017) User-driven design of decision support systems for polycentric environmental resources management. *Environmental Modelling and Software* 88: 58–73.

4
LIMITS AND THRESHOLDS

Setting global, local and regional safe operating spaces

John Dearing

Limits and thresholds: the context

The roots of this chapter lie in the post-war ideas around systems – entities defined in terms of their different parts interacting through flows of energy, matter or information. A system changes, or adapts, to variations in external influences through negative and positive feedback loops (see Reyers and Selomane, this volume). The book, *Limits to Growth* (Meadows et al., 1972) included a first attempt to use systems models to simulate the global effects of resource depletion and pollution on economic development, and demonstrated how feedback mechanisms could slow or even reverse exponential growth during the twenty-first century. While not universally accepted, the basic ideas in *Limits to Growth* provide the basis for studies on human wellbeing and the natural environment in the context of global economic growth.

Since the 1960s, other scientific approaches have explored systems and how they can become unstable and fail if they cross certain limits or thresholds. The earliest, René Thom's catastrophe theory, introduced mathematical concepts for system instability that later spawned chaos theory and the application of critical transition theory (Scheffer, 2009). Ecologists, including Holling (1973) and May (1972), developed theoretical models for alternate steady states, ecological resilience and food web networks. These early studies of systems fed into the fields now referred to as complexity science and resilience theory.

In parallel, global institutions incorporated these scientific developments into policy statements. The UN Conference on the Human Environment (1972), the UN Rio Earth Summit (1992), the UN Millennium Development Goals (2000), the International Geosphere-Biosphere Amsterdam Declaration (2001), the UN Rio+20 Summit (2012), through to the UN Sustainable Development Goals (2015), brought together the concerns of environmentalists over uncontrolled development, particularly the idea of non-linear, abrupt shifts and a need to recognise the existence of limits. In 2005, the Millennium Ecosystem Assessment (MA) highlighted the dramatic loss of diversity, the degradation of ecosystem services and increased risk of non-linear changes, the consequent barriers to reducing poverty, hunger and disease, and therefore the need for significant changes in policies, institutions and practices (MA, 2005). The ESPA Programme (2009–2018) was designed to provide the interdisciplinary research and evidence base for addressing the MA findings.

Coincident with the start of the ESPA Programme, Johan Rockström and colleagues introduced new concepts: planetary boundaries and safe operating spaces. Rockström et al. (2009a) highlighted global-scale boundaries for nine biophysical processes: climate change, biodiversity loss, biogeochemical flows (N and P cycles), freshwater use, stratosphere ozone, atmospheric aerosol loading, ocean acidification, land use change and chemical pollution. They argued that these planetary life-support systems, and their associated processes, broadly define a safe operating space for human development. Rockström et al. (2009b) developed the conceptual basis for the boundaries. Drawing on Scheffer et al. (2001), they proposed a classification of system changes – from smooth 'linear' changes to 'non-linear' changes that may also be smooth through time, but may also involve abrupt change as thresholds or tipping points are reached.

One particular type of non-linear change that has generated much concern for environmentalists, and increasingly policy-makers, occurs when the system shifts non-linearly and rapidly towards a new steady state but crosses an unstable equilibrium that then represents a barrier to reversibility. Attempts to reverse the system back to its starting point show hysteresis, or a lagged effect, because reversals in the external conditions have little impact on the system until they have gone far beyond the point of the initial threshold. In this last case, Rockström et al.

BOX 4.1 RELATIONSHIPS BETWEEN POVERTY ALLEVIATION AND ECOSYSTEM SERVICES

Many theoretical and empirical relationships between human wellbeing or poverty alleviation (PA) and the quality or abundance of ecosystem services (ES) have been proposed. Here, they are shown using the planetary boundary concepts with PA on the x-axis (control variable) and ES on the y-axis (response variable), but whether they are control or response variables depends on the context. ES may represent aggregated services but, more realistically, a sub-set of provisioning, regulating, supporting or cultural services. (a) *Linear* – the direction and elasticity (or strength) of direct relationships. Low and high positive elasticity are associated with weakly and strongly coupled social-ecological systems, respectively. Negative elasticity describes situations where PA succeeds even as ES decline, or the reverse where poverty increases as ES improve. (b) *Parabolic non-linear* – the trajectory, often relatively gradual, whereby (i) regulating ES (e.g. water quality) first declines with agricultural

Limits and thresholds 57

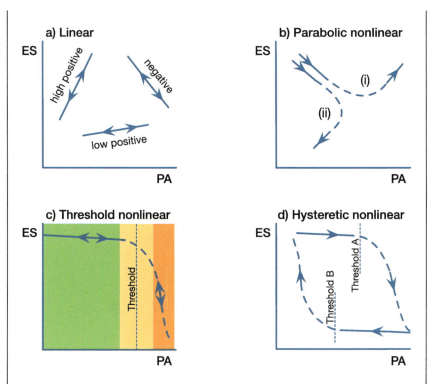

FIGURE 4.1 theoretical and empirical relationships between human wellbeing or poverty alleviation (PA) and the quality or abundance of ecosystem services (ES).

intensification and then improves as regulatory frameworks improve with PA; (ii) PA causes regulating ES (e.g. forest cover/biodiversity) to decline, eventually feeding back to reduce provisioning ES (e.g. forest products) and increase poverty, and where regional resource exploitation leads to growing inequalities in wellbeing. (c) *Threshold non-linear* – crossing a threshold causes a relatively rapid decline in ES – for example, the loss of wheat yield (provisioning ES) as investment in larger shrimp farms causes widespread soil salinisation. The example uses the definition of 'safe, cautionary and dangerous operating spaces' (green, yellow and orange), which in theory may be reversible. (d) *Hysteretic non-linear* – in contrast to (c), threshold responses between ES and PA may be irreversible or time-lagged – for example, the loss of fish stocks (provisioning ES) as technological investment in fish catch methods transgresses threshold A; fish stock recovery requires fishing efforts to be reversed beyond threshold A to threshold B, with losses of income or livelihoods (after Daw et al., 2016; Dearing unpublished; Scheffer et al., 2001; Steffen et al., 2015; Zhang et al., 2015).

(2009a) tapped into real fears that continued degradation of biophysical conditions could result in global change that was not only unanticipated and rapid but would be effectively irreversible. This led to the authors defining a 'safe' space where the risk of transgressing a potentially damaging biophysical threshold, as defined scientifically, was minimised (see Figure 4.1, (c) and (d)). Boundaries of safe spaces are not defined at the threshold value but by the lower end of the range of driving conditions (Figure 4.1 (c)). In theory, this allows time for society to react to early warning signals of an imminent tipping point. Expert judgement and literature reviews in 2009 concluded that three systems, climate change, biodiversity loss and biogeochemical flows, already exceeded safe boundaries.

The planetary boundaries concept includes key processes that have relevance to the ESPA programme: the paths taken by the linked human–environment system or its components over time; the effects of changes in external conditions on single process or on the interaction of processes; and the risk of crossing thresholds and moving to alternate steady states (Willcock et al., 2016). This chapter reviews recent relevant research and draws conclusions relevant to ecosystem services and poverty.

Extending and updating the planetary boundaries

The planetary boundaries work has been immensely influential but not without critics, who have pointed to the treatment of the nine control variables as independent when several are clearly interdependent; to the lack of social or economic context; and to the non-explicit determination of the boundaries (e.g. Nordhaus et al., 2012).

As anticipated, a number of more recent studies have updated the key boundaries (Carpenter and Bennett, 2011; Running, 2012). Mace et al. (2014) focused on biodiversity and showed that extinction rates and species richness are weak metrics for biodiversity loss as it affects humanity. Instead, their analysis points to genetic diversity, functional diversity and biome integrity as more useful indicators of ecosystem conditions that underlie persistent and productive life-support systems, such as forest biomes and biogeochemical cycling. While challenges remain, particularly in understanding the drivers or control variables of biome change and the presence of thresholds, they proposed taking a stronger systems-based approach and considering the role of biodiversity in moderating other boundaries and understanding the cross-scale relationship between sub-global biomes and biodiversity.

Steffen et al.'s (2015) planetary boundaries update did adopt a more systems-based approach, recognising the interdependence of boundaries and the importance of spatial scale. They discuss the links to societal needs, especially in terms of UN Sustainable Development Goals, which imply the need for a stable functioning Earth System.

A major innovation in Steffen et al.'s (2015) paper was to link global and regional scales through sub-global dynamics that are important for global functioning. Where they can be mapped, certain regions have already exceeded a safe boundary (Figure 4.2). For phosphorus and nitrogen, these include many of the agricultural

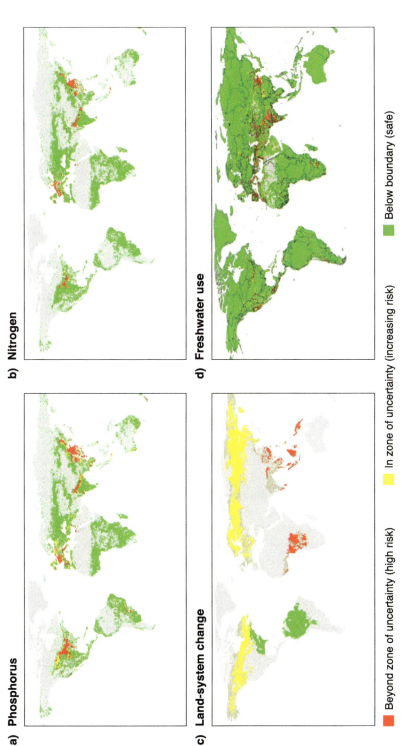

FIGURE 4.2 The global distributions and current status of the planetary boundary control variables for (a) biogeochemical flows – phosphorus (P), (b) biogeochemical flows – nitrogen (N), (c) land-system change and (d) freshwater use. Green areas are within the safe boundary; yellow areas are within the zone of uncertainty (increasing risk); and red areas are beyond the zone of uncertainty (high risk) (see also Figure 4.1). Grey areas in (a) and (b) are areas where P and N fertilisers are not applied, in (c) are areas not covered by major forest biomes, and in (d) are areas where river flow is very low so that environmental flows are not allocated.

Source: After Steffen et al., 2015; reproduced with permission from AAAS.

areas of North America, Europe, the Ganges plain and China. For land system change, the high-risk areas are deforested forest biomes in Africa and Southeast Asia. For freshwater use, the high-risk areas are predominantly in California, Central America, the Mediterranean region, the Middle East, South Asia and north-east China. While the planetary boundaries framework was not designed to be downscaled or disaggregated to smaller levels, the 'planetary boundary thinking' is clearly relevant to achieving development goals at the smaller scales/levels (e.g. regions, catchments) where most policy actions are designed and implemented.

Regional safe and just operating spaces

The first planetary boundary study to 'think' in a regional development context (Dearing et al., 2014) argued that the sustainability of local ecosystem services is often a more urgent socio-environmental need than understanding the cumulative effects of environmental degradation at the planetary scale. Raworth (2012) had already extended the planetary boundary concept to include a normative 'social foundation', which together with the scientifically defined 'environmental ceiling' created by the boundaries, defined a doughnut-shaped operating space that was both 'safe' and 'just'. Dearing et al. (2014) applied this to two Chinese rural lake-catchment systems in Yunnan Province and the lower Yangtze basin (Erhai and Shucheng) where multi-decadal time-series for several ecosystem services were available. The classification of system behaviours (linear, non-linear, threshold and early warning signals) allowed safe, cautionary and dangerous spaces to be defined in real time-series (Figure 4.3(a)). Published data for local social conditions (e.g. access to education, health care, piped drinking water) were used to assess the extent to which regional social norms had been achieved.

In both locations, a social foundation was found to be close to fully met except for access to piped water (Erhai and Shucheng), energy (Erhai) and modern sanitation (Shucheng). Yet the regulating services that had already crossed a safe boundary into cautionary or dangerous spaces included water quality (Figure 4.3(b)). The findings underline the massive challenge for water and soil management in achieving the complete alleviation of poverty while protecting or restoring water resources. Indeed, at Erhai, a previous study (Wang et al., 2012) showed that the aquatic ecosystem passed a critical transition in 2001 as it changed from a relatively clear water, mesotrophic state to a turbid water eutrophic state in a matter of months (Figure 4.3(a)), water quality 1 and 2). More than fifteen years on, and despite implementation of measures to reduce nutrient loading from farming and sewage plants, the lake shows no evidence (Wang, personal communication) of tipping back to the initial state: a real-world example of a system undergoing hysteresis (Figure 4.1(d)).

An assessment of safe and just operating spaces in South Africa (Cole et al., 2014) took a different approach, combining global boundaries, national limits and local thresholds to create a national 'barometer' of sustainable development. Climate change, freshwater use, marine harvesting and biodiversity loss all exceeded their

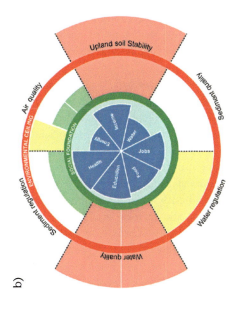
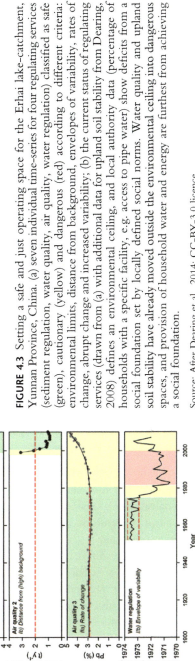

FIGURE 4.3 Setting a safe and just operating space for the Erhai lake-catchment, Yunnan Province, China. (a) seven individual time-series for four regulating services (sediment regulation, water quality, air quality, water regulation) classified as safe (green), cautionary (yellow) and dangerous (red) according to different criteria: environmental limits, distance from background, envelopes of variability, rates of change, abrupt change and increased variability; (b) the current status of regulating services (drawn from (a) with additional data for upland soil stability from Dearing, 2008) defines an environmental ceiling, and local authority data (percentage of households with a specific facility, e.g. access to pipe water) show deficits from a social foundation set by locally defined social norms. Water quality and upland soil stability have already moved outside the environmental ceiling into dangerous spaces, and provision of household water and energy are furthest from achieving a social foundation.

Source: After Dearing et al., 2014; CC-BY-3.0 licence.

safe boundaries, while the greatest social deprivations were personal safety, income and jobs. Disaggregated results showed that environmental stress varies significantly but is generally increasing (Cole et al., 2017). In contrast, social deprivation is generally decreasing but with notable exceptions, such as food security in six provinces. Historically disadvantaged provinces show the most deprivation overall. The 'barometers' and trends help communicate the range of challenges for provincial governments as they try to implement the UN Sustainable Development Goals.

More research is needed to develop a universal approach to setting, and then delivering, local and regional safe and just operating spaces. Even accepting Rockström et al.'s (2009b) stance that 'ecological and biophysical boundaries should be non-negotiable' (2009b SI, p.5), there is much scope for how the social foundations for just spaces are configured socially and economically through governance. In this respect, the issue of ecosystem governance may be less about equity and more about justice (Sikor et al., 2014). Empirical justice analysis takes a broad scan of moral concerns and ethical positions, and pays attention to the roles of all stakeholders today and across generations (see also Dawson et al., this volume). Configuring new spaces may require transformative changes in social norms, behaviours, governance and management. Pereira et al. (2015) promote several principles for multi-stakeholder learning and collaboration: emancipation and empowerment, ensuring reflexivity, knowledge co-creation, transformative learning and nurturing innovations. But a major challenge, and one that goes to the heart of the ESPA programme, is to understand how social and biophysical factors depend upon each other.

Interactions between ecosystem services and poverty

These configurations of planetary boundaries and safe and just operating spaces are valuable for communicating the risks of transgressing biophysical limits and thresholds. But they all fail to define limits and thresholds in terms of a social-ecological system (SES) and fall short of providing a basis for designing policy that can adapt or transform the whole system to a more sustainable or desirable state. Thus the challenge is to find metrics of SES behaviour that define the paths towards limits and thresholds. Such an approach has been previously recognised as 'syndromes' (e.g. Schellnhuber et al., 1997), 'archetypes' (e.g. Eisenack, 2012) and 'green-loop' to 'red-loop' transitions (Cumming et al., 2014). These functional descriptions all aim to provide a level of generality about the key interactions that determine a system's path. For example, the Sahel syndrome (Schellnhuber et al., 1997) describes a dysfunctional SES defined by positive feedbacks that drive overgrazing and soil erosion; the archetypes of Moral Hazard or Poverty Trap (Eisenack, 2012) define barriers to climate adaptation; and different sets of population, technological and ecological feedback mechanisms define transitions in agricultural systems (Cumming et al., 2014). These are clearly valuable for providing static, implicit or conceptual assessments of social-ecological dynamics.

However, functional descriptions based largely on contemporaneous interactions are not the best guide for assessing the likelihood of transgressing limits and thresholds in real situations through time. Where the challenge is to assess temporal dynamics explicitly, one approach is to map recent social and ecological changes onto theoretical links between ecosystem services and poverty alleviation.

As a starting point, Daw et al. (2016) mapped out 'elasticity in ecosystem services', a concept akin to 'price elasticity' in economics (Figure 4.1(a)). This represents a set of plausible relationships between human wellbeing and ecosystem quality ranging from predictable, linear ones where human wellbeing is more or less strongly linked either positively or negatively to ecosystem quality, to non-linear ones where human wellbeing may show unpredictable responses to changes in ecosystem services. The authors also developed a framework for understanding the relationships based on a linear flow chain, by which ecosystems are coupled to wellbeing through several steps: ecosystem stocks, flows, goods, value, shared contributions and wellbeing.

However, although the Daw et al. (2016) framework is designed to underpin the theoretical linear-non-linear elasticities, in practice it is restricted to linear understanding. Feedbacks are not explicitly studied in this ESPA project set in East African coastal communities, and it would have been interesting to see the likely feedbacks (however tentative) added to their comprehensive model of the chain of multiple flows. The lack of a temporal dimension makes this difficult, and means that the empirical application here is limited to qualitative assessments of elasticity.

The inherent weakness of linear frameworks (e.g. Wei et al., 2012) is clear from studies that have used time-series to observe the dynamic coupling between wellbeing and ecosystem services (Box 4.1). An ESPA project set in the lower Yangtze basin (Dearing et al., 2012; Zhang et al., 2015) reconstructed historical regulating ecosystem services from analyses of lake sediments. Combining these with social and economic records illustrated the long-term trade-off between provisioning and regulating (and many cultural) services as a result of actions to alleviate poverty (Figure 4.1(b)). Economic growth over the past 60 years through land intensification and urban development was paralleled by steep rises in provisioning services but steep losses in a range of regulating ecosystem services, mainly since the 1980s (Figure 4.4(a)). Of special concern are water quality services that have already passed critical transitions in several areas. Viewed collectively, the results suggest that the regional social–ecological system passed a tipping point in the late 1970s and is now in a transient phase heading towards a new steady state. Across the region, the long-term relationship between economic growth and ecological degradation (Figure 4.4(b)) shows no sign of decoupling, as demanded by the need to reverse an unsustainable trajectory. Although improved environmental policies and regulation after the late 1980s helped to stabilize losses of biodiversity and regulating services, such as soil stability, agricultural intensification continues to cause widespread pollution of water and air (Zhang et al., 2015).

64 J Dearing

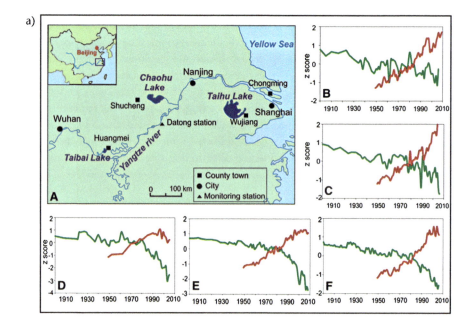

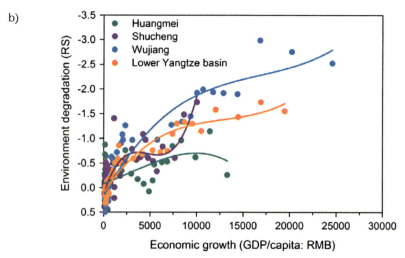

FIGURE 4.4 Poverty alleviation and ecosystem service dynamics in the lower Yangtze basin, eastern China. (a) Relationships between time-series of regulating (green) and provisioning (red) ecosystem services in the twentieth and twenty-first centuries for different locations and aggregated for the whole basin, showing widespread trade-offs between successful land use intensification and environmental degradation; (b) relationship between regional economic wealth and regulating services for the same locations 1950–2010, showing little evidence for a downturn in environmental degradation with greater poverty alleviation.

Source: Zhang et al., 2015; CC-BY-3.0 licence.

Similar results were revealed within the ESPA DELTAS project focused on the Bangladesh coastal zone (Hossain et al., 2016). Since the 1980s, increasing gross domestic product and *per capita* income have mirrored rising levels of food and inland fish production, which has led to a reduction of ~17% in the population below the poverty line. At the same time, non-food ecosystem services such as water availability, water quality and land stability have deteriorated. Conversion of rice fields to shrimp farms is almost certainly a factor in increasing soil and surface water salinity, while water availability, shrimp farming and maintenance of biodiversity appear to have passed tipping points in the 1970s–1980s. As with the lower Yangtze basin, the point at which growing economic wealth might be expected to feed back into effective environmental protection (Zhang et al., 2015 and Figure 4.1(b)) has not yet been reached, at least for water resources.

Using the same methodology, the Belmont Forum DELTAS project produces similar temporal dynamics in the Amazon, Ganges–Brahmaputra–Meghna (GBM) and Mekong deltas (de Araujo Barbosa et al., 2016). Combining these findings with the lower Yangtze basin and the Bangladesh coastal zone (smaller than GBM) provides evidence of a widespread trade-off between rising food production and deteriorating regulating services as poverty is alleviated (Figure 4.5). The recent slowing down in production levels may be linked to the loss of regulating services: an unsustainable trajectory now brought to a head by negative feedback (Raudsepp-Hearne et al., 2010).

Applying Daw et al.'s (2016) elasticity concept to these delta systems classifies them as having high negative (or inverse) elasticity, but with different elasticities (low vs high) through time as local thresholds are transgressed. In contrast, Suich et al. (2015) found ESPA studies tending towards direct elasticities, with impacts on ecosystem services and poverty correlated either positively or negatively. But importantly they noted that the empirical studies were usually incomplete in terms of the range of ecosystem services, with most focusing on provisioning, rather than regulating, services. It will be difficult to apply the elasticity concept in the absence of time-series, or detailed qualitative information over time for multiple ecosystem services. The strong uni-directionality of the empirical relationship between provisioning and regulating services (Figure 4.5) may underline the lack of case studies, but may call into question the validity of elastic and reversible relationships. The priority of paying greater attention to long-term drivers (Fischer et al., 2015) is certainly borne out in these studies.

Can historical perspectives, based on time-series, provide information about whether a threshold change is imminent: essentially providing an early warning signal that the system is moving out of safe space? Much work has been undertaken in the search for properties of real or modelled time-series, such as increased variance, which indicate 'critical slowing down' or 'flickering' of the system as it loses resilience and becomes unstable (e.g. Biggs et al., 2009; Scheffer et al., 2012). But the evidence across the ESPA projects is equivocal. In the Bangladesh coastal system (Hossain et al., 2017a), the results were variable with no clear indication of impending shifts. In Yunnan Province, China, the apparent variability prior to

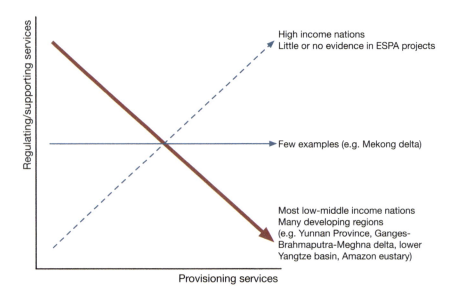

FIGURE 4.5 Schematic empirical relationships between provisioning and regulating/supporting ecosystem services as poverty is alleviated, showing the apparent main direction and prevalence (thick solid line – most common; thin solid line – less common; dotted line – rare or no evidence). The most common and inverse relationship represents a trade-off between poverty alleviation and environmental degradation (e.g. lower Yangtze basin, Bangladesh coastal zone and the Amazon estuary). Data from some regions (e.g. Mekong delta) indicate that poverty alleviation may be linked to a greater extraction of provisioning goods without incurring losses of regulating services. However, on current evidence, there is little or no evidence for provisioning services to be positively associated with regulating/supporting services.

a critical transition in the lake ecosystem owed as much to the quality of the dataset as it did to actual system instability (Wang et al., 2012). Only in the lower Yangtze basin (Zhang et al., 2015) was widespread rising variability in regulating and provisioning services interpreted as a possible signal of regional instability. These findings are driving the search for early warning signals based on the structural properties of the system, such as connectedness (de Araujo Barbosa et al., 2016; Doncaster et al., 2016; Zhang et al., 2015), rather than the frequency properties of time-series.

Overall, a typology of social-ecological dynamics, supported by both theory and metrics, is becoming better defined; and a language that includes linear, non-linear, feedbacks, thresholds, hysteresis and early warning signals is valuable for taking stock of current conditions and anticipating future changes (see Reyers and Selomane, this volume). The evidence from case-studies points to a need to identify safe and just spaces in purely dynamical terms, asking how society and communities have interacted with the natural environment, and whether the trajectory of interactions is heading towards desirable or undesirable states. To design policy that achieves this, it will be helpful to combine empirical assessments with tools and models that communicate the likely effects of alternative decisions.

Simulating limits, trade-offs and safe spaces

The modelling and simulation of future limits and safe operating spaces for real SES is in its infancy. Verburg et al.'s (2016) review makes the point that models for management often ignore feedbacks and thresholds, while models describing social-ecological dynamics often lack direct relevance to decision making. Nevertheless, a few ESPA projects have made significant advances in the development and use of simulation models that capture both realistic dynamics and management options.

Daw et al. (2015) combined participatory conceptual modelling, ecological modelling, interactive models and qualitative scenarios to explore trade-offs in a Kenyan coastal fishery. The EcoSim fisheries model was used as a conceptual systems model, and a simple mathematical model is used to simulate flows of benefits to different resource users under different scenarios. Comprehensive bivariate outputs (phase plots) map out a range of linear and non-linear relationships that define different kinds of trade-offs (Box 4.1). A classification of the relationships according to strongly held 'sacred' and 'secular' values gives 'routine', 'tragic' and 'taboo' trade-offs depending on which groups of stakeholders are involved. For example, a socially acceptable win-win for the whole community between conservation of fish stocks and profitability gained from fewer, larger fish may mask the trade-off for women who typically rely on small, cheap fish for income. The study introduces a novel approach to capturing the complexities in the biophysical system that produce trade-offs and clearly demonstrates how stakeholders can be brought into the learning process through the application of such simple, 'toy' models (Galafassi et al., 2017). Feedback mechanisms are alluded to in the conceptual model, and it would have been interesting to understand how they are incorporated into the interactive toy models.

Hossain et al. (2017a) used a systems dynamic model to make a first attempt at operationalising the safe operating spaces concept for the Bangladesh coastal zone. Like Daw et al. (2015), a conceptual model produced in collaboration with stakeholders summarised the main social and ecological components including provisioning and regulating services, basic farm economics, land-use shifts between cropping and shrimp farming, and farm incomes as the indicator of wellbeing. The connections between the components were defined from regression analyses of time-series (Hossain et al., 2017b) and from estimated functional relationships where data were sparse or absent. Partial validation of the model was achieved through comparison of outputs against historical trends in subsets of data. Eight 'what if' scenarios produced simulated outputs for different combinations of climate change, subsidy level, sea-level rise and water flows in the Ganges. A dangerous operating space was defined when the system moves outside its historical envelope of variability. The overarching message is that a safe operating space requires a temperature rise of less than 2°C, as agreed within the 2015 Paris Agreement, but there are still risks to regulating services, especially increasing soil salinity. In this respect, the model illustrates unintended consequences of farm subsidies in the form of a positive feedback loop, which tends to encourage over-use of fertiliser and irrigation.

The Bangladesh coastal zone model uses only simple social-ecological couplings that restrict its decision-making value. Cooper (2017) built on the approaches used

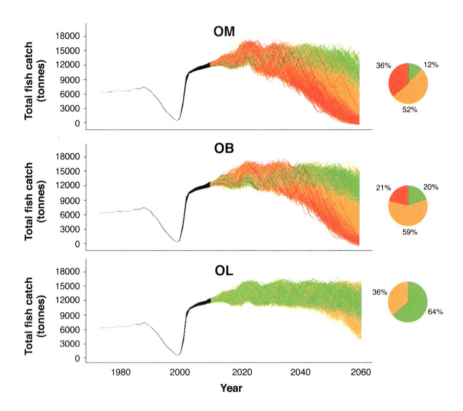

FIGURE 4.6 Simulating future annual catches in the Chilika lagoon fishery, eastern India, using a systems dynamic model with each trajectory defined as safe and just (green), cautionary (yellow) or dangerous (red) with respect to the maximum sustainable yield in 2050–2060. Annual fish catch time-series (N = 1000 per scenario) produced by spectrums of driver interactions under three governance scenarios: OM – only the tidal outlet maintained by dredging; OB – as OM with fishing bans in the tidal outlet; OL – as OM with limits on the number of new fishers allowed to join each fishing fleet. The historical record of fish catch, 1973–2009 (black), shows the fluctuating values caused by a lack of dredging. The findings illustrate the increasing probability of long-term safe and just trajectories (percentages shown in the pie-charts) from OM to OL, as governance becomes stronger.

Source: Cooper, 2017, reproduced with permission.

by both Daw et al. (2015) and Hossain et al. (2017a), embedding a process-based fisheries model within a comprehensive SES dynamic model that allows assessment of future safe spaces as boundary conditions, like climate change (cf. Scheffer et al., 2015). Application to the Chilika lagoonal fishery in eastern India showed that the model can simulate previous abrupt shifts in fish catch. Forward modelling from 2010 to 2060 (Figure 4.6) for three sets of management options determined by stakeholders generated alternative future trajectories, defined as safe, cautionary or dangerous with respect to fishery yield. A further step analysed all the trajectories that end in safe spaces and determined a 'core' set of management options, such as the number of fishers and motorboats that, if implemented today, give good probabilities for desirable outcomes.

Conclusions

By definition, the sustainable management of ecosystem services for poverty alleviation must confront both the natural limits imposed by environmental systems and the implications for the wellbeing of people. Thus, setting limits and defining safe and just spaces for complex SES are powerful and potentially durable concepts. But they necessitate theorising, observing, analysing and simulating system dynamics in ways that are inevitably challenging. These concepts, and the findings that flow from their application, also require a means to be delivered effectively to policy-makers. Thus, important questions are: how well have ESPA projects risen to these challenges and what have we learned?

In terms of theorising, the classification of the temporal relationships between poverty alleviation and ecosystem services is a major advance, and could go further by matching the range of elasticities to the many social-ecological theories that exist. Where social-ecological dynamics have been explored empirically, there is a contrast between those that focus on contemporary conditions and those that utilise time-series. The former tend to produce a deep understanding of the coupling between wellbeing and ecosystem services embedded in current circumstances, especially in terms of cultural and governance factors. The latter produce clear representations of trade-offs, thresholds and phase transitions over recent history, but usually at the expense of understanding the causal nature, or otherwise, of the relationships portrayed.

Future studies will benefit from combining the two approaches within the same regional context: on their own, neither is sufficient. Nevertheless, where concepts and theory have been supported by empirical data there are clear conclusions. Many regions in Africa and Asia are deemed to have exceeded safe limits for phosphorus, nitrogen, land use or freshwater use, and smart water management is vital in the two rural communities in China where safe limits have been downscaled. The elasticity concept clearly provides a powerful descriptor of past and present dynamics, and potentially a new means for determining trade-offs and safe regional boundaries. On current evidence, several large tropical deltaic systems with negative elasticity lie in transient phases beyond safe operating spaces, moving towards potentially undesirable or dangerous zones. Similarly, multi-decadal trends in indicators of ecosystem services and human wellbeing point to widespread non-stationary dynamics governed by slowly changing variables, declining resilience (for example to anticipated changes in climate) and with an increased likelihood of systemic instability or threshold changes.

In terms of delivering the results to policy-makers, the evidence is less clear because few studies in this field have covered the full 'science-discovery' to 'solution-driven' spectrum. Developing visual communication tools that can convey limits, trade-offs and safe spaces to policy-makers has been helpful at global, regional and local scales, and outputs from simulation models have been portrayed figuratively. However, a new challenge will be to communicate information derived from system dynamics where visual expression alone is insufficient. Participatory approaches, with stakeholders involved in knowledge co-production, are essential for creating appropriate policy (see Dawson et al.; Buytaert et al., this volume), but where vital knowledge stems from understanding the meaning and implications of system dynamics, it may be necessary to accept that local communities do not have sufficient capacity to ask all the necessary questions, for example, about thresholds and limits. Attempts to raise intellectual capacities through, for example, complexity workshops (ESPA, 2014) and dedicated bi-lingual websites (e.g. www.complexity.soton.ac.uk) are valuable but in their infancy.

The relatively short timescale for ESPA research is necessarily limiting the scale of findings in this area. But there may also be a certain reluctance to pursue systems-based methods to achieve solutions to development problems. It has been argued that systems-based resilience theory should be central to sustainable development thinking (Brown, 2016; Leach et al., 2010; Ramalingam, 2013), but it is perhaps not as dominant as its advocates would like. As Redman (2014: 3) says: 'Simply put, sustainability prioritizes outcomes; resilience prioritizes process'. It's the difference between goal- or path-orientated approaches and open-ended, emergent perspectives. Researchers may still be viewing outcomes against future scenarios as more beguiling than providing process-based advice to stakeholders on being resilient and sustainable over coming years and decades. Outputs from the ESPA and related programmes have now demonstrated the value of studying process-based limits and thresholds within a development context – laying down the challenge for new studies.

Acknowledgements

The author wishes to thank Dr Gregory Cooper, Dr Craig Hutton and the editors for providing feedback on earlier versions of the manuscript, and to Alix Dearing for proofreading. Gregory Cooper also gave his permission to reproduce Figure 4.6 from his PhD thesis.

References

(ESPA outputs marked with '★')

Biggs R, Carpenter SR and Brock WA. (2009) Turning back from the brink: detecting an impending regime shift in time to avert it. *Proceedings of the National Academy of Sciences* 106: 826–831.
Brown K. (2016) *Resilience, Development and Global Change*. London: Routledge.
Carpenter SR and Bennett EM. (2011) Reconsideration of the planetary boundary for phosphorus. *Environmental Research Letters* 6: 014009.
Cole MJ, Bailey RM and New MG. (2014) Tracking sustainable development with a national barometer for South Africa using a downscaled 'safe and just space' framework. *Proceedings of the National Academy of Sciences* 111: E4399–E4408.
Cole MJ, Bailey RM and New MG. (2017) Spatial variability in sustainable development trajectories in South Africa: provincial level safe and just operating spaces. *Sustainability Science* 12: 829–848.
Cooper GS. (2017) Social-ecological tipping points in world deltas: designing a safe and just operating space for the Chilika lagoon fishery, India. Unpublished PhD thesis, University of Southampton, 334 pp.
Cumming GS, Buerkert A, Hoffmann EM, et al. (2014) Implications of agricultural transitions and urbanization for ecosystem services. *Nature* 515: 50–57.
★Daw TM, Coulthard S, Cheung WWL, et al. (2015) Evaluating taboo trade-offs in ecosystems services and human well-being. *Proceedings of the National Academy of Sciences* 112: 6949–6954.
★Daw TM, Hicks CC, Brown K, et al. (2016) Elasticity in ecosystem services: exploring the variable relationship between ecosystems and human well-being. *Ecology and Society* 21: 11.
de Araujo Barbosa CC, Dearing J, Szabo S, et al. (2016) Evolutionary social and biogeophysical changes in the Amazon, Ganges–Brahmaputra–Meghna and Mekong deltas. *Sustainability Science* 11: 555–574.
Dearing JA. (2008) Landscape change and resilience theory: a palaeoenvironmental assessment from Yunnan, SW China. *The Holocene* 18: 117–127.
★Dearing JA, Wang R, Zhang K, et al. (2014) Safe and just operating spaces for regional social-ecological systems. *Global Environmental Change* 28: 227–238.
★Dearing JA, Yang X, Dong X, et al. (2012) Extending the timescale and range of ecosystem services through paleoenvironmental analyses, exemplified in the lower Yangtze basin. *Proceedings of the National Academy of Sciences* 109: E1111–E1120.
Doncaster CP, Alonso Chávez V, Viguier C, et al. (2016) Early warning of critical transitions in biodiversity from compositional disorder. *Ecology* 97: 3079–3090.
Eisenack K. (2012) Archetypes of adaptation to climate change. In: Glaser M, Krause G, Ratter BMW, et al. (eds) *Human-Nature Interactions in the Anthropocene: Potentials of Social-Ecological Systems Analysis*. New York: Routledge, 107–122.
★ESPA. (2014) *ESPA Complexity Workshop, 8–9 July 2014, London*. Available at: http://bit.ly/ESPAComplexity.
★Fischer J, Gardner TA, Bennett EM, et al. (2015) Advancing sustainability through mainstreaming a social-ecological systems perspective. *Current Opinion in Environmental Sustainability* 14: 144–149.
★Galafassi D, Daw TM, Munyi L, et al. (2017) Learning about social-ecological trade-offs. *Ecology and Society* 22: 2.
Holling CS. (1973) Resilience and stability of ecological systems. *Annual Review of Ecology and Systematics* 4: 1–23.

*Hossain MS, Dearing JA, Eigenbrod F, et al. (2017a) Operationalizing safe operating space for regional social-ecological systems. *Science of the Total Environment* 584–585: 673–682.

*Hossain MS, Dearing JA, Rahman MM, et al. (2016) Recent changes in ecosystem services and human well-being in the Bangladesh coastal zone. *Regional Environmental Change* 16: 429–443.

*Hossain MS, Eigenbrod F, Amoako Johnson F, et al. (2017b) Unravelling the inter-relationships between ecosystem services and human wellbeing in the Bangladesh delta. *International Journal of Sustainable Development and World Ecology* 24: 120–134.

Leach M, Scoones I and Stirling AC. (2010) *Dynamic Sustainabilities: Technology, Environment, Social Justice*. London: Earthscan.

MA. (2005) *Millennium Ecosystem Assessment, 2005. Ecosystems and Human Well-Being: Synthesis*. Washington, DC: Island Press.

Mace GM, Reyers B, Alkemade R, et al. (2014) Approaches to defining a planetary boundary for biodiversity. *Global Environmental Change* 28: 289–297.

May RM. (1972) Will a large complex system be stable? *Nature* 238: 413–414.

Meadows DH, Meadows DL, Randers J, et al. (1972) *The Limits to Growth*. New York: Universe Books.

Nordhaus T, Shellenberger M and Blomqvist L. (2012) *The planetary boundaries hypothesis: a review of the evidence*. Oakland, CA: The Breakthrough Institute, 1–42.

*Pereira L, Karpouzoglou T, Doshi S, et al. (2015) Organising a safe space for navigating social-ecological transformations to sustainability. *International Journal of Environmental Research and Public Health* 12: 6027–6044.

Ramalingam B. (2013) *Aid on the Edge of Chaos: Rethinking International Cooperation in a Complex World*. Oxford: Oxford University Press.

Raudsepp-Hearne C, Peterson GD, Tengö M, et al. (2010) Untangling the environmentalist's paradox: why is human well-being increasing as ecosystem services degrade? *BioScience* 60: 576–589.

Raworth K. (2012) A safe and just space for humanity: can we live within the doughnut? *Oxfam Policy and Practice: Climate Change and Resilience* 8: 1–26.

Redman CL. (2014) Should sustainability and resilience be combined or remain distinct pursuits? *Ecology and Society* 19: 37.

Rockström J, Steffen W, Noone K, et al. (2009a) A safe operating space for humanity. *Nature* 461: 472–475.

Rockström J, Steffen W, Noone K, et al. (2009b) Planetary boundaries: exploring the safe operating space for humanity. *Ecology and Society* 14: 32.

Running SW. (2012) A measurable planetary boundary for the biosphere. *Science* 337: 1458–1459.

Scheffer M. (2009) *Critical Transitions in Nature and Society*. Princeton, NJ and Oxford: Princeton University Press.

Scheffer M, Barrett S, Carpenter SR, et al. (2015) Creating a safe operating space for iconic ecosystems. *Science* 347: 1317–1319.

Scheffer M, Carpenter S, Foley JA, et al. (2001) Catastrophic shifts in ecosystems. *Nature* 413: 591–596.

Scheffer M, Carpenter SR, Lenton TM, et al. (2012) Anticipating critical transitions. *Science* 338: 344–348.

Schellnhuber H-J, Block A, Cassel-Gintz M, et al. (1997) Syndromes of global change. *GAIA – Ecological Perspectives for Science and Society* 6: 19–34.

*Sikor T, Martin A, Fisher J, et al. (2014) Toward an empirical analysis of justice in ecosystem governance. *Conservation Letters* 7: 524–532.

*Steffen W, Richardson K, Rockström J, et al. (2015) Planetary boundaries: guiding human development on a changing planet. *Science* 347: 1259855.
*Suich H, Howe C and Mace G. (2015) Ecosystem services and poverty alleviation: a review of the empirical links. *Ecosystem Services* 12: 137–147.
Verburg PH, Dearing JA, Dyke JG, et al. (2016) Methods and approaches to modelling the Anthropocene. *Global Environmental Change* 39: 328–340.
*Wang R, Dearing JA, Langdon PG, et al. (2012) Flickering gives early warning signals of a critical transition to a eutrophic lake state. *Nature* 492: 419–422.
*Wei Y, Ison R, Colvin J, et al. (2012) Reframing water governance: a multi-perspective study of an over-engineered catchment in China. *Journal of Environmental Planning and Management* 55: 297–318.
*Willcock S, Hossain S and Poppy GM. (2016) Managing complex systems to enhance sustainability. In: Solan M and Whiteley NM (eds) *Stressors in the Marine Environment*. Oxford: Oxford University Press, 301–312.
*Zhang K, Dearing JA, Dawson TP, et al. (2015) Poverty alleviation strategies in eastern China lead to critical ecological dynamics. *Science of the Total Environment* 506–507: 164–181.

PART II
Ongoing and rapid system changes

In this section, five chapters examine changes in social-ecological systems with reference to implications for environmental services and human wellbeing. The ongoing growth of human populations, shifts in age distribution, household size, wealth distribution and patterns of movement, including planned and unplanned migration, are all important factors influencing the interactions between people and the ecosystems they depend upon. As Adger and Fortnam (Chapter 5) describe, ecosystem management has the potential to either buffer or amplify the welfare consequences of population changes and migration, but the poorest and most vulnerable groups of people are much more likely to be losers, so deserving particular attention in planning and policy processes. Land-use change is most often a response to demands for increased production for growing human populations, and intensification for production has been the key trend in recent decades that, as Martin and colleagues (Chapter 6) describe, has many consequences that are often negative for ecosystem services that were not the focus of management. The immediate outcomes of intensification may be positive for both yields and aggregate incomes, but these benefits are often transient and miss the poorest and most vulnerable people completely.

Over half the global population are now living in urban areas, and urbanisation is expected to continue to increase through this century, so understanding the rural–urban continuum, especially with regards to ecosystem services and wellbeing, is ever more relevant. Marshall and colleagues (Chapter 7) examine peri-urban areas where change is often rapid and unplanned. Even as incomes increase, there are unintended and mostly negative consequences for the poorest, who suffer the most from ecosystem change and degradation, such as exposure to environmental hazards, and are often unable to access new sources of income and livelihoods. Urban areas also create huge demands for ecosystem services from nearby as well as from more distant areas, creating new pressures on even quite distant ecosystems.

The consequences of such linkages across ecosystems and their communities are examined closely in the contexts of forests and water systems by Whittaker and colleagues (Chapter 8). These systems are complicated in terms of both biophysical and socio-political factors, and the evidence is that, despite their attraction, simple payment for ecosystem service schemes often fails for predictable reasons. Instead, emerging practices among multi-stakeholder groups show that more lasting agreements based on reciprocity and cooperation could better succeed.

Ecosystems can of course also be restored, either with the intention to reverse degradation, or to re-establish the structure and function of an earlier, untransformed ecosystem. As Cameron (Chapter 9) reviews, wholesale restoration is difficult, costly and time consuming; however, there are other narrower restoration goals, such as efforts to restore certain kinds of ecosystem or biodiversity conditions that are cost effective and may more easily be achieved. While these efforts have been applied in many contexts, they are often narrowly focused and the evidence-base is weak and disorganised, leading to many instances of unintended consequences, especially for groups of services and communities who were not part of the plan.

5
INTERACTIONS OF MIGRATION AND POPULATION DYNAMICS WITH ECOSYSTEM SERVICES

W Neil Adger and Matt Fortnam

Introduction

The demand and supply of ecosystem services interacts with population dynamics within social-ecological systems. Yet the intricacies of population dynamics are ignored or lost in aggregation in many analyses and models. The decline in ecosystem services globally is partly explained by the issue of scale: greater human population in aggregate, and the changing distribution of these populations across different ecological regions, leads to greater pressure on ecosystems for productive use, pressure on habitats for settlement or agriculture, and greater pollution. But studies have demonstrated that only considering the total number of people has a limited role in explaining specific aspects of resource decline, and indeed high population density can in itself create the incentives for sustainable resource use. Hence a critical examination of the relationship between ecosystem services and population dynamics reveals key demographic processes. In particular, we emphasise here the role of migration as a social phenomenon predominantly of deliberate, voluntary change of residence, either permanently or temporarily, that has complex interactions with wellbeing, poverty and ecosystem services that are transformative of individuals and societies.

The analysis of interactions between ecological and social dynamics suggests that because ecosystem services are variable in space and time, human populations adapt to such processes through their own mobility. Rapid demographic and environment changes interact with development interventions with likely consequences for ecosystem service use and wellbeing. We highlight, in particular, that the dominant migration flows observed globally, especially from rural to urban areas, have profound consequences for ecosystem service access. This chapter outlines such relationships and suggests that development planning and interventions need to account for the spatial distribution of populations, the structure of populations and their mobility and migration patterns.

Spatiotemporal variability, mobility and ecosystem services

Mobility of ecosystem services and contemporary response strategies

Ecosystem services are mostly researched, particularly in terrestrial environments, as ecosystems or linked social-ecological systems situated in a place. Typically, a system is bounded geographically to an area within which ecosystem services and institutional arrangements are assessed (Pascual et al., 2017). Many studies involve snapshots of one or two ecosystem services at a single moment in time. Yet, ecosystem services are highly variable and mobile in space and time (Renard et al., 2015).

Environmental processes vary temporally and spatially: hence the services they provide are also variable. Rather than a steady, linear supply, which is often assumed in assessments, ecosystem service provision is dependent on dynamic, non-linear relationships between ecosystem stocks and flows (Koch et al., 2009). For example, marine ecosystems fluctuate daily, seasonally and inter-annually in response to seasonal oceanographic changes due to physical-chemical conditions and diurnal and seasonal vertical and lateral migrations of marine life (Drakou et al., 2017). Similarly, seasonal and erratic rainfall and climate extremes drive fluctuations in water and forage availability in drylands, resulting in mass migrations of wildlife and livestock (Fernandez-Gimenez and Le Febre, 2006). Because of this variability, ecosystem service benefits often only manifest at very specific times in annual or other temporal cycles, for both provisioning and regulating services. For instance, wave attenuation capacities are affected by intra-annual changes in the density and biomass of seagrasses (Chen et al., 2007).

Ecosystem service variability can create uneven patterns of income and consumption in natural resource-dependent households, which leads to seasonal or periodic poverty. Because of climatic seasons, farming households often have periods of the year for harvesting and selling crops, income from which is saved and used over the intervening months, and periods of hardship when savings are spent and crops have not matured for sale. Similarly, unpredictable variability in climate and ecosystem service supply increases the risk of households falling into, or failing to escape, poverty. In rural coastal Bangladesh, for example, households living in persistent poverty tend to have high seasonal variability in their incomes. This suggests that ecosystem service variability and seasonality poses risks to households falling into poverty and can limit the potential of ecosystem services to provide pathways out of poverty. For example, variability and declining overall forest integrity for the Sunderban mangrove forests in Bangladesh projected over the coming decades (Payo et al., 2016) challenges the role of ecosystem services as a safety net for coastal populations.

Human mobility is a key social response for dealing with such spatial and temporal variability in ecosystem services, income and consumption. Figure 5.1 shows temporal and spatial patterns of mobility in fisheries and pastoralist social-ecological systems. Livelihood studies have documented the critical role of migration in reducing vulnerability and poverty in low-income countries (Ellis, 1998). Seasonal migration enables households to benefit from seasonal patterns of food production and labour demand elsewhere to cope with local variability at home (de Haan, 1999). Many small-scale fishers in developing countries move in response to the seasonal movement or availability of fish to maintain their income (Figure 5.1(a)). On Lake Victoria, East Africa, about 60,000 fishers, around half of all boat crew, move from beach to beach for 2–3-month periods to access higher productivity fishing grounds and landing sites that command higher prices (Nunan et al., 2012).

Circular migration can help households diversify their livelihoods to cope with seasonal variability in climate and ecosystem services, such as when farmers take non-farm jobs in the city during the offseason. In India, approximately 20 million people temporarily migrate each year, mostly from drought-prone areas with rainfed agriculture to irrigated cropland (Deshingkar, 2006). Circular migration is driven by economic, cultural and social factors, as well as ecosystem service variability. Pastoralists, for instance, move, not just to access more productive pastures, but to reach markets and interact with other families and tribes to build social ties and make social exchanges such as marriage (Fernandez-Gimenez and Le Febre, 2006). Rotational migration involves movement to avoid or respond to ecosystem service overexploitation. Slash-and-burn agriculture in Amazonia, rotation of livestock between pastures to avoid overgrazing, and rotation of fishing activity within a space provide examples of this type of mobility. Beitl (2015), for example, observed how artisanal shellfish harvesters in the coastal mangrove swamps of Ecuador move to new grounds when their catch rates fall below average, with potential benefits of allowing habitats and stocks to recover. Such mobile practices are often deeply embedded in social practices and entwined in strategies that secure livelihoods (de Haan, 1999).

Livelihood mobility occurs across a range of scales (Figure 5.1(a),(b)). In the small-scale fisheries, some mobility is daily and localised, such as when fishers travel to the shoreline by foot or motor vehicle and to local fishing grounds by boat. Many fishers, however, migrate to distant waters to take advantage of spatial and temporal variability in fisheries productivity across seascape or jurisdictional and national boundaries. Similarly, the scale of transhuman pastoralism can vary from a limited landscape such as a valley to large-scale transboundary areas.

Mobility and flexibility is a well-documented livelihood strategy to cope and adapt to environmental variability, yet the interconnections between ecosystem services and livelihood mobility have not been considered in ecosystem service research, despite the obvious implications for ecosystem service uses and experiences on the transit routes and sites of out- and in-migration.

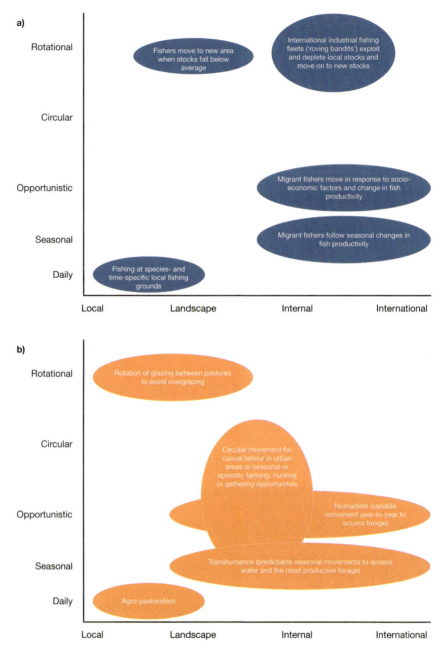

FIGURE 5.1 Spatial and temporal variability and mobility of (a) fisheries and (b) rangeland ecosystem services and livelihoods.

Challenges to governing mobile ecosystem services and livelihoods

Ecosystem management is often organised as common pool resource institutions, such as co-managed or community-based protected areas, based on local governance creating a vested interest in the provision and sustainable management of local ecosystem services. Mobile ecosystem services and human populations, however, challenge this governance model by disconnecting resources and resource users from the place of management. For example, in the Western Indian Ocean, marine protected areas and local fisheries enforcement have been established to address declining fish stocks. However, fishers cross local and national boundaries in search of mobile fish stocks, making monitoring the movement of migrants (Wanyonyi et al., 2011) and the management of fishing effort in a demarcated area problematic (Nunan et al., 2012). Berkes et al. (2006) describe mobile fleets of fishers and traders as roving bandits, who target and deplete stocks of valuable marine species and then move to new areas to exploit other stocks. Small-scale, local governance arrangements do not match the scale of mobility of these fisheries driven by global demand and technological changes in fishing practices. Migrant fishers then have little incentive to participate in management institutions that depend on attachment to place and, in a globalised world, the rate that new markets and technologies emerge outpaces the ability of local institutions to adapt.

Place-based protected areas often struggle to conserve mobile fisheries and wildlife as they are too small, scattered or disparate to match the behaviour of migratory species, and enforcement and monitoring outside of the protected areas is too weak. Common pool resource management institutions are therefore effective at managing species that are sedentary or not very mobile at local or landscape levels, but not for highly mobile ecosystem services and livelihoods.

Common property institutions that constrain mobility may also be counterproductive for poverty alleviation in some contexts, given the critical connections between human mobility, livelihoods and ecosystem services for the wellbeing of the poor. In pastoral systems, for instance, common property resource institutions are often mismatched with the changing availabilities of forage and water over space and time, and thus the needs of pastoralism (Brottem et al., 2014). In fisheries, migrant access to a fishery may be impeded by permits, licences or membership of local institutions.

Mobile actors are often excluded or unable to participate in local governance. The creation of co-management arrangements on Lake Victoria sought the participation of key stakeholders in decision making and management. However, given the mobility of the boat crews, their effective participation was problematic, with co-management instead dominated by powerful boat owners (Nunan et al., 2012). Co-management literature provides little guidance on how to deal with such mobile resource users. The large-scale and/or transboundary movement of pastoralists is also often not considered in conservation and natural resource management, which tends to target sedentary agricultural populations that are in conflict with pastoralists (Binot et al., 2009). Conditions of high rainfall and forage variability require flexible rules and limited social boundaries to maintain pastoral mobility (Brottem et al., 2014); this is at odds with the dominant place-based management of ecosystem services.

Ecosystem management institutions have not yet evolved to cope with the complexity and diversity of ecosystem service mobility. Berkes et al. (2006) suggest multi-level governance as a solution. This would involve managing ecosystem services and connecting institutions across local to international levels, and accounting for the interests and views of migrants in decision making. Mobile ecosystem services and resource users can potentially be integrated into multi-level governance systems: experience from schemes such as the international Coral Triangle Initiative involving six countries suggests that coordination is challenging even to avoid conflicts and maintain regulatory cohesion (Fidelman et al., 2014).

Migration decisions, migration outcomes and ecosystem services

Migration as a social system

Migration is a multifaceted social system that has complex interactions with wellbeing, poverty and trajectories of capital accumulation. Voluntary migration encompasses choice: permanent movement to exploit economic opportunities, both domestically and internationally, and circular movements of people between source and destination areas. Movement of people to urban centres within their own countries represents the single largest contemporary migration flow. But some migration arises from a lack of agency and choice: involuntary displacement due to conflict, coercion by governments or because of environmental degradation.

Does voluntary migration represent a universal pathway out of poverty for those involved in it? Most migration theories and empirical studies point to the motivations for migration as involving expectations of increased wellbeing, both in economic and social terms. When individuals leave home and form new households in distant locations, economic models conceptualise this action as an intrahousehold contract so that migration compensates for or benefits the household overall (Taylor, 1999). It is well established that migration, at the aggregate level, increases economic growth in, and economic linkages between, source and destination areas through remittance income (de Haas, 2005), and increases wellbeing and life satisfaction among those moving location (Nowok et al., 2013). The evidence is diverse across the social and economic sciences.

Dimensions of the migration–ecosystem service relationship involve issues such as how remittance income is invested, and how new populations in rural frontiers or in urban areas access ecosystem services, including the role of ecosystem services in creating wellbeing for migrant populations. Most migration-environment research focuses on the relative influence of resource scarcity, extreme events and environmental change on individual decision making or on aggregate flows of people, or the prospect of migration as adaptation to environmental harm (reviewed in Adger et al., 2015). The key parameters of how ecosystem services, environmental change and migration interact within social-ecological systems is not conceptualised in consistent or comprehensive ways. Here we examine each of the issues in turn.

Ecosystem services in source-destination linkages

Migration leads to increased economic linkages between where people move from, and where they eventually reside: source and destination areas. Indeed, migration studies have shown that most individuals leave households to gain employment and resources to return to their original households. Remittance flows from temporary or international migration sources are maintained over many years, which stems from migrants wanting the fall-back option of returning to their place of origin and to ensure the maintenance of land and other assets that they may inherit. Remittance income, unlike seasonally variable resources or agriculture-dependent livelihoods, is often constant over the course of the year, and hence can smooth income or consumption levels (Ellis, 1998). More importantly, remittance income tends to be invested in capital, such as in human capital through education or entrepreneurship, rather than being used principally for consumption (Hoddinott, 1994). Thus seasonal and circular migration have several interactions with ecosystem services. The out-migration of adults clearly reduces labour in source areas, making the exploitation of ecosystem services more difficult, but this is offset if adults travel back for important harvest times or to maintain ecosystems. Perhaps most importantly, remittance income can be invested in ecosystem-conserving technologies, or in greater exploitation and degradation of ecosystem services.

The evidence suggests that both ecosystem service enhancement and ecosystem service degradation result from temporary migration and investment of remittance income. Qin (2010) shows, for example, that out-migration of household members in rural parts of Chongqing region of China enhances the wellbeing of those households compared to those without migrant sources of income. However, among migrant households, there is some land abandonment due to labour shortages, which may explain the rise in forest cover in the region from 10% in the 1960s to 24% by 2008. Contrary conclusions are drawn by Gray and Bilsborrow (2014) from analysis in rural Ecuador, where agricultural areas have increased rather than being abandoned as a response to labour out-migration. In fact, there is evidence that out-migration can result in investment in sustainability. Hunter et al. (2014) show that temporary migration from rural areas in South Africa allows investment in natural capital by those households involved. Not all remittance investment leads to greater sustainability, however. Adger et al. (2002) documented how remittance flows supported the expansion of high-value but risky conversion of mangrove areas to aquaculture in northern Vietnam.

Ecosystem services in migration decisions

So while migration affects the demand and supply of ecosystem services, how important are ecosystem services for decisions concerning migration? Migration decision-making models show that the principal drivers of decisions to move are related to economic and educational opportunities, and barriers and risks to staying and going (Black et al., 2011). Ecosystem services play a role in such calculus, because they affect the landscapes of opportunity and risk in both source and destination areas. Migration decisions involve social disruption and feelings of loss and grief concerning places where people leave. Some of this is associated with place and place utility: in effect, cultural ecosystem services are part of the landscape of meaning and attachment of places people leave. Sense of place and attachment to place emerge from interactions with the physical and biological environment as well as through social relations: ecosystems have value through those relations in places (Masterson et al., 2017). Adams (2016), for example, explains how farming populations remain in upland Peruvian highlands due to cultural ecosystem services, such as perceptions of land and landscape, whereas standard models and calculus would suggest otherwise. Similarly, Mortreux and Barnett (2009) document the cultural and attachment reasons for populations deciding not to migrate internationally from Tuvalu in the Pacific. In other words, ecosystem services beyond their material value maintain value and indeed maintain populations within landscapes of social-ecological interaction.

Does migration lead to pressure on ecosystem services?

Temporary and circular migration from rural areas to cities and urban centres remains the single most prevalent migration flow globally. It has, then, significant and offsetting roles in the maintenance of ecosystem services: migration may enhance poverty alleviation, but the interaction with ecosystem services depends on how investments directly affect the exploitation and sustainability of resources.

While global migration flows are dominated by rural–urban movement, continued movement to new resource frontiers, particularly to forest frontiers, directly affects ecosystem services. López et al. (2006) argue that high fertility rates among remote farming communities in Latin American forest frontiers have a disproportionate impact on forest conversion, and that forest frontier migrants remain the main proximate cause of deforestation. López-Carr and Burgdorfer (2013) suggest that large family sizes also generate high levels of next-generation migration to new frontier areas. The effect of migration to forest frontiers on rates of habitat decline is, however, a complicated picture: in many remote forest frontiers, such as in Amazonia, there is evidence of continued depopulation as people move to urban areas for greater economic opportunities (Parry et al., 2010), yet rural-to-frontier migration remains a major trend. The impact of such migration flows on ecosystem services relates to how frontier migrants gain access to and knowledge about ecosystem services in their new locations, and whether their effects on ecosystem services are above average for the aggregate population.

There is much evidence on how habitat loss from land conversion reduces local ecological knowledge in frontier environments: Kai et al. (2014) show how younger populations can identify fewer forest species than older generations in forest frontiers in China. But new migrants gain knowledge through experimentation and experience. Muchagata and Brown (2000) show how migrant farmers in eastern Amazonia gain detailed taxonomic knowledge of their forest and pasture environments. Meyfroidt (2013) shows, however, that moves towards sustainable land use practices in Vietnam significantly lagged behind any new knowledge of environmental degradation and increasing scarcity of ecosystem services.

Given that knowledge and access to ecosystem services is not sufficient for conservation practices in new populations, other incentives come into play. Jones et al. (2018) provide evidence that new migrant populations in forest frontiers in Madagascar are attracted by land availability, but are no more likely than established populations to clear forest land: in other words, they are not so-called exceptional forest degraders. Garrett et al. (2017) suggest for frontier agriculture in Amazonia that agricultural intensification opportunities need to align with activities that bring non-material wellbeing and build on the identities of the farming communities, rather than relying on out-migration to bring about a forest transition.

Role of migration and displacement associated with loss of ecosystem services

How does the loss of ecosystem services affect migration processes – do they amplify or attenuate ongoing and established migration flows? Loss of ecosystem services may occur due to either sudden-onset natural hazards or long-term modifying processes, such as land degradation or sea level rise. The distinction is important, because natural hazards are a major source of involuntary displacement of populations. By contrast, long-term ecosystem degradation interacts with economic factors leading to conscious decisions to migrate from such areas (Renaud et al., 2011).

Displacement is a common phenomenon, with about 26 million people forced to vacate their homes and settlements every year because of disaster events such as floods, tsunamis, tropical storms, droughts or wildfires (IDMC, 2015). In addition to loss of infrastructure, loss of shelter and risk to life, these events disrupt the provision of ecosystem services, with the potential to displace people. For example, a drought may affect crop and livestock productivity, causing food insecurity or famine that displaces local populations. The exposure of a population to a hazard is also affected by the loss of regulatory services. For example, two million people were displaced by the 2004 Asian tsunami; settlements, water resources and cultivated areas were better protected where mangrove forests stood compared to deforested areas (Kathiresan and Rajendran, 2005). Displacement due to shocks is usually, however, short-term and short-distance, with most people returning to their home as soon as ecosystem services recover and livelihoods are viable (Black et al., 2013).

Changes in ecosystem services alter the relative advantages and disadvantages of areas for in- and out-migration. Given current global environmental change trends, the influence of ecosystem service status on migration is expected to increase in the future (Black et al., 2011). In drylands, for example, residents may choose to leave as land degradation causes loss of soil nutrients, food and water for humans and livestock. Indeed, de Sherbinin et al. (2012) found that the most dominant source of out-migration in developing countries between 1970 and 2000 was from marginal drylands and drought-prone regions. Small island states threatened by sea level rise and regions affected by increasingly frequent and severe climate hazards are also often cited as potential places from which international migration will increase (de Sherbinin et al., 2012).

Environmental risks and degraded regulating ecosystem services contribute to involuntary migration through a number of intervening variables. First, migration is driven by multiple, interacting political, social, economic, demographic and environmental signals, such as resource scarcity, which interact in multi-causal ways. Attributing migration to environmental dimensions is therefore neither possible, nor fruitful (Black et al., 2011; Renaud et al., 2011). Second, empirical studies of climate-related hazards and other environmental drivers have shown both increasing and decreasing migration outcomes (Table 5.1). Land degradation, for example, triggered migration in cases in Kenya and Guatemala but reduced human mobility in cases in Uganda and Mali. The examples in Table 5.1 also demonstrate that migration can decrease among some groups in the population and increase among others concurrently: migration outcomes vary within localities, differentiated by gender, class and income. In effect, migration is a household-level strategy for spreading risk and gaining income and resources: environmental shocks therefore act to dampen and reduce opportunities for migration as a livelihood strategy (Adger et al., 2002; Call et al., 2017).

Vulnerability to environmental risks and mobility have been shown to have an inverse relationship: those that are most vulnerable to environmental change have the least resources to migrate to less exposed sites (Black et al., 2013). Ecosystem service loss may reduce the resources available for vulnerable populations to move, while those with the means migrate, temporarily or permanently, to areas with more favourable ecosystem service availability. Some empirical studies support this perspective. Call et al. (2017), for example, found that environmental variability observed in Bangladesh over two decades disrupted livelihood mobility rather than displaced people (Table 5.1).

The increasing influence of environmental drivers on migration decisions means that ecosystem management has the potential to play an important role in amplifying or dampening migration. Policies and interventions aimed at addressing or reducing vulnerability to environmental change may maintain ecosystem services and wellbeing in an area and therefore discourage migration. Mangrove planting, for example, can reduce exposure to storms and tidal surges and therefore reduce the risk of displacement. Given the complex interaction between human and environment factors in determining migration trends, an ecosystem service lens may offer

TABLE 5.1 Migration outcomes of ecosystem service losses and environmental shocks

Location	Environmental shock or change	Key ecosystem service effects	Impact on migration	
Vietnam (Dun, 2011)	Increasing frequency of extreme **floods** events	Destruction of crops	↑	Triggered household or individual migration
Ethiopia (Gray and Mueller, 2012)	**Drought**	Loss of livestock and crops	↑	Men's labour migration more than doubled under severe drought as a coping strategy
			↓	Female marriage migration decreased by half under moderate drought, reflecting decreased ability to finance wedding
Bangladesh (Call et al., 2017)	**Precipitation, temperature** and **flooding** variability	Destruction of crops and reduced productivity	↓	Floods decreased temporary migration in aftermath
			↓	Persistent heavy precipitation decreased migration
			↑	Increased temperatures increased temporary migration
Kenya and Uganda (Gray, 2011)	**Soil degradation**	Reduced soil quality	↓	Significantly reduced migration in Kenya
			↑	Marginally increased migration in Uganda
Bangladesh (Paul, 2005)	**Tornado**	Loss of crops and cattle	—	No migration due to distribution of disaster relief
Ghana (van der Geest, 2011)	**Drought and slow onset environmental degradation**	Soil fertility	↓	During worst droughts of late 1970s and early 1980s, migration decreased
			↑	Increased out-migration due to push of land scarcity and soil infertility and, more importantly, pull of fertile land

new insights on the role of environmental factors in pushing and pulling people to migrate. At the same time, if migration and vulnerability are inverse, common property institutions may inadvertently contribute to trapping vulnerable populations by inhibiting mobility.

Wider population dynamics and ecosystem services

Migration and mobility are part of wider demographic transitions and population dynamics. While migration alters the spatial pattern of population density, it is also embedded in demographic trajectories: migration rates are partly determined by the availability of working-age individuals, dependency ratios and resource pressures (Hugo, 2011). Hence, resource pressure, through demand for provisioning ecosystem services and impacts on regulating ecosystem services, is related to population density or other elements of population structure. There are several population structure factors that affect ecosystem services, resource demand and their locally dependent population: age profile, household size and dependency ratios. Changing demographic structures have profound effects on ecosystem services (Liu et al., 2003).

Demand for provisioning ecosystem services changes over the life course, with peak consumption typically correlated with periods when individuals are at lifetime peak income levels. The single most significant demographic factor for burdens on ecosystem services, however, is the observed reduction of average household size in virtually all regions of the world. Liu et al. (2003), for example, showed that countries with biodiversity hotspots had higher levels of household formation (i.e. the same population but living in smaller-sized households) in the 15 years to 2000, which increased urban sprawl and pressures on biodiversity. Similarly, Kaye et al. (2006) show that small household size directly affects biogeochemical flows and pollution loading, and Cardillo et al. (2004) argue that population density is a factor in localised extinctions of carnivore populations. Hence, the structure of populations has interacting effects with ecosystem services.

Ecosystem services and demographic change further interact through how economic security facilitates or stalls demographic transitions. There is a well-recognised link between poverty and fertility choice, but with scattered evidence of the causal nature of relationships: for example, in the relationship between increased insecurity associated with environmental decline and high fertility rates. López-Carr and Burgdorfer (2013), for example, observed high levels of fertility in remote forest frontier environments in Latin America caused by economic insecurity. The general evidence on fertility shows that drivers of higher than replacement fertility levels in societies are around social conformity and expectations on one hand and economic drivers, such as economic or environmental insecurity, on the other. The impact of ecosystem service decline and accessibility on fertility remains indeterminate, but most theory and empirical evidence points to how ecosystem service decline potentially leads to livelihood insecurity in disadvantaged populations (Daw et al., 2011), and such insecurity potentially stalls poverty alleviation, with knock-on effects on migration, fertility choice and other human responses.

Frontiers of research on migration, mobility and population dynamics

The interactions between ecosystem services, migration and wider demographic trends are highly complex and dynamic, and ecosystem services are more usefully viewed in terms of social-ecological systems rather than static resources in terrestrial landscapes. Migration systems have indeed their own dynamics, and while environmental change and risks influence the main drivers of migration, movement continues despite environmental risks in both source and destination areas. Insights into migratory flows, population dynamics and resource pressures point to three emerging scientific frontiers on ecosystem services, migration and population dynamics.

First, the major demographic transitions under way around the world mean ageing populations, larger urban populations and different relationships between urban and non-built landscapes everywhere. Cities are becoming denser in some areas, and more extensive in others: but everywhere they are drawing on wider ranges of ecosystem services and have evolving links to hinterlands and global economic markets (Seto et al., 2012; Marshall et al., this volume). In this global context, the provision of urban ecosystem services is the critical challenge for cities, as recognised within city plans and international initiatives up to the urban Sustainable Development Goal. Migration, rather than natural population growth, drives the expansion of cities in Asia and Africa in particular. In these contexts, the ability of new migrant populations to access safe environments, clean water and green spaces has been shown to be critical to their wellbeing, and to making migration a sustainable route out of poverty (Roy et al., 2016). How ecosystem services can be managed for urban expansion through green infrastructure and other routes, and the role of technology in providing nature experiences to urban residents, for example, is a critical research arena.

Second, ecosystem services remain critical for pathways out of poverty and for influencing why populations persist in environments where there are incentives for depopulation, not least marginal agricultural areas. de Sherbinin et al. (2012) showed how, globally, 50–100 million people migrated from each of mountain and dryland regions between 1970 and 2000. Populations persist in these regions, in part, because of the value of ecosystem services to those populations, not least in their sense of place and cultural importance (Adams, 2016). Thus, research on how ecosystem services interact with long-term population movements, and the value of regulating services in avoiding involuntary migration, is a further research frontier.

Third, the evidence in this area suggests that many interventions for management of ecosystem services may be challenged because they fail to account for mobility, both of ecosystem processes and the distributions of populations accessing them.

These challenges have already been noted, for example in terms of the telecoupling of cause and consequence of actions and ecosystem processes (Pascual et al., 2017; Rieb et al., 2017). But further, increasing mobility may challenge traditional collective action and co-management of ecosystems: as people move in and out of areas, the boundaries of communities, users and resources are tested and breached. Hence migration and population dynamics are a key challenge for ecosystem service science: it needs to embrace the full spectrum of relevant social sciences, from demography to the sociology and human geography of place.

Acknowledgements

This chapter draws on research under Assessing Health, Livelihoods, Ecosystem Services and Poverty Alleviation in Populous Deltas (NERC Grant No. NE/J000892/1), part of the Ecosystem Services for Poverty Alleviation programme; and on Deltas, Vulnerability and Climate Change: Migration and Adaptation project (IDRC 107642) under the Collaborative Adaptation Research Initiative in Africa and Asia Programme, with financial support from the UK Government's Department for International Development and the International Development Research Centre, Canada. We thank Helen Adams and the editors for constructive comments. This version remains solely our responsibility.

References

(ESPA outputs marked with '★')

Adams H. (2016) Why populations persist: mobility, place attachment and climate change. *Population and Environment* 37: 429–448.
Adger WN, Arnell NW, Black R, et al. (2015) Focus on environmental risks and migration: causes and consequences. *Environmental Research Letters* 10: 060201.
Adger WN, Kelly PM, Winkels A, et al. (2002) Migration, remittances, livelihood trajectories, and social resilience. *Ambio* 31: 358–366.
Beitl CM. (2015) Mobility in the mangroves: catch rates, daily decisions, and dynamics of artisanal fishing in a coastal commons. *Applied Geography* 59: 98–106.
Berkes F, Hughes TP, Steneck RS, et al. (2006) Globalization, roving bandits, and marine resources. *Science* 311: 1557–1558.
Binot A, Hanon L, Joiris DV, et al. (2009) The challenge of participatory natural resource management with mobile herders at the scale of a Sub-Saharan African protected area. *Biodiversity and Conservation* 18: 2645.
Black R, Adger WN, Arnell NW, et al. (2011) The effect of environmental change on human migration. *Global Environmental Change* 21: S3–S11.
Black R, Arnell NW, Adger WN, et al. (2013) Migration, immobility and displacement outcomes following extreme events. *Environmental Science and Policy* 27: S32–S43.
Brottem L, Turner MD, Butt B, et al. (2014) Biophysical variability and pastoral rights to resources: West African transhumance revisited. *Human Ecology* 42: 351–365.
Call MA, Gray C, Yunus M, et al. (2017) Disruption, not displacement: environmental variability and temporary migration in Bangladesh. *Global Environmental Change* 46: 157–165.

Cardillo M, Purvis A, Sechrest W, et al. (2004) Human population density and extinction risk in the world's carnivores. *PLoS Biology* 2: e197.

Chen S-N, Sanford LP, Koch EW, et al. (2007) A nearshore model to investigate the effects of seagrass bed geometry on wave attenuation and suspended sediment transport. *Estuaries and Coasts* 30: 296–310.

*Daw T, Brown K, Rosendo S, et al. (2011) Applying the ecosystem services concept to poverty alleviation: the need to disaggregate human well-being. *Environmental Conservation* 38: 370–379.

de Haan A. (1999) Livelihoods and poverty: the role of migration – a critical review of the migration literature. *The Journal of Development Studies* 36: 1–47.

de Haas H. (2005) International migration, remittances and development: myths and facts. *Third World Quarterly* 26: 1269–1284.

de Sherbinin A, Levy M, Adamo S, et al. (2012) Migration and risk: net migration in marginal ecosystems and hazardous areas. *Environmental Research Letters* 7: 045602.

Deshingkar P. (2006) Internal migration, poverty and development in Asia. *ODI Briefing Papers* 11.

Drakou EG, Pendleton L, Effron M, et al. (2017) When ecosystems and their services are not co-located: oceans and coasts. *ICES Journal of Marine Science* 74: 1531–1539.

Dun O. (2011) Migration and displacement triggered by floods in the Mekong Delta. *International Migration* 49: e200–e223.

Ellis F. (1998) Household strategies and rural livelihood diversification. *The Journal of Development Studies* 35: 1–38.

Fernandez-Gimenez ME and Le Febre S. (2006) Mobility in pastoral systems: dynamic flux or downward trend? *International Journal of Sustainable Development and World Ecology* 13: 341–362.

Fidelman P, Evans LS, Foale S, et al. (2014) Coalition cohesion for regional marine governance: a stakeholder analysis of the Coral Triangle Initiative. *Ocean and Coastal Management* 95: 117–128.

Garrett RD, Gardner TA, Morello TF, et al. (2017) Explaining the persistence of low income and environmentally degrading land uses in the Brazilian Amazon. *Ecology and Society* 22: 27.

Gray C and Mueller V. (2012) Drought and population mobility in rural Ethiopia. *World Development* 40: 134–145.

Gray CL. (2011) Soil quality and human migration in Kenya and Uganda. *Global Environmental Change* 21: 421–430.

Gray CL and Bilsborrow RE. (2014) Consequences of out-migration for land use in rural Ecuador. *Land Use Policy* 36: 182–191.

Hoddinott J. (1994) A model of migration and remittances applied to Western Kenya. *Oxford Economic Papers* 46: 459–476.

Hugo G. (2011) Future demographic change and its interactions with migration and climate change. *Global Environmental Change* 21: S21-S33.

Hunter LM, Nawrotzki R, Leyk S, et al. (2014) Rural outmigration, natural capital, and livelihoods in South Africa. *Population, Space and Place* 20: 402–420.

IDMC. (2015) Global Estimates 2015: people displaced by disasters. Geneva: Internal Displacement Monitoring Centre, Norwegian Refugee Council, Oslo, Norway.

*Jones JPG, Mandimbiniaina R, Kelly R, et al. (2018) Human migration to the forest frontier: implications for land use change and conservation management. *Geo: Geography and Environment* [in press].

Kai Z, Woan TS, Jie L, et al. (2014) Shifting baselines on a tropical forest frontier: extirpations drive declines in local ecological knowledge. *PLoS ONE* 9: e86598.

Kathiresan K and Rajendran N. (2005) Coastal mangrove forests mitigated tsunami. *Estuarine, Coastal and Shelf Science* 65: 601–606.

Kaye JP, Groffman PM, Grimm NB, et al. (2006) A distinct urban biogeochemistry? *Trends in Ecology and Evolution* 21: 192–199.

Koch EW, Barbier EB, Silliman BR, et al. (2009) Non-linearity in ecosystem services: temporal and spatial variability in coastal protection. *Frontiers in Ecology and the Environment* 7: 29–37.

Liu J, Daily GC, Ehrlich PR, et al. (2003) Effects of household dynamics on resource consumption and biodiversity. *Nature* 421: 530–533.

López E, Bocco G, Mendoza M, et al. (2006) Peasant emigration and land-use change at the watershed level: a GIS-based approach in Central Mexico. *Agricultural Systems* 90: 62–78.

López-Carr D and Burgdorfer J. (2013) Deforestation drivers: population, migration, and tropical land use. *Environment: Science and Policy for Sustainable Development* 55: 3–11.

Masterson V, Stedman R, Enqvist J, et al. (2017) The contribution of sense of place to social-ecological systems research: a review and research agenda. *Ecology and Society* 22: 49.

Meyfroidt P. (2013) Environmental cognitions, land change and social-ecological feedbacks: local case studies of forest transition in Vietnam. *Human Ecology* 41: 367–392.

Mortreux C and Barnett J. (2009) Climate change, migration and adaptation in Funafuti, Tuvalu. *Global Environmental Change* 19: 105–112.

Muchagata M and Brown K. (2000) Colonist farmers' perceptions of fertility and the frontier environment in eastern Amazonia. *Agriculture and Human Values* 17: 371–384.

Nowok B, Van Ham M, Findlay AM, et al. (2013) Does migration make you happy? A longitudinal study of internal migration and subjective well-being. *Environment and Planning A* 45: 986–1002.

Nunan F, Luomba J, Lwenya C, et al. (2012) Finding space for participation: fisherfolk mobility and co-management of Lake Victoria fisheries. *Environmental Management* 50: 204–216.

Parry L, Day B, Amaral S, et al. (2010) Drivers of rural exodus from Amazonian headwaters. *Population and Environment* 32: 137–176.

★Pascual U, Palomo I, Adams WM, et al. (2017) Off-stage ecosystem service burdens: a blind spot for global sustainability. *Environmental Research Letters* 12: 075001.

Paul BK. (2005) Evidence against disaster-induced migration: the 2004 tornado in north-central Bangladesh. *Disasters* 29: 370–385.

★Payo A, Mukhopadhyay A, Hazra S, et al. (2016) Projected changes in area of the Sundarban mangrove forest in Bangladesh due to SLR by 2100. *Climatic Change* 139: 279–291.

Qin H. (2010) Rural-to-urban labor migration, household livelihoods, and the rural environment in Chongqing Municipality, Southwest China. *Human Ecology* 38: 675–690.

Renard D, Rhemtulla JM and Bennett EM. (2015) Historical dynamics in ecosystem service bundles. *Proceedings of the National Academy of Sciences* 112: 13411–13416.

Renaud FG, Dun O, Warner K, et al. (2011) A decision framework for environmentally induced migration. *International Migration* 49: e5–e29.

Rieb JT, Chaplin-Kramer R, Daily GC, et al. (2017) When, where, and how nature matters for ecosystem services: challenges for the next generation of ecosystem service models. *BioScience* 67: 820–833.

★Roy M, Cawood S, Hulme D, et al., eds. (2016) *Urban Poverty and Climate Change: Life in the Slums of Asia, Africa and Latin America.* London: Routledge.

Seto KC, Reenberg A, Boone CG, et al. (2012) Urban land teleconnections and sustainability. *Proceedings of the National Academy of Sciences* 109: 7687–7692.

Taylor EJ. (1999) The new economics of labour migration and the role of remittances in the migration process. *International Migration* 37: 63–88.

van der Geest K. (2011) North-south migration in Ghana: what role for the environment? *International Migration* 49: e69–e94.

Wanyonyi I, Crona B and Rosendo S. (2011) *Migrant Fishers and Fishing in the Western Indian Ocean: Socio-Economic Dynamics and Implications for Management.* Zanzibar, Tanzania: WIOMSA.

6
LAND USE INTENSIFICATION

The promise of sustainability and the reality of trade-offs

Adrian Martin, Brendan Coolsaet, Esteve Corbera, Neil Dawson, Janet Fisher, Phil Franks, Ole Mertz, Unai Pascual, Laura Vang Rasmussen and Casey Ryan

Introduction

There are seemingly compelling reasons to intensify land-based production systems (Godfray et al., 2010), and yet the benefits of higher productivity have too often been accompanied by substantial, detrimental contributions to environmental change at local to global scales (Foley et al., 2005; Laurance et al., 2014; Poppy et al., 2014; Rockström et al., 2009). By 2050 there will be an estimated 9 billion people on the planet which, along with changing dietary preferences such as increasing meat consumption, could require a doubling of demand for food crop production between 2005 and 2050 (Tilman et al., 2011). This global estimate hides greater regional pressures with increased demand for cereal crops of 150% or more in sub-Saharan African countries such as Ethiopia, Ghana and Tanzania (Franks et al., 2017). Achieving food security will be made more difficult by the increasing competition for land arising from other urgent and important local and global challenges, including demand for land for biodiversity conservation (e.g. protected areas) and for energy security (e.g. biofuels). Given the increasing competition for land, large-scale expansion of agriculture is no longer the preferred option in many places, leaving four alternative and potentially complementary strategies for future food security: (1) increasing yields through intensification; (2) reducing demand by eliminating overconsumption and reducing meat consumption; (3) reducing wastage, estimated at 1.3 billion tonnes of food lost annually post-harvest (Gustavsson et al., 2011); and (4) improving distribution. While priorities vary from country to country, the land use intensification option has generally been pursued most vigorously to date and continues to feature prominently in global environment and development strategies (DeClerck et al., 2016; Rockström et al., 2017). Land-use intensification, including the target to double the productivity of smallholders by 2030, is seen as fundamental to achieve the UN Sustainable Development Goals of ending hunger (SDG2) and achieving sustainable use of terrestrial ecosystems (SDG15).

Land use intensification has been central for human development throughout history and will play a role in addressing future challenges. However, while some strongly advocate intensification as a way to deliver gains for both human welfare and the environment (e.g. Cohn et al., 2014; Stevenson et al., 2013), this has become hotly debated. In the case of agriculture, some forms of intensification are found not to spare land from agricultural expansion and to lead to a range of negative environmental impacts (Hertel et al., 2014; Phelps et al., 2013). For these reasons, the call now is for 'sustainable intensification', a concept that is generally understood to mean increasing the productivity of land while reducing or eliminating adverse environmental impacts (Godfray and Garnett, 2014; Pretty and Bharucha, 2014; Rockström et al., 2017). Just as there is a debate about the effectiveness of land-use intensification for achieving environmental goals, so too there is a debate about its relationship with poverty. While evidence has accrued that economic growth from agricultural intensification is effective for poverty elimination (de Janvry and Sadoulet, 2009; Thirtle et al., 2003), recent studies have questioned this, both in terms of the short-term effects on the poor (Dawson et al., 2016) and the vulnerability of poorer groups to longer-term environmental degradation (Dearing et al., 2014).

This chapter reviews recent published research that investigates the combined effects of intensification on both ecosystem services and human wellbeing in low- and middle-income countries. Our analysis combines a more descriptive summary of findings across a sample of 60 cases, reported in 53 publications (1997–2017), with a more detailed study of a small number of exemplary cases.

Conceptualising land use intensification

Land use intensification is broadly defined as activities undertaken with the intention of enhancing the productivity or profitability per unit area of rural land use, including intensification of particular land uses as well as changes between land uses. Most research concerns cases of agricultural intensification, but there were a few cases of terrestrial aquaculture and agroforestry. Based on our sample, we identify four broad types of land use intensification.

1 *Land use conversion.* Predominantly conversion from fallow systems to permanent cropland, but also other changes, e.g. conversion from rain-fed to irrigated and from annual crops to plantations.
2 *Increased inputs.* Primarily physical inputs, including irrigation, chemicals, machinery and labour, but also new knowledge and skills, thus potentially including conservation agriculture as a form of intensification.

3   *Crop or product change.* Involving new types and often higher-yielding varieties of crops, and normally involving specialisation or monocropping and a shift from subsistence to cash-cropping.
4   *Mixed intensification.* More complex combinations of the previous three types.

These land use intensification *activities* produce outcome pathways that incorporate inter-connected social and ecological impacts (Figure 6.1). Local and global *drivers* initiate intensification activities that play out in particular places. Indirect local drivers include markets, governance and population while indirect global drivers include economic globalisation and climate change. While *outcome pathways* are complex, dynamic and context-dependent, we employ the language of social-ecological trade-offs and synergies to summarise these as win-win, lose-lose and win-lose pathways. This simplification should not lose sight of the underlying complexity, but is useful for identifying and describing emerging patterns in the scientific literature.

Outcomes from land use intensification – including trade-offs – are given meaning by social *values* and may thus be perceived and experienced in diverse ways by different social groups. Ultimately, the values and meanings attached to outcomes are determinants of *policy responses* in the context of key societal objectives such as food security. For example, growing evidence that the use of neonicotinoid pesticides contributes to declines in flying insect populations has coincided with

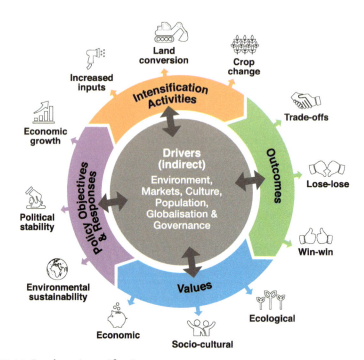

FIGURE 6.1 Land use intensification process.

wider appreciation of the value of pollinators. This is leading to policy responses that ban or limit the use of such pesticides, thus changing options for future intensification. This example refers mainly to economic preferences, but values involve many types of preferences, including social and cultural ones. Poverty elimination is a primary value in the context of ecosystem services and leads to a consideration of whether, and in what circumstances, land use intensification can produce pathways out of poverty. These elements (drivers, activities, outcomes, values and responses) are not envisaged to be connected in simple linear relationships, but rather involve complex, dynamic and multi-dimensional system changes that cannot be well accounted for through simple causal links (Erb et al., 2013).

Land use intensification outcomes

We identify and discuss three main themes relating to ecosystem services and wellbeing. First, we consider a central feature of the ecosystem services literature: the use of typologies of multiple ecosystem and human wellbeing outcomes, following the conceptual framework of the Millennium Ecosystem Assessment (MA, 2005). Second, we discuss multiple ecosystem service trade-offs (Howe et al., 2014). Third, we consider an important (but less common) trend towards disaggregation of human wellbeing outcomes to identify winners and losers (Daw et al., 2011). Finally, we try to draw together findings across these three themes to identify the contribution of ESPA research into land use intensification to an understanding of the connections between changes to ecosystem services and to human wellbeing.

Measuring multiple outcomes

Land use intensification studies tend to focus on singular outcomes, such as responses of crop yields to changing inputs, and mainly focus on either ecological or social outcomes in isolation (Rasmussen et al., 2017a). Figure 6.2 summarises the outcome variables adopted in the smaller (but growing) body of work that reports on both social and ecological outcomes. It reveals both the limitations and strengths of the research. In terms of limitations, a small number of more traditional measures continue to dominate (van Vliet et al., 2012). 85% of the 60 studies we reviewed reported on food production, generally classified as a provisioning ecosystem service; 92% of studies reported on income as a poverty variable, which we classify here as a human wellbeing outcome, with the reservation that income is only an intermediate means to achieve desired ways of being. Given our selection of the ecosystem services literature, it is surprising to find that relatively few studies describe any other provisioning or regulating ecosystem services, and fewer still describe cultural ecosystem services (Figure 6.2). Biodiversity and supporting services (notably soil formation) are more frequently included.

This bias in what is measured has strong implications for judgements about the sustainability of intensification. On the one hand, the outcome indicators that the research community most often measure (food production and income) are the variables that appear most likely to respond positively to land use intensification – this is intuitively what one would expect and is confirmed by our review findings (Figure 6.3). On the other hand, certain indicators of sustainability that are widely recognised as important outcomes of land use (e.g. water purification, water regulation) are infrequently described but, when they are, record negative outcomes

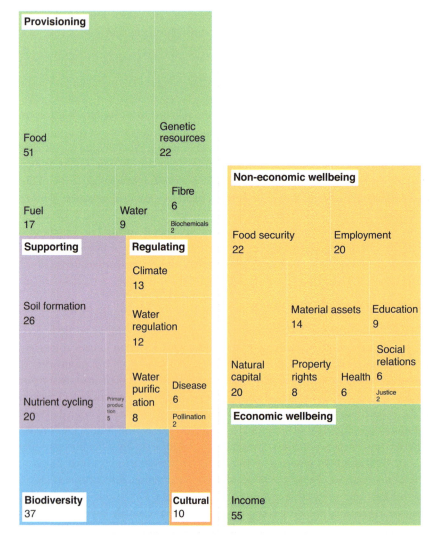

FIGURE 6.2 Number of cases reporting different measures of ecosystem services and human wellbeing. Note: cultural ecosystem services amalgamate categories of cultural heritage, spiritual and religious, recreation and ecotourism, aesthetic and educational, and sense of place.

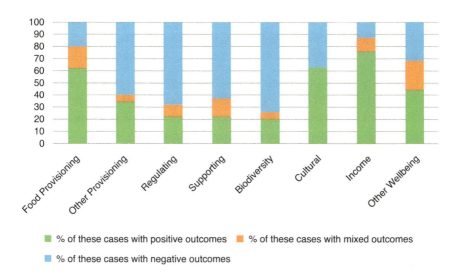

FIGURE 6.3 Proportion of studies reporting positive and negative outcomes for different categories of ecosystem services and human wellbeing.

in the majority of cases. Connecting these limitations suggests a reporting bias towards measures that one would expect to gain from intensification (e.g. production yields) and against measures that are more likely to show losses (such as water regulation). Studies reporting on cultural ecosystem services remain rare and the positive outcomes in Figure 6.3 may well reflect the very small number of observations. Our finding is that the logic and discourse that supports mainstream land use intensification policies is not currently subject to adequate scientific scrutiny (Figure 6.2).

This limitation in the evidence is not surprising, given that it would be impractical to study multiple ecosystem services and human wellbeing outcomes in most research projects. Regardless of this, the literature we reviewed provides a more complete picture of the outcomes of land use intensification, including the observation that, when measured, impacts on biodiversity, supporting ecosystem services and regulating ecosystem services are more often negative than positive. By contrast, impacts on both economic and non-economic measures of human wellbeing are often reported as positive – the so-called environmentalist's paradox (Raudsepp-Hearne et al., 2010). However, this finding is largely limited to economic measures of wellbeing and only a few cases attempt to show the distribution of benefits among different groups. A case from Mozambique (Box 6.1) shows that the use of multi-dimensional measures of wellbeing provides a more nuanced understanding of outcome pathways, demonstrating, for example, that only some aspects of wellbeing are directly responsive to land use intensification.

BOX 6.1 IMPACTS OF LAND USE INTENSIFICATION ON MULTI-DIMENSIONAL WELLBEING, MOZAMBIQUE

The ESPA-ACES project explored three case studies in Mozambique and examined how multi-dimensional wellbeing and inequality changed with three common land use intensification activities: intensification of smallholder commercial agriculture, small-scale charcoal production and subsistence cultivation.

The study used the conceptual framework of Erb et al. (2013) to analyse differences across multi-dimensional land-use intensity gradients, including three dimensions of land use intensification: (1) inputs to the production system (e.g. land, technology); (2) outputs from the production system (e.g. product yields); and (3) modifications to system properties and functions (e.g. soil quality and biodiversity). Site-specific measurements of inputs, outputs and system-level modifications were used to create three multi-dimensional gradients, and villages were classified *post hoc* along the gradients. The project also applied the Multi-dimensional Poverty Index (Alkire and Seth, 2016), measuring 15 indicators of wellbeing to reflect the multiple deprivations the poor face in terms of health, living standards and education.

Multi-dimensional wellbeing improved with intensification of both commercial and subsistence agriculture, suggesting that socioeconomic benefits from agricultural intensification and expansion may overcome localised environmental trade-offs, at least in the short term. However, some regulating services may be being undermined by intensification, as smallholders reported more climate shocks in the most deforested areas and a loss of bird predators of crop pests. In contrast, a boom–bust pattern of wellbeing was observed following charcoal intensification, whereby multi-dimensional wellbeing initially increased but subsequently declined. There were limited productive investment opportunities for charcoal-derived income, due to unconducive national policies, and hence resource extraction and related income were unsustainable.

In all sites, intensification only improved endogenous aspects of a household's wellbeing where beneficial outcomes are mediated by a household's agency (e.g. housing material, affordability of healthcare). Exogenous benefits that are beyond the agency of a single household, such as the construction of a village borehole, require additional structural support, irrespective of land use intensification.

Source: case contributed by ESPA-ACES project team (http://bit.ly/ESPA-ACES)

Trade-offs

We consider three types of trade-off: first, ecological trade-offs between the flow of different ecosystem services; second, trade-offs between different measures of human wellbeing; and third, social-ecological trade-offs between human wellbeing outcomes and ecosystem services outcomes. These primary forms of trade-off all involve social trade-offs, because different groups of people prefer different sets of outcomes and all types of trade-offs therefore produce winners and losers (Rodríguez et al., 2006; Sikor, 2013).

Ecological trade-offs between the production of different ecosystem services are dominated by cases in which land use intensification leads to increased food production at the expense of regulating and supporting ecosystem services and biodiversity. Our sample of literature contained 31 cases reporting gains in food provisioning. Of these, 26 report on at least one other ecosystem service, as summarised in Table 6.1.

Such trade-offs between provisioning and other ecosystem services are examined in a case study from China (Box 6.2). A key finding here is that losses to regulating ecosystem services often play out slowly but then appear to reach a critical stage at which feedback systems operate and regime shift occurs. This is also a key finding in a case study of shrimp farming in Bangladesh (Hossain et al., 2016, 2017; Islam et al., 2015; Szabo et al., 2016), in which ecosystem degradation accelerates due to feedbacks. In this case, land use changes that caused salination led to even more land being converted to shrimp production, leading to further salinity and soil degradation. This represents a significant threat to the poor, because the shift away from land-based farming is capital-intensive, attracting wealthier farmers and externalising environmental impacts on poorer rice farmers. Understanding trade-off dynamics requires research that captures change over extended time periods (Dearing, this volume).

Trade-offs between different human wellbeing outcomes have been less well studied to date, and this may be reflected in our review. Table 6.2 reports on the 41 cases that found land use intensification to have a positive effect on local agricultural incomes. Broadly speaking it suggests that, where other indicators of (non-economic)

TABLE 6.1 How increased food production trades off with ecosystem services. This table reports only outcomes for different ecosystem services for the cases that identified positive benefits for food

	Positive outcomes	*Mixed outcomes*	*Negative outcomes*
Non-food provisioning	6	1	4
Regulating	2	1	10
Cultural	3	0	2
Supporting or biodiversity	7	6	11

> **BOX 6.2 AGRICULTURAL INTENSIFICATION IN CHINA: TRADE-OFFS BETWEEN PROVISIONING AND REGULATING ECOSYSTEM SERVICES**
>
> During the second half of the twentieth century, China achieved food self-sufficiency but this involved costs to the environment that highlight trade-offs between provisioning and regulating ecosystem services. Dearing et al. (2014) and Zhang et al. (2015) find that degradation of regulating ecosystem services follows non-linear transition pathways, with notable tipping points or regime shifts. The risk of rapid reduction in regulating services appears to be linked to high levels of system connectedness arising from reduced landscape diversity. Centrally planned land use intensification increased system connectedness up until the mid-1980s. There was then a period of diversification (reduced connectedness) due to the shift from top-down planning to household responsibility for farm planning. However, this trend has now been overshadowed by economic globalisation and a renewed trend towards greater connectedness as farmers respond to the same market signals.
>
> The effects of these trade-offs often involve time lags, with collapses in regulating services coming much later than initial gains in provisioning services. Such lags provide important insight into the 'environmentalist's paradox' – wellbeing gains may be achieved despite losses of ecosystem services if the real effects of environmental degradation have not yet occurred. Finally, there is evidence of negative feedback systems – past losses of ecosystem services are becoming evident, and in turn this leads to accelerated ecological degradation. For example, farmers suffering from reduced yields due to soil acidification respond by increasing their use of fertilisers.

wellbeing are also measured, these are often positive too. As an example, the two cases that reported on gender outcomes found that positive effects on income were linked to positive effects on social relations (specifically gender equality in these cases) because land use intensification led to greater income earning opportunities for women, which improved their autonomy and social standing (Agoramoorthy et al., 2012; Dahal et al., 2009).

However, this does not mean that income is a reliable proxy measure for multi-dimensional wellbeing outcomes. In Mozambique (Box 6.1), land use intensification mainly led to improvements in those aspects of wellbeing that involved household control over income. We also find cases where rising income from land use intensification actually led to reduced food security, for example in upland Laos, where intensification of crop production has been found to lead to poorer nutritional outcomes (Box 6.3). Such cases challenge simple notions of synergy between income growth and other measures of human wellbeing.

TABLE 6.2 How increased income is associated with changes in non-economic human wellbeing outcomes. This table reports only on cases that find land use intensification to have a positive effect on local incomes

	Positive outcomes	*Mixed outcomes*	*Negative outcomes*
Education	6	2	0
Food security	9	0	3
Natural capital (e.g. land, livestock)	10	1	2
Material assets	4	4	1
Employment	8	7	0
Health	1	1	1
Social relations	2	1	0
Property rights	1	4	0
Justice	1	0	0

In order to further explore *social-ecological trade-offs* we looked at the pair-wise social and ecological outcomes for each of the 61 cases. The most common paired outcome, found in 23% of cases, is for gains in wellbeing (most commonly income) to be accompanied by losses in ecosystem services. These included water quality (Dearing et al., 2014; Hossain et al., 2016, 2017), carbon storage (Börner et al., 2007), trees in the landscape (Rahman et al., 2016; Wood et al., 2016) and biodiversity (Okubo et al., 2010; Renwick et al., 2014). In a further 10% of cases, gains in wellbeing were accompanied by mixed outcomes for ecosystem services. Only in 17% of cases do we find 'win-win' paired outcomes, dominated by measures of food production and income.

These observations of trade-offs are crude, in the sense that they mainly observe co-outcomes rather than establishing causal pathways. Nevertheless, the overall picture is important: considering the relatively small body of research that investigates both ecosystem services and wellbeing outcomes, win-win outcomes remain quite rare, and positive outcomes for income and food production are frequently associated with negative outcomes for other ecosystem services.

Disaggregated outcomes

All trade-offs ultimately have a social outcome, because different groups value different ecosystem services in different ways. This means that the outcomes of land use intensification will typically involve winners and losers, and thus any serious attempt to understand connections between ecosystem services and poverty alleviation needs to disaggregate outcome measures in ways that reveal impacts on

BOX 6.3 LAND USE INTENSIFICATION AND DISAGGREGATED WELLBEING OUTCOMES IN UPLAND LAOS

This case focuses on three villages around the Nam Et-Phou Louey National Protected Area in north-eastern Laos. Land use intensification has involved adoption of a new cash crop, reduced fallow times and increased inputs, partly driven by the desire to 'spare' land for tiger conservation. Maize was introduced in 2010, under contract farming arrangements, and villages further from the park's core have integrated maize production into their shifting cultivation systems, whereas Phon Song village has adopted continuous maize cultivation due to land constraints.

Using a Multi-dimensional Poverty Index, it was found that poverty rates had fallen rapidly, from 59% in 2004 to 20% in 2014, but this had been accompanied by reductions in food security. In Phon Song, with the most intensified landscape, there were significantly fewer wild foods, including rodents – 77% of villagers never replace this lost protein source through market-bought meat. Thus, the most intensified landscapes in this region may be the least well nourished. Disaggregated analysis found that inequalities in income were increasing and were closely linked to access to land. When park boundaries were demarcated in 2000, customary land rights became formalised and this favoured households with the most farm labour and those with social connections. This initial condition of inequality is now being amplified – for example, wealthier households are better able to encroach upon park land.

This case illustrates feedback systems that connect changes to ecosystem services and human wellbeing. Land use change contributes (among other drivers) to the commercialisation of farming households, and this is entwined with cultural change that includes a decline in forests as places of spiritual significance – even animist ethnic groups now present domestic rather than forest goods as gifts to their ancestors. Economic and cultural change is shifting the values attached to ecosystem qualities, such that wild plants and animals that were once viewed as provisioning services are increasingly viewed as pests and weeds. In Phon Song, the use of rodenticides and herbicides is becoming more common as a result and researchers observe a co-evolving relationship between cultural and ecological diversity. In this village, the reduction of fallow periods is already leading to falling yields, causing farmers to take loans to intensify inputs, and also leading to widespread illicit forest clearance in the Total Protection Zone. Therefore, it is questionable whether intensification here is sustainable, either for future food production or sparing land for conservation.

Source: Broegaard et al. (2017), Dawson et al. (2017a,b), Rasmussen et al. (2017b)

economically and socially marginal groups. A study from Rwanda, for example, finds that national data on farm incomes is a poor indicator of the wellbeing outcomes for the poor (Dawson et al., 2016). It is therefore surprising that only 11 of our 61 cases reported disaggregated analysis of wellbeing outcomes. Those that do explicitly consider the impacts on marginalised groups (Dawson et al., 2016, 2017b; Dearing et al., 2014; Hossain et al., 2016; Islam et al., 2015) confirm that poor people are less able to access benefits from land use intensification due to a range of institutional and structural barriers to accessing land, capital and expertise. Furthermore, they show that environmental outcomes of land use intensification can be particularly damaging for small farmers and fishers (Hossain et al., 2016; Islam et al., 2015; Box 6.2). One of the emerging findings from studies of disaggregated outcomes of land use intensification is that where inequity is deepened, this not only undermines poverty alleviation objectives but can also undermine long-term ecological sustainability (Dawson et al., 2017b; Martin, 2017). In the example from Laos (Box 6.3), inequitable access to land is amplified by land use intensification and local perceptions of inequity are eroding the legitimacy of the protected area boundaries.

Social-ecological outcome pathways

While we cannot derive rigorous generalisations, we observe that social-ecological outcomes are associated with the type of land use intensification activity. In particular, case studies that primarily involve increasing inputs to land-based production systems are more often associated with positive social-ecological outcomes compared with cases of crop change and land conversion. Indeed most cases involving 'increased input' intensification activities (11 out of 20) report decisively positive human wellbeing outcomes while only 3 out of these 20 report decisively negative wellbeing outcomes. There is an even split between those reporting positive and negative ecosystem service outcomes (8 out of 20 each). Such summary findings are important to note and to follow up in further research, but many cases are likely to involve hidden impacts of intensification. For example, because outcomes are scale dependent, in terms of the time taken to manifest themselves, and in terms of the spatial distribution of benefits and costs, land use intensification may bring wellbeing benefits in one place while transferring costs to other places (Pascual et al., 2017). Thus, if we want to better understand bundled social-ecological outcomes we need to be careful about what we measure, the length of time we measure it for, and the level of aggregation. If we want to understand how land use intensification can contribute to pathways out of poverty, we need longer-term and cross-scale work to understand how losses to key ecosystem services, particularly regulating services, can be avoided (Dearing, this volume).

Considering 'crop change' and 'land conversion' cases, we find anecdotal evidence of fewer positive outcomes for either wellbeing or ecosystem services, and more 'lose-lose' outcomes with negative impacts for both. More research is needed to confirm such trends, though we can still learn from example cases. The 'lose-lose' cases in our sample demonstrate that the pathways leading to these outcomes are quite varied. For example, we see pathways in which the negative impact on ecosystem services comes soonest and appears to be the cause of negative impacts on the wellbeing of smallholders, e.g. where soil salinisation ultimately undermines livelihoods of the less wealthy, or where deforestation from charcoal intensification ultimately undermines local income. But we also see cases where negative ecological and social outcomes appear in parallel from early on – for example, research in forest-agriculture mosaic landscapes in Rwanda shows how economically and socially marginalised groups were immediately disadvantaged by the government's Crop Intensification Programme, particularly through economic barriers to compliance, reduced tenure security and prohibition of traditional agriculture (Dawson, 2015; Dawson et al., 2016).

The presence of multiple outcome pathways reflects the importance of particular contexts in determining outcomes of land use intensification. For example, in the Laos case the spatial context was crucial, with different outcomes for villages located in different zones of the protected area. In Mozambique, national policy context was important in terms of which dimensions of human wellbeing outcome were affected by land use intensification. However, we also tentatively discern some regularities across categories of outcome pathways. Considering lose-lose categories, we first observe that these tend to directly or indirectly involve increased crop specialisation, with a shift towards monocultures of cash crops – for example, maize cropping in Laos, shrimp production in Bangladesh and tea crops in Rwanda. These changes have been associated with quite rapid impacts – for example, pests that feed on maize, concentration of land holdings in the Rwanda and Laos cases and acceleration of salinisation in the Bangladesh case. Second, drivers of land use intensification often leave marginal groups with limited choices. In Rwanda, government policy has dictated crop change; in Laos, the reservation of land for conservation has driven the switch to continuous maize cropping. A common factor in these cases is that the smallest landholders lack command of the assets needed to succeed with the induced crop change. Thus, a repeated observation is that negative wellbeing outcomes arise from an inability to make necessary intensification of inputs, including investment in labour, fertilisers and pesticides (Aragona and Orr, 2011; Dawson et al., 2016; Jakovac et al., 2015, 2016; Shaver et al., 2015). Finally, we observe that costs are often transferred to the poorest groups as an indirect result of intensification by other farmers, e.g. through increased risk of pests due to the reduction of genetic diversity.

Conclusions

We introduced this chapter by highlighting expectations for land use intensification to deliver on poverty alleviation and environmental protection goals. Our review shows that we are still some way from understanding the extent to which such 'sustainable intensification' is being achieved in practice, or indeed how it can be achieved in future. An uncritical and summary review of the evidence as a whole might conclude that land use intensification leads to improvements in human wellbeing despite losses to biodiversity and ecosystem services. However, a deeper exploration makes it clear that we need more research that considers multiple ecosystem services and human wellbeing dimensions, and the multiple and non-linear timing of impacts, as well as finer-grained social levels where impacts are differentiated.

Despite limitations, our research through this lens of integrated social-ecological enquiry reveals few cases of 'win-win' outcomes from land use intensification, and that some apparent wins hide a more complex picture. Where impacts on biodiversity, regulating and supporting ecosystem services are measured (which in itself is not common), the outcomes are more often seen to be negative. Furthermore, in several cases declining ecosystem services are accompanied by losses in wellbeing for some groups of people. These cases suggest multiple and complex pathways to 'lose-lose' outcomes that will benefit from further research. Losses to ecosystem services can lead to losses in human wellbeing, but the reverse causality also appears possible as well as less linear relationships. Equity is in some cases a mediating factor, showing that particular elements of human wellbeing can feed back on ecosystem governance.

While the evidence is limited, the literature suggests that many negative outcomes from intensification are partially predictable. For example, that the poorest will have least access to land, credit and other necessary factors of commercialised agricultural production; and that a progressive shift to landscape level monoculture will increase the demand for soil nutrients and the threat posed by pests and diseases. It is likely predictable that removing or reducing fallow periods will increase the resources needed to deal with weeds; and that heavy irrigation in arid areas will produce salinisation, or that changing large areas of land to saline aquaculture will lead to salinisation problems for adjacent paddy fields; and it is predictable that rolling back or abandoning some forms of intensification when they turn out to be disappointing can be difficult. What is less clear is the pace at which such effects will play out, the kinds of feedback systems that may lead to rapid and irreversible change, and the social and political response to these.

The research and practice communities can contribute to achievement of land use-related SDGs in two main ways. First, we can better use the available knowledge – for example, incorporating new findings related to the differentiated impacts on marginalised groups. But second, to further advance our understanding of sustainable intensification, there has to be a paradigm shift in how we approach and evaluate the outcomes of intensification efforts. Judging purely on production and income increases is inadequate.

References

(ESPA outputs marked with '★')

Agoramoorthy G, Hsu MJ and Shieh P. (2012) India's women-led vegetable cultivation improves economic and environmental sustainability. *Scottish Geographical Journal* 128: 87–99.

Alkire S and Seth S. (2016) Identifying destitution through linked subsets of multi-dimensionally poor: an ordinal approach. *OPHI Working Paper 99*. University of Oxford.

Aragona FB and Orr B. (2011) Agricultural intensification, monocultures, and economic failure: the case of onion production in the Tipajara watershed on the eastern slope of the Bolivian Andes. *Journal of Sustainable Agriculture* 35: 467–492.

Börner J, Mendoza A and Vosti SA. (2007) Ecosystem services, agriculture, and rural poverty in the Eastern Brazilian Amazon: interrelationships and policy prescriptions. *Ecological Economics* 64: 356–373.

★Broegaard RB, Rasmussen LV, Dawson N, et al. (2017) Wild food collection and nutrition under commercial agriculture expansion in agriculture-forest landscapes. *Forest Policy and Economics* 84: 92–101.

Cohn AS, Mosnier A, Havlík P, et al. (2014) Cattle ranching intensification in Brazil can reduce global greenhouse gas emissions by sparing land from deforestation. *Proceedings of the National Academy of Sciences* 111: 7236–7241.

Dahal BM, Nyborg I, Sitaula BK, et al. (2009) Agricultural intensification: food insecurity to income security in a mid-hill watershed of Nepal. *International Journal of Agricultural Sustainability* 7: 249–260.

★Daw T, Brown K, Rosendo S, et al. (2011) Applying the ecosystem services concept to poverty alleviation: the need to disaggregate human well-being. *Environmental Conservation* 38: 370–379.

★Dawson N. (2015) Bringing context to poverty in rural Rwanda: added value and challenges of mixed methods approaches. In: Roelen K and Camfield L (eds) *Mixed Methods Research in Poverty and Vulnerability: Sharing Ideas and Learning Lessons*. London: Palgrave Macmillan, 61–86.

★Dawson N, Grogan K, Martin A, et al. (2017a) Environmental justice research shows the importance of social feedbacks in ecosystem service trade-offs. *Ecology and Society* 22: 12.

★Dawson N, Martin A and Danielsen F. (2017b) Assessing equity in protected area governance: approaches to promote just and effective conservation. *Conservation Letters*.

★Dawson N, Martin A and Sikor T. (2016) Green revolution in sub-Saharan Africa: implications of imposed innovation for the wellbeing of rural smallholders. *World Development* 78: 204–218.

★Dearing JA, Wang R, Zhang K, et al. (2014) Safe and just operating spaces for regional social-ecological systems. *Global Environmental Change* 28: 227–238.

DeClerck F, Jones S, Attwood S, et al. (2016) Agricultural ecosystems and their services: the vanguard of sustainability? *Current Opinion in Environmental Sustainability* 23: 92–99.

de Janvry A and Sadoulet E. (2009) Agricultural growth and poverty reduction: additional evidence. *The World Bank Research Observer* 25: 1–20.

Erb K-H, Haberl H, Jepsen MR, et al. (2013) A conceptual framework for analysing and measuring land-use intensity. *Current Opinion in Environmental Sustainability* 5: 464–470.

Foley Ja, Defries R, Asner GP, et al. (2005) Global consequences of land use. *Science* 309: 570–574.

Franks P, Hou-Jones X, Fikreyesus D, et al. (2017) Reconciling forest conservation with food production in sub-Saharan Africa: case studies from Ethiopia, Ghana and Tanzania. *IIED Research Report*. London.

Godfray HCJ, Beddington JR, Crute IR, et al. (2010) Food security: the challenge of feeding 9 billion people. *Science* 327: 812–818.

Godfray HCJ and Garnett T. (2014) Food security and sustainable intensification. *Philosophical Transactions of the Royal Society B: Biological Sciences* 369: 20120273.

Gustavsson J, Cederberg C, Sonesson U, et al. (2011) Global Food Losses and Food Waste: Extent Causes and Prevention. Rome, Italy: FAO, 37 pp.

Hertel TW, Ramankutty N and Baldos ULC. (2014) Global market integration increases likelihood that a future African Green Revolution could increase crop land use and CO_2 emissions. *Proceedings of the National Academy of Sciences* 111: 13799–13804.

*Hossain MS, Dearing JA, Rahman MM, et al. (2016) Recent changes in ecosystem services and human well-being in the Bangladesh coastal zone. *Regional Environmental Change* 16: 429–443.

*Hossain MS, Eigenbrod F, Amoako Johnson F, et al. (2017) Unravelling the inter-relationships between ecosystem services and human wellbeing in the Bangladesh delta. *International Journal of Sustainable Development and World Ecology* 24: 120–134.

*Howe C, Suich H, Vira B, et al. (2014) Creating win-wins from trade-offs? Ecosystem services for human well-being: a meta-analysis of ecosystem service trade-offs and synergies in the real world. *Global Environmental Change* 28: 263–275.

*Islam GT, Islam AS, Shopan AA, et al. (2015) Implications of agricultural land use change to ecosystem services in the Ganges delta. *Journal of Environmental Management* 161: 443–452.

Jakovac CC, Peña-Claros M, Kuyper TW, et al. (2015) Loss of secondary-forest resilience by land-use intensification in the Amazon. *Journal of Ecology* 103: 67–77.

Jakovac CC, Peña-Claros M, Mesquita RC, et al. (2016) Swiddens under transition: consequences of agricultural intensification in the Amazon. *Agriculture, Ecosystems & Environment* 218: 116–125.

Laurance WF, Sayer J and Cassman KG. (2014) Agricultural expansion and its impacts on tropical nature. *Trends in Ecology and Evolution* 29: 107–116.

MA. (2005) *Millennium Ecosystem Assessment, 2005. Ecosystems and Human Well-Being: Synthesis*. Washington, DC: Island Press.

*Martin A. (2017) *Just Conservation: Biodiversity, Wellbeing and Sustainability*. Abingdon, UK: Routledge.

Okubo S, Harashina K, Muhamad D, et al. (2010) Traditional perennial crop-based agroforestry in West Java: the tradeoff between on-farm biodiversity and income. *Agroforestry Systems* 80: 17–31.

*Pascual U, Palomo I, Adams WM, et al. (2017) Off-stage ecosystem service burdens: a blind spot for global sustainability. *Environmental Research Letters* 12: 075001.

Phelps J, Carrasco LR, Webb EL, et al. (2013) Agricultural intensification escalates future conservation costs. *Proceedings of the National Academy of Sciences* 110: 7601–7606.

*Poppy GM, Chiotha S, Eigenbrod F, et al. (2014) Food security in a perfect storm: using the ecosystem services framework to increase understanding. *Philosophical Transactions of the Royal Society B: Biological Sciences* 369.

Pretty J and Bharucha ZP. (2014) Sustainable intensification in agricultural systems. *Annals of Botany* 114: 1571–1596.

Rahman SA, Sunderland T, Kshatriya M, et al. (2016) Towards productive landscapes: trade-offs in tree-cover and income across a matrix of smallholder agricultural land-use systems. *Land Use Policy* 58: 152–164.

Rasmussen LV, Bierbaum R, Oldekop JA, et al. (2017a) Bridging the practitioner–researcher divide: indicators to track environmental, economic, and sociocultural sustainability of agricultural commodity production. *Global Environmental Change* 42: 33–46.

*Rasmussen LV, Christensen AE, Danielsen F, et al. (2017b) From food to pest: conversion factors determine switches between ecosystem services and disservices. *Ambio* 46: 173–183.

Raudsepp-Hearne C, Peterson GD, Tengö M, et al. (2010) Untangling the environmentalist's paradox: why is human well-being increasing as ecosystem services degrade? *BioScience* 60: 576–589.

Renwick AR, Vickery JA, Potts SG, et al. (2014) Achieving production and conservation simultaneously in tropical agricultural landscapes. *Agriculture, Ecosystems & Environment* 192: 130–134.

Rockström J, Steffen W, Noone K, et al. (2009) A safe operating space for humanity. *Nature* 461: 472–475.

Rockström J, Williams J, Daily G, et al. (2017) Sustainable intensification of agriculture for human prosperity and global sustainability. *Ambio* 46: 4–17.

Rodríguez J, Beard Jr TD, Bennett E, et al. (2006) Trade-offs across space, time, and ecosystem services. *Ecology and Society* 11: 28.

Shaver I, Chain-Guadarrama A, Cleary KA, et al. (2015) Coupled social and ecological outcomes of agricultural intensification in Costa Rica and the future of biodiversity conservation in tropical agricultural regions. *Global Environmental Change* 32: 74–86.

*Sikor T, ed. (2013) *The Justices and Injustices of Ecosystem Services*. Abingdon, UK: Routledge.

Stevenson JR, Villoria N, Byerlee D, et al. (2013) Green Revolution research saved an estimated 18 to 27 million hectares from being brought into agricultural production. *Proceedings of the National Academy of Sciences* 110: 8363–8368.

*Szabo S, Hossain MS, Adger WN, et al. (2016) Soil salinity, household wealth and food insecurity in tropical deltas: evidence from south-west coast of Bangladesh. *Sustainability Science* 11: 411–421.

Thirtle C, Lin L and Piesse J. (2003) The impact of research-led agricultural productivity growth on poverty reduction in Africa, Asia and Latin America. *World Development* 31: 1959–1975.

Tilman D, Balzer C, Hill J, et al. (2011) Global food demand and the sustainable intensification of agriculture. *Proceedings of the National Academy of Sciences* 108: 20260–20264.

van Vliet N, Mertz O, Heinimann A, et al. (2012) Trends, drivers and impacts of changes in swidden cultivation in tropical forest-agriculture frontiers: a global assessment. *Global Environmental Change* 22: 418–429.

Wood SL, Rhemtulla JM and Coomes OT. (2016) Intensification of tropical fallow-based agriculture: trading-off ecosystem services for economic gain in shifting cultivation landscapes? *Agriculture, Ecosystems & Environment* 215: 47–56.

*Zhang K, Dearing JA, Dawson TP, et al. (2015) Poverty alleviation strategies in eastern China lead to critical ecological dynamics. *Science of the Total Environment* 506–507: 164–181.

# 7
ECOSYSTEM SERVICES AND POVERTY ALLEVIATION IN URBANISING CONTEXTS

Fiona Marshall, Jonathan Dolley, Ramila Bisht, Ritu Priya, Linda Waldman, Priyanie Amerasinghe and Pritpal Randhawa

Introduction

The world's urban population is expected to rise from 3.9 to 6.4 billion people between 2014 and 2050, with 90% of this increase in Asia and Africa (UN, 2014). While the impacts of urbanisation on ecosystems and the dependence of urban populations on ecosystem services are acknowledged (Gómez-Baggethun et al., 2013), the complex nature of the interactions involved and the diverse implications for human wellbeing are poorly understood, risking missed opportunities for managing urban ecosystems more sustainably. As direct and visible dependence on ecosystems for livelihoods declines, so urban development policies have tended to neglect ecosystem management, and communication strategies to raise awareness among urban publics become challenging. This dissociation of urban development from ecosystems makes it difficult for urban communities to understand and manage urbanisation sustainably, at the same time as they remain highly dependent on their ecological hinterlands (Seto et al., 2013).

Academic and policy interest in urban ecosystems and ecosystem services has grown rapidly since the late 1990s (Bolund and Hunhammar, 1999; Botkin and Beveridge, 1997). A body of urban ecosystem services literature (see Andersson et al., 2014; Baró et al., 2017; Elmqvist et al., 2013; Gaston et al., 2013; Gómez-Baggethun and Barton, 2013; Haase et al., 2014a,b; Kremer et al., 2016) has emerged amidst rising concerns about the environmental impacts of urbanisation (largely in North America and Europe), as cities appropriated ecosystem services from near and distant ecosystems (Folke et al., 1997; Rees and Wackernagel, 1996). Scholars also recognised that there was an important role for ecosystems within urban areas to contribute to biodiversity and human wellbeing (Bolund and Hunhammar, 1999) and potentially even reduce impacts of urbanisation on distant ecosystems (Gaston et al., 2013).

Nevertheless, urban ecosystem services research remains a relatively new field. A recent review of urban assessments found that most were concerned with Europe, North America and China, and focused on ecosystem services generated in urban areas by forested areas, mixed land use and urban green infrastructure such as parks (Haase et al., 2014b). This is consistent with Bolund and Hunhammar's (1999: 294) definition of urban ecosystems as 'all natural green and blue areas in the city, including in this definition street trees and ponds'. However, following the Millennium Ecosystem Assessment (MA, 2005), a wider range of services has been shown to be provided by urban ecosystems, including 'supporting (e.g. soil formation and nutrient cycling), provisioning (e.g. urban food production), regulating (e.g. local climate and flood regulation) and cultural (e.g. aesthetic, sense of place and health benefits of green space and wildlife' (Davies et al., 2011 as quoted in Gaston et al., 2013).

The focus of urban ecosystem services research has widened to incorporate a multi-scale social-ecological systems approach going beyond 'ecology *in* cities' to examine 'the ecology *of* cities' (Gómez-Baggethun et al., 2013: 177; see also Seitzinger et al., 2012). This brings a greater emphasis onto the close linkages between urbanisation processes and ecosystems which span or interact across the traditional boundaries between urban and rural. This highlights ecosystem services produced across the rural–urban continuum within city-regions – particularly those associated with peri-urban agricultural ecosystems (e.g. Deutsch et al., 2013; Lin et al., 2015) – and the dynamic rural–urban linkages emerging around urbanising places from small towns to megacities and urban corridors (Elmqvist et al., 2013; Gómez-Baggethun and Barton, 2013). The ecosystem services framework can, however, provide a useful common language for co-management of ecosystems across urban areas and their hinterlands (Kremer et al., 2016).

However, there has been little attention in urban ecosystem literature to equity in needs and demands for, and access to, ecosystem service benefits, including those that directly support food and water security (Haase et al., 2014b). In contrast, the literature on ecosystem services and poverty alleviation, which has emerged in parallel to the urban ecosystems literature, focuses attention on the Global South and the role of ecosystem services in poverty alleviation and social justice. However, until recently, this literature has dealt mainly with rural systems and their interaction with a narrow range of poverty indicators such as income and assets (Suich et al., 2015).

Research by the Ecosystem Services for Poverty Alleviation (ESPA) programme has bridged the gap between the northern-focused urban ecosystems literature and its emergent interest in the rural–urban continuum, and the rural-centric ecosystem services and poverty alleviation literatures. In this chapter we review relevant research in urbanising contexts, which is still relatively sparse, arguing that the expanding peri-urban interface is a critical frontier for learning about interconnected ecosystems and livelihood transitions and merits more attention (Marshall, 2016). We examine how an enhanced understanding of peri-urban dynamics, coupled with alliance building and multi-stakeholder dialogue concerning cross-scale implications of current development interventions, can reveal possibilities for creating synergies across the rural–urban continuum in support of integrated urban environmental, human wellbeing and economic development goals.

Peri-urban ecosystem transformations

Rural-urban linkages in the Global South are increasingly shaped and transformed by processes of peri-urbanisation (Seto et al., 2013). Global, national, regional and urban political economies drive peri-urban transformations through their influence on patterns of investment, consumption, employment, migration, urban planning priorities and environmental legislation, and implementation of regulations. These transformations are characterised by a range of land use and livelihood changes and socio-economic and institutional dynamics. For these reasons, we define the peri-urban interface not simply by location in relation to urban centres, but in terms of the juxtaposition of rural and urban activities, institutions and/or land uses (Marshall et al., 2009).

Peri-urban places on the margins of large metropolitan areas are often characterised by a mosaic of land uses, including agriculture, common land and forest, alongside industry, urban infrastructure, informal settlements, exclusive gated communities, urban parks and golf courses (Box 7.1). There are also typically flows of urban waste from the city's core to the peripheries in the form of landfill sites and waste treatment facilities; air pollution, illegal extraction of groundwater by industries and disposal of untreated industrial and domestic waste in open space, under the ground and in rivers or other water bodies (Marshall et al., 2009; STEPS Centre and Sarai, 2010). At the other end of the peri-urban spectrum are rural villages. Here the peri-urban context is a juxtaposition of urban and rural

---

BOX 7.1 PERI-URBAN AGRICULTURE, ECOSYSTEM SERVICES AND HUMAN WELLBEING IN INDIA

Building on a longer programme of transdisciplinary research in peri-urban India (Marshall et al., 1999, 2003, 2005; Singh et al., 2010; te Lintelo et al., 2002), fieldwork activities were conducted in the village of Karhera as part of the 'risks and responses to urban futures' project in 2014–2015. Karhera lies between Delhi and Ghaziabad in the National Capital Region in India, and many of its inhabitants still depend on agriculture for their livelihoods.

Driven by the broader trajectory of urban development, land-use change in Karhera has been substantial and rapid. Nearby areas have become informal industrial clusters, the government has acquired land for infrastructure construction and for setting up a City Forest park, and land has been sold informally to private builders for informal settlements (Bisht et al., 2016).

Economic opportunities for peri-urban residents have changed as local factory work and other jobs have become available, attracting migrants and resulting in an increasingly heterogeneous population.

Upstream industries have depleted and polluted the water flow along the Hindon River, which runs through Karhera, and provided a source of drinking, bathing and irrigation water to the community in the past. Lack of regulation due to the area's ambiguous administrative status as neither rural nor urban has allowed local industries relocated from urban areas to pollute local groundwater and soils. The City Forest park project, initiated by the Ghaziabad City development authority, has enclosed former common land used by local farmers. This has resulted in a sought-after cultural ecosystem service being available to paying urbanites, but has increased pressure on depleted groundwater resources and reduced access to agricultural land and other forest ecosystem services.

Access to expanding urban markets for fresh vegetables (especially spinach) has improved livelihoods for many farmers, who have changed from mixed farming of staple crops and livestock to intensive spinach farming (see STEPS Centre, 2016). This has significantly reduced material poverty for many landed and tenant farming households, providing incomes higher than are available in informal factory work. This comes with trade-offs, however. Industrial air and water pollution contaminate crops, posing food safety threats to both peri-urban and urban consumers. Village *johads* (traditional communal ponds) and innovative waste water reuse practices for irrigation largely disappeared when a new supply of piped water was temporarily supplied, but the new water infrastructure soon became inadequate due to competing demands, lack of maintenance and a growing population. When traditional practices were reinstated, new problems of faecal contamination arose due to inadequate sewage and waste disposal services. The increased intensity and duration of work is physically demanding, and women often bear the heaviest burden as they work in fields while the men sell the produce at markets (Waldman et al., 2017). This exposes them to health risks from the polluted water, as they apply it to their crops, and also poses a threat to food safety for urban consumers. The poorest urban consumers are likely to be most at risk as they are unable to afford expensive certified organic produce or foreign imported foods to replace the nutritional value of locally grown leafy vegetables (Marshall and Randhawa, 2017). Finally, the move away from mixed farming to intensive vegetable production also has implications for the feedbacks to peri-urban ecosystems, as crop yields are supported by higher use of chemical inputs and intensive year-round cultivation, with the likelihood of declining soil fertility and structure. There is little support for small-scale farmers in peri-urban areas, despite the critical role they play in multiple dimensions of food security (Marshall and Randhawa, 2017).

BOX 7.2 A RURAL-URBAN RECIPROCAL WATER AGREEMENT IN INDIA

Kovacs et al. (2016) report on a case study of a 'reciprocal water agreement' (RWA) between urban and rural communities in Himachal Pradesh, India.

An increasingly unreliable water supply due to changing rainfall and snowfall patterns had put pressure on water quality and cost, which prompted the Palampur town Municipal Council (MC) to place greater value on the high quality and more reliable water supply from the neighbouring upstream Bohal spring. The recharge zone for this spring lies within a forest area used by three villages to support their livelihoods. In response to increasing flash floods and declines in firewood availability, these upstream villages had developed informal management arrangements to protect local forest ecosystems in order to preserve the ecosystem services supporting firewood, leaf fodder, flash flood prevention and spring water recharge.

Development of the RWA was facilitated by the German Development Agency, GIZ, and the State Government of Himachal Pradesh in order to create a decentralised formal arrangement for management of water supply to the town. Negotiations between the town and upstream villages led to the creation of a formal rural organisation for forest management (Village Forest Development Society – VFDS). The RWA was set up between the VFDS and the MC, which was required to pay an annual fee to the VFDS for protecting the forest in order to maintain the spring water supply. The MC had the right to monitor this activity and end the RWA if the forest was not properly protected in accordance with the agreed plan.

Despite initial signs of success, the changes in governance have negatively impacted the rural communities' ability to manage access to and use of the forest over the long term. After the facilitators of the RWA stepped back from direct involvement the RWA continued to work well from the perspective of the MC, maintaining the quantity and quality of water supply to the town from the spring. The rural communities upstream, however, faced internal conflicts over differing perceptions of the RWA, competing agendas of different households and villages, increasing pressure from outside commercial actors with their own agenda for hydropower and infrastructure development, and the VFDS became increasingly dysfunctional. In addition, the RWA payments didn't contribute significantly to the livelihoods of the majority of villagers, and the contribution of forest ecosystem services to poverty alleviation was no different than before the formalisation of forest protection measures.

institutions, often created to service the increasing demands of urban consumers. For example, shared ecosystems such as water catchments may provide direct ecosystem services to rural communities whose activities also have impacts on the indirect flow of ecosystem services to the town (see Box 7.2). Here, the juxtaposition of urban and rural institutions and activities is seen in the extension of municipal governance arrangements into ecological hinterlands, in attempts to manage the trade-offs and synergies between rural livelihoods and urban demand for ecosystem services, such as water security.

Institutional challenges for managing peri-urban ecosystems

Institutionally and legally, the peri-urban interface is often governed by complex administrative arrangements and may fall outside the purview of both rural and urban governments (Marshall et al., 2009). Often emergent formal urban-style governance structures co-exist alongside partially dismantled yet persistent formal and informal rural arrangements, coupled with institutional ambiguity concerning which agencies are responsible for regulation of pollution, provision of public services and infrastructure and the management of agricultural support programmes. Bureaucratic oversight of the peri-urban area can be non-existent for activities that do not fall into strictly urban or rural activities and jurisdictions. Simultaneously, however, it can result in legal pluralism as both urban and rural laws and institutions are applied *ad hoc* (Dupont, 2007; Narain and Nischal, 2007). These complex and overlapping jurisdictional arrangements can lead to 'organised irresponsibility', where environmental regulations are lax and can be readily flouted. This is compounded by the fact that traditional environmental management structures tend to decline in the transition from 'rural' to 'urban' status. New formal urban institutions are slow to evolve, often siloed, and involve a shift in decision making to distant authorities. This often leaves an institutional vacuum and neglect of ecosystem service-based livelihoods. At the same time, the growth of new informal, market-based arrangements lacks the structures for ecosystem management (Moench and Gyawali, 2008), and has little or no incentive to consider ecosystem services for the poor.

Another set of challenges emerges from the fact that, in comparison with many traditional rural settings, peri-urban ecosystems are disconnected from people who receive ecosystem service benefits. When there is also less interdependence between community members who are accessing and utilising them, many of the established mechanisms for community-based management are ineffective (Moench and Gyawali, 2008). As new diversified livelihood and market opportunities open, it is no longer a requirement to contribute to ecosystem management to benefit from these. The traditional direct links to ecosystems will remain for some, but additional demands on ecosystems emerge from local and non-local users to meet formal and informal market demands.

Peri-urban ecosystem services and poverty linkages

Peri-urban ecosystems and the services they provide support peri-urban livelihoods, and can contribute to urban food and water security, air and water purification, flood control, urban heat island reduction and cultural and religious practices (Dubbeling, 2013; Marshall et al., 2009, 2017; Moench and Gyawali, 2008). The multiple and changing pressures on peri-urban ecosystems are reflected in shifting relationships between ecosystem services and poverty, with new issues emerging which are neither urban nor rural. In urbanising contexts, the pressures on ecosystems will change along with the nature of the ecosystem services. While direct access to provisioning ecosystem services (arguably a core focus in rural contexts) remains important, the pressures on peri-urban ecosystems that affect regulating services (such as water purification or flood control) are of growing concern, because of increasing and widespread implications for human health (through, for example, poor air and water quality and food safety).

Urban development and redevelopment bring new pressures on ecosystems, and peri-urban communities themselves are also transformed through migration, land-use change and changing employment opportunities. A complex set of new opportunities and exclusions emerge which drive changes in ecosystem services-based livelihoods and have implications for the degradation and maintenance of peri-urban ecosystems. As highlighted by Adger and Fortnam (this volume), migration and urban expansion is a critical area for ecosystem services research.

The case study of Karhera (Box 7.1) illustrates some of the complex flows of benefits, risks and feedbacks which link ecosystem services and multiple aspects of human wellbeing in a rapidly urbanising peri-urban context. For those peri-urban residents who depend directly on ecosystem services for their livelihoods, the relationships with poverty alleviation can also be quite distinct from rural contexts. Peri-urban ecosystems may not only act as a safety net for the poorest, but also provide potential pathways out of poverty. An increasing proportion of households operate with livelihood strategies that depend on a mixed economy between the urban and rural, and often formal and informal sectors (Moench and Gyawali, 2008). Within the livelihood mix of a peri-urban community (or even a single household), agriculture and temporary urban employment may both be important. But as the Karhera example demonstrates, direct dependence on peri-urban ecosystem services can provide pathways out of poverty for some. In rapidly urbanising peri-urban contexts, the potential contribution of agriculture to peri-urban livelihoods often increases significantly as farmers adjust and intensify agricultural practices, responding to growing urban markets for fresh perishable produce. This increases the potential contribution of agriculture to peri-urban livelihoods and opens a pathway out of material poverty for many who would otherwise find themselves trapped in low-wage factory work under poor conditions. There are many potential direct interventions that could help to maintain peri-urban ecosystem services, such as promotion of decentralised technologies; revival of communal water resources; and increased rainwater harvesting and support for safe and appropriate waste water re-use (Amerasinghe et al., 2013; Nanninga et al., 2012). However, rapid depletion and degradation of peri-urban ecosystems by mainstream development interventions, ambiguous governance arrangements and the limited power and agency of local communities to manage their local ecosystems, has resulted in trade-offs between reducing material poverty and other aspects of wellbeing, with longer-term adverse implications for middle-class and wealthy urban residents too.

The Karhera case exemplifies the rather chaotic evolution and neglect of ecosystem service and poverty interactions in many rapidly urbanising contexts. By way of contrast, our second example (Box 7.2) illustrates that unintended consequences can result from deliberate interventions made by municipal authorities who recognise the dependence on distant ecosystems to meet increasing urban demand for resources. Here a municipal corporation has recognised the need for enhanced ecosystem management to secure urban water supplies, and has attempted to bring together environmental concerns and livelihoods of forest communities. In this case, formalising a reciprocal arrangement to manage this rural–urban linkage did not simplify the complex local negotiations. Nor did it protect rural communities from outside pressures. Instead it gave rise to 'multifaceted difficulties for the upstream hamlets, which has impeded the functionality of their forest management committee' (Kovacs et al., 2016: 1). This highlights the importance of understanding local politics and their histories, and in particular recognising and being adaptive to changes in local governance arrangements that result from interactions with urban institutions.

Enhancing pro-poor peri-urban ecosystem management and building synergies across the rural–urban continuum

Our case studies demonstrate the need to better understand the processes through which policy and institutional challenges, and political dynamics across scales, interact to influence environmental management in transitional places, and create barriers and opportunities for creating synergies with poverty alleviation goals. They also illustrate the need to work with local and state governments to explore possibilities for integrated urban planning that extend beyond city limits. This type of re-visioning of city regions to incorporate environment, health and development perspectives also raises more fundamental issues about consumption patterns, carrying capacity of cities and the extent to which urban development should impose on rural ecosystems.

To be effective, environmental management and resource-sharing initiatives across the rural–urban continuum must include sustained engagement with communities, with local contexts and with local social, cultural, economic and political drivers and dynamics. Complex interactions between environment, poverty and health will rapidly evolve in these uncharted development trajectories, and interventions based on singular prescriptive solutions are rarely effective (Marshall et al., 2015; Randhawa and Marshall, 2014).

In settings with such complex social structure and conflicts of interest, differential impacts across social segments are bound to occur, most often to the disadvantage of the more marginalised and powerless. Increasingly heterogeneous peri-urban communities and a lack of social cohesion can add to the challenges of addressing these exclusionary processes, through difficulties in mobilising people in response to environmental and poverty issues (Waldman et al., 2017). In addition, where local citizen activism is present, initiatives with a focus on environmental, health and livelihood issues of the poor tend to be isolated from each other. Recent research (Priya et al., 2017) has explored possibilities for building alliances to enhance the agency of the peri-urban poor, and revealed the emergence of a distinctive peri-urban civil society activism in Delhi. This is distinct from the 'environmentalism of the poor' practiced by rural and forest dwelling groups; from the dominant elite urban 'green development' practices and discourses of 'bourgeois environmentalism'; as well as from the urban politics of the poor' (Priya et al., 2017). It thus reflects the possibility of creating bridges across sectional interests – rural and urban, red and green ideological streams – and across classes.

A framework for analysing ecosystem service and poverty alleviation interactions in urbanising contexts

Critical to developing policy and planning, which can realise synergies between peri-urban ecosystem management and other urban development goals, will be a re-conceptualisation 'of cities and their hinterlands as interconnected ecosystem service landscapes' (Kremer et al., 2016). As discussed above, urban contexts have some distinctive features which must be central to this re-conceptualisation.

Our framework places poor and marginalised communities, whose livelihoods are directly dependent on ecosystem services, at the centre of our analysis. This approach provides a means of analysing social differentiation in the contribution of ecosystem services to wellbeing within communities and across scales (see Fisher et al., 2014). However, we propose three additional lines of enquiry.

First, an explicit focus on how the transition of governance systems and institutional structures mediate ecosystem services interactions for the poor. This includes attention to the impact of the wider *political economy* and of *peri-urban transformations* (including changing governance arrangements, increasingly heterogeneous populations, the juxtaposition of informal and formal institutions) on how ecosystem services are both accessed and utilised by diverse urban and peri-urban stakeholders.

Second, a focus on how ecosystem services can impact the health and wellbeing of diverse urban and peri-urban communities in both positive and negative ways. For example, our Karhera case study clearly illustrates how in polluted peri-urban ecosystems there may be benefits to material aspects of wellbeing through food provisioning, but adverse impacts on health (Waldman et al., 2017).

Last, we draw on insights from Dorward's (2014) analysis, which highlights the dynamic nature of ecosystems services, linked to changing livelihoods within broader

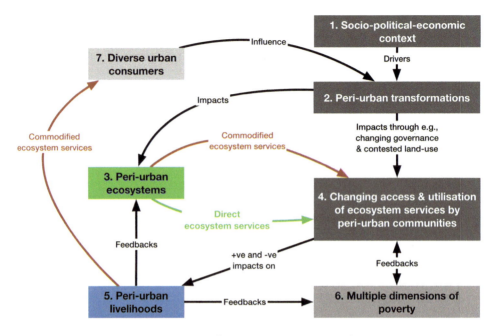

FIGURE 7.1 Ecosystem services–poverty alleviation interactions in urbanising contexts.

structures which themselves are also changing – and illustrated in our case studies by changing threats and opportunities and livelihoods in flux, with multiple feedback implications for peri-urban ecosystems.

Figure 7.1 draws on the empirical work and related literatures discussed above, to highlight key features of ecosystem services and poverty alleviation interactions in urban development and redevelopment. It represents the changing access to and utilisation of ecosystem services by poor and marginalised peri-urban communities (4) and the multiple ways that this impacts on livelihoods (5), and relates to the health and wellbeing of peri-urban and urban residents and to environmental integrity across temporal and spatial scales. The green arrows indicate direct flows of ecosystem services where communities are 'dwelling in' or in close contact with the ecosystems providing the services. The red arrow indicates the indirect flow of services which are provided as commodities and/or transported to consumers (7) distanced from the ecosystem (e.g. food and water) or experienced through travel as destinations rather than a dwelling place (e.g. cultural). This distinction is adapted to the peri-urban context from Cumming et al.'s (2014) notion of red-loop/green-loop dynamics in agricultural transitions and urbanisation.

The diagram highlights the impact of peri-urban transformations (2) – driven by the broader socio-political-economic context of urban development (1) – on how peri-urban communities access and utilise ecosystem services (4). These impacts include, for example, changing governance arrangements and contested land use in peri-urban areas which influence the access of peri-urban communities to ecosystem services and the ways in which these can support livelihood strategies (5). In many cases peri-urban transformations (2) also directly impact peri-urban ecosystems (3), as infrastructure developments and urban pollution degrade ecosystems and urban greening projects transform forest, scrub, wetland and agro-ecosystems for cultural uses. All these impacts have implications for multiple dimensions of poverty (6) through the contribution of ecosystem services to changing patterns of peri-urban livelihoods (5), which in turn produce feedbacks to peri-urban ecosystems (3) as, for example, agricultural practices change or households become more or less dependent upon gathering firewood from forests. Outcomes for diverse urban consumers (7), particularly the urban poor who are often unable to substitute local provisioning services for more expensive imported commodities, are also linked to the impacts of transformations on peri-urban ecosystems and livelihoods through their role in providing commodified ecosystem services such as food, water and cultural services.

Conclusions

Processes of urbanisation are implicated in worsening environmental degradation and poverty, while at the same time cities often drive growth and innovation. Essential connections between people and the environment are often obscured in the drive for economic growth, infrastructural development and mainstream initiatives for clean and green urban centres. As in rural contexts, urban and peri-urban ecosystem services have critical roles to play in underpinning sustainable development, and will be key to building 'resilient' towns and cities. However, the commodification of ecosystem services as they move across the rural–urban continuum detracts the attention of urban residents from the multiple roles of peri-urban ecosystem services, including disaster risk management; reduction of heat island effects; air and water purification; and food and water security. As a result, the degradation of urban and peri-urban ecosystems and intense competition for land use has multiple negative impacts across temporal and spatial scales and social groups.

Neoliberal reordering of urbanising places, rising land prices, complex local governance arrangements, jurisdictional ambiguity and poor environmental regulation are among the many challenges for improved environmental management. Traditional environmental management structures, in the transition from 'rural' to 'urban' status, often leave an institutional vacuum and neglect for ecosystem services-based livelihoods, and the growth of informal market-based arrangements lacks structures for ecosystem services management.

Increasingly heterogeneous communities, which can lack social cohesion, and a disconnection between peri-urban ecosystems and their multiple beneficiaries, present difficulties for establishing effective management/adaptive co-management approaches. In addition, local citizen activism on environmental, food security and health issues of the poor tend to be isolated from each other, although emergent forms of peri-urban activism may be important for creating new alliances across interest groups, sectors and scales.

Dynamic urbanising contexts highlight the need to shift from singular technocratic approaches to service provision and 'clean up and control' approaches for urban environmental management, promoting instead flexible, creative approaches, engaging with communities on the ground and seeking ways of incorporating subaltern experiential knowledge into adaptive management processes. Both our case studies highlight the need to recognise and address the distinctive institutional challenges of environmental management in peri-urban contexts, understanding local politics and context-specific governance mechanisms that are appropriate for facilitating negotiations between ecosystem services and poverty alleviation trade-offs among multiple groups across the rural–urban continuum.

Ecosystem service and poverty interactions present distinctive challenges and opportunities in peri-urban contexts. For example, contrary to claims that ecosystem services function mainly as a safety net to prevent increasing poverty, we find that in some peri-urban settings they offer potential pathways out of poverty. Peri-urban agri-ecosystem services can support significant increases in income as a main or supplementary source of peri-urban livelihoods, but there are trade-offs in terms of adverse effects on health. Tackling environment, poverty and health issues together, through unpacking their links to peri-urban ecosystem services, offers the opportunity to both reduce peri-urban poverty and enhance the health and wellbeing of peri-urban and urban residents by, for example, supporting innovative ways to overcome these trade-offs.

Research to date suggests that there are some immediate opportunities to reduce trade-offs while maintaining or even improving peri-urban ecosystems, and building synergies across the rural-urban continuum (Bhatt et al., 2016; Marshall et al., 2017). For example, in the case of peri-urban farming – to consider the preservation of land most suitable for agriculture for production of crops for local markets that will be affordable for the urban poor; to recognise the adverse impacts of polluting and extracting industries on agriculture; to support the development of decentralised technologies to improve the efficiency of water resource use, its quality and access by the poor; and linking urban waste recycling to food production.

Major progress beyond this is likely to require greater formal recognition of the value of peri-urban ecosystem services, looking beyond cultural services and cosmetic improvements. Here more work is required to reframe debates, demonstrating the implications of poor ecosystem management and the potential benefits of alternative strategies across all social groups. Current local, national and international interest in 'sustainable' urbanisation, 'city regions' and urban resilience (Ernstson et al., 2010; Jennings et al., 2015; Meerow et al., 2016; Seeliger and Turok, 2013) provides opportunities to integrate such insights into current initiatives and create dialogue to reframe wider debates. A key advantage of working in transitional peri-urban contexts is that they enable rapid learning, evaluation and potential scaling-up of successful initiatives.

Acknowledgement

The authors gratefully acknowledge helpful inputs from Jorn Scharlemann.

References

(ESPA outputs marked with '★')

Amerasinghe P, Bhardwaj RM, Scott C, et al. (2013) Urban wastewater and agricultural reuse challenges in India. IWMI.

Andersson E, Barthel S, Borgström S, et al. (2014) Reconnecting cities to the biosphere: stewardship of green infrastructure and urban ecosystem services. *Ambio* 43: 445–453.

Baró F, Gómez-Baggethun E and Haase D. (2017) Ecosystem service bundles along the urban-rural gradient: insights for landscape planning and management. *Ecosystem Services* 24: 147–159.

Bhatt S, Singh A and Mani N. (2016) Peri-Urban Agriculture and Ecosystems: Resilient Narratives. Gorakhpur, India: Gorakhpur Environmental Action Group (GEAG).

★Bisht R, Bhonagiri A, Waldman L, et al. (2016) *Karhera: A Photo Book*. Brighton, UK: STEPS Centre. Available at: http://bit.ly/KarheraPB

Bolund P and Hunhammar S. (1999) Ecosystem services in urban areas. *Ecological Economics* 29: 293–301.

Botkin DB and Beveridge CE. (1997) Cities as environments. *Urban Ecosystems* 1: 3–19.

Cumming GS, Buerkert A, Hoffmann EM, et al. (2014) Implications of agricultural transitions and urbanization for ecosystem services. *Nature* 515: 50–57.

Davies L, Kwiatkowski L, Gaston KJ, et al. (2011) UK National Ecosystem Assessment: Technical Report. Cambridge, UK: UNEP-WCMC.

Deutsch L, Dyball R and Steffen W. (2013) Feeding cities: food security and ecosystem support in an urbanizing world. In: Elmqvist T, Fragkias M, Goodness J, et al. (eds) *Urbanization, Biodiversity and Ecosystem Services: Challenges and Opportunities*. Dordrecht, The Netherlands, Heidelberg, Germany, New York, London: Springer Netherlands, 505–537.

★Dorward AR. (2014) Livelisystems: a conceptual framework integrating social, ecosystem, development, and evolutionary theory. *Ecology and Society* 19.

Dubbeling M. (2013) Scoping paper feeding into the development of UNEP's position on urban and peri-urban agriculture. Leusden: RUAF Foundation.

Dupont V. (2007) Conflicting stakes and governance in the peripheries of large Indian metropolises – An introduction. *Cities* 24: 89–94.

Elmqvist T, Fragkias M, Goodness J, et al., eds. (2013) *Urbanization, Biodiversity and Ecosystem Services: Challenges and Opportunities*. Dordrecht, The Netherlands: Springer Netherlands.

Ernstson H, van der Leeuw SE, Redman CL, et al. (2010) Urban transitions: on urban resilience and human-dominated ecosystems. *Ambio* 39: 531–545.

★Fisher JA, Patenaude G, Giri K, et al. (2014) Understanding the relationships between ecosystem services and poverty alleviation: a conceptual framework. *Ecosystem Services* 7: 34–45.

Folke C, Jansson Å, Larsson J, et al. (1997) Ecosystem appropriation by cities. *Ambio* 26: 167–172.

Gaston KJ, Ávila-Jiménez ML and Edmondson JL. (2013) REVIEW: managing urban ecosystems for goods and services. *Journal of Applied Ecology* 50: 830–840.

Gómez-Baggethun E and Barton DN. (2013) Classifying and valuing ecosystem services for urban planning. *Ecological Economics* 86: 235–245.

Gómez-Baggethun E, Gren Å, Barton DN, et al. (2013) Urban ecosystem services. In: Elmqvist T, Fragkias M, Goodness J, et al. (eds) *Urbanization, Biodiversity and Ecosystem Services: Challenges and Opportunities*. Dordrecht, The Netherlands, Heidelberg, Germany, New York, London: Springer Netherlands, 175–251.

Haase D, Frantzeskaki N and Elmqvist T. (2014a) Ecosystem services in urban landscapes: Practical applications and governance implications. *Ambio* 43: 407–412.

Haase D, Larondelle N, Andersson E, et al. (2014b) A quantitative review of urban ecosystem service assessments: concepts, models, and implementation. *Ambio* 43: 413–433.

Jennings S, Cottee J, Curtis T, et al. (2015) Food in an Urbanised World: The Role of City Region Food Systems in Resilience and Sustainable Development. *Report on Food in an Urbanized World Conference, 4th February 2015*. International Sustainability Unit.

*Kovacs EK, Kumar C, Agarwal C, et al. (2016) The politics of negotiation and implementation: a reciprocal water access agreement in the Himalayan foothills, India. *Ecology and Society* 21: 37.

Kremer P, Hamstead Z, Haase D, et al. (2016) Key insights for the future of urban ecosystem services research. *Ecology and Society* 21.

Lin BB, Philpott SM and Jha S. (2015) The future of urban agriculture and biodiversity-ecosystem services: challenges and next steps. *Basic and Applied Ecology* 16: 189–201.

MA. (2005) *Millennium Ecosystem Assessment, 2005. Ecosystems and Human Well-Being: Synthesis*. Washington, DC: Island Press.

*Marshall F. (2016) Recognising sustainability frontiers in the peri-urban interface. *South Asian Water Studies* 6: 98–102.

Marshall F, Agarwal R, Lintelo Dt, et al. (2003) Heavy metal contamination of vegetables in Delhi. London: UK Department for International Development.

Marshall F, Bell JNB, Stonehouse J, et al. (1999) The Impacts and Policy Implication of Air Pollution on Agriculture in urban and peri-urban areas of developing countries: a case study from India. London: UK Department for International Development.

*Marshall F, Dolley J, Randhawa P, et al. (2017) Why peri-urban ecosystem services matter for urban policy (policy briefing). Brighton, UK: STEPS Centre.

Marshall F, Agarwal R, Ghose C, et al. (2005) Contaminated irrigation water and food safety for the urban and peri-urban poor: appropriate measures for monitoring and control from field research in India. *Briefing Paper*. London: UK Department for International Development.

Marshall F, Pandey P, Randhawa P, et al. (2015) Rethinking urban waste management in India. *STEPS Centre Policy Brief*. Brighton, UK: STEPS Centre.

*Marshall F and Randhawa P. (2017) India's peri-urban frontier: rural-urban transformations and food security. London: IIED.

Marshall F, Waldman L, MacGregor H, et al. (2009) On the edge of sustainability: perspectives on peri-urban dynamics. *STEPS Working Paper*. Brighton, UK: STEPS Centre.

Meerow S, Newell JP and Stults M. (2016) Defining urban resilience: a review. *Landscape and Urban Planning* 147: 38–49.

*Moench M and Gyawali D. (2008) Desakota: reinterpreting the urban-rural continuum. *Final Report Desakota II A*. Swindon, UK: Natural Environment Research Council.

Nanninga TA, Bisschops I, López E, et al. (2012) Discussion on sustainable water technologies for peri-urban areas of Mexico City: balancing urbanization and environmental conservation. *Water* 4: 739–758.

Narain V and Nischal S. (2007) The peri-urban interface in Shahpur Khurd and Karnera, India. *Environment and Urbanization* 19: 261–273.

*Priya R, Bisht R, Randhawa P, et al. (2017) Local environmentalism in peri-urban spaces in India: emergent ecological democracy? *STEPS Working Paper*. Brighton, UK: STEPS Centre.

Randhawa P and Marshall F. (2014) Policy transformations and translations: lessons for sustainable water management in peri-urban Delhi, India. *Environment and Planning C: Government and Policy* 32: 93–107.

Rees W and Wackernagel M. (1996) Urban ecological footprints: why cities cannot be sustainable – and why they are a key to sustainability. *Environmental Impact Assessment Review* 16: 223–248.

Seeliger L and Turok I. (2013) Towards sustainable cities: extending resilience with insights from vulnerability and transition theory. *Sustainability* 5: 2108–2128.

Seitzinger SP, Svedin U, Crumley CL, et al. (2012) Planetary stewardship in an urbanizing world: beyond city limits. *Ambio* 41: 787–794.

Seto KC, Parnell S and Elmqvist T. (2013) A global outlook on urbanization. In: Elmqvist T, Fragkias M, Goodness J, et al. (eds) *Urbanization, Biodiversity and Ecosystem Services: Challenges and Opportunities*. Dordrecht, The Netherlands, Heidelberg, Germany, New York, London: Springer Netherlands, 1–12.

Singh A, Sharma RK, Agrawal M, et al. (2010) Health risk assessment of heavy metals via dietary intake of foodstuffs from the wastewater irrigated site of a dry tropical area of India. *Food and Chemical Toxicology* 48: 611–619.

*STEPS Centre. (2016) *What Does the Future Hold for Delhi's Urban Farmers?* Available at: https://steps-centre.org/blog/what-does-the-future-hold-for-delhis-urban-farmers/

STEPS Centre and Sarai. (2010) Contesting sustainabilities in the peri-urban interface. *STEPS Research Report*. Brighton, UK: STEPS Centre.

*Suich H, Howe C and Mace G. (2015) Ecosystem services and poverty alleviation: a review of the empirical links. *Ecosystem Services* 12: 137–147.

te Lintelo D, Marshall F and Bhupal DS. (2002) Urban food: the role of urban and peri-urban agriculture in India: a case study from Delhi. *Food Nutrition and Agriculture (FAO)* 29: 4–13.

UN. (2014) *World Urbanization Prospects: The 2014 Revision*. United Nations, Department of Economic and Social Affairs, Population Division.

*Waldman L, Bisht R, Saharia R, et al. (2017) Peri-urbanism in globalizing India: a study of pollution, health and community awareness. *International Journal of Environmental Research and Public Health* 14: 980.

8
RECIPROCAL COMMITMENTS FOR ADDRESSING FOREST–WATER RELATIONSHIPS

Lana Whittaker, Eszter K Kovacs and Bhaskar Vira

Introduction

Forests provide a multitude of ecosystem services. These services include the provision of a range of products which provide direct use values; climate regulation, carbon sequestration and supporting services such as nutrient cycling; as well as a range of cultural services, including recreational spaces. Increasingly, the importance of forests in relation to the regulation and maintenance of hydrological flows has been recognised. For example, the 2002 Shiga Declaration on Forests and Water recognised the importance of forest–water interactions and the need for further research to develop both bio-physical and socio-economic understandings of these interactions. Numerous meetings on forests and water have been held since, and in 2015 the Food and Agricultural Organization (FAO) launched a five-year Forests and Water Action Plan, which aims to increase knowledge and support for policies for forest–water interactions and management. The Collaborative Partnership on Forests, under the Global Forest Expert Panel initiative, is currently coordinating a global scientific assessment on forests and water, which is expected to report in 2018.

In this context of growing awareness and research into forest–water relationships, this chapter reviews the links between forests, water and people, with a focus on how these interactions impact poverty alleviation and human wellbeing (see Coulthard et al., this volume, for a discussion of these terms). Partly driven by the impacts of population growth and pressures on land, and influenced by changing precipitation regimes and climate patterns, forest–water systems are increasingly becoming stress points, where multiple competing uses have to be reconciled and managed through a more hydrologically sensitive approach to forest planning and management. We first examine how land-use change within forest- and tree-based landscapes influences water availability, and explore associated impacts on ecosystem services and human wellbeing. Second, we highlight the trade-offs in forest–water social-ecological systems that arise from processes and patterns of human land and water use. Making visible these trade-offs generates a broad awareness of interlinkages and potential impacts, so that unintended consequences of actions in relation to forest, land and water use can be anticipated, and avoided where possible. Third, we consider management and governance options that seek to address and manage trade-offs through recognising interdependence and reciprocity in both ecological and social systems. We review interventions, which include mutual obligations and social relations, market-mediated interventions (such as payments for ecosystem/watershed services) and broader reciprocal (watershed) agreements. Finally, we reflect on prospects for the future management of tree–water interactions with particular attention to human wellbeing.

Throughout the chapter, we draw on available knowledge and evidence from the ESPA programme. While our understandings of forest–water interactions have improved greatly due to an intensification of research efforts, decision making for planning, urbanisation and development still frequently takes place in the absence of hard evidence and long-term monitoring of social and environmental change. This creates a fundamental tension between 'science' and 'policy' (or lack thereof). A growing understanding of complex social-ecological systems suggests that the 'science' behind forest–water relationships will remain highly context-dependent, making generalisation difficult and precluding simple policy prescriptions. Despite these caveats, the interaction of forests and land use with the hydrological cycle, and the essentiality of water for forests and all life, makes this issue a critical element of the integrated approach to environment, wellbeing and human prosperity that underpins the Sustainable Development Goals agenda.

Forest–water relationship

The relationship between forests and water is reciprocal: forests depend on sufficient water to survive, but forests also play a significant role in regulating the hydrological cycle. The exact nature and extent of this role has, over the years, generated much discussion (see for example, Bruijnzeel, 2004; Hamilton, 1987; Hamilton and King, 1983), but relationships between forests and water are now recognised to be complex and context-dependent. The quality of forests, forest stand type and composition, geohydrology and meteorological conditions are all relevant factors that affect long-term ecological state and water availability across watersheds, catchments and larger landscapes.

Forests affect water quality, quantity (yield) and the timing of flows, including seasonality (Brauman et al., 2007; Brogna et al., 2017), providing influences on the hydrological system which ultimately impact people, understood as (differentiated) water users and their diverse needs. The role of forests in ensuring water quality is the least disputed of these three relationships (Postel and Thompson, 2005). The characteristics of forest soils, and the fact that leaf litter dissipates raindrop energy, leads to high water infiltration rates and little surface run-off, minimising surface erosion and reducing the quantity of sediment in water (Ellison et al., 2017; Neary et al., 2009). Combined with the capacity of forests to trap and filter pollutants, this results in forests producing high-quality water, reducing the need for treatment before the water is consumed by downstream users (Creed et al., 2016).

The relationships between forests and water yield and flows are more disputed. Compared to other vegetation types, forests intercept precipitation and consume high quantities of water due to evapotranspiration. Consequently, decreased forest cover is commonly associated with increased water yield and *vice versa* (Farley et al., 2005; Filoso et al., 2017). The view that there is a trade-off between tree densities and water availability has emerged (Ilstedt et al., 2016). The relationship between tree cover and water yield is, however, mediated by multiple factors including tree age (younger forests use more water), tree species (deciduous trees may have less of a negative effect on water yield than pine trees, for example) and tree-density (Ellison et al., 2017; Filoso et al., 2017; Ilstedt et al., 2016; Wattenbach et al., 2007).

Most importantly, and often overlooked in analyses of the forest–water relationship, it is essential to understand the 'alternative state' against which forested landscapes are being considered. If forests, or semi-natural vegetation, are potentially threatened with conversion to, for instance, suburban housing (see Box 8.1), the question of water yield and flows in these catchments needs to be considered in relation to these two alternative states, not some idealised land-use system that is 'best' for water. Similarly, if a degraded landscape is being brought under tree cover via an afforestation programme, what matters is the net impact of more trees in this landscape relative to the earlier state, and in relation to plausible alternative land uses.

In locations with seasonal rainfall, the seasonal distribution of water flows is of greater importance to livelihoods than annual water yield (Bruijnzeel, 2004; Ellison et al., 2017). By promoting infiltration, forests increase the moisture content of soil, recharge groundwater and help the gradual release of water (Brogna et al., 2017), thereby moderating peak and base flows (Neary et al., 2009). The removal of forest cover can lead to soil degradation and reduced infiltration, which can reduce groundwater and dry season flows (Ellison et al., 2017). If the soil is not degraded and rainfall can infiltrate, then the reduction in the water lost to evapotranspiration due to forest removal may increase dry season flows (Bruijnzeel, 2004; Ellison et al., 2017). Again, this relationship is mediated by multiple factors, including tree species and soil characteristics (see Ghimire et al., 2013).

Forests also moderate peak flows (Neary et al., 2009), and thus an additional regulating service provided by forests is hazard mitigation (Brauman et al., 2007). Forest loss results in reduced infiltration and increased run-off, which promotes floods (Ellison et al., 2017). The role of forests in reducing floods is, however, limited in high-intensity rainfall events, when soil saturation leads to surface run-off, especially in shallow soils on steep slopes (FAO, 2008). Mangrove forests play a different protective role, acting as a buffer against cyclones and storm surges (Sakib et al., 2015).

These relationships between forests and water typically take place at the scale of a catchment or watershed, where the upstream and downstream flows are dominant. However, recent work has highlighted that forests also affect water in upwind and downwind locations (Keys et al., 2012). Evapotranspiration recharges atmospheric moisture, contributing to rainfall both locally and in distant locations (Ellison et al., 2017). Ellison et al. (2012) consequently argued that, globally, the presence of forests leads to increased water yields. Significant reductions in tree cover reduce evapotranspiration, affecting rainfall downwind (Ellison et al., 2017). The extent and scale of these upwind and downwind relationships, and how they complement or negate upstream and downstream flows within watersheds, remain the subject of considerable discussion, and need careful investigation in specific empirical contexts.

Key drivers affecting the forest–water relationship

The relationships between forests and water described above are increasingly affected by multiple drivers (Figure 8.1). *Climate change* will affect the extent and intensity of rainfall (Ellison et al., 2017). Increased temperatures have already affected the quantity and duration of snowpacks (Jones et al., 2010) and led to water scarcity and consequent conflict (Bhusal and Subedi, 2014; Buytaert et al., 2014). Increased temperatures will also affect evapotranspiration rates.

Demographic change affects both the total demand for forests, land and water and its geographical distribution. For example, Buytaert and Bievre (2012) modelled future water use in the tropical Andes and found population growth to be the determining factor in future water scarcity; while Rideout et al. (2013) found that population density and proximity to roads, as well as soil type, were significant predictors of mangrove loss in Kenya. *Economic and trade drivers* influence the choice of land-use. Notably, Geist and Lambin (2002) found that in 152 cases of tropical deforestation, 96% could be explained through agricultural expansion as a proximate cause; and economic factors, including urbanisation and the growth of timber markets, were the underlying cause in 81% of cases.

Urbanisation can lead to the destruction of forests, the degradation of soils and the creation of impervious surfaces which reduce infiltration rates (Neary et al., 2009), and can also decrease water quality (Foley et al., 2005). At the same time, urbanisation creates larger constituencies of downstream resource users with dependence on upstream actors, increasing the need for upstream landscapes to be managed in a way that maintains water quality and quantity (see 'Reciprocal commitments' below, and also Marshall et al., this volume).

Trade-offs in the forest–water relationship

Development and urbanisation processes give rise to a number of impacts and consequences whereby trade-offs between alternative land-use options and land users at a number of scales become inevitable, affecting lives and livelihoods. In

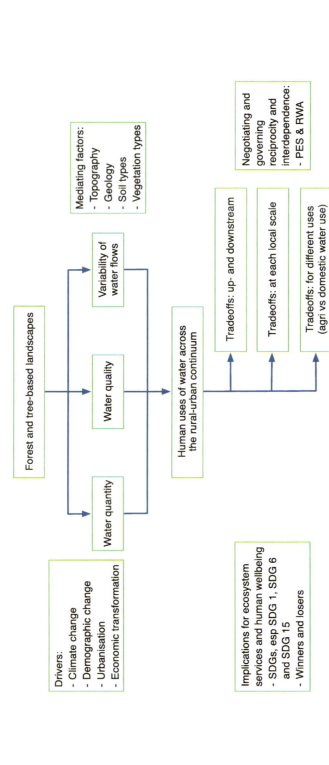

FIGURE 8.1 Summary figure showing forest–water relationships.

particular, trade-offs occur between the economic gains of non-forest land use and the maintenance of healthy watersheds and the wellbeing of the inhabitants (Leimona et al., 2015). Although deforestation for agriculture and logging has economic benefits, the increased use of these provisioning services comes at the expense of forest cover, which can impact hydrological regulating services and water supply.

Trade-offs may also occur between the pursuit of material wellbeing and ecosystem services. Findings from the ESPA deltas project demonstrate these trade-offs in coastal Bangladesh, where dams in upstream areas and polderisation produced an environment favourable to shrimp farming, which decreased mangrove forest cover and then led to decreased accessibility of forest products due to regulations (Hossain et al., 2016). Conversion to shrimp farming further increased soil and water salinity, reducing mangrove diversity and making shrimp farming more favourable. Conversion to shrimp farming does not, however, necessarily reduce poverty, as in many cases employment opportunities are reduced as profits are reaped by the few (elite capture) and people are negatively affected by increased salinisation (Nicholls et al., 2016). Thus, trade-offs in land and water use, hydrological services and wellbeing occur across space and time.

Trade-offs between different uses of water within a watershed occur as the use of, or removal of, water for one purpose may affect the quantity and quality of water available for other uses and users. Such trade-offs have been documented across the Himalayas (see Box 8.1).

Trade-offs also occur between hydrologically connected up- and downstream users of forests and water. Changes to forests in upstream areas may benefit the upstream inhabitants, but can negatively affect the quantity and quality of water received by downstream users, fuelling conflict. In the Santa Cruz valleys in Bolivia, cloud forests being cleared for agriculture and cattle grazing has led to increased sedimentation and contaminated water supplies (Asquith, 2011, 2013). The 1.5 million urban residents of Santa Cruz rely on this water supply, as do soy producers in the lowlands (Asquith, 2011). Urbanisation in downstream locations brings these trade-offs to light. For example, greater seasonal water scarcity has given rise to an elevated number of conflicts between upstream (usually villagers) and downstream (usually town) settlements and water users, with a number of water-sharing and development interventions necessary for the mediation of these overlapping needs and rights claims (see Box 8.1). As inhabitants in upstream locations are typically poorer than downstream water users (Pagiola et al., 2005), it is always necessary to consider the power dynamics in how these trade-offs play out and are negotiated (Howe et al., 2014).

Trade-offs can also occur within communities of both up- and downstream users. The use of ecosystem services within communities is neither homogenous nor equitable. The poor tend to have a more immediate interface and dependency on natural resources and ecosystem services (Fisher et al., 2013), for example through fuelwood extraction from forests or direct water consumption from springs. Indeed, ESPA studies have shown that the use of ecosystem services may be determined

BOX 8.1 POLITICAL ECONOMY OF WATER SECURITY, ECOSYSTEM SERVICES AND LIVELIHOODS IN THE WESTERN HIMALAYAS

Overview

ESPA research examined the relationship between water supply and urbanisation across six small town case studies located through the Himalayas: Palampur and Rajgarh in Himachal Pradesh, India; Mussoorie and Nainital in Uttarakhand, India; and Bidur and Dhulikhel in Nepal. At each, we examined water source routes and capacities, up- and downstream demands for water and arising land-use change, and governance trends around water resources.

Trade-offs

Between water-uses and land

Migration from rural areas to small towns results in the rapid growth and expansion of these settlements, heightening water demand and consumption. These dynamics extend beyond town boundaries as villages and communities along water routes are impacted by greater water extraction for urban areas, particularly as their own (rural) water demands have increased due to changes in the agricultural system, especially through the planting of thirstier cash crops (for example in Rajgarh, Himachal Pradesh). At Nainital, unplanned and informal urbanisation led to the construction of houses on ground that is key to the recharge of the town's central lake, which is also the town's main source of drinking water. Protecting this upstream area from further encroachment and land-use change remains critical for the long-term sustainability of Nainital's water source, but illustrates well the trade-offs between housing, poverty and water. The long-term protection of the lake has become a cause of sustained civil society advocacy and action; public interest litigation with the intent to safeguard the lake is before the state court (at the time of writing, Nov. 2017).

Between water-users

Across our case study areas, we documented increased conflict between the demands of rural and urban water users even where shared access agreements existed, such as among community drinking water associations at Bidur and Dhulikhel in Nepal. This conflict arose due to the greater extraction and demand of urban settlements, and a lack of adequate consultation and negotiation (and in some cases, compensation or the development of alternatives) with upstream settlements. Many small towns in the lower Himalayas are also popular tourist attractions during the driest and hottest months, leading to significant water shortages. The predominantly urban tourist base imposes high water consumption demands, particularly through the hotel sector, to the detriment of permanent inhabitants and rural water users.

Reciprocal water access agreements (RWAs)

Palampur in Himachal Pradesh, India, is a small town whose water supply to the central areas of the town flow from an upstream spring that emanates from a community-managed forest. Through the past decade, this forest had been severely over-logged. With the aid of external negotiators, an RWA agreement was implemented between three upstream hamlets and the Palampur Municipal Council (MC), imposing land-use and access restrictions on the forest area in exchange for a relatively small yearly payment. Prolonged engagement and research into the institutional dynamics before and after the agreement show the difficulty faced by small villages in maintaining RWAs after successful inception, which speaks to the power asymmetries that tend to exist between up- and downstream contractors as well as within communities (Kovacs et al., 2016). Interestingly, environmental conditionality in the form of long-term monitoring of either the forest or water is not deemed of great importance to the MC, such that it is not undertaken.

Distribution of benefits

In the urban settlements we have studied in India and Nepal, there is wide variation in the ability of downstream consumers to access water. In Rajgarh, for example, the costs of physical connections to the mains pipeline exclude some of the poorest households from access to water supply. In some cases, there is recognition of the variation in ability to pay; for example, the Dhulikhel Water Users' Committee in Nepal has agreed a progressive tariff structure, so that those who consume more water pay proportionately more per unit of use, while the poorest consumers (who typically consume less) pay a lower rate.

---

by a range of socio-economic factors, including household income, the gender of the household head and land tenure (Hamann et al., 2016) and cultural identity such as caste in India (Lakerveld et al., 2015). Reductions in the availability of these services, or reduced access to them, will therefore disproportionately affect these social groups. Moreover, the impacts of change are differentially experienced, with lower socio-economic classes typically bearing a greater burden. For example, the effects of mangrove loss on household vulnerability and security are not equally spread. Hajra et al. (2017) found that within the Indian Sundarban Delta community, the poor are more likely to experience material and human losses following hazards, including inundation and surges, land erosion and soil salinisation. Moreover, repeated losses make households more vulnerable to future losses.

Interventions to influence biophysical trade-offs in the water–forest relationship may similarly result in uneven impacts on up- and downstream communities, making the negotiation of socio-economic trade-offs a key issue. As Lakerveld et al. (2015: 64) write and show in their study of community forest management in India: '"ecosystem services" do not automatically flow from ecosystems to human beings, but are largely co-produced through human labour, capital and technologies'. At catchment and basin scale, the growing interdependence of users and the need for mediated solutions have resulted in greater interest in reciprocal commitments that achieve mutually beneficial collective action for the management/protection of the forest–water regime. These commitments are reviewed in the following section.

Reciprocal commitments

A growing number of 'reciprocal' approaches recognise the biophysical and socio-economic interconnectivity between settlements and ecosystems, and the interdependence of users across these landscapes. In these approaches, interventions aim to align the behaviour of different actors in order to achieve desired land-use management that mitigates, reduces or reverses the loss of watershed services, and/or conserves forest. While the efficacy of forest restoration to maintain or improve watershed services is highly variable, contextually dependent and on the whole uncertain (Filoso et al., 2017), reciprocal forest–water agreements recognise the reliance of communities on both forests and water, together and separately. This mutual interdependence has been mediated in a number of different ways, and this section will draw on a growing number of examples that have been developed and introduced in recent times.

Mediation through established social practices

Mutual obligations may exist across social-ecological landscapes due to long-established traditions of sharing and reciprocity, with an understanding of mutual interdependence. These may often rely on tacit knowledge and historic relations. These relations may, however, be threatened due to new pressures, and may need to be reinforced or reinvigorated, and in some cases, formalised. For example, in Mustang district, Nepal, water was used to irrigate cropland and local communities managed water through cooperative management practices. Increased water scarcity due to changes in snowfall and precipitation alongside changed demands for water, including from domestic use and hydropower, led to increased conflict among communities (Bhusal and Subedi, 2014; Buytaert et al., 2014). In response, communities have developed management techniques to share water. For example, for several decades the two villages of Dhakarjong and Phalyak divided the river into five portions to share between them. Due to problems that arose with this approach, the communities now share the river by days; the stream is diverted to

Phalyak for three days and Dhakarjong for two. Although this has not completely resolved tension (Bhusal and Subedi, 2014), the example illustrates the mutually negotiated reciprocal arrangements that can exist without 'outside' interference.

Interventions for watershed services

Investments in watershed services link actors within a watershed, connecting upstream service providers and downstream communities (Vogl et al., 2017). They are increasingly used to ensure water quantity and quality. In 2013 alone, globally these investments amounted to US$12.3 billion (Bennett and Carroll, 2014). Here we consider two key forms of interventions: payments for ecosystem services (PES) and reciprocal water agreements (RWAs).

Mediation through quasi-markets (PES schemes)

PES schemes to ensure the provision of hydrological services from tree-based landscapes typically take the form of downstream water users paying upstream service providers to maintain the provision of a high-quality water supply. For example, in Costa Rica's Pago por Servicios Ambientales programme, land users are paid for certain land uses, including planting trees and forest conservation, with payment coming from a national fund, reflecting the value of services to downstream users (Pagiola et al., 2005). In Mexico's Payment for Hydrological Environmental Services Program, fees from charges to water users are used to pay forest owners to conserve the forest in areas where commercial forestry is not financially viable (Muñoz-Piña et al., 2008). The payments to upstream providers must be higher than the benefits they would receive from alternative land use and lower than the value of the water supply to downstream users (Pagiola et al., 2005).

Water funds are another type of PES scheme that focus on the demand for hydrological services by (often wealthy and organised) downstream communities (Goldman-Benner et al., 2012). Although there are a variety of water funds, they share three common traits: a funding mechanism to fund watershed conservation, a governance mechanism for planning and decision making, and a management mechanism to ensure conservation occurs (Bremer et al., 2016). The first water fund was initiated in 2000 in Quito, Ecuador. In 2011, the Latin American Water Funds Partnership was established, and there are now 19 water funds across 7 countries in Latin America.

Using PES to ensure the provision of hydrological services is not, however, straightforward. It has already been established that relationships between forests and water are complex and often uncertain. Moreover, assessing the value of services is problematic due to overlapping services and service ambiguity (Ojea et al., 2012). For these reasons, PES programmes usually fail to ensure that payments are conditional on the observable delivery of environmental benefits, such as increased water supply or the maintenance of forest, and usually rely on actions or behaviours that are assumed to result in an improvement in these services. Monitoring presents another layer of difficulty, as communities are frequently unable or ill-equipped to maintain monitoring practices. It is also rare that land use can be linked directly with environmental factors to be monitored, at timescales relevant to PES agreements.

Mediation through RWAs

RWAs are explicit agreements between stakeholders in a landscape, but not always subject to the strict terms that are supposed to underpin PES regimes. Here, reciprocity is explicitly recognised and subject to some form of negotiated agreement, which might include obligations for all parties in terms of behaviour and/or rewards/punishments. Two ESPA-funded projects provide useful insights into the functioning of RWAs. In Bolivia, the NGO Fundación Natura Bolivia has facilitated a number of RWAs. Upstream farmers have signed contracts with downstream water users to conserve their forests, in return for compensation such as beehives and fruit trees paid for by downstream users (Asquith, 2011). To date, 195,000 water users have signed contracts with 4,500 upstream landowners to conserve 210,000 ha of forests (Asquith, 2016). These agreements build on pre-existing social norms which encourage reciprocity and co-operation (Grillos, 2017). RWAs were also used in Palampur, India, as detailed in Box 8.1.

Outside of the ESPA portfolio, there is evidence that multi-stakeholder forums for negotiating and agreeing mutual obligations within urban watersheds and catchments can sustain high-impact uses (such as tourism), while maintaining watershed integrity and water quality (Blanchard et al., 2015). In the Wasatch watershed, above Salt Lake City, an extra-territorial regulatory authority allows planners to impose restrictions on certain types of activity and development within the watershed, such as cattle grazing (ibid.). The authority does, however, permit recreation and public use under a socially negotiated settlement managed through the Mountain Accord, a multi-stakeholder forum which includes both conservation and development minded actors, as well as civic and regulatory authorities.

Importantly, these RWAs demonstrate that watershed management objectives can be achieved, and maintained, without needing the intervention of market-type mechanisms such as PES.

Outcomes for poverty alleviation

The conceptual framework presented by Fisher et al. (2014) emphasises the importance of social differentiation in access to ecosystem services. The framework also disaggregates poverty alleviation into poverty reduction and poverty prevention. Ecosystem services are more likely to prevent poverty than reduce it (Fisher et al., 2013), with the prevention of poverty typically stemming from the provision of forest products (provisioning services) (Fisher et al., 2014). It is thus imperative that the consequences of the management of forests for hydrological services for poverty alleviation and wellbeing are considered.

PES schemes are expected to alleviate poverty by providing an income to upstream land users, with an assumption that upstream land users are poor (Pagiola et al., 2005). However, this is not necessarily the case. Notably, many of the participants in Costa Rica's Pago por Servicios Ambientales programme were relatively well-off urban dwellers (Pagiola et al., 2005). Moreover, upstream communities are not homogenous; even if many inhabitants can be classified as poor, different levels of poverty can exist (ibid.). For forest–water management regimes to alleviate poverty, the poor must benefit; however, the poor may be excluded from PES. For example, Muñoz-Piña et al. (2008) find in Mexico's Payment for Hydrological Environmental Services Program that the 'very highly marginalised' were less well represented in the programme than the 'highly marginalised'. The same can occur in RWAs. In Bolivia, Grillos (2017) found that material wealth and social embeddedness predicted participation in RWAs, while environmental attitudes did not. Importantly, Grillos (2017) found that participation was skewed towards wealthier members of the community. Thus, as reported in a number of other interventions in relation to rural natural resource management (Vira et al., 2012), there is a potential tendency towards elite capture and the distribution of benefits being skewed towards those who are already well-off, and have the capacity to participate in ecosystem management programmes.

The equity of the distribution of benefits among downstream users must also be considered. Although downstream users are likely to be better off than upstream service providers, still there will be variation in poverty levels within the downstream community (Pagiola et al., 2005). In the urban settlements that we have studied in India and Nepal, this is evident from the wide variation in the ability of downstream consumers to access water (see Box 8.1).

Towards water-sensitive forest- and tree-based landscape management to reduce poverty and improve human wellbeing

The interdependence of rural and urban dwellers across forest–water systems, and their mutual reliance on land use, water and associated systems of natural resources, requires the adoption of 'water-sensitive' approaches to the management of forest- and tree-based landscapes. A starting point is the recognition of what we call 'critical water zones' across the landscape, those specific locations which are identifiable as impacting the hydrological system, and where changes in the patterns of land use can result in variations in hydrological regimes. Once these critical water zones have been identified, the potential pressures that might result in a change of state need to be understood, as well as the likely impacts of these changes on the hydrological system. If there are drivers that are reducing the water-bearing capacity of these landscapes, management interventions may be required to reverse these trends, including the use of regulatory instruments and/or negotiated (reciprocal) agreements to counteract some of these pressures.

Such an idealised approach to water management is complicated by the reality of the political economy context for decision making in many countries, where existing interests have a stake in maintaining the *status quo* (even if this is ecologically unsustainable), and power is exercised unequally (and not always in a transparent manner). Accountability can sometimes be enforced through the mobilisation of citizens' voices, including the use of the judiciary in defence of the public interest (see Box 8.1), but these cases are not widespread. In too many examples across our case studies, decisions that are made, or being proposed, reflect conventional and existing solutions to perceived needs for large-scale and high-impact infrastructure development, failing to respond to the social and ecological particularities of forest–water systems, and the potential for more locally appropriate interventions that respect insights from local and expert knowledge about ecosystem service dynamics in particular places.

The decision-making context is further complicated by the lack of long-term data and monitoring of social and ecological systems. These decision environments present significant challenges to scientists who work on sophisticated models of the forest–hydrological system, but are unable to verify their understanding of plausible systemic relationships in the absence of adequate empirical information, which is today further complicated by a more rapidly changing climate. For the decision maker, this lack of scientific data does not obviate the immediacy of choice. Even doing nothing is a choice – not to intervene. In such a 'data-poor' environment, decision making has to use 'best available' knowledge, in a form of adaptive management, while also investing in better monitoring and measurement of key variables (also see Buytaert et al., this volume). Experts, and those who are advising the decision process, also need to adopt an attitude of well-informed 'experimentation', transferring their understanding from similar social-ecological systems to decide on plausible interventions, and ensuring that they are willing to change course if the evidence suggests that the desired impacts are not forthcoming.

This agenda for a new management paradigm, which is informed by ESPA and other evidence on forest–water relationships, requires a significant shift in the risk-averse mindset that characterises administrative decision making in both the forest bureaucracy and among water engineers, and is not necessarily easy to achieve under current governance systems. Finding ways to empower stakeholders to take action in support of water-sensitive forest management, and promoting an enabling management framework for local application and empowerment, within spatially nested structures of decision making, is an aspirational goal but one that will require committed and imaginative leadership.

References

(ESPA outputs marked with '★')

★Asquith N. (2011) Reciprocal agreements for water: an environmental management revolution in the Santa Cruz valleys. *Revista: Harvard Review of Latin America* XI: 58–60.
★Asquith N. (2013) Investing in Latin America's water factories: incentives and institutions for climate compatible development. *Revista: Harvard Review of Latin America* XII: 21–24.

Asquith N. (2016) Watershared: adaptation, mitigation, watershed protection and economic development in Latin America. *Inside stories on climate compatible development*. Climate & Development Knowledge Network (CDKN).

Bennett G and Carroll N. (2014) *Gaining Depth: State of Watershed Investments 2014*. Washington, DC: Forest Trends' Ecosystem Marketplace.

Bhusal J and Subedi B. (2014) Climate change induced water conflict in the Himalayas: a case study from Mustang, Nepal. *Ecopersia* 2: 585–595.

Blanchard L, Vira B and Briefer L. (2015) The lost narrative: ecosystem service narratives and the missing Wasatch watershed conservation story. *Ecosystem Services* 16: 105–111.

Brauman KA, Daily GC, Duarte TKe, et al. (2007) The nature and value of ecosystem services: an overview highlighting hydrologic services. *Annual Review of Environment and Resources* 32: 67–98.

Bremer LL, Auerbach DA, Goldstein JH, et al. (2016) One size does not fit all: natural infrastructure investments within the Latin American Water Funds Partnership. *Ecosystem Services* 17: 217–236.

Brogna D, Vincke C, Brostaux Y, et al. (2017) How does forest cover impact water flows and ecosystem services? Insights from 'real-life' catchments in Wallonia (Belgium). *Ecological Indicators* 72: 675–685.

Bruijnzeel LA. (2004) Hydrological functions of tropical forests: not seeing the soil for the trees? *Agriculture, Ecosystems and Environment* 104: 185–228.

*Buytaert W and Bievre BD. (2012) Water for cities: the impact of climate change and demographic growth in the tropical Andes. *Water Resources Research* 48: 1–13.

*Buytaert W, Zulkafli Z, Grainger S, et al. (2014) Citizen science in hydrology and water resources: opportunities for knowledge generation, ecosystem service management, and sustainable development. *Frontiers in Earth Science* 2: 26.

Creed IF, Weber M, Accatino F, et al. (2016) Managing forests for water in the anthropocene – the best kept secret services of forest ecosystems. *Forests* 7: 60.

Ellison D, Futter MN and Bishop K. (2012) On the forest cover-water yield debate: from demand- to supply-side thinking. *Global Change Biology* 18: 806–820.

Ellison D, Morris CE, Locatelli B, et al. (2017) Trees, forests and water: cool insights for a hot world. *Global Environmental Change* 43: 51–61.

FAO. (2008) *Forests and Water: A Thematic Study Prepared in the Framework of the Global Forest Resources Assessment 2005*. Rome, Italy: FAO.

Farley KA, Jobbágy EG and Jackson RB. (2005) Effects of afforestation on water yield: a global synthesis with implications for policy. *Global Change Biology* 11: 1565–1576.

Filoso S, Bezerra MO, Weiss KCB, et al. (2017) Impacts of forest restoration on water yield: a systematic review. *PLoS ONE* 12: 1–26.

*Fisher JA, Patenaude G, Giri K, et al. (2014) Understanding the relationships between ecosystem services and poverty alleviation: a conceptual framework. *Ecosystem Services* 7: 34–45.

*Fisher JA, Patenaude G, Meir P, et al. (2013) Strengthening conceptual foundations: analysing frameworks for ecosystem services and poverty alleviation research. *Global Environmental Change* 23: 1098–1111.

Foley Ja, Defries R, Asner GP, et al. (2005) Global consequences of land use. *Science* 309: 570–574.

Geist HJ and Lambin EF. (2002) Proximate causes and underlying driving forces of tropical deforestation. *BioScience* 52: 143–150.

Ghimire CP, Bonell M, Bruijnzeel LA, et al. (2013) Reforesting severely degraded grassland in the Lesser Himalaya of Nepal: effects on soil hydraulic conductivity and overland flow production. *Journal of Geophysical Research: Earth Surface* 118: 2528–2545.

Goldman-Benner RL, Benitez S, Boucher T, et al. (2012) Water funds and payments for ecosystem services: practice learns from theory and theory can learn from practice. *Oryx* 46: 55–63.

★Grillos T. (2017) Economic vs non-material incentives for participation in an in-kind payments for ecosystem services program in Bolivia. *Ecological Economics* 131: 178–190.

★Hajra R, Szabo S, Tessler Z, et al. (2017) Unravelling the association between the impact of natural hazards and household poverty: evidence from the Indian Sundarban delta. *Sustainability Science* 12: 453–464.

★Hamann M, Biggs R and Reyers B. (2016) An exploration of human well-being bundles as identifiers of ecosystem service use patterns. *PLoS ONE* 11: e0163476.

Hamilton L. (1987) What are the impacts of Himalayan deforestation on the Ganges–Brahmaputra lowlands and delta? Assumptions and facts. *Mountain Research and Development* 7: 256–263.

Hamilton L and King PN. (1983) *Tropical Forested Watersheds: Hydrologic and Soils Response to Major Uses or Conversions.* Boulder, CO: West View Press.

★Hossain MS, Dearing JA, Rahman MM, et al. (2016) Recent changes in ecosystem services and human well-being in the Bangladesh coastal zone. *Regional Environmental Change* 16: 429–443.

★Howe C, Suich H, Vira B, et al. (2014) Creating win-wins from trade-offs? Ecosystem services for human well-being: a meta-analysis of ecosystem service trade-offs and synergies in the real world. *Global Environmental Change* 28: 263–275.

Ilstedt U, Bargués Tobella A, Bazié HR, et al. (2016) Intermediate tree cover can maximize groundwater recharge in the seasonally dry tropics. *Scientific Reports* 6: 21930.

Jones J, Achterman GL, Augustine LA, et al. (2010) Hydrologic effects of a changing forested landscape- challenges for the hydrological sciences. *Hydrological Processes* 2274: 2267–2274.

Keys PW, Van Der Ent RJ, Gordon LJ, et al. (2012) Analyzing precipitationsheds to understand the vulnerability of rainfall dependent regions. *Biogeosciences* 9: 733–746.

★Kovacs EK, Kumar C, Agarwal C, et al. (2016) The politics of negotiation and implementation: a reciprocal water access agreement in the Himalayan foothills, India. *Ecology and Society* 21: 37.

Lakerveld RP, Lele S, Crane TA, et al. (2015) The social distribution of provisioning forest ecosystem services: evidence and insights from Odisha, India. *Ecosystem Services* 14: 56–66.

Leimona B, Lusiana B, van Noordwijk M, et al. (2015) Boundary work: knowledge co-production for negotiating payment for watershed services in Indonesia. *Ecosystem Services* 15: 45–62.

Muñoz-Piña C, Guevara A, Torres JM, et al. (2008) Paying for the hydrological services of Mexico's forests: analysis, negotiations and results. *Ecological Economics* 65: 725–736.

Neary DG, Ice GG and Jackson CR. (2009) Linkages between forest soils and water quality and quantity. *Forest Ecology and Management* 258: 2269–2281.

★Nicholls RJ, Hutton CW, Lázár AN, et al. (2016) Integrated assessment of social and environmental sustainability dynamics in the Ganges–Brahmaputra–Meghna delta, Bangladesh. *Estuarine, Coastal and Shelf Science* 183: 370–381.

Ojea E, Martin-Ortega J and Chiabai A. (2012) Defining and classifying ecosystem services for economic valuation: the case of forest water services. *Environmental Science and Policy* 19–20: 1–15.

Pagiola S, Arcenas A and Platais G. (2005) Can payments for environmental services help reduce poverty? An exploration of the issues and the evidence to date from Latin America. *World Development* 33: 237–253.

Postel SL and Thompson BH. (2005) Watershed protection: capturing the benefits of nature's water supply services. *Natural Resources Forum* 29: 98–108.

*Rideout AJR, Joshi NP, Viergever KM, et al. (2013) Making predictions of mangrove deforestation: a comparison of two methods in Kenya. *Global Change Biology* 19: 3493–3501.

*Sakib M, Nihal F, Haque A, et al. (2015) Sundarban as a buffer against storm surge flooding. *World Journal of Engineering and Technology* 3: 59–64.

*Vira B, Adams B, Agarwal C, et al. (2012) Negotiating trade-offs: choices about ecosystem services for poverty alleviation. *Economic and Political Weekly* 47: 67–75.

Vogl AL, Goldstein JH, Daily GC, et al. (2017) Mainstreaming investments in watershed services to enhance water security: barriers and opportunities. *Environmental Science and Policy* 75: 19–27.

Wattenbach M, Zebisch M, Hattermann F, et al. (2007) Hydrological impact assessment of afforestation and change in tree-species composition – a regional case study for the Federal State of Brandenburg (Germany). *Journal of Hydrology* 346: 1–17.

9
RESTORATION OF ECOSYSTEMS AND ECOSYSTEM SERVICES

Alison Cameron

Introduction

Habitat degradation, loss and fragmentation result in a wide range of biophysical, socio-economic and wellbeing consequences, and outcomes vary for different social and demographic groups. The FAO estimates that one-third of the world's population suffers directly from ecosystem degradation, with many of these living in drier regions. As the area of degraded land has grown, so has concern over loss of production and regulating ecosystem services. Many ecosystems are affected, and humanity's demands on our planet are now extending beyond sustainable limits (Dearing et al., 2014; Mace et al., 2014; Steffen et al., 2015; Dearing, this volume). In response, there is a rapidly escalating policy focus on ecosystem restoration (Box 9.1). However, case studies highlight the challenges of designing restoration programmes that are in line with sustainable development goals, and effective in both restoring ecosystem services and alleviating poverty. There is an urgent need to better understand opportunities and limitations for ecosystem restoration, to sustain or improve ecosystem services. It is also critical to evaluate the potential of both the restoration process and the restored ecosystems to contribute to poverty alleviation.

This chapter reviews restoration projects from the ecosystem services and poverty alleviation literature, with a focus on research from the ESPA programme. The world's poor rely on services from a wide range of ecosystems, and ecosystem restoration is being conducted across many different ecosystems, tackling a spectacular range of problems with a huge diversity of activities. While aiming to provide a broad overview, this review focuses on the terrestrial biome, including reforestation, afforestation and re-greening of terrestrial land (Box 9.2), and excluding rehabilitation, remediation and reclamation. However, the findings from these are broadly relevant to other ecosystems and restoration methods (e.g. re-wetting peatlands, re-seeding coral reefs). This review also focuses on large-scale restoration, due to the recent emergence of many such projects and their

BOX 9.1 POLICY AND FUNDING FOR ECOSYSTEM RESTORATION

Since their creation in 1992 three of the United Nations Conventions have developed significant policy, institutional and funding instruments not only to halt degradation, but to reverse it, providing a major stimulus for large-scale restoration projects. While the United Nations Framework Convention for Climate Change (UNFCCC) Clean Development Mechanism funds afforestation and reforestation, it has been criticised for not incorporating ecological restoration (Ma et al., 2014). However, since 2010, the UNFCCC Green Climate Fund has supported increasing numbers of ecosystem restoration and rehabilitation projects. The Bonn Challenge, launched in 2011 by the UNFCCC, called for the restoration of 150 million hectares by 2020, and in 2014 the New York Declaration on Forests (NYDF) extended this to 350 million hectares by 2030. The 2015 Paris Agreement will be critical to meeting these ambitions as it promotes more flexibility on climate change mitigation actions through Intended Nationally Determined Contributions, many of which contain pledges to meet ambitious ecosystem restoration goals. The United Nations Convention to Combat Deforestation (UNCCD) has just launched its Land Degradation Neutrality fund. Three of 24 cross-cutting themes identified by the United Nations Convention on Biological Diversity (CBD) focus on ecosystem restoration, while the CBD's Aichi Biodiversity Targets 14 and 15 directly link restoration with ecosystem services and address poverty alleviation. The Intergovernmental Science-Policy Platform on Biodiversity and Ecosystem Services (IPBES) will finalise its Land Degradation and Restoration Assessment in 2018. The World Bank's Biocarbon Fund portfolio includes projects in 16 countries across five continents, restoring 150,000 hectares of degraded lands through afforestation and reforestation activities, many contributing to UNFCCC targets.

potential impacts. Relatively few ESPA projects have directly studied restoration, but many have produced relevant and generalisable findings.

Ecosystem restoration

Although ecosystem restoration is taking place in all ecosystems all over the world, two substantial biases exist in the ecological restoration literature. Most case studies come from the United States, Australia and Europe (Jones and Schmitz, 2009; Wortley et al., 2013), and most evidence of relationships between biodiversity, ecosystem functioning and ecosystem services comes from studies of biodiversity loss and degradation, rather than from restoration.

> **BOX 9.2 DEFINITIONS**
>
> *Ecological restoration* is 'the process of assisting the recovery of an ecosystem that has been degraded, damaged or destroyed', with an overall aim to restore ecological integrity measured against an appropriate 'reference model' (McDonald et al., 2016: 9).
>
> *Reforestation* refers to re-establishment of forest on land that had recent tree cover, whereas *afforestation* refers to establishing forest on land that has been without forest for much longer (the UNFCCC uses a threshold of >50 years).
>
> *Re-greening* encompasses a range of farmer-managed methods to increase tree and shrub cover, for example in agroforestry where 'farmers protect and manage the growth of trees and shrubs that regenerate naturally in their fields' (Reij and Winterbottom, 2015: 4).
>
> *Rehabilitation*, *remediation* and *reclamation* usually refer to projects initiated to improve severely degraded or contaminated sites – for example, former mining sites. Due to the relative expense these most often aim for partial restoration, or an alternative end state that will restore only a limited set of ecological attributes or services.

International investment in restoration activity is also biased, with reviews of past restoration projects (e.g. Jones and Schmitz, 2009) and announcements of large-scale ecosystem restoration projects revealing a historical and increasing focus on forest and arid land restoration initiatives. New extensive reforestation efforts include Initiative 20 × 20, aiming to restore 20 million hectares of land in 11 countries in Latin America and the Caribbean, and AFR100, aiming to restore 100 million hectares of land in over 20 African countries (Ding et al., 2017). Further to this are large-scale re-greening projects such as the Green Belt Movement in Kenya (Brooks, 2017) and farmer-managed re-greening of Sahel regions (case study below).

Aspirations, goals and targets

Aspirations for ecosystem restoration projects range from modest improvement of key ecosystem functions and services, through to complete restoration of native biodiversity and habitat structure, with an implicit goal to restore the full range of associated ecosystem functions and services.

Setting goals and targets, and monitoring progress towards them, is undoubtedly challenging. Nearly all restoration projects set area-based targets for restoration, but these are weak metrics in isolation and additional goals need to be carefully selected depending on the nature of the project. For example, since the 1960s South Korea has greatly increased its stock of trees while the total forested area has slightly declined (Wolosin, 2017). Therefore, additional measures such as canopy cover, forest volume, stocking rate and carbon stocks are useful metrics of forest restoration.

A review of over 200 restoration projects found that nearly all restoration projects have clearly defined quantifiable goals relating to ecosystem structure and biodiversity, and that these are frequently monitored; however, ecosystem function goals are less specific and less frequently monitored, and ecosystem services goals even less so (Hallett et al., 2013). Driven by evolving ecosystem service frameworks (Pascual and Howe; Reyers and Selomane, both this volume), restoration projects are increasingly looking beyond simple goals such as erosion control, or restoration of a narrow range of provisioning services (e.g. timber, crops, fisheries), and are developing creative approaches to restoring a more diverse portfolio of ecosystem services. Quantitative models of ecosystem services, which could support goal setting, are developing rapidly. However, these are still limited to a sub-set of services, mostly focused on carbon (e.g. Gress et al., 2017; Willcock et al., 2016b), and are data-demanding and technically challenging to apply (Willcock et al., 2016a). The better-developed models have mostly been parameterised from studies in degraded systems and so should be used with caution in the restoration context. A further complication is the growing interest in bundles of ecosystem services which commonly include primary productivity (e.g. carbon sequestration, timber or agriculture), hydrological services (quantity and quality of water) and mitigation of extreme events (e.g. floods, droughts, cyclone damage, storm surges). Assessing potential trade-offs and synergies within, and the total benefits from, such bundles is extremely challenging (e.g. Martin et al.; Whittaker et al., both this volume).

While social goals are widely incorporated into restoration projects these are rarely quantitative, and Hallett et al. (2013) found that only 27% of social goals were measured.

Restoration methods

After defining project goals and targets, the key challenge is to select appropriate methods and effectively balance investment of limited resources. While site-based ecological interventions are often more obvious to observers, restoration projects involve a balance of on- and off-site, and ecological and social, components.

Active ecological interventions are designed to drive succession and increase the pace of restoration, often promoting yields of a limited number of ecosystem services (e.g. timber production). Examples of the most active restoration methods include: preparing land, producing saplings in nurseries, planting and follow-up care for saplings, manually restoring meanders in river systems or transplanting cultivated corals to degraded reefs. Such active restoration measures are often beneficial in highly degraded ecosystems, particularly those that have entered alternative stable states (e.g. where soils have been compacted, hard pans have formed, topsoil has been lost or invasive species dominate) (Holl and Aide, 2011). Mid-intensity actions are designed to enhance succession – such as strategic enrichment planting of saplings, supplementing the depleted seed stocks of degraded forests, seeding coral reefs and controlling invasive species. The technical aspects of active ecosystem restoration are by necessity highly specific to the ecosystem, the history of its degradation and scale of their use. When founded on good ecological knowledge, active restoration usually accelerates ecosystem recovery although it can slow recovery or redirect it to a different end point if poorly designed (Holl and Aide, 2011).

Passive restoration options invest comparatively little in site management, and rely almost entirely on the natural regeneration capacity of the ecosystem. They capitalise on reduced external pressures (e.g. land abandonment), or focus effort on controlling damaging external pressures or drivers of degradation (e.g. preventing fires in terrestrial systems, preventing destructive fishing practices, preventing the arrival of invasive species). Globally, passive restoration is more widespread than active restoration (Chazdon, 2014), and has been found to be more successful than passive restoration in restoring habitat structure and biodiversity in tropical forest habitats (Crouzeilles et al., 2017). A review of 240 restoration studies documented rapid natural recovery taking place over decades for aquatic systems, to half a century for forest ecosystems (Jones and Schmitz, 2009). In combination, these findings provide an optimistic outlook for large-scale passive restoration.

Data on the relative costs of active and passive restoration are sparse, and analytical methods vary considerably (de Groot et al., 2013; Nebhöver et al., 2011), but passive restoration is usually more cost effective (e.g. Bullock et al., 2011; Zahawi et al., 2014). The most intensive interventions are restricted to small-scale projects due to the relatively high costs which may limit their use at larger scales.

Drivers of degradation

Trade-offs and interactions between ecological and socio-economic interventions to mitigate the drivers of degradation are complex and context specific. Even the most active ecological interventions will struggle to balance restoration gains against degradation losses if direct and indirect drivers of degradation are not addressed. However, only dealing with drivers of degradation will not lead to passive ecological recovery if the ecosystem is stuck in an alternative stable state. A major challenge is that, while individual site-based restoration projects can identify and address some direct drivers of degradation (e.g. through enforcement of resource management regulations, and by engaging local communities in projects), many indirect drivers (e.g. population growth, economic markets) can only be addressed by longer-term and larger-scale government or intergovernmental policies.

Poverty is thought to influence many indirect (population growth, migration) and direct (urbanisation, infrastructure, agriculture) drivers of degradation (MA, 2005), but these relationships are still relatively poorly understood. Although the poor are generally more dependent on biodiversity and ecosystem services, a wide range of relationships including feedbacks exist and disaggregation of socio-ecological data is necessary to fully understand drivers of degradation in any single system (Vira and Kontoleon, 2012; Coulthard et al., this volume). Failure to understand the interactions of different drivers can result in the poor being unfairly targeted with land-use restrictions. For example, there has been a widespread perception that communal land management by poor communities in Zimbabwe resulted in desiccation and environmental degradation. However, longer-term studies of groundwater decline found that rainfall was the strongest determinant, with anthropogenic land-use change of secondary importance and groundwater abstraction playing a trivial role (Lovell et al., 2002).

Where resources, expertise and institutional frameworks allow, there can be very constructive synergies. For example, active reforestation projects offer temporary employment (e.g. collecting seeds, working in tree nurseries, planting), providing alternative incomes, helping to buffer people from poverty and local drivers of degradation until ecosystem services and associated wellbeing benefits are realised in the longer term. However, restoration will only be sustainable if the ecosystem services and associated wellbeing benefits are restored to levels sufficient to incentivise maintenance of the newly restored ecosystem.

Outright failures of restoration are rarely published (Zedler, 2007), but disappointing performance of ecosystem restoration initiatives often seems to stem from an extreme focus on a single approach, with successes characterised by more balance (e.g. Crouzeilles et al., 2017).

Mapping knowledge of ecosystem and ecosystem services restoration using the ecosystem services framework

Biodiversity, ecosystem functions and ecosystem services

Ecosystem restoration often has multiple goals – for example, to increase ecosystem service yields, improve resilience to disruptions such as natural disasters and to long-term changes such as climate change; ultimately to enhance and secure human wellbeing. However, it is often not clear how to balance investment in ecosystem recovery to return the desired balance of different ecosystem services. For example, how might investment in soil conservation and restoration, or in enhancing biodiversity, affect balance within and between the groups of regulating and provisioning services? Restoration of habitat structure (e.g. reforestation) is the most common goal. Biodiversity is frequently a priority, but while there is strong evidence that biodiversity underpins yields of many ecosystem services, caution is required extrapolating conclusions from experiments with relatively small numbers of species, or studies of natural systems which are predominantly being degraded rather than restored, as communities may not reassemble in the reverse order to which they dis-assemble through degradation (Cardinale et al., 2012).

The MA (2005: 11) stated that 'it is rare that all of the biodiversity and services of a system can be restored'. In a meta-analysis assessing biodiversity and ecosystem services restoration, Rey-Benayas et al. (2009) find that across 89 projects, representing a wide range of terrestrial and marine ecosystems, biodiversity and ecosystem services, increased on average to 86 and 80%, respectively of their non-degraded comparators. Jones and Schmitz (2009) demonstrate that recovery times vary according to the intensity of perturbation and the ecosystem, so it seems likely that more time and greater investment could improve these outcomes further. Determining the potential benefits of attempting to fully restore biodiversity remains a major frontier for research, and the answer seems to be very specific to the ecosystem and services in question. Some ecosystem services (food and timber production) are maximised in anthropogenic landscapes (e.g. intensive agriculture and forestry) with very low levels of biodiversity, but require intensive management (e.g. weed and pest control) and inputs (e.g. fertiliser). Numerous experiments have shown a positive, but saturating, relationship between biodiversity and ecosystem functioning. However, deep-sea case studies indicate that some ecosystem functions may respond exponentially to increased biodiversity (TEEB, 2010). Whatever the shape of the response function in a system, it seems likely that resilience to future environmental change may be enhanced if apparently 'redundant' species are restored and maintained within ecosystems (Oliver et al., 2016).

A final, and significant, limitation of these studies is that ecosystem services are really co-created by provision of the service and the social requirement for the service (Cardinale et al., 2012; Lakerveld et al., 2015). A service that is produced but not used is not a service. It is therefore of limited use, as most studies have done to date, to investigate the relationship between biodiversity and gross yields of potential ecosystem services.

Can ecosystem restoration alleviate poverty?

A number of studies (e.g. Fisher and Christopher, 2007) have examined changes in ecosystem components, such as biodiversity, to socio-economic indicators of poverty. For example, Leisher et al. (2010) identify ten biodiversity conservation mechanisms (community timber enterprises, nature-based tourism, fish spillover, protected area jobs, agroforestry and agrobiodiversity conservation, non-timber forest products, payments for environmental services (PES), mangrove restoration and grasslands management) for which there is empirical evidence of poverty reduction benefits to the rural poor. They conclude that sometimes these 'provide modest poverty reduction benefits or a safety net to keep people from falling deeper into poverty, and sometimes when upended, a few can become poverty traps' (Leisher et al., 2010: 1), but find a 'limited number of studies that generated hard evidence of poverty impacts' (ibid., p. 2). More recently Roe et al. (2014) found that the most commonly identified processes by which biodiversity affects poverty are through direct use, supporting subsistence needs and income generation. However, the study outlines many complex linkages that are difficult to precisely define and quantify, identifying disease and human–wildlife conflict as needing further attention, and a substantial knowledge gap relating to the sustainability of biodiversity use.

Due to the challenges inherent in determining and measuring wellbeing benefits from ecosystem services (Daw et al., 2016), many ecosystem restoration projects state aspirations to increase wealth or wellbeing of the poor, but few set clear targets (Hallett et al., 2013). Even when economic or wellbeing targets are clear, projects vary in their efforts to ensure that benefits are delivered to target groups. Most effort has been focused on targeting distributions of cash or in-kind incentives towards poverty alleviation (e.g. through PES and conditional transfer agreements). No restoration studies have researched the step-by-step relationships between restoration action, ecosystem condition, ecosystem processes, through to ecosystem services and on to associated disaggregated economic and wellbeing outcomes. However, Reyers and Selomane (this volume) provide a useful starting point for projects wishing to address these gaps.

While more research is needed, it is critical to develop guidelines for emerging policy and programmes, and it is clear that ecosystem restoration will not simply reverse declines in ecosystem services and wellbeing. For example, Howe et al. (2014) could not identify a generalisable context for win-win scenarios. Apparent beneficiaries of environmental degradation, described by the 'Environmentalist's paradox', whereby welfare gains appear to outweigh ecosystem services losses from environmental degradation, are likely only experiencing short- to medium-term gains (Zhang et al., 2015; Martin et al., this volume). As the short-term winners become losers, motivation for ecosystem restoration should increase. In fact, many restoration projects are successful when targeting highly degraded ecosystems, where opportunity costs are relatively low (Ding et al., 2017; Huxham et al., 2015).

Finally, there are indications that the poorest groups of people, having already lost out from ecosystem degradation, may be vulnerable to further losses through restoration. This is because the poor are often denied access to ecosystem services upon which they are disproportionately and highly dependent, and lack resources to invest in alternatives. Among conservation measures with some evidence of positively affecting poverty, those widely regarded as potential mechanisms for incentivising ecosystem restoration lie at the lower end of the benefits scale (Leisher et al., 2010). In Madagascar, Poudyal et al. (2016) find a pilot REDD+ social safeguard scheme biased towards families with power, food security and accessibility, after not effectively identifying the poorest households who are bearing the highest losses from increasing forest protection. Such projects may therefore be widening socio-economic inequities.

While the poor may not exercise much political or economic power, they can have great influence on their local environments, and negative-feedback loops resulting from failures to address inequities may explain many instances of restoration failure or deepening degradation. If the costs of restoration (e.g. income or ecosystem service losses to the community) outweigh the benefits (e.g. from compensation schemes or alternative livelihoods), local stakeholders can easily undermine restoration programs. Poor communities with few alternatives may be effectively forced to continue to engage in destructive practices such as burning, grazing or over-extraction (Ding et al., 2017). These findings highlight the importance of collecting pre-project (i.e. pre-restoration) baseline data for both ecosystem and wellbeing metrics, and for disaggregated evaluation of outcomes.

For projects relying on PES to incentivise restoration, McDermott et al. (2013) outline the importance of considering who sets the agenda, and establishing transparent and inclusive procedures to ensure equitable distribution of costs and benefits associated with a project (also see Dawson et al.; Nunan et al., both this volume). The Trees for Global Benefit project, a Carbon PES project in Uganda, highlights several trade-offs between restoration goals and sustainable development goals. The conservation and carbon sequestration objectives of the implementing organisation mean that farmers are only supported to plant indigenous species, although they might obtain greater short-term benefits from fast-growing exotics or improved varieties of fruit trees (Schreckenberg et al., 2013).

Large-scale restoration programmes in practice

Re-greening Africa's Sahel Region

Through much of the last century, anti-desertification programmes in the dry lands of sub-Saharan Africa focused unsuccessfully on active restoration. Seedling planting projects in this region were expensive, and suffered very low survival rates. However, since 1980, examples of large-scale creation of new agroforestry parklands have emerged in the West African Sahel. These are the result of farmer-managed regeneration, where natural regeneration is assisted by promoting re-sprouting of tree stumps and roots that have remained after land clearing. Motivated by a combination of environmental, economic and political crisis in the 1980s, 5 million hectares of agricultural land in Niger have been re-greened (Reij et al., 2009). When trees were perceived to belong to the state, farmers had less incentive to manage them, but when governance weakened through political instability and forestry services declined, farmers began claiming ownership of the trees on their farms, self-organising to protect their trees from livestock and reviving traditional low-cost agroforestry practices. Increased tree densities have increased grain yields, fodder availability, fuelwood and timber, and non-timber products, with the net result of improving food security and incomes (Reij and Garrity, 2016). This demonstrates the vast potential for low-cost restoration where drivers of degradation, in this case maladapted institutional frameworks, can be addressed.

China's Sloping Land Conversion Program

Between 1949 and 1979, 38 million hectares of natural habitat were converted for agriculture in China. The associated environmental degradation led to severe erosion, sandstorms, droughts and floods, and lack of forest resources, culminating in the Yellow River drought in 1997, and Yangtze River flood in 1998, and by 1998 erosion affected 38% of the nation's land area (Delang and Yuan, 2015). Regulating ecosystem services (air quality regulation, soil stability, sediment regulation, water purification and biodiversity) declined through the twentieth century in the Yangtze River basin, while provisioning services (crop production, agricultural goods) rose (Dearing et al., 2012; Zhang et al., 2015).

One response has been the Sloping Land Conversion Program (SLCP), the world's largest ecological restoration project and largest PES project (also see Porras and Asquith, this volume). Launched in 1999, its main goals were to improve regulating ecosystem services, principally to reduce soil erosion and flooding. Farmers were compensated with cash, grain and seedlings for taking land on steep slopes out of agricultural production and converting it to 'ecological' (timber-producing) or 'economic' (orchards and other non-timber products) forestry, or to grassland. Subsidy levels were set by soil fertility (a proxy for agricultural income loss), and durations ranged from 5 years for 'ecological' to 2 years for grassland restoration. Restoration methods included ceasing agricultural activity, excluding grazing, planting grasses and trees, and allowing natural vegetation to regenerate.

Positive outcomes have been decreases in soil erosion (Uchida et al., 2007) and increases in above- (Wolosin, 2017) and below-ground (Song et al., 2014) carbon stocks. Although perceived as beneficial, it is harder to determine the contribution of SLCP to flood mitigation, as complementary wetland restoration initiatives have also contributed to hydrological regulation and there is much variation across China. On the negative side, few of the restored forests are highly biodiverse, and there is concern that while the afforestation monoculture components have increased production services (timber, pulp, fuel wood), this is strongly traded off with regulating services (Xu, 2011).

The SLCP's success is primarily due to the significant ecosystem service (and disservice) differential between the degraded and reforested conditions, supported by the differential in agricultural yield between flatter, more fertile land (the intended ultimate beneficiary) and more sloping, less productive, agricultural land targeted for conversion by the scheme. Upstream farmers were sufficiently compensated, and downstream agricultural intensification was supported by the resulting sedimentation and flooding regulation. The programme was particularly attractive to farmers because its objectives combined reforestation and restoration of ecological integrity with poverty alleviation (Delang and Yuan, 2015).

A critical factor for its success in poverty alleviation is that, in contrast to many rural development or PES programmes, much of the funding was distributed directly to households (this is further elaborated by Porras and Asquith, this volume). Furthermore, by addressing surplus production of grain in some regions, which was lowering farmer incomes, the programme helped to even out inequities between urban and rural populations and eastern and western provinces. Overall, Liu et al. (2010) found that the SLCP had significant positive effects on household incomes. Drawing on a number of economic studies, Delang and Yuan (2015: 63) concluded that 'for a majority of the program plots, farmers received more in payments after entering the [SLCP] program than they had received from planting crops'. In general, farmers who converted more degraded, less productive, land have made the greatest gains, and as poverty has been associated with land quality this should include the poorest farmers.

The overall design challenge for large-scale restoration projects is to develop a simple and efficient programme that is equitable and effective. As simple tiered rates and durations of compensation were applied, instances of over- and under-compensation have been identified, but overpayments exceed underpayments providing some margin for error. While the project has been successful in alleviating poverty, accessibility has been identified as a bias, with larger land conversion quotas being allocated to villages with better connections to local forest bureaus (Li et al., 2006).

As the SLCP started to withdraw subsidies from 2015 onwards, there are concerns over the extent to which restoration will be maintained. It is hoped that after the initial subsidised period, where farmers had to invest a lot of labour in converting their land, labour will be diverted to other off-site income-generation activities, and that this, along with some productivity from the restored land, will offset the loss of subsidies and ensure the persistence of the new forest cover.

While the programme seems to be an overall success, it is notable that there are a range of systematic offstage (distant, diffuse and delayed) ecosystem service burdens (as per Pascual et al., 2017). Within China this includes the associated effects of migration of rural labour to urban areas, and internationally includes increased demand for imported timber from countries such as Madagascar, which has experienced devastating effects from illegal trade in rosewood (Zhu, 2017).

Conclusions

Studies of the effects of ecosystem degradation on ecosystem services, and of rewards, incentives or PES designed to maintain and enhance ecosystem services, have demonstrated that it is extremely challenging to design sustainable development activities that are equitable, inclusive and just. Hence, it is important to learn from case studies, but also to fill the substantial knowledge gaps.

The ecosystem services framework provides common ground for trans-disciplinary research and project design, but substantial challenges remain for improving the effectiveness of ecosystem restoration. Ecosystem services are dependent upon ecosystem functions, which in turn depend upon the biophysical qualities (e.g. biodiversity, soil type, topography) and functions of an ecosystem. However, there is considerable uncertainty about the strengths and importance of these interactions. Even where these relationships have been well studied through ecosystem degradation, ecosystem restoration often does not simply reverse the loss of ecosystem services, or the associated economic and wellbeing outcomes.

As it is increasingly recognised that social-ecological systems have the capacity to self-correct, so an improved understanding of the social aspects will support the design of restoration interventions. Consensus is emerging that, while site-based restoration activities are important, ecosystem restoration requires a policy focus to reduce the drivers of degradation. If emerging policy stimulates well-designed interventions, it is possible that low-intensity, less costly, passive, ecological intervention may be necessary, except where ecosystems have settled in an undesirable alternative stable state.

Disaggregation of costs and effects is a particular challenge, across all scales of restoration projects. Small-scale restoration initiatives are often components of larger conservation, forestry or agricultural extension projects, with integrated objectives, institutional frameworks and governance structures. Large-scale programmes, such as China's SLCP, are complicated by simultaneous ecosystem degradation and restoration across the landscape, driven by a great diversity of policies and projects.

While poverty is not listed as one of the drivers of land-use change, it is increasingly recognised that poverty interacts with many of the indirect and direct drivers of ecosystem degradation. Given the higher level of direct dependence of poor communities on the natural environment, and that the poor are frequently trapped on, or marginalised onto, poorer land, meeting current large-scale and rapid ecosystem restoration goals must directly engage the poor. Large-scale restoration projects may benefit from economy of scale and better access to capital (Ding et al., 2017). However, as there is no 'one-size-fits-all' solution in ecological restoration, we must develop appropriate adaptations to deal with the greater diversity of socio-ecological relationships that exist within their influence.

Improved understanding of trade-offs between ecosystem services, better understanding of and accounting for co-production of ecosystem services, disaggregation of wellbeing and economic data, to tailor ecosystem restoration interventions to a greater range of socio-ecological dynamics, can all be facilitated by emerging social-ecological systems approaches to the ecosystem services framework (Reyers and Selomane, this volume). Exercising key principles of equity and transparency through project planning and implementation (Schreckenberg et al., 2016), to understand who uses what within an ecosystem and the consequences of intervention (e.g. Brown and Fortnam, this volume), is particularly critical to ensure that interventions do not further disadvantage the poor.

This will require further state-of-the art collaborations, between biophysical, social and economic scientists, and between scientists and practitioners. Meanwhile, pragmatic use of emerging conceptual frameworks can support decision makers to identify conditions under which restoration can provide sustainable development pathways.

References

(ESPA outputs marked with '★')

Brooks MC. (2017) Grassroots leadership for ecological sustainability, empowerment, and political change. In: Brooks JS and Normore AH (eds) *Leading Against the Grain: Lessons for Creating Just and Equitable Schools*. New York: Teachers College Press, 14–22.

Bullock JM, Aronson J, Newton AC, et al. (2011) Restoration of ecosystem services and biodiversity: conflicts and opportunities. *Trends in Ecology and Evolution* 26: 541–549.

Cardinale BJ, Duffy JE, Gonzalez A, et al. (2012) Biodiversity loss and its impact on humanity. *Nature* 486: 59–67.

Chazdon RL. (2014) *Second Growth: The Promise of Tropical Forest Regeneration in an Age of Deforestation.* Chicago, IL: University of Chicago Press.

Crouzeilles R, Ferreira MS, Chazdon RL, et al. (2017) Ecological restoration success is higher for natural regeneration than for active restoration in tropical forests. *Science Advances* 3: e1701345.

*Daw TM, Hicks CC, Brown K, et al. (2016) Elasticity in ecosystem services: exploring the variable relationship between ecosystems and human well-being. *Ecology and Society* 21: 11.

*Dearing JA, Wang R, Zhang K, et al. (2014) Safe and just operating spaces for regional social-ecological systems. *Global Environmental Change* 28: 227–238.

*Dearing JA, Yang X, Dong X, et al. (2012) Extending the timescale and range of ecosystem services through paleoenvironmental analyses, exemplified in the lower Yangtze basin. *Proceedings of the National Academy of Sciences* 109: E1111–E1120.

de Groot RS, Blignaut J, Van Der Ploeg S, et al. (2013) Benefits of investing in ecosystem restoration. *Conservation Biology* 27: 1286–1293.

Delang CO and Yuan Z. (2015) *China's Grain for Green Program: A Review of the Largest Ecological Restoration and Rural Development Program in the World.* Cham, Switzerland: Springer International.

Ding H, Faruqi S, Carlos Altamirano J, et al. (2017) *Roots of Prosperity: The Economics and Finance of Restoring Land.* Washington, DC: World Resources Institute, 80.

Fisher B and Christopher T. (2007) Poverty and biodiversity: measuring the overlap of human poverty and the biodiversity hotspots. *Ecological Economics* 62: 93–101.

*Gress SK, Huxham M, Kairo JG, et al. (2017) Evaluating, predicting and mapping below-ground carbon stores in Kenyan mangroves. *Global Change Biology* 23: 224–234.

Hallett LM, Diver S, Eitzel MV, et al. (2013) Do we practice what we preach? Goal setting for ecological restoration. *Restoration Ecology* 21: 312–319.

Holl KD and Aide TM. (2011) When and where to actively restore ecosystems? *Forest Ecology and Management* 261: 1558–1563.

*Howe C, Suich H, Vira B, et al. (2014) Creating win-wins from trade-offs? Ecosystem services for human well-being: a meta-analysis of ecosystem service trade-offs and synergies in the real world. *Global Environmental Change* 28: 263–275.

*Huxham M, Emerton L, Kairo J, et al. (2015) Applying climate compatible development and economic valuation to coastal management: a case study of Kenya's mangrove forests. *Journal of Environmental Management* 157: 168–181.

Jones HP and Schmitz OJ. (2009) Rapid recovery of damaged ecosystems. *PLoS ONE* 4: e5653.

Lakerveld RP, Lele S, Crane TA, et al. (2015) The social distribution of provisioning forest ecosystem services: evidence and insights from Odisha, India. *Ecosystem Services* 14: 56–66.

Leisher C, Sanjayan M, Blockhus J, et al. (2010) Does conserving biodiversity work to reduce poverty. A state of knowledge review. Report by The Nature Conservancy, Cambridge University, UK and IIED, 26.

Li DY, Bo FM and Tao JL. (2006) The achievements, effects and development countermeasures of the Returning Land for Farming to Forestry Project in Hunan. *Hunan Forestry Science and Technology* 33: 1–5.

*Liu C, Lu J and Yin R. (2010) An estimation of the effects of China's priority forestry programs on farmers' income. *Environmental Management* 45: 526–540.

Lovell C, Mandondo A and Moriarty P. (2002) The question of scale in integrated natural resource management. *Conservation Ecology* 5: 25.

MA. (2005) *Millennium Ecosystem Assessment, 2005. Ecosystems and Human Well-Being: Biodiversity Synthesis.* Washington, DC: Island Press.

Ma M, Haapanen T, Singh RB, et al. (2014) Integrating ecological restoration into CDM forestry projects. *Environmental Science and Policy* 38: 143–153.

*McDermott M, Mahanty S and Schreckenberg K. (2013) Examining equity: a multi-dimensional framework for assessing equity in payments for ecosystem services. *Environmental Science and Policy* 33: 416–427.

McDonald T, Gann G, Jonson J, et al. (2016*) International Standards for the Practice of Ecological Restoration – Including Principles and Key Concepts.* Washington, DC: Society for Ecological Restoration.

Mace GM, Reyers B, Alkemade R, et al. (2014) Approaches to defining a planetary boundary for biodiversity. *Global Environmental Change* 28: 289–297.

Nebhöver C, Aronson J, Blignaut J, et al. (2011) Investing in ecological infrastructure. In: ten Brink P (ed.) *The Economics of Ecosystems and Biodiversity: National and International Policy Making.* London and Washington, DC: Earthscan, 401–448.

Oliver TH, Heard MS, Isaac NJB, et al. (2016) A synthesis is emerging between biodiversity-ecosystem function and ecological resilience research: reply to Mori. *Trends in Ecology and Evolution* 31: 89–92.

*Pascual U, Palomo I, Adams WM, et al. (2017) Off-stage ecosystem service burdens: a blind spot for global sustainability. *Environmental Research Letters* 12: 075001.

*Poudyal M, Ramamonjisoa B, Hockley N, et al. (2016) Can REDD+ social safeguards reach the 'right' people? Lessons from Madagascar. *Global Environmental Change* 37: 31–42.

Reij C and Garrity D. (2016) Scaling up farmer-managed natural regeneration in Africa to restore degraded landscapes. *Biotropica* 48: 834–843.

Reij C, Tappan G and Smale M. (2009) Agroenvironmental transformation in the Sahel: another kind of 'Green Revolution'. *IFPRI Discussion Paper 00914.* Washington, DC: International Food Policy Research Institute (IFPRI).

Reij C and Winterbottom R. (2015) *Scaling Up Regreening: Six Steps to Success. A Practical Approach to Forest and Landscape Restoration.* Washington, DC: World Resources Institute.

Rey-Benayas JM, Newton AC, Diaz A, et al. (2009) Enhancement of biodiversity and ecosystem services by ecological restoration: a meta-analysis. *Science* 325: 1121–1124.

*Roe D, Fancourt M, Sandbrook C, et al. (2014) Which components or attributes of biodiversity influence which dimensions of poverty? *Environmental Evidence* 3: 3.

*Schreckenberg K, Franks P, Martin A, et al. (2016) Unpacking equity for protected area conservation. *Parks* 22: 11–26.

*Schreckenberg K, Mwayafu D and Nyamutale R. (2013) *Finding Equity in Carbon Sequestration. A Case Study of the Trees for Global Benefits Project, Uganda.* Uganda Coalition for Sustainable Development.

Song X, Peng C, Zhou G, et al. (2014) Chinese Grain for Green Program led to highly increased soil organic carbon levels: a meta-analysis. *Scientific Reports* 4: 1–7.

*Steffen W, Richardson K, Rockström J, et al. (2015) Planetary boundaries: guiding human development on a changing planet. *Science* 347: 1259855.

TEEB. (2010) *The Economics of Ecosystems and Biodiversity: Ecological and Economic Foundations*, ed. Pushpam Kumar. London and Washington, DC: Earthscan.

Uchida EMI, Farnsworth HF, Fellow S, et al. (2007) Are the poor benefiting from China's land conservation program? *Environment and Development Economics* 12: 593 620.

Vira B and Kontoleon A. (2012) Dependence of the poor on biodiversity: which poor, what biodiversity? In: Roe D, Elliott J, Sandbrook C, et al. (eds) *Biodiversity Conservation and Poverty Alleviation: Exploring the Evidence for a Link.* 1st edn. London: Wiley, 52–84.

★Willcock S, Hooftman D, Sitas N, et al. (2016a) Do ecosystem service maps and models meet stakeholders' needs? A preliminary survey across sub-Saharan Africa. *Ecosystem Services* 18: 110–117.

★Willcock S, Phillips OL, Platts PJ, et al. (2016b) Land cover change and carbon emissions over 100 years in an African biodiversity hotspot. *Global Change Biology* 22: 2787–2800.

Wolosin M. (2017) Large-scale forestation for climate mitigation: lessons from South Korea, China, and India. San Francisco, CA: Climate and Land Use Alliance, 60.

Wortley L, Hero JM and Howes M. (2013) Evaluating ecological restoration success: a review of the literature. *Restoration Ecology* 21: 537–543.

Xu J. (2011) China's new forests aren't as green as they seem. *Nature* 477: 371.

Zahawi RA, Reid JL and Holl KD. (2014) Hidden costs of passive restoration. *Restoration Ecology* 22: 284–287.

Zedler JB. (2007) Success: an unclear, subjective descriptor of restoration outcomes. *Ecological Restoration* 25: 162–168.

★Zhang K, Dearing JA, Dawson TP, et al. (2015) Poverty alleviation strategies in eastern China lead to critical ecological dynamics. *Science of the Total Environment* 506–507: 164–181.

Zhu A. (2017) Rosewood occidentalism and orientalism in Madagascar. *Geoforum* 86: 1–12.

PART III
Improving governance

The chapters in this section all deal with governance, a fundamentally political process which determines who has access to and can benefit from ecosystem services. As Nunan and colleagues (Chapter 10) outline, no single approach, whether community-based, private sector or state-led, can definitively deliver the desired win-win of enhancing wellbeing while sustaining the environment. However, a lack of coordination between local, national and international decision-making levels, and between different sectors within government, continues to frustrate attempts to govern ecosystems in the holistic manner required to resolve inevitable trade-offs, anticipate and adapt to changing circumstances. The important role of informal institutions in governing natural resources is often overlooked and power dynamics underplayed. While meaningful participation of resource users in decisions about the environment on which they depend is widely espoused, providing a voice to marginalised people remains a challenge. In this respect, Buytaert and colleagues (Chapter 11) are optimistic that widespread adoption of new information and communication technologies can support more participatory governance by facilitating an inclusive process of knowledge co-generation. Not only do low-cost and robust sensors facilitate data collection by resource users, but participatory modelling and visualisation techniques also enable their involvement in data processing and extracting knowledge. Mobile phones increasingly enable all societal groups to access and share information widely and in real time. New technologies thus have the potential to be disruptive – in both negative and positive sense – of existing social structures and connections between actors.

The next three chapters highlight the fact that both market-based and regulatory approaches to resource governance need to be carefully designed to avoid negative impacts on poorer and marginalised groups. In Chapter 12, Menton and Bennett review the evolution of payments for ecosystem services (PES) schemes from a purely market-based approach for achieving often quite narrow ecosystem service objectives, to one that seeks to reward environmental stewardship in a more holistic manner. Conventional PES schemes can negatively impact poorer households by insufficiently compensating the costs of land-use change or by imposing conditionality requirements which exclude them from potential benefits. Porras and Asquith (Chapter 13) argue that conditional transfer schemes like PES have the potential to realise environmental protection at a much more significant scale by learning from social protection schemes. They suggest that a focus on poverty alleviation could attract greater political and budgetary support for conditional transfer schemes with environmental objectives. While there may be some trade-offs between sites with high poverty levels and those where the environment is most at risk, this approach could also promote greater integration across siloed government departments. Woodhouse and colleagues (Chapter 14) argue that integration of social and environmental goals is also needed in the case of protected areas. Far from being a simple technical instrument for resource management, protected areas should be understood as social and political processes. To properly mitigate or compensate the frequent negative impacts of protected areas on local people requires consideration of wellbeing in its broadest sense, and effective participation by local stakeholders from the point of inception.

10
GOVERNING FOR ECOSYSTEM HEALTH AND HUMAN WELLBEING

Fiona Nunan, Mary Menton, Constance McDermott and Kate Schreckenberg

Introduction

Governance mediates the relationships between ecosystem services and human wellbeing, shaping the degree to which those services alleviate or exacerbate poverty (Suich et al., 2015). Indeed, the term ecosystem 'service' implies service to or for someone, involving potential trade-offs regarding which services, at whose cost or benefit, at what scale, from global (e.g. climate regulation) to local (e.g. food security) and for which social groups (McDermott et al., 2013). The decision-making processes that allocate access to ecosystems and ecosystem services are thus inherently political.

The terms 'ecosystem governance' and 'governance of ecosystem services' highlight the diversity of services that may be derived from an ecosystem in a way that the more common sectoral perspective (e.g. forest governance or fisheries governance) may not. This diversity of services, however, may lead to trade-offs being experienced between different uses and stakeholders, with ecosystem governance being concerned with the resolution of trade-offs (Sikor et al., 2014). One key area of trade-offs explicit in literature is between conservation and livelihood objectives and outcomes. We use this recognition of trade-offs as an organising framework for the chapter, considering first ecosystem-focused approaches, then rights-based approaches and lastly, participatory approaches to governance. We then turn to two overarching areas of concern within the literature, on the relevance of scale and multiple administrative levels (multi-level governance) and the importance of informal, or socially embedded, institutions.

For the purpose of this chapter, we consider natural resource governance to be

> ... the norms, institutions, and processes that determine how power and responsibilities over natural resources are exercised, how decisions are taken

and how citizens – including women, men, youth, indigenous peoples and local communities – secure access to, participate in, and are impacted by the management of natural resources.

Campese (2016: 7)

The chapter is informed by a systematic mapping of literature related to governance of ecosystem services and renewable natural resources for improved wellbeing and poverty alleviation. Themes emerging from the coding of 872 papers included: institutions, instruments, power and participation/community-based governance. We further draw on interviews with 23 projects funded by the Ecosystem Services for Poverty Alleviation (ESPA) programme, and a workshop with partners from government and non-government actors across a range of sectors from both North and South. Our aim is to explore what is known about the nature and performance of governance arrangements, systems and processes at multiple levels for ecosystem health and poverty alleviation.

Ecosystem-focused approaches: regulatory vs market-based approaches to governing access and use

Some ecosystem governance approaches focus primarily on protecting or conserving ecosystem health. Aimed at reducing the environmental impacts of natural resource use and/or land-cover change, these are often divided into two main categories based on whether they focus on 'carrots' (market-based incentives for desired behaviour) or 'sticks' (regulatory approaches: command-and-control policies, rules and regulations) or some combination of the two (Börner et al., 2015). The regulatory approach includes legal frameworks, land-use or environmental policies that control use (e.g. restrictions on the species and size of trees that can be logged, controls on fishing gear used or seasonal bans for particular species) and enforcement of these rules and regulations. Protected areas, which restrict natural resource use, are a regulatory approach applied across the globe. While protected areas can have benefits for biodiversity and ecosystem services, they have variable implications for poverty and wellbeing (see Coulthard et al., this volume). Weaknesses in protected area effectiveness are often linked to their failures to account for human wellbeing and dependence on ecosystem services from the protected area. The very poor are often disproportionately affected by restrictions over access to natural resources, through protected area status or other measures (Bidaud et al., 2017; Bluwstein et al., 2016; Dawson and Martin, 2015). This exposes them to fines and sanctions if caught collecting products illegally, which they can ill-afford. For conservation to succeed, governance structures must support local participation in conservation initiatives, as seen in the case of Great Apes species conservation (Sandbrook and Roe, 2012).

Market-based governance initiatives, designed to incentivise sustainability through the provision of market rewards, have generated considerable debate in the literature. Although they provide financial incentives for sustainable use, they focus primarily on environmental outcomes and the effects on wellbeing are often not central considerations in their design. Of particular importance, from a poverty perspective, is the critique that market-based instruments, such as certification or Payment for Ecosystem Services (PES) schemes, are neo-liberal tools which further entrench the existing inequalities of a global capitalist system (see also Menton and Bennett, this volume). They have widespread implications for power dynamics, access and equitable participation in governance processes. For example, a review of the evidence on four certification schemes focused on forests, fair trade and carbon found that without deliberative efforts to support local access and benefit-sharing, these schemes tend to favour large-scale and/or high-capacity producers and reinforce existing market inequalities (McDermott, 2013). Similar effects were found in a case study of biodiversity offsets in Madagascar, governed by the Business and Biodiversity Offsets Programme and associated international standards (Bidaud et al., 2017). Such challenges are also associated with PES, particularly when reliant on monetisation or marketisation of ecosystem services (Kovacs et al., 2016; Muradian et al., 2013). With regard to REDD+, researchers have highlighted how an excessive focus on 'technical' issues related to carbon measurement and accounting – which lies at the core of performance-based payments for emissions reductions – obscures power imbalances and favours the interests of external actors and investors over local communities (Patenaude and Lewis, 2014; Sikor, 2013a). These findings demonstrate that although market-based type instruments may deliver on efficiency, they do not necessarily delivery on equity and poverty alleviation (see also Box 10.1).

To inform the development of an approach that may deliver more equitable outcomes, Sikor (2013b) argues that three 'design elements' are critical for shaping social justice: scale of implementation, methodology to measure ecosystem services and the nature of benefits. He finds that 'safeguards', such as those associated with REDD+, are remedial and inadequate to address systemic design issues, for example that favour external control, commodification of ecosystem services and monetary benefits over local actors, knowledge and values. Local participation in the design of such schemes is generally seen as important, as is the need to design schemes explicitly to generate local benefit (Hejnowicz et al., 2015; Locatelli et al., 2014).

Equity, justice and rights-based approaches

There is growing interest in rights-based approaches to governance where wellbeing, equity and rights are central considerations in the design and implementation of interventions. Research on justice and equity suggests that whatever institutional approach is pursued for the governance of land and resources, it is critical that it be situated in a broader understanding of the distribution of power and resources across multiple social scales (McDermott et al., 2013; Sikor, 2013a; see also Dawson et al., this volume).

Equity and justice framings can be helpful for both researchers and practitioners to conceptualise social challenges such as poverty alleviation much more broadly, by recognising that what is 'fair' and 'just' is socially contested, that poverty is relative and its causes and manifestations highly diverse, and that resource conservation and poverty alleviation require trade-offs. For example, McDermott et al. (2013) distinguish between procedural equity, which refers to equity in decision-making processes; distributive equity, as in equity in the distribution of costs and benefits; and contextual equity, as in the equity of the overall environmental and socio-political context. A conservation intervention may invest heavily in procedural equity by bringing a wide group of stakeholders to the negotiating table, but if stakeholders vary in their relative capacities and freedoms to defend their interests and values, this could lead to highly unequal material and non-material outcomes. Many efforts to alleviate poverty do not explicitly address such trade-offs. Likewise, much research on the impacts of conservation interventions does not disaggregate social data adequately to identify precisely who benefits and loses (Daw et al., 2011). For example, a given governance strategy may raise average incomes (e.g. Liu et al., 2010), but these gains may serve to make the relatively well-off richer while excluding the poorest and most vulnerable (e.g. Kovacs et al., 2016; Muradian et al., 2013).

The emergence of 'rights-based' governance has grown from such conceptual foundations. While such an approach cannot eliminate all trade-offs, it does attempt to ensure that all interventions identify and respect the rights of all affected actors. In the case of Indigenous people, for example, the process of Free, Prior and Informed Consent (FPIC) is supposed to protect their land and resource rights. However, there remains lack of clarity about ownership by Indigenous people of sub-surface minerals and stored forest carbon, and the FPIC process is applied variably in different sectors (Mahanty and McDermott, 2013).

Participatory and decentralised approaches are widespread but imperfect

Participatory approaches to natural resource governance encompass a wide range of strategies aimed at improving the effectiveness and/or equity of ecosystem conservation. Such arrangements include community-based natural resource management, community-based forest management and community-based conservation, and collaborative arrangements, with communities working with other actors, such as government departments or the private sector. The participation of communities in community-based approaches to natural resource management, however, has been interpreted and approached differently within initiatives, sometimes involving no more than communication with local communities without meaningful devolution of power (Shackleton et al., 2010). Many community-based approaches are introduced through top-down initiative, while others are rooted in customary norms and practices. In addition to encouraging the participation of resource users

BOX 10.1 COMBINING REGULATORY AND MARKET-BASED APPROACHES TO CONSERVE BIODIVERSITY: AT WHAT COST TO WELLBEING?

The Corridor Ankeniheny-Zahamena (CAZ) protected area in Madagascar exemplifies the trend towards combining regulatory and market-based governance instruments, and highlights the challenge of linking improvements in ecosystem services with improved local wellbeing. Recognising that conserving biodiversity for global benefit may impose costs on local people, the World Bank prescribes a safeguarding process. Contrary to expectations, Poudyal et al. (2016) find that the best predictor for people to be identified as being eligible for safeguard payments is not their likely dependence on the forest but rather their socio-political power, with membership of the community forest association committee being the highest predictor. Compared with other ways of providing livelihood benefits to park-adjacent populations, MacKinnon et al. (2017) find safeguards to be the most expensive option delivering the least funds to the community but, unlike other approaches, benefiting individual households. Benefits linked to conservation agreements provide the greatest proportion of funds to the community level (ibid.). Using hypothetical scenarios, Rakotonarivo et al. (2017) find that a household's experience of the reality of the impacts of forest protection affects their willingness to accept any kind of compensatory activity in exchange for giving up their rights to clear forest for agriculture. These studies highlight the need to consider who benefits and who loses from the establishment of a protected area, and how best to deliver compensatory activities. They also illustrate the interlinked nature of community-, national- and international-level governance, as the funds available to support communities around CAZ are dependent on the level of income the government can obtain through REDD+ agreements, in turn based on calculations of by how much CAZ will reduce shifting cultivation and hence carbon emissions.

in governance, many countries have devolved power and responsibilities from central to local government. However, a lack of power and resources received by lower levels of government often constrains their ability to undertake their governance functions (Larson and Soto, 2008).

There is mixed evidence regarding whether community-based governance arrangements have a positive effect on ecosystem and poverty alleviation outcomes. Focusing on forest areas in East Africa and South Asia, Persha et al. (2011) find that only 27% of 84 cases studied have positive outcomes for both biodiversity and livelihoods, and that these win-win situations are more likely when local forest

BOX 10.2 COMPARING NATURAL RESOURCE GOVERNANCE SYSTEMS IN TANZANIA

Patenaude and Lewis (2014) compared the impacts on ecosystem services and on poverty alleviation of four prominent resource governance systems in Tanzania: Community Based Forest Management (CBFM), Joint Forest Management, Wildlife Management Areas and *ngitili* enclosures, a traditional land husbandry technique practised by some Sukuma pastoralists. In comparing these approaches, they conclude that *ngitili* and CBFM are the most successful in terms of outcomes for ecosystem health and poverty alleviation, and attribute this to decisions being made at the local level, with perceptions of equitable benefit-sharing among community members. Where decisions are made at other levels a lack of ownership or understanding may contribute to non-compliance or perhaps inappropriate or ineffective decisions. The authors stress the benefits of flexibility in institutional arrangements, so that systems reflect the local context and preferences. They conclude by making four recommendations for REDD+ in Tanzania, which have resonance for governance of ecosystem services for poverty alleviation more broadly:

1. A decentralised approach to governance should be adopted that aims to promote democratisation rather than tasked with reducing government expenditure.
2. There must be a commitment for fair benefit distribution.
3. Cooperation between agencies is essential, across programmes (horizontal) and between actors and administrative levels (vertical).
4. Governance structures should build on existing traditional systems, which would support buy-in by communities and simplify the operation of the governance system.

users participate in forest rulemaking. Reviewing 165 protected areas around the world, Oldekop et al. (2016) also find that a win-win relationship between socio-economic and biodiversity outcomes is more likely where protected areas adopt co-management and empower local people. In Tanzania, community-based forest management approaches offer the greatest potential to deliver on both ecosystem health and poverty alleviation (see Box 10.2).

A lack of baseline information and the challenges of finding counterfactuals make it very difficult to determine the precise impact of community forest management on either forest status or livelihoods. In Madagascar, where 15% of natural forest is managed in community forests, Rasolofoson et al. (2015) used a matching approach to show that community forest management overall has no apparent impact on deforestation; however, a reduction in deforestation was found in those community forest sites which do not allow commercial use of forest products. In terms of household livelihoods, the team found that community forest management had neither negative nor positive impacts on household livelihoods; however, households closer to the forest and with higher education levels do obtain significant benefits (Rasolofoson et al., 2017).

Such findings chime with earlier work by McDermott and Schreckenberg (2009), which emphasises the need to understand who within communities benefits from community forestry, finding that it is more likely to generate positive change at community level rather than directly benefiting poor and marginalised households. Understanding who benefits is not just important in contexts of decentralisation. For example, interventions to reduce the use of illegal fishing gear on the Kenyan coast may improve the number of large expensive fish but have a negative impact on the wellbeing of women who are reliant on selling smaller fish (Abunge et al., 2013). Although women may have very different expectations of the outcomes of governance interventions than men (Keane et al., 2016), their perspectives are often not considered (see Brown and Fortnam, this volume).

The importance of community-level benefits is highlighted in many studies. In Tanzania, Gross-Camp (2017) finds that although households in villages participating in community forestry do not experience significant changes in wellbeing, they are nevertheless very supportive of the community forestry process, valuing it as a means of securing the land for the community and protecting it from use by outsiders. A similar focus on collective goals of securing resources for the future and aesthetic benefits is an important motivating factor for community participation in marine protected areas in the Philippines (Chaigneau and Brown, 2016).

One of the challenges of participatory approaches is that governments may be unwilling to devolve power to communities in a meaningful way, as was found in a study of Wildlife Management Areas (WMAs) in Tanzania (Bluwstein et al., 2016). Although ostensibly community-owned, WMAs give limited space for popular participation in rule-making (Bluwstein et al., 2016). This centralised control of power and resources is seen in the maintenance of the conservation narrative, with no alternative land uses being considered over time. This is manifested in 'territorialization', the setting of territories and marking of boundaries, where 'decades of consecutive conservation projects have continuously territorialized the landscape despite failures in the processes of demarcating, controlling, and managing conservation interventions' (Bluwstein and Lund, 2018: 2). The governance framework and purpose therefore go unchallenged over time.

Centralised control and power are also evident in the lack of downward accountability of formal structures to communities. This means that local communities often lack full knowledge and understanding of, and engagement with, what is going on (Bluwstein et al., 2016; Moyo et al., 2016). In the case of WMAs, Bluwstein et al. (2016) argue that although villagers can elect and remove representatives to the inter-village community-based organisation formed to manage the WMA, the establishment of this body above the level of village government means that villagers' power is undermined. This lack of knowledge and engagement encourages resource users to utilise informal institutions rather than, or in combination with, formal structures and systems.

Governance at scale: multi-level and multi-actor

All of the above approaches occur within a context of governance at multiple scales, involving multiple actors with different, at times conflicting, interests. A multi-level governance perspective recognises interactions among a complex network of actors and institutions that go beyond a state-centric interpretation of governance. Such a perspective recognises the challenge of scale in natural resource governance, referring in particular to spatial scale, but also to temporal scale and the range of analysis (Gibson et al., 2000). Scale is challenging because ecosystems may cross administrative boundaries, provide multiple services (governed by multiple sectors) and are affected by decisions and actions at multiple administrative levels, from local to international. This multiplicity of actors, policies, rules and levels suggests that interactions between actors within and across levels are essential for effective governance, yet such interactions tend to be piecemeal, often project or activity-driven and are rarely at a level for sustained and effective integrated governance. Given this complexity, multi-level governance systems may lack legitimacy in the eyes of resource users and struggle to deliver on accountability and transparency of decision making (Termeer et al., 2010).

A multi-scale perspective is ever more critical in the context of globalisation, where the 'local' is increasingly embedded in external flows of materials, capital (e.g. in the form of remittances), investments and the larger-scale dynamics of international governance and trade. However, as Zoomers and Otsuki (2017) argue, too many resource governance interventions have focused their environmental and social strategies and assessments exclusively at the project or very local level, thereby missing many of the core drivers of poverty and its long-term alleviation.

Ecosystems tend to be governed through separate natural resource sectors (forestry, fisheries, environment and water, for example). These often operate in 'silos', with only limited cooperation and coordination (Reed et al., 2016). Sectors have their own cultures, ways of doing things, budgets, objectives and plans. The requirements of, and constraints on, sectors limit willingness and capacity to coordinate and cooperate with other sectors and actors. One of the challenges at the local level is the creation of multiple user groups or committees, sometimes associated with specific donor-funded projects, calling into question the long-term sustainability and effectiveness of such structures.

Landscape approaches are a specific type of multi-level governance. Ranging from Integrated Conservation and Development Projects to Integrated Water Resources Management and Eco-agriculture, landscape approaches seek to overcome disciplinary boundaries and reconcile social and environmental agendas (Reed et al., 2016). In a systematic review of landscape approaches, Reed et al. (2016) argue that the approach differs from preceding attempts to tackle issues such as poverty alleviation and biodiversity loss by explicitly acknowledging that it is not possible to always satisfy all stakeholders. They identify five elements of effective landscape approaches: evaluating progress, establishing good governance, evolving away from panacea solutions, engaging multiple stakeholders and embracing dynamic processes (Reed et al., 2016: 2544).

International processes, such as the Convention on Biological Diversity or REDD+ under the UNFCCC, bring different implications for governance at the local and national levels. Despite concern over the top-down nature of these initiatives, international processes can open avenues of access to the decision-making process for local people. For example, the rights of indigenous peoples to FPIC are often explicitly recognised by international policy documents. While respect for indigenous rights in REDD+ has been far from perfect, it has in some cases, served as an avenue for indigenous peoples' strategy to 'import power' to the UNFCCC and have their rights taken into consideration (Wallbott, 2014).

Informal institutions remain critical for governance of ecosystem services

Institutions, often referred to as 'rules of the game' (North, 1990: 3), facilitate access to decision making and access to resources, and both shape and are shaped by governance arrangements and outcomes (Ostrom, 1990). Institutions are often differentiated between formal and informal; or bureaucratic, 'those formalised arrangements based on explicit organisational structures, contracts and legal rights, often introduced by governments or development agencies' (Cleaver, 2002: 13), and socially embedded, 'those based on culture, social organisation and daily practice institutions' (ibid.). Common property literature, for example associated with Elinor Ostrom's design principles (Ostrom, 1990), has tended to focus on how institutions can be designed for effective governance of common pool resources. Alternative perspectives, informed by political ecology and sociological institutionalism (Nunan et al., 2015), place more emphasis on the importance of socially embedded institutions, including institutions not necessarily designed for natural resource governance, such as gendered norms and kinship.

Literature referring to informal, or socially embedded, institutions often focuses on how institutions mediate livelihoods as well as governance, though governance and livelihoods are closely connected. Critical Institutionalism highlights the role of socially embedded institutions and reflects '(i) complexity of institutions entwined in everyday social life; (ii) their historical formation; and (iii) the interplay between the traditional and the modern, formal and informal arrangements' (Hall et al., 2014: 73). Cleaver's (2002) 'institutional bricolage' provides further insight into which institutions matter for natural resource governance and livelihoods by demonstrating how people piece together new institutions from existing institutions, whether formal or informal, to gain and maintain access to resources. An example of a Critical Institutionalism analysis of governance arrangements within inland fisheries, by Nunan et al. (2015), demonstrates how the composition and function of co-management structures is affected by power relations, gender relations and norms, and kinship. Such institutions then affect how natural resources are governed and the outcomes in terms of the level of exploitation. They also affect who benefits: local people, migrants, men, women and people of different ethnicities.

A key finding in relation to the design and introduction of new institutions for natural resource governance is that this does not take place in an institutional vacuum. The existing plethora of formal and informal institutions affects how any new institutional arrangements are received, shaped and responded to (de Koning, 2014). This means that new institutional arrangements may look quite different between locations and over time. Furthermore, where new institutional arrangements, such as those related to decentralisation, are not fully implemented or supported, pre-existing institutions, particularly informal institutions, may remain important in determining access to resources and making decisions with consequences for the health of ecosystems. For example, in Kyrgyzstan, although Pasture Users Associations were introduced in 2009, they are not recognised as legitimate by local herders who operate outside of the governance mandate of those formal institutions, making their own decisions on where to graze animals and how many animals to pasture (Isaeva and Shigaeva, 2017). In a similar vein, and informed by research on institutions and natural resource governance, Patenaude and Lewis (2014) argue that building new governance structures on existing traditional systems is important for ensuring buy-in and operational simplicity.

One of the most important institutions determining the extent to which individuals and communities can control the benefits they derive from ecosystems is tenure. The 'bundle of rights' concept recognises that traditional tenure systems typically have layered rights to resources, ranging from the right to access a resource to the right to manage it and exclude others (Schlager and Ostrom, 1992). While over two billion people live in lands held under customary tenure (Alden Wiley, 2016), only one fifth of these are formally recognised (RRI, 2015). In some countries, requirements that land must be actively used to be owned can discourage farmers from practising traditional long-fallow systems which may provide many ecosystem services (Zwartendijk et al., 2017). Martin et al. (2016) argue that changing the formal tenure of indigenous territories to enable local control over land use would help to redress the power imbalance and make relationships more equal.

Conclusions

We conclude that there is no one governance approach that can definitively deliver on improved ecosystem health and human wellbeing. However, it is clear that the nature of involvement of resource users, particularly of women and the poor, in governance arrangements and processes is critical. Involvement, or participation, must be meaningful – that is, it must be sustained and have influence over decision making. This has proved far from easy to achieve as such participation challenges the power of government, the private sector and community members with greater social status and wealth. Yet, governments, the private sector and wealthier members of communities must also play a role in natural resource governance.

From this, we can learn that governance arrangements should be locally specific, developed and shaped by those involved in the social-ecological system, with potential to change over time in response to changing circumstances and new information. More effective governance for ecosystem health and poverty alleviation must challenge power relations and power dynamics within and across levels of governance.

A further conclusion is that much governance of ecosystems remains sectorally focused, even where ecosystem-based approaches are espoused, with forest management being mainly concerned with trees and fisheries management with fish. Ecosystem governance implies a more holistic approach to the governance of renewable natural resources, one that brings potential trade-offs to the fore and is concerned with resolving such trade-offs. A step towards such an approach would be greater cooperation and coordination between actors involved, including between parts and levels of government. This would also enable movement towards a more adaptive, responsive approach to governance, more able to respond to change and new information, as well as to cope with uncertainty.

These lessons are summarised in a set of governance principles outlined in Box 10.3. There are multiple examples of sets of natural resource governance principles (see, for example, Lockwood et al., 2010); however, this set provides a succinct summary of key points from the chapter.

This portrayal of how governance arrangements and processes need to progress suggests that there are two key outstanding areas of research: (i) how meaningful and sustained participation of all stakeholder groups in ecosystem governance, particularly of more marginalised groups, can be encouraged; and (ii) how greater coordination of policy and practice within and between administrative levels can be facilitated. To deliver on more effective and meaningful participation for pro-poor policy and practice, which also delivers on improved ecosystem health, we need to understand how the dominance of more powerful actors can be effectively challenged. This includes attention to government – resource-user relations, and to investigating how new governance arrangements and approaches can more effectively and appropriately take into account existing institutions, including customary governance systems. To deliver on greater cooperation and coordination within and between areas of policy and practice, evidence on the potential incentives and mechanisms for such practice is needed, with examples of what such cooperation and coordination might look like.

Finally, there is very little evidence available on the wider governance impacts from ecosystem governance. The plethora of participatory natural resource governance initiatives might, for example, be expected to empower people and incentivise engagement with broader governance systems, with the potential to improve accountability and planning. Investigation into whether such wider benefits exist, or how they could be encouraged, is needed. This could strengthen links between ecosystem governance and other governance systems and embed ecosystem governance arrangements in wider governance, leading to greater sustainability and coordination.

BOX 10.3 GOVERNANCE PRINCIPLES

While the literature reviewed in this chapter highlights the fact that there are no hard-and-fast rules about which governance arrangements achieve the best outcomes for ecosystem services and wellbeing in which contexts, there is widespread agreement that certain principles are important in all cases:

Accountability: Kairu et al. (2018) find that the 'implementation gap' between Kenya's progressive 2005 Forest Act and Participatory Forest Management on the ground is in part caused by forest officers having greater upward accountability (expressed in their role of forest law enforcers) than downward accountability as community facilitators.

Participation: Participation of resource users in the governance of ecosystems, whether through customary or new community-based approaches, can improve livelihood and ecosystem health outcomes (Patenaude and Lewis, 2014), but must be meaningful and sustained.

Adaptive management: There is increasing understanding that governance systems must be adaptive, able to cope with often rapid changes in the local context. For example, the expansion of hydro-power interests in the Himalayan foothills posed a real challenge to the nascent reciprocal water access agreement being negotiated between the small town of Palampur and upstream communities (Kovacs et al., 2016).

Information: Several studies highlight the need for good information to support effective and fair governance. In discussing the uncertain boundaries of Tanzania's Wildlife Management Areas, Bluwstein and Lund (2018: 461) note that 'the people drawing a map wield great power and can easily err'. Buytaert et al. (2014) argue that the availability of better and cheaper technology could potentially give citizens access to data that enable them to participate more effectively in decision making (see also Buytaert et al., this volume).

Capacity-building: Linked to the recognition of the need for adaptive management comes the need for ongoing capacity-building. Whether decentralising resource management to the local level or establishing a reciprocal water agreement (Kovacs et al., 2016), both community members and staff of facilitating government or non-government organisations need training to initiate and support sustainable interventions.

References

(ESPA outputs marked with '★')

★Abunge C, Coulthard S and Daw TM. (2013) Connecting marine ecosystem services to human well-being: insights from participatory well-being assessment in Kenya. *Ambio* 42: 1010–1021.

Alden Wiley L. (2016) Customary tenure: remaking property for the 21st century. In: Graziadei M and Smith L (eds) *Comparative Property Law: Global Perspectives*. Cheltenham, UK: Edward Elgar.

★Bidaud C, Schreckenberg K, Rabeharison M, et al. (2017) The sweet and the bitter: Intertwined positive and negative social impacts of a biodiversity offset. *Conservation and Society* 15: 1–13.

★Bluwstein J and Lund JF. (2018) Territoriality by conservation in the Selous–Niassa Corridor in Tanzania. *World Development* 101: 453–465.

★Bluwstein J, Moyo F and Kicheleri RP. (2016) Austere conservation: understanding conflicts over resource governance in Tanzanian wildlife management areas. *Conservation and Society* 14: 218–231.

Börner J, Marinho E and Wunder S. (2015) Mixing carrots and sticks to conserve forests in the Brazilian Amazon: a spatial probabilistic modeling approach. *PLoS ONE* 10: p.e0116846.

★Buytaert W, Zulkafli Z, Grainger S, et al. (2014) Citizen science in hydrology and water resources: opportunities for knowledge generation, ecosystem service management, and sustainable development. *Frontiers in Earth Science* 2: 26.

Campese J. (2016) Natural Resource Governance Framework Assessment Guide: learning for improved natural resource governance. *IUCN/CEESP NRGF Working Paper*. Gland, Switzerland: IUCN and CEESP.

★Chaigneau T and Brown K. (2016) Challenging the win-win discourse on conservation and development: analyzing support for marine protected areas. *Ecology and Society* 21: 36.

Cleaver F. (2002) Reinventing institutions: bricolage and the social embeddedness of natural resource management. *European Journal of Development Research* 14: 11–30.

★Daw T, Brown K, Rosendo S, et al. (2011) Applying the ecosystem services concept to poverty alleviation: the need to disaggregate human well-being. *Environmental Conservation* 38: 370–379.

★Dawson N and Martin A. (2015) Assessing the contribution of ecosystem services to human wellbeing: a disaggregated study in western Rwanda. *Ecological Economics* 117: 62–72.

de Koning J. (2014) Unpredictable outcomes in forestry – governance institutions in practice. *Society and Natural Resources* 27: 358–371.

Gibson CC, Ostrom E and Ahn TK. (2000) The concept of scale and the human dimensions of global change: a survey. *Ecological Economics* 32: 217–239.

★Gross-Camp N. (2017) Tanzania's community forests: their impact on human well-being and persistence in spite of the lack of benefit. *Ecology and Society* 22: 37.

Hall K, Cleaver F, Franks T, et al. (2014) Capturing critical institutionalism: a synthesis of key themes and debates. *European Journal of Development Research* 26: 71–86.

★Hejnowicz AP, Kennedy H, Rudd MA, et al. (2015) Harnessing the climate mitigation, conservation and poverty alleviation potential of seagrasses: prospects for developing blue carbon initiatives and payment for ecosystem service programmes. *Frontiers in Marine Science* 2: 32.

*Isaeva A and Shigaeva J. (2017) Soviet legacy in the operation of pasture governance institutions in present-day Kyrgyzstan. *Journal of Alpine Research* 105–1.

Kairu A, Upton C, Huxham M, et al. (2018) From shiny shoes to muddy reality: understanding how meso-state actors negotiate the implementation gap in participatory forest management. *Society and Natural Resources* 31: 74–88.

*Keane A, Gurd H, Kaelo D, et al. (2016) Gender differentiated preferences for a community-based conservation initiative. *PLoS ONE* 11: e0152432.

*Kovacs EK, Kumar C, Agarwal C, et al. (2016) The politics of negotiation and implementation: a reciprocal water access agreement in the Himalayan foothills, India. *Ecology and Society* 21: 37.

Larson AM and Soto F. (2008) Decentralization of natural resource governance regimes. *Annual Review of Environment and Resources*. 33: 213–239.

*Liu C, Lu J and Yin R. (2010) An estimation of the effects of China's priority forestry programs on farmers' income. *Environmental Management* 45: 526–540.

*Locatelli T, Binet T, Kairo JG, et al. (2014) Turning the tide: how blue carbon and payments for ecosystem services (PES) might help save mangrove forests. *Ambio* 43: 981–995.

Lockwood M, Davidson JAC, et al. (2010) Governance principles for natural resource management. *Society and Natural Resources* 23: 986–1001.

*McDermott CL. (2013) Certification and equity: applying an 'equity framework' to compare certification schemes across product sectors and scales. *Environmental Science and Policy* 33: 428–437.

*McDermott M, Mahanty S and Schreckenberg K. (2013) Examining equity: a multidimensional framework for assessing equity in payments for ecosystem services. *Environmental Science and Policy* 33: 416–427.

McDermott M and Schreckenberg K. (2009) Equity in community forestry: insights from North and South. *International Forestry Review* 11: 157–170.

*MacKinnon J, Andriamaro L, Rambeloson A, et al. (2017) Costs of delivery approaches for providing livelihood projects to local communities as part of REDD+ programs: an analysis from Madagascar. *Environmental Conservation*: 1–9.

*Mahanty S and McDermott CL. (2013) How does Free, Prior and Informed Consent (FPIC) impact social equity? Lessons from mining and forestry and their implications for REDD+. *Land Use Policy* 35: 406–416.

*Martin A, Coolsaet B, Corbera E, et al. (2016) Justice and conservation: the need to incorporate recognition. *Biological Conservation* 197: 254–261.

*Moyo F, Ijumba J and Lund JF. (2016) Failure by design? Revisiting Tanzania's flagship wildlife management area Burunge. *Conservation and Society* 14: 232–242.

*Muradian R, Arsel M, Pellegrini L, et al. (2013) Payments for ecosystem services and the fatal attraction of win-win solutions. *Conservation Letters* 6: 274–279.

North DC. (1990) *Institutions, Institutional Change and Economic Performance*. Cambridge, UK: Cambridge University Press.

Nunan F, Hara M and Onyango P. (2015) Institutions and co-management in East African inland and Malawi fisheries: a critical perspective. *World Development* 70: 203–2014.

Oldekop JA, Holmes G, Harris WE, et al. (2016) A global assessment of the social and conservation outcomes of protected areas. *Conservation Biology* 30: 133–141.

Ostrom E. (1990) *Governing the Commons: The Evolution of Institutions for Collective Action*. Cambridge, UK: Cambridge University Press.

*Patenaude G and Lewis K. (2014) The impacts of Tanzania's natural resource management programmes for ecosystem services and poverty alleviation. *International Forestry Review* 16: 459–473.

Persha L, Agrawal A and Chhatre A. (2011) Social and ecological synergy: local rulemaking, forest livelihoods, and biodiversity conservation. *Science* 331: 1606–1608.

★Poudyal M, Ramamonjisoa B, Hockley N, et al. (2016) Can REDD+ social safeguards reach the 'right' people? Lessons from Madagascar. *Global Environmental Change* 37: 31–42.

★Rakotonarivo OS, Jacobsen JB, Larsen HO, et al. (2017) Qualitative and quantitative evidence on the true local welfare costs of forest conservation in madagascar: are discrete choice experiments a valid ex ante tool? *World Development* 94: 478–491.

★Rasolofoson RA, Ferraro PJ, Jenkins CN, et al. (2015) Effectiveness of community forest management at reducing deforestation in Madagascar. *Biological Conservation* 184: 271–277.

★Rasolofoson RA, Ferraro PJ, Ruta G, et al. (2017) Impacts of community forest management on human economic well-being across Magadascar. *Conservation Letters* 10: 346–353.

Reed J, Van Vianen J, Deakin EL, et al. (2016) Integrated landscape approaches to managing social and environmental issues in the tropics: learning from the past to guide the future. *Global Change Biology* 22: 2540–2554.

RRI. (2015) *Who Owns the World's Land?* Washington, DC: Rights and Resources Initiative.

Sandbrook C and Roe D. (2012) Species conservation and poverty alleviation – the case of great apes in Africa. In: Roe D, Elliott J, Sandbrook C abnd Walpole M (eds) *Biodiversity Conservation and Poverty Alleviation: Exploring the Evidence for a Link*. Chichester, UK: Wiley, 173–190.

Schlager E and Ostrom E. (1992) Property rights regimes and natural resources: a conceptual analysis. *Land Economics* 68: 249–262.

Shackleton CM, Willis TJ, Brown K, et al. (2010) Reflecting on the next generation of models for community-based natural resources management. *Environmental Conservation* 37: 1–4.

★Sikor T, ed. (2013a) *The Justices and Injustices of Ecosystem Services*. Abingdon, UK: Routledge.

★Sikor T. (2013b) REDD+: justice effects of technical design. In: Sikor T (ed.) *The Justices and Injustices of Ecosystem Services*. Abingdon, UK: Routledge, 46–68.

★Sikor T, Martin A, Fisher J, et al. (2014) Toward an empirical analysis of justice in ecosystem governance. *Conservation Letters* 7: 524–532.

★Suich H, Howe C and Mace G. (2015) Ecosystem services and poverty alleviation: a review of the empirical links. *Ecosystem Services* 12: 137–147.

Termeer CJAM, Dewulf A and van Lieshout M. (2010) Disentangling scale approaches in governance research: comparing monocentric, multilevel, and adaptive governance. *Ecology and Society* 15: 29.

Wallbott L. (2014) Indigenous peoples in UN REDD+ negotiations: 'Importing power' and lobbying for rights through discursive interplay management. *Ecology and Society* 19: 21.

Zoomers EBA and Otsuki K. (2017) Addressing the impacts of large-scale land investments: re-engaging with livelihood research. *Geoforum* 83: 164–171.

★Zwartendijk BW, van Meerveld HJ, Ghimire CP, et al. (2017) Rebuilding soil hydrological functioning after swidden agriculture in eastern Madagascar. *Agriculture, Ecosystems and Environment* 239: 101–111.

11
CO-GENERATING KNOWLEDGE ON ECOSYSTEM SERVICES AND THE ROLE OF NEW TECHNOLOGIES

Wouter Buytaert, Boris F Ochoa-Tocachi, David M Hannah, Julian Clark and Art Dewulf

Introduction: evidence-based governance of ecosystem services

Much of the global research on the interface between ecosystem services and sustainable development is driven by the need for a better scientific evidence base to support decision making and policy (e.g. Balian et al., 2016). In many developing regions in particular, the natural processes that determine the magnitude and spatiotemporal dynamics of ecosystem services are still poorly characterised (e.g. Wohl et al., 2012). Perhaps even less is known about the way people interact with these services, and how this determines their livelihoods and poverty status (e.g. Doswald et al., 2014). This makes it pertinent to reflect on the process of generating data, evidence and knowledge on ecosystem services, and on how this process can be improved to maximise the potential for poverty alleviation.

This is particularly relevant because of the transformative potential of new technologies to this process, and the accelerating adoption of such new technologies by the poor. In particular, information and communication technology (ICT), such as mobile phones and computer-based social networks can be instrumental in the collection, analysis and sharing of information. At the same time, an exponentially increasing amount of information is becoming available online. A significant amount of this information relates to ecosystem services: witness for instance the boom in satellite-based earth observation, which provides great opportunities to create relevant scientific knowledge to support management of ecosystem services.

However, technological development also has a more fundamental impact on the way that ecosystem service-relevant knowledge is created, how it flows between different actors, how it influences power relations and negotiation strategies, and thus how it influences decisions and policy-making. This is particularly the case for technologies and approaches, such as collaborative governance, participatory action research and citizen science, that disrupt conventional knowledge generation processes.

In this chapter we reflect on the current state of science and the gaps in understanding of processes of knowledge creation on ecosystem services and their relation to poverty. We then outline a conceptual framework to discuss future opportunities to support and improve the process by which knowledge is generated, how it influences decision making and how it can be used in poverty-alleviation contexts.

Opportunities for poverty alleviation

Poverty is a multi-dimensional phenomenon, impeding groups of people from undertaking the actions and activities that they want to engage in, and being who they want to be, thereby realising the kind of life they have 'reason to value' (Sen, 1999: 87; see also Coulthard et al., this volume). The required capabilities to take these actions relate to different concrete dimensions of quality of life, such as avoiding hunger, being educated, escaping premature death or being an accepted and respected member of society.

In many regions in the world and developing countries in particular, these dimensions depend on a variety of ecosystem services, including provisioning (e.g. drinking water), regulating (e.g. biocontrol of pests), supporting (e.g. habitat provision) and cultural services (e.g. religious heritage sites). Based on their access to and use of these services, people can take individual decisions on how to manage ecosystems to improve their quality of life. By making more efficient use of ecosystem services, individual benefits can be increased. By considering impacts on the long-term availability of these services, individual decisions can also contribute to more sustainable management of these services. Access to relevant information and knowledge about ecosystem services is therefore a key element in supporting individual decisions that relate to the alleviation of an individual's poverty.

However, people's capabilities to escape poverty also relate to the opportunities they have to actively participate in shaping their livelihoods beyond their individual decisions and in the struggle over the conditions that allow or impede them to do so. Because there are many interdependencies in social-ecological systems, and because many ecosystem services have common pool resource characteristics (Ostrom et al., 1999), collective decision-making arrangements on ecosystem services can have an important impact on livelihoods. For instance, trade-offs often have to be made within and between different ecosystem services, whereby prioritising one service compromises the production of others (for example, carbon uptake versus water use by forests; water use upstream and downstream in a watershed). Ecosystem services that have common pool resource characteristics (e.g. water, communal land) also run a risk of overexploitation or unsustainable use, which has to be addressed through some form of collective knowledge generation and monitoring arrangement. Environmental information can support collective choice and monitoring arrangements between ecosystem service users and/or public authorities. The usefulness of this information increases when these actors are involved in generating this knowledge (Dewulf et al., 2005), for example, to use it legitimately to assess different management scenarios.

The dynamics of both individual and collective decision making on ecosystem services depend on people's entitlements. These are alternative sets of utilities derived from environmental goods and services over which social actors have legitimate effective command, and which are instrumental in achieving wellbeing (Leach et al., 1999). People's entitlements are related to their identity and position in social networks (e.g. gender, age, ethnicity and social class), and to the nature of local institutional rules and norms. They determine the conditions of access to natural resources as well as opportunities for their use, exchange and valorisation.

Marginalised and excluded members of communities may have their access to, and their possibility to, valorise ecosystem services restricted, while other community members may benefit at their expense. These entitlements and their impact on poverty and wellbeing are therefore critical processes to understand in any attempt at leveraging ecosystem services for poverty alleviation. They are intrinsically related to institutional processes, because this is where stakeholders mutually learn and struggle over issues of access to, legitimacy of use, and conditions for valorisation of natural resources.

It is also key in poverty alleviation to improve the voice and participation of poor groups in these learning processes and struggles, and to support them in finding more effective strategies, to change the rules of entitlement in their favour. The access of people in poverty to the relevant knowledge can give them advantage when negotiating individual access to ecosystem services, and increase their voice in collective decision making about ecosystem services. It can also support them in negotiating the monitoring of institutional arrangements that give them access to ecosystem services. This can help to reduce exploitation or abuse of ecosystem services by those that are better off or have more power in the negotiation process. Lastly, continuous access to relevant knowledge and information about the current state of ecosystem services and potential changes (e.g. induced by environmental degradation and climate change) also supports the poor to adapt to changing conditions, and more generally to support adaptive governance of ecosystem services.

Knowledge co-generation in polycentric governance systems

Given the importance of information and knowledge generation on ecosystem services in the poverty-alleviation process, it is crucial to understand the processes of such knowledge generation in the social-ecological system in which people interact with ecosystem services. The work of Nobel Laureate Elinor Ostrom on the governance of natural resources triggered an increasing recognition that social-ecological systems, especially in developing contexts, are often characterised by multiple centres of decision making across different scales, thereby relying on a distribution of responsibilities, multiple sources of information, and co-generation of knowledge (e.g. Buytaert et al., 2016; Folke et al., 2005). As a result, a highly structured, hierarchical and top-down paradigm of governing (e.g. integrated river basin management, Lankford and Hepworth, 2010), may not be an optimal model for such systems.

Instead, a polycentric approach to natural resources management has been proposed as a potential alternative to tightly integrated (e.g. state-centralised) management systems (Lankford and Hepworth, 2010). Even if they are less streamlined than centralised systems, polycentric approaches to governance tend to 'enhance innovation, learning, adaptation, trustworthiness, levels of cooperation of participants, and the achievement of more effective, equitable, and sustainable outcomes at multiple scales' (Ostrom, 2010: 552).

Polycentric governance also recognises much more explicitly the existence of different types of knowledge within the social-ecological system in addition to scientific knowledge, i.e. local (indigenous) knowledge and hybridised knowledge forms. As a result, this stresses the concept of knowledge co-generation and its benefits, such as a stronger emphasis on the indigenous knowledge of marginalised groups, and explicit recognition of concepts such as access, participation and negotiating power within the process of knowledge generation.

The role of technology in knowledge co-generation

Technology can play a potentially transformative role in the process of knowledge co-generation. Perhaps the most conspicuous adoption of ICT among the poor is the rapid uptake of mobile phones (Lu et al., 2016a,b). Mobile phones enable a plethora of new direct information flows, including calls, text messages and informative apps. Indirectly they also foster interaction and knowledge exchange by enabling the use of social media and other peer-to-peer interactions. Increasingly, these channels are used by actors with a specific agenda or purpose within the context of ecosystem services, for instance to support farming practices, or to implement early warning systems. However, these technologies may also be used to influence decision making less directly, for example, through publicity and commercial applications.

The advent of social networks and other 'interactive' ICT applications also enables a more structural form of knowledge co-generation. The development of computerised decision support systems in natural resources management dates back several decades. However, such systems have often been criticised for being strongly supply-driven, and rigidly oriented towards a very specific problem or use (Karpouzoglou et al., 2016; Zulkafli et al., 2017). Recent ICTs have a potential to change this, and to break open the traditional unidirectional flow of information from the system to an end-user into a multidirectional flow of information between various actors, by integrating social networking technologies and similar application over networks such as the internet. Such 'second generation' decision-support systems are sometimes referred to as 'environmental virtual observatories', because they provide an opportunity to enhance conventional information about the environment with virtual technologies (Buytaert et al., 2012).

Lastly, a broader range of technologies supports new methods for data collection. These can range from easily accessible datasets in the public domain, such as satellite imagery and governmental monitoring records, to low-cost and robust sensors connected to the Internet. These technologies enable data collection and processing by stakeholders that are not traditional analysts or scientists. This promotes new and 'alternative' approaches to information collection and knowledge generation, such as participatory monitoring and modelling, participatory action research and citizen science.

Much of this evolution is occurring in the broader environmental realm. For instance, one of the most active areas of citizen science is biodiversity assessments, while it also underpins grassroots action on water quality (Buytaert et al., 2014) and some of the biggest online environmental datasets, such as the Open Street Map. As such, it is a force to be reckoned with in the context of ecosystem services assessment, and increasingly in the context of sustainable development and poverty alleviation.

A conceptual framework to analyse knowledge co-generation

As argued above, knowledge generation in the context of managing ecosystem services for poverty alleviation is often a complex, multi-directional and iterative process of interactions between different stakeholders. Here, we provide a simple conceptual framework to guide our discussion on the dynamics of knowledge co-generation and the role of new technologies in this process.

We identify three major steps in the process of creating actionable knowledge in which new technologies can be instrumental: the collection of new observations; the processing of these observations and extraction of knowledge; and the interaction between different actors ('communication') on the newly created knowledge. Such interaction may raise new questions and identify needs for further knowledge, resulting in an iterative process of knowledge generation conceptualised in Figure 11.1. Especially in polycentric systems, it is likely that the knowledge generation process is not linear, but consists of many iterations, feedback loops and shortcuts between individual actors. This would result in secondary and parallel loops of knowledge generation in addition to the main loop represented in Figure 11.1. The existence of such secondary loops is probably a major characteristic of the knowledge co-generation process.

In the following sections, we apply our conceptual framework to the portfolio of literature emanating from the Ecosystem Services for Poverty Alleviation (ESPA) programme, and discuss how ESPA activities have created new insights into the co-generation of knowledge relating to ecosystem services.

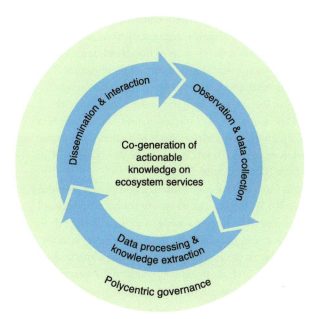

FIGURE 11.1 Conceptual overview of the knowledge co-generation process in a polycentric system.

Observations and data collection

Several ESPA projects have experimented with, and developed, new methods to enhance the observation of ecosystem processes, and to alleviate the issue of data scarcity that is endemic in many development contexts.

One set of projects is mostly concerned with exploring new data sources. Satellite imagery, in particular, is a promising new source of information on ecosystem processes as diverse as mangrove forest extent and disappearance (Kirui et al., 2013), soil salinisation of river deltas (Amoako Johnson et al., 2016) and spatiotemporal patterns of precipitation (Futter et al., 2015). The spatiotemporal coverage of satellite imagery is particularly relevant to identifying spatial and temporal patterns of change and variability, especially in regions where local observations are difficult to make (e.g. conflict areas, mountain regions), and where institutional capacity for data collection is low. However, major problems remain with regard to coarse resolutions and uncertainties, especially for processes such as precipitation that rely on proxy measurements – for example, cloud top temperature and related variables, with imperfect correlations to the variable of interest (Futter et al., 2015). Nevertheless, these studies and, in particular, methods and approaches that are specifically tailored for data-scarce regions (Pandeya et al., 2016), provide a direct contribution to the globally recognised need for better quantitative data about natural processes (e.g. Wohl et al., 2012).

Novel methods for data collection leverage new technologies in unexpected and unintended ways – for instance, using data from the mobile phone network to track migration patterns in the context of floods in Bangladesh (Lu et al., 2016a,b; and Box 11.1). The increasing adoption of mobile phones and ICT also facilitates the collection of natural and social science information, both from the scientist's perspective (e.g. online storage and processing) and from the participant's perspective (e.g. online surveys, email questionnaires). An example of the latter is the deployment of a participatory video process to facilitate the understanding of local wellbeing in four villages in rural Tanzania in the context of community-based forest management (Gross-Camp, 2017).

A more radical form of data collection in a co-creation context is that of citizen science (Haklay, 2013). Because of its strong reliance on technology, citizen science is often associated with data collection in developed regions (e.g. bird counting). However, the possibility to leverage citizen science in a developing country context is receiving increasing attention as a method to support participatory action research and to promote inclusion (Buytaert et al., 2014). One promising example is a participatory hydrological monitoring network in the Andes (iMHEA by its Spanish abbreviation), which generates data on water resources to evaluate the impacts of land use change and other human interventions. By bringing together community members, users of soil and water, policy makers and scientists, this new generation of hydrological information has the potential to extrapolate results and inform actions in a regional data-scarce context (Ochoa-Tocachi et al., 2016). This case also exemplifies the use of new technologies such as robust, low-cost sensors, automatic data transmission and interactive mobile phone applications (Buytaert et al., 2014). This increasing access to environmental data collection techniques, which is driven by low-cost sensors and similar technology, has important consequences for the knowledge-generation process. For example, it can influence (and potentially reduce) monopolies on data access, and in negotiating access to natural resources (Buytaert et al., 2016).

At the same time, these technological developments can also incur risks. The disruptive nature of technology can result in a realignment of social structures and practices because of the availability of information and new connections between actors. For instance, the availability of online models can reduce land value or impact existing social practices. It is therefore paramount that researchers and implementers are aware of these pitfalls and, in particular, the risk of increasing imbalances in information access (Buytaert et al., 2014).

Data processing and knowledge extraction

Raw observational evidence often needs to be processed to convert it into relevant and actionable knowledge for decision makers. The type and level of processing is very diverse, and may range from direct visualisation to complex analysis and processing using computational models, such as in weather forecasts (Grainger

BOX 11.1 DETECTING MIGRATION PATTERNS AS CLIMATE ADAPTATION STRATEGIES WITH MOBILE PHONE NETWORK DATA

The low elevation and highly climate-stressed south coast of Bangladesh is likely to suffer from climate-related migration trajectories, with unprecedented complexity and dynamism resulting from both extreme weather events and slow-onset climatic stressors (Martin et al., 2014). Conventional survey-based research may be insufficient to track such migration patterns, the study of which could benefit from more rapid, cost-effective and accurate tools processing detailed mobility data over a larger range of temporal and spatial scales (Lu et al., 2016b). Lu et al. (2016a) report on a collaboration between the International Centre for Climate Change and Development (ICCCAD), Flowminder, Grameenphone, Telenor Research, United Nations University and the Bangladeshi Ministry of Disaster Management and Relief, to understand climate-induced migration and displacement in Bangladesh. They accessed mobile network operator call detail records, which contain for each subscriber the location of the closest mobile phone tower at the time of each call, text message or data download. By using two de-identified datasets, one covering a period of three months and the other a period of two years, they analysed the directionality and seasonality of migration patterns on both local and national scales, and investigated behavioural responses in the population exposed to cyclone Mahasen. Because of the large sample size and detailed spatiotemporal resolution, mobile phone data allow for characterisation of locally and contextualised mobility patterns as well as identification of anomalies before and after climate shocks. Although the use of such data has limitations – for example, uncertainty in the representation of vulnerable groups such as women, children and the poorest – they provide a novel tool to complement other information sources (Wesolowski et al., 2012). For instance, they have potential to indicate when and where impacts of disasters have occurred, support audits of the effectiveness of early-warning programmes and overcome potential biases in the selection of post-disaster damage sites for humanitarian interventions (Lu et al., 2016b).

et al., 2016). Although data processing and algorithm development are most typically associated with the realm of scientists, new and increasingly participatory methods for doing so are emerging.

Among these, participatory modelling has emerged as a way to incorporate views and insights from local, non-scientist experts into a conceptual model. This is particularly relevant in an ecosystem services context. Local experts tend to have an in-depth understanding of the natural processes occurring in an ecosystem, albeit often in a qualitative manner. A joint approach to conceptualising a social-ecological system may be instrumental to incorporate such indigenous knowledge in evidence generation (e.g. Dewulf et al., 2005). However, methods and tools to do so are still scarce and often strongly context dependent and idiosyncratic. Within the context of the ESPA programme, Daw et al. (2015) and Galafassi et al. (2017) used participatory modelling with stakeholders to understand and build a conceptual model of the trade-offs that are inherently present in the balancing of different ecosystem services. They used a 'toy model' to support discussions and to construct

BOX 11.2 A PARTICIPATORY SOCIAL-ECOLOGICAL MODELLING APPROACH TO ASSESS TABOO TRADE-OFFS

The small-scale tropical fishery at Nyali, Mombasa, Kenya is a social-ecological system that includes different primary stakeholders that use and impact on the natural ecosystem. McClanahan (2010) identified that a reduction in fishing intensity could result in a win-win scenario between profitability and conservation. However, this solution at the aggregate scale overlooked trade-offs with food production, employment and wellbeing of marginalised women who have limited visibility and voice in governance (Matsue et al., 2014). Daw et al. (2015) applied a participatory framework to identify and consider some of these 'taboo' trade-offs in ecosystem services and human wellbeing hidden within apparent win-win situations. First, focus group discussions with five primary stakeholder groups (fishery users) explored their perceptions of wellbeing and their dependence on the system (Abunge et al., 2013; Galafassi et al., 2017). Second, 15 years of biological and fisheries data collected from ecological monitoring, landing site surveys and online databases were assimilated through an ecological model to provide expected ecosystem responses to diverse fishing effort scenarios. Third, participatory conceptual modelling with secondary stakeholders (staff from local government and non-governmental organisations, and representatives of fishery and tourism interests) regarded as local experts, identified social and ecological linkages, feedbacks and drivers of the system. These data sources were integrated into a simplified social-ecological 'toy model' and a set of narrative scenarios of possible futures. Local learning assessment, through entry and exit questionnaires, observation and follow-up qualitative interviews, evidenced an expansion in local systemic understanding of the nature and dynamics of trade-offs. An explicit consideration of trade-offs, values and possible taboos can ultimately support socially equitable and sustainable decision making. Such a combination of participatory modelling and scenario development has the potential to enhance transparency, accountability, relevance and trustworthiness in the management of social-ecological systems (Daw et al., 2015).

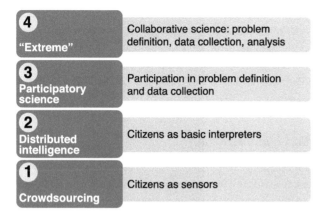

FIGURE 11.2 Levels of participation in citizen science as identified by Haklay (2013) and explored in a poverty alleviation context by Buytaert et al. (2014).

and evaluate future scenarios (see also Box 11.2). Applications of participatory modelling in the context of improving models of infectious diseases can be found in Grant et al. (2016).

New technologies can also be instrumental in facilitating participatory approaches to data processing, and need further exploration. For instance, Ramirez-Gomez et al. (2015) developed techniques based on participatory Geographic Information Systems (PGIS), combining mapping and focus group discussions, to involve indigenous peoples in the lower Caquetá River basin in Colombia in the analysis of changes in the location and stocks of provisioning ecosystem services. They recommend using PGIS in data-scarce scenarios and for building common mapping information.

Related to such participatory approaches, citizen science is also promoted as a powerful tool for interactive data processing and knowledge extraction. Although the concept is more commonly associated with data collection, citizen science can promote the involvement of stakeholders at all stages of the knowledge-generation process, including during the problem identification and analysis phases. This more inclusive form of knowledge generation has been referred to as 'extreme' citizen science (Haklay, 2013; and Figure 11.2), and is particularly appropriate in a context of sustainable development (Buytaert et al., 2014).

A potential issue with citizen science, and related participatory approaches developed within a scientific context, is their reliance on the traditional scientific method, which is not necessarily compatible with forms of indigenous knowledge that are common in a poverty context. Overcoming these issues may require more holistic approaches of inclusive knowledge generation. Collins et al. (2009) and Wei et al. (2012) pursued the building of 'learning systems' to create an incipient social learning platform to address the pitfalls of classic paradigms in water resources management, which fail to address the 'wicked' nature of policy making in regions that are characterised by large institutional complexity and informality. Such platforms tend to be less centralised and aim for a more organic and 'messy' form of learning and knowledge creation. From that perspective, such learning systems are closely aligned to the recognition of polycentricity in natural resources management systems (Buytaert et al., 2016; Lankford and Hepworth, 2010).

Knowledge dissemination and interaction

The scientific community increasingly recognises the need to improve the way in which potentially complex information is being conveyed to stakeholders (Grainger et al., 2016). This is particularly relevant in a poverty-alleviation context, in which the background and educational level of actors tend to be highly variable and insufficiently tailored information may disadvantage the poor. Knowledge dissemination activities that rely on technology or present a learning curve, such as computer-based decision-support systems and mobile phones, can run the risk of being hijacked by elites with better access and an educational advantage. In such contexts, it is paramount to co-design knowledge dissemination systems, and to evaluate the usefulness, usability and accessibility of such systems.

Zulkafli et al. (2017) implemented a comprehensive study of user-centred design of a computer-based interface to convey hydro-meteorological information in a farmer community in the Peruvian Andes (Box 11.3). Other authors have studied the evaluation of environmental information and interaction between scientists and stakeholders. For instance, Willcock et al. (2016) evaluated the relevance of ecosystem service maps and models to meet stakeholders' needs in the context of ecosystem services in sub-Saharan Africa, identifying significant deficiencies in the currently available information.

More complex issues arise when data contain large uncertainties or are more difficult for non-scientists to grasp (e.g. highly dimensional datasets such as precipitation, or abstract concepts such as biodiversity). New technologies such as interactive visualisations, infographics and social media hold promise to enhance the flow of information between actors in a complex, multi-layered social-ecological system; however, exploring their potential within the context of ecosystem service management for poverty alleviation is still in its infancy (Grainger et al., 2016). The same holds for more complex and intangible aspects of knowledge dissemination, such as trustworthiness, credibility, reliability and their impact on power relations, and poverty-alleviation efforts in general. The dynamics of social media interaction, for example, involve personalisation, amplification, polarisation and dispersion of information through networks, which is likely to create hypes and to reinforce convictions among like-minded people (Stevens et al., 2016). While some studies investigating ICT for development show a positive correlation between ICT and social capital (including boosting trust and credibility) (e.g. Thapa et al., 2012), others are much more cautionary (e.g. Ahmed, 2018).

> **BOX 11.3 USER-DRIVEN DESIGN OF A DECISION-SUPPORT SYSTEM FOR POLYCENTRIC ECOSYSTEM MANAGEMENT**
>
> Upstream/downstream water users in Lima, Peru, are adapting to water scarcity at various levels, from communities to regional decision makers. The diverse interests and interactions of decision makers result in local water and pastoral land management decisions being influenced by larger, more formal, decision-making structures beyond the community scale (Buytaert et al., 2016). Some institutions have reflected on the importance of scientific evidence to support and balance policy design, but environmental decision support systems (EDSS) are commonly single actor-oriented and science-driven (Karpouzoglou et al., 2016). Zulkafli et al. (2017) developed and applied a framework for an iterative research and collaborative design process of EDSS based on a more complete understanding of the contextual decision-making structures and practices. First, an immersive field-based discovery phase identified up to 23 different entities existing in a polycentric governance arrangement where data, information and knowledge on water resources have been generated, owned and shared separately. Second, an iterative participatory design phase leveraged the interdisciplinary nature of the involved actors and research team (for instance, visualisation for non-technical audiences, Grainger et al., 2016) for rapid conceptual design, parallel prototyping and user testing. The different users were formalised in a set of profile personas with connected interests, agendas, roles, decision-making processes and goals, and requirement criteria for useful (relevant), usable (intuitive) and unobstructed (exchangeable) information. These requirements were clustered in data-driven (e.g. mapping and monitoring), model-driven (e.g. indices) and communication- and knowledge-driven (e.g. uncodified knowledge exchange) EDSS solutions and translated into web-tools. The integration of collaborative design, user-tailoring and regional and international interests in the data and knowledge generated and owned locally could potentially shift power balances in support of polycentric ecosystem management, particularly for marginalised actors. This contrasts with top-down approaches that might have required a forced change in how decision makers access and use information (Zulkafli et al., 2017).

Conclusions

The presented evidence and insights highlight the strong potential for new technologies to support an inclusive process of knowledge co-generation on ecosystem services that benefits poverty alleviation. Here we created a framework to analyse the knowledge generation process in three stages, i.e. data collection, data processing and knowledge extraction, and knowledge communication and dissemination. The portfolio of ESPA projects has generated new approaches and evidence in each of these stages. New approaches to participatory monitoring and the development of low-cost and robust sensors can enhance participation in the data collection stage. These activities bear a strong resemblance to the concept of 'citizen science', and only recently is its potential in a context of poverty alleviation being explored.

Participatory modelling and the valorisation of indigenous knowledge are examples of approaches that promote inclusiveness in the stage of data processing and knowledge extraction from raw observations. Lastly, the increasing adoption of ICTs by the poor creates significant potential to improve the access to relevant information and its sharing between actors, thus supporting a more decentralised and participatory process. An important factor here is the need for tailored visualisation of environmental data, including the role of infographics.

Reflecting on these processes, we perceive a strong parallel between the potential for technology to support decentralised forms of evidence generation on the one hand, and the existence of polycentric governance processes in many social-ecological processes related to ecosystem services on the other. These parallels can be leveraged for poverty alleviation. Knowledge generation in social-ecological processes is a continuous and strongly iterative process, which is further enhanced by the increasingly real-time nature of observations and predictions. This can stimulate participation in knowledge generation and reduce the knowledge gap. Inevitably, such development also incurs risks that need to be evaluated and addressed, such as the re-alignment of social structures and practices because of newly introduced information and new connections between actors.

References

(ESPA outputs marked with '★')

★Abunge C, Coulthard S and Daw TM. (2013) Connecting marine ecosystem services to human well-being: insights from participatory well-being assessment in Kenya. *Ambio* 42: 1010–1021.

Ahmed Z. (2018) Explaining the unpredictability: a social capital perspective on ICT intervention. *International Journal of Information Management* 38: 175–186.

★Amoako Johnson F, Hutton CW, Hornby D, et al. (2016) Is shrimp farming a successful adaptation to salinity intrusion? A geospatial associative analysis of poverty in the populous Ganges–Brahmaputra–Meghna Delta of Bangladesh. *Sustainability Science* 11: 423–439.

Balian EV, Drius L, Eggermont H, et al. (2016) Supporting evidence-based policy on biodiversity and ecosystem services: recommendations for effective policy briefs. *Evidence and Policy* 12: 431–451.

★Buytaert W, Baez S, Bustamante M, et al. (2012) Web-based environmental simulation: bridging the gap between scientific modeling and decision-making. *Environmental Science and Technology* 46: 1971–1976.

★Buytaert W, Dewulf A, De Bièvre B, et al. (2016) Citizen science for water resources management: toward polycentric monitoring and governance? *Journal of Water Resources Planning and Management* 142: 01816002.

*Buytaert W, Zulkafli Z, Grainger S, et al. (2014) Citizen science in hydrology and water resources: opportunities for knowledge generation, ecosystem service management, and sustainable development. *Frontiers in Earth Science* 2: 26.

*Collins K, Colvin J and Ison R. (2009) Building 'learning catchments' for integrated catchment managing: designing learning systems based on experiences in the UK and South Africa. *Water Science and Technology* 59: 687–693.

*Daw TM, Coulthard S, Cheung WWL, et al. (2015) Evaluating taboo trade-offs in ecosystems services and human well-being. *Proceedings of the National Academy of Sciences* 112: 6949–6954.

Dewulf A, Craps M, Bouwen R, et al. (2005) Integrated management of natural resources: dealing with ambiguous issues, multiple actors and diverging frames. *Water Science and Technology* 52: 115–124.

Doswald N, Munroe R, Roe D, et al. (2014) Effectiveness of ecosystem-based approaches for adaptation: review of the evidence-base. *Climate and Development* 6: 185–201.

Folke C, Hahn T, Olsson P, et al. (2005) Adaptive governance of social-ecological systems. *Annual Review of Environment and Resources* 30: 441–473.

*Futter MN, Whitehead PG, Sarkar S, et al. (2015) Rainfall runoff modelling of the Upper Ganga and Brahmaputra basins using PERSiST. *Environmental Science: Processes & Impacts* 17: 1070–1081.

*Galafassi D, Daw TM, Munyi L, et al. (2017) Learning about social-ecological trade-offs. *Ecology and Society* 22: 2.

*Grainger S, Buytaert W and Mao F. (2016) Environmental data visualisation for non-scientific contexts: literature review and design framework. *Environmental Modelling and Software* 85: 299–318.

*Grant C, Lo Iacono G, Dzingirai V, et al. (2016) Moving interdisciplinary science forward: integrating participatory modelling with mathematical modelling of zoonotic disease in Africa. *Infectious Diseases of Poverty* 5: 17.

*Gross-Camp N. (2017) Tanzania's community forests: their impact on human well-being and persistence in spite of the lack of benefit. *Ecology and Society* 22: 37.

Haklay M. (2013) Citizen science and volunteered geographic information: overview and typology of participation. In: Sui D, Elwood S and Goodchild M (eds) *Crowdsourcing Geographic Knowledge: Volunteered Geographic Information (VGI) in Theory and Practice*. Dordrecht, The Netherlands: Springer Netherlands, 105–122.

*Karpouzoglou T, Zulkafli Z, Grainger S, et al. (2016) Environmental Virtual Observatories (EVOs): prospects for knowledge co-creation and resilience in the Information Age. *Current Opinion in Environmental Sustainability* 18: 40–48.

*Kirui KB, Kairo JG, Bosire J, et al. (2013) Mapping of mangrove forest land cover change along the Kenya coastline using Landsat imagery. *Ocean and Coastal Management* 83: 19–24.

Lankford B and Hepworth N. (2010) The cathedral and the bazaar: monocentric and polycentric river basin management. *Water Alternatives* 3: 82–101.

Leach M, Mearns R and Scoones I. (1999) Environmental entitlements: dynamics and institutions in community-based natural resource management. *World Development* 27: 225–247.

*Lu X, Wrathall DJ, Sundsøy PR, et al. (2016a) Unveiling hidden migration and mobility patterns in climate stressed regions: a longitudinal study of six million anonymous mobile phone users in Bangladesh. *Global Environmental Change* 38: 1–7.

*Lu X, Wrathall DJ, Sundsøy PR, et al. (2016b) Detecting climate adaptation with mobile network data in Bangladesh: anomalies in communication, mobility and consumption patterns during cyclone Mahasen. *Climatic Change* 138: 505–519.

McClanahan TR. (2010) Effects of fisheries closures and gear restrictions on fishing income in a Kenyan coral reef. *Conservation Biology* 24: 1519–1528.

Martin M, Billah M, Siddiqui T, et al. (2014) Climate-related migration in rural Bangladesh: a behavioural model. *Population and Environment* 36: 85–110.

Matsue N, Daw T and Garrett L. (2014) Women fish traders on the Kenyan coast: livelihoods, bargaining power, and participation in management. *Coastal Management* 42: 531–554.

★Ochoa-Tocachi BF, Buytaert W, De Bièvre B, et al. (2016) Impacts of land use on the hydrological response of tropical Andean catchments. *Hydrological Processes* 30: 4074–4089.

Ostrom E. (2010) Polycentric systems for coping with collective action and global environmental change. *Global Environmental Change* 20: 550–557.

Ostrom E, Burger J, Field CB, et al. (1999) Revisiting the commons: local lessons, global challenges. *Science* 284: 278–282.

★Pandeya B, Buytaert W, Zulkafli Z, et al. (2016) A comparative analysis of ecosystem services valuation approaches for application at the local scale and in data scarce regions. *Ecosystem Services* 22: 250–259.

★Ramirez-Gomez SOI, Torres-Vitolas CA, Schreckenberg K, et al. (2015) Analysis of ecosystem services provision in the Colombian Amazon using participatory research and mapping techniques. *Ecosystem Services* 13: 93–107.

Sen A. (1999) *Development as Freedom*. Oxford: Oxford University Press.

Stevens TM, Aarts N, Termeer C, et al. (2016) Social media as a new playing field for the governance of agro-food sustainability. *Current Opinion in Environmental Sustainability* 18: 99–106.

Thapa D, Sein MK and Sæbø Ø. (2012) Building collective capabilities through ICT in a mountain region of Nepal: where social capital leads to collective action. *Information Technology for Development* 18: 5–22.

★Wei Y, Ison R, Colvin J, et al. (2012) Reframing water governance: a multi-perspective study of an over-engineered catchment in China. *Journal of Environmental Planning and Management* 55: 297–318.

Wesolowski A, Eagle N, Tatem AJ, et al. (2012) Quantifying the impact of human mobility on malaria. *Science* 338: 267–270.

★Willcock S, Hooftman D, Sitas N, et al. (2016) Do ecosystem service maps and models meet stakeholders' needs? A preliminary survey across sub-Saharan Africa. *Ecosystem Services* 18: 110–117.

Wohl E, Barros A, Brunsell N, et al. (2012) The hydrology of the humid tropics. *Nature Climate Change* 2: 655–662.

★Zulkafli Z, Perez K, Vitolo C, et al. (2017) User-driven design of decision support systems for polycentric environmental resources management. *Environmental Modelling and Software* 88: 58–73.

12

PES

Payments for ecosystem services and poverty alleviation?

Mary Menton and Aoife Bennett

Introduction

Many ecosystem governance approaches seek to change land-use or natural resource use patterns in order to reduce environmental degradation. Some use command-and-control regulations or 'sticks' that restrict access to and use of ecosystems, while others employ 'incentive-based mechanisms' (or 'carrots') to change behaviours, or a combination of the two (Börner et al., 2015; Nunan et al., this volume). Incentive-based instruments are 'assumed to allow social actors more freedom to coordinate among themselves in pursuit of societal goals' (Jordan et al., 2005: 497). The umbrella of incentive-based instruments includes mechanisms ranging from subsidies and taxes to conditional transfers, and can be market or non-market based. In this chapter, we focus on one of the most ubiquitous incentive-based governance instruments applied to ecosystem services in recent years: payments for ecosystem services (PES). Some argue that there are very specific conditions necessary for PES: a voluntary agreement or contract between a buyer and a provider, conditional upon provision of a well-defined ecosystem service (as per Wunder, 2005). However, in many cases PES has become a generic term for initiatives that transfer benefits or rewards to providers/stewards of ecosystem services, whether these be via cash payments, in-kind transfers or provision of services (e.g. training in new farming techniques, access to health care). Over time, frameworks for understanding ecosystem services have evolved (see Pascual and Howe, this volume) and, in parallel, definitions of and concepts behind PES have changed. In this chapter, we explore several key questions: (i) how have definitions of PES evolved and changed over time (and what are the theoretical and practical implications)? (ii) Can environment-centred and pro-poor focused outcomes of PES projects be better harmonised towards an environmental/poverty win-win scenario? (iii) What are the power, equity and justice challenges for PES? And (iv) What are the 'lessons learned' from the theoretical and on-the-ground realities of PES to date towards effective and sustained pro-poor PES mechanisms in the future?

How have definitions of PES evolved and changed over time?

The term PES has evolved over time and is used to describe a wide range of interventions that aim to change behaviours that lead to environmental degradation through incentive-based mechanisms. PES arose from the recognition that although all humans derive benefits from 'services', such as water, the onus often falls on people in rural areas and in developing countries to steward the world's remaining natural services (WCED, 1987). For example, for people downstream in cities to have clean water, people upstream in the mountains must not contaminate it; however, this may prevent them from fishing or irrigating their lands in the most efficient ways for them, so there are opportunity costs to stewardship. Theoretically therefore, the buyer compensates or rewards the steward for protecting the ecosystem or the specific ecosystem services.

The conundrum of how to appropriately compensate stewards (ecosystem services 'providers') resulted in a steep increase in attention to the valuation of ecosystem services, for the purpose of quantifying the opportunity costs of stewardship. Much of the early literature on PES focused on questions of ecosystem services valuation, willingness-to-pay and opportunity costs (Engel et al., 2008; Pagiola et al., 2005). Over time, the focus has shifted increasingly towards social issues beyond monetary value and markets (see Box 12.1).

To date, there is consensus neither about the definition of PES nor the conditions necessary for its implementation. The most widely cited definition, by Wunder (2005), states that PES requires five key criteria to be met:

- a voluntary transaction where a
- well-defined ecosystem service (or land-use likely to secure that service) is being
- 'bought' by (at least one) buyer from a
- (at least one) provider
- if, and only if, the provider secures ecosystem service provision (conditionality).

This perspective sees PES as a means to enact the Coase Theorem, that trade in externalities can lead to efficient outcomes if transaction costs are low. However, some assert that this definition is too narrow because very few successful on-the-ground examples of such 'true-PES' actually exist. According to Engel (2016), two basic types of PES can be distinguished: Coasean PES result from a direct negotiation between ecosystem service beneficiaries and ecosystem service providers. Alternatively, Pigouvian PES resemble an environmental subsidy, where payments are made by a government agency out of specified user fees (e.g. a water charge) or taken as a tax. However, many existing and most new PES schemes represent hybrids of the two.

Although PES is often labelled a 'market-based' mechanism and critics question its 'commodity fetishism' (Kosoy and Corbera, 2010) and its dependence on neoliberal market-based incentives, in many cases PES is not market-based. Corbera et al. (2007) maintain that PES often contravenes the purist (i.e. Wunder, 2005) definition as there are no 'actual markets where ecosystem services are sold to service buyers' (p.366). The nature of ecosystem services, some of which are privately

---

BOX 12.1 EVOLUTION OF RESEARCH ON PES: CHANGING PREVALENCE OF KEYWORDS

Based on a keyword search in Web of Science carried out on 19 December 2017, we trace the changes in the proportion of articles in the PES literature that address different themes. Articles with PES in the title/abstract began to appear in 2004 and gained momentum in 2007, quickly numbering hundreds of papers per year. REDD+ (Reducing Emissions from Deforestation and Degradation) became a substantial contributor to the PES literature base from 2008. REDD+ articles appear to have peaked in 2014, yet still represent approximately half of the papers on PES and/or REDD+. Over time, papers that mention poverty and/or wellbeing have decreased in relative prevalence compared with those that look at power and/or institutions. Themes of equity and justice have grown in relative prevalence since 2008, and are now on a par with the number of papers mentioning poverty and/or wellbeing. The language of 'trade-offs' and 'win-wins' has been used in 10–15% of papers since 2012. The shift in keywords present in the PES literature reflects a change in the perceived importance of particular aspects of PES: PES is no longer put forth as a simple and efficient mechanism for protecting ecosystem services, and authors continue to debate the social context and conditions necessary for positive outcomes.

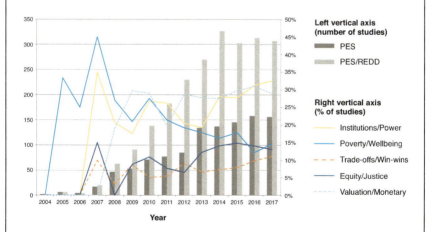

FIGURE 12.1 Evolution of PES and REDD+ publications from 2004–2017.

owned while others are public goods or communally owned, creates barriers to market conditions. In many cases, the commodity is ill-defined and governments act as intermediaries by mobilising resources from consumers to a government fund (Corbera et al., 2007).

Some assert that high transaction costs and the role of the state in defining or allocating property rights over the resources/ecosystems linked to ecosystem services means that Coase Theorem does not entirely apply to the reality of PES, which should therefore not be considered a market-based instrument (Tacconi, 2012). Additionally, case studies across the globe highlight both the methodological issues with a theoretical and practical market-based approach that involves the state, as well as cautioning against attribution of any observed changes in behaviour of the participants only to the PES (market) mechanism itself (Kumar and Muradian, 2009). Rather, these authors demonstrate that even those cases that seem stoically market-based, actually involve a myriad of specific socio-political and economic circumstances that are inherently dynamic over time and space, interacting with PES carrots and sticks in different ways that ultimately produce specific types of PES hybrids.

As a result of these observed complexities, the ecosystem services concept began to increasingly acknowledge the role of human agency, political processes and power. The PES literature has seen a shift away from adherence to 'true-PES' market-based models towards emphasis on institutions, power and equity and a widening of the concept to include what some consider to be 'PES-like' initiatives. Indeed Wunder (2015) himself expanded his definition to acknowledge many of the constraints to 'true-PES' in practice. The theoretical and practical shift in PES from a large-scale, market-based mechanism, to one which seeks to merge ecosystem service protection with poverty alleviation at a more local (project-based) level, has led to thinking about a move away from direct compensation for specific ecosystem services to one which approaches the problem with a more holistic institutional approach (Hejnowicz et al., 2015; Shelley, 2011).

The emphasis on 'payments' in PES is considered problematic by some, as many projects depend upon reciprocal agreements or 'rewards' that are not directly conditional upon measured outcomes (Whittaker et al., this volume; Kovacs et al., 2016). In some countries, the use of the term 'payments' sparks opposition to PES (e.g. Bolivia, Asquith and Vargas, 2007). A recent PES law in Peru is labelled the Law on Compensation Mechanisms for Ecosystem Services (Law 30215, June 2014) (Government of Peru, 2014) as a result of objections to the term 'payments'. Some have proposed a shift in language towards the use of the term 'Rewards for Ecosystem Service Stewardship' (Shelley, 2011) as a term that more accurately reflects the types of mechanisms carried out under the PES-umbrella.

PES is seen by some as an exchange of incentives or rewards or even reciprocal agreements (Asquith and Vargas, 2007). PES thus represents a transfer of resources (e.g. money, education, infrastructure) between social actors (e.g. individuals, governments, non-governmental organizations) that 'aims to create incentives to align individual and/or collective land use decisions with the social interest in the management of natural resources' (Muradian et al., 2010: 1205). For Kosoy and

Corbera (2010), PES could alleviate poverty by creating an 'urban–rural compact' that transfers resources from 'consumers' to 'providers'. Muradian et al. (2010) propose that economic incentives are just one of many drivers that may influence behavioural patterns in relation to land use and the stewardship of ecosystem services, such that PES must be flexible enough to account for:

- the importance of economic incentives: the relative role of the payment/transfer in guiding behaviour
- direction of transfer: extent of intermediaries' involvement in the process
- degree of commodification: extent to which the ecosystem service can be assessed/acquired in measurable quantities.

The PES literature studies such a range of interventions that the picture of what PES is, what it should be and what its impacts are becomes blurred. For example, some studies of PES include reciprocal watershed agreements (RWA), and REDD+ (Reducing Emissions from Deforestation and Degradation) was described as 'the largest PES experiment in the world' (Corbera, 2012). Whether or not RWA and REDD+ are 'true-PES', they nevertheless provide insights that are relevant to moving PES forward and which we draw on below.

The impact of payment type and conditionality on PES outcomes

Early interest in PES arose from the belief that the dependence on conditional payments made the PES model institutionally simpler and more technical in nature than Integrated Conservation and Development Projects (ICDPs), which were widespread but considered relatively ineffective (Ferraro, 2001). As outlined by Porras and Asquith (this volume), PES is often considered one form of a broader set of mechanisms called conditional transfers. Conditionality of PES requires: contracts/negotiations that are linked to measurement of performance, monitoring of said performance and rewards/sanctions based on performance (Engel et al., 2008). Yet, as Fisher (2013) highlights, conditionality is rarely enacted in full and it obscures the importance of justice outcomes. Payment based on performance means there are prerequisites to participation in PES projects that may not be available to all actors: wealth is an influencing factor in project participation (which links to concerns about power and elite capture) (Fisher, 2013). Conditionality can also be problematic for more technical reasons – the outcomes sought by PES are often multi-dimensional and difficult to measure.

It is important to distinguish between PES initiatives that condition payments based on actions (e.g. conversion to conservation agriculture; planting of trees on farms) and those that are conditional on outcomes (e.g. reductions in deforestation rates, improvements in water quality). While some projects support actions that build assets like agroforestry (Porras et al., 2013; see also Box 12.2) and apiculture (Asquith et al., 2008), others focus on restricting activities, as Shelley (2011) discusses,

> ### BOX 12.2 PES IN COSTA RICA: MANAGING TRADE-OFFS
>
> Costa Rica's PES programme is one of the earliest examples of large-scale PES. Starting in 1997, the programme paid farmers for carbon storage, watershed protection and conserving biodiversity. Payments were for actions designed to bring ecosystem service benefits but not for actual outcomes in terms of ecosystem provision.
>
> In ecological terms, the programme has been a success, covering almost 1 million ha of land since 1997 and increasing forest cover from a low of 21% in the 1980s to 50% by 2012. In socio-economic terms, the programme tried to encourage small- and medium-sized property owners by facilitating access for smaller producers. At first, areas with a low social development index were targeted, but after finding that benefits were captured by wealthier people in these areas, the system now weights applications from small (<50 ha) properties higher than others. Transaction costs for small producers were lowered by providing group contracts, decentralising the administrative offices where applications could be made and simplifying the contracts. The introduction of asset-building agroforestry and reforestation activities was more attractive to small producers than use-constraining activities like forest protection. However, smaller properties come with a trade-off as they may result in a more fragmented landscape, leading to lower ecosystem service outcomes. Another trade-off facing the programme is balancing the desire to introduce better indicators for ecosystem services against the increased cost of such monitoring systems.
>
> Source: Porras et al. (2013)

while others use a mixed approach (e.g. Bolsa Floresta in Brazil, Viana, 2008). Indeed as Shelley (2011) points out, in some cases, it may be more straightforward to monitor actions and behaviours instead of outcomes, such that true conditionality can become prohibitively expensive. For example, monitoring the number of trees a household planted along a riparian zone is easier than monitoring water quality and attributing changes to a particular household's actions.

Some argue that projects should 'bundle' services so that several ecosystem services and multiple social aspects could be included in the same project (Hejnowicz et al., 2015). Others argue that it is better to 'stack' them, whereby separate payments/schemes are made for different ecosystem services from the same place (Reed et al., 2017). Given the interconnectedness of ecosystem services and processes, bundling, stacking and single-service projects need to address risks of double-counting and additionality in project design and implementation in order to maintain environmental impact and economic efficiency (Hejnowicz et al., 2015).

PES initiatives also differ in the ways they distribute payments/rewards: some are individual/household based (e.g. China's SLCP, Liu et al., 2010; Costa Rica's national PES, Porras et al., 2013), others focus on community/collective rewards (e.g. Mexico's hydrological PES project in ejidos, Kerr et al., 2014) and others implement a combination (e.g. Bolsa Floresta, Viana, 2008). In cases where landscape-level changes are sought, collectively distributed payments/rewards may be more realistic than household/individual payments (Kerr et al., 2014). Kaczan et al. (2017) found that group participation in design and the presence of group-coordinating mechanisms increased the impact of PES projects and helped reduce the free-rider effect and other problems inherent in collective rewards. In their Agent Based Model of the potential to use agglomeration payments (where participants receive bonus payments when a neighbour joins the project) for PES schemes focused on conservation agriculture, Bell et al. (2016) found that agglomeration payments increased adoption and efficiency by decreasing the cost of payments and monitoring.

Furthermore, not all land-use/resource-use decisions are linked to rewards, and changes in these behaviours cannot always be 'compensated' with payments/rewards. Keane et al. (2016) found that PES projects assume that behavioural changes can be adequately compensated, but this is often not the case, particularly for women and other marginalised groups. Payments are often based on opportunity costs that are calculated without attention to the social and cultural values of ecosystem services, and based on static/baseline household poverty levels which mask changes in opportunity costs over time (Van Hecken et al., 2015). In some cases, payments fail to cover the calculated opportunity costs (Kosoy et al., 2007), let alone the more nuanced interpretations of the 'cost' of changing behaviours.

Pro-poor vs environment-centred PES: poverty alleviation as co-benefit, a pre-requisite or a cause of trade-offs?

Even though some of the earliest examples of PES included poverty alleviation as specific objectives or assumed co-benefits, some authors insist that PES was conceptualised 'as a mechanism to improve the efficiency of natural resource management, and not as a mechanism for poverty reduction' (Pagiola et al., 2005: 239). According to Wunder (2013: 231), the shift towards inclusion of pro-poor objectives in PES arose because 'While user-financed PES programs tend to focus on their environmental goals, government-financed programs often *de facto* come to politically drift into win-win spheres of multiple side-objectives, such as poverty alleviation, regional development, or electoral motives.' Some believe that there are inevitable trade-offs between the two objectives of environmental effectiveness and poverty alleviation, and hesitate to endorse a win-win discourse (Engel, 2016; Pagiola et al., 2005; Vira et al., 2012). Nevertheless, Pagiola et al. (2005) conclude that there can be important synergies between PES and poverty reduction when programme design is well thought out and local conditions are favourable.

Despite a lack of consensus regarding the pro-poor origins of PES, concern over its wellbeing outcomes is at the core of many papers on PES. Sikor (2013) highlights concerns over the 'justices and injustices' linked to ecosystem services, and finds that the design of PES can have different justice outcomes (also see Dawson et al., this volume). According to Pascual et al. (2014) (among others), procedural fairness in PES can promote synergies between environmental and equity objectives so that PES can be socially progressive and can successfully integrate environmental and poverty alleviation goals. Those prioritising environmental outcomes tend to see participation as a transaction cost whereas a procedural justice lens would require participation (Fisher, 2013).

The debates around socio-environmental safeguards and co-benefits in REDD+ are particularly relevant to questions around pro-poor vs pro-environment outcomes. While REDD+ could bring income to the poor, the poor run the risk of suffering from elite capture, loss of access to land and lack of voice in decision-making (Peskett et al., 2008). There are concerns that national REDD+ programmes could 'recentralise' control of forest and land, thereby negatively affecting local peoples' rights and livelihoods (Phelps et al., 2010). Tenure security and effective participation of local communities are seen as means to ensure both pro-poor and pro-environment outcomes (Chhatre et al., 2012). If REDD+ ignores the capacity of local people to contribute to local development, it could repeat the environmental vs poverty trade-offs found in previous schemes (e.g. ICDPs, land-use policies) (Pokorny et al., 2013). Visseren-Hamakers et al. (2012) assert that these non-carbon values are critical to the legitimacy and effectiveness of REDD+ and should be seen as prerequisites and not 'co-benefits'.

However, in a systematic review of the literature, Samii et al. (2014: 7) found 'little reason for optimism for the potential of current PES approaches to achieve both environmental conservation and poverty reduction benefits jointly'. Pokorny et al. (2013) found that forest conservation initiatives in the Amazon that focused on environmental objectives tended to create barriers to forest use, while pro-poor initiatives showed ambivalent results for environmental outcomes. A randomised control trial of an avoided deforestation PES project in Uganda found environmental benefits (lower rates of tree cover loss in project communities compared with controls), but ambiguous results for poverty (household expenditures neither increased nor decreased) (Jayachandran et al., 2017). Yet some studies found benefits for both the environment and poverty alleviation. Liu et al. (2010) found improved income for farmers in China's SLCP which had some success in converting agricultural lands back to forest. In Cambodia, Clements et al. (2010) found increased income from a bird-nest protection programme, with simultaneous increases in bird populations.

Beyond the question of win-wins vs trade-offs, it is still unclear whether or not PES leads to pro-poor outcomes. In their review, Börner et al. (2017) found no consistent trend in poverty alleviation impacts. While aggregate-level evaluations may indicate positive/negative outcomes, assessments of the poverty alleviation components of PES initiatives must recognise that there are likely to be winners and losers, and any indicators of wellbeing must be disaggregated to account for differentiated outcomes (Daw et al., 2011).

Power, equity and justice: who participates? Who wins?

PES is inherently political (Van Hecken et al., 2015). As Muradian et al. (2013) assert, PES is 'part of broader structures of power.' Different groups can influence the design and implementation of PES payment schemes, thereby influencing their effectiveness and distributional outcomes (Muradian et al., 2013). The 'providers' of ecosystem services comprise a range of actors, from rural households who – for example – maintain forest cover, to communities involved in watershed protection to developing countries whose reductions in deforestation are rewarded under REDD+. Participation of different groups in PES, and barriers to participation, are at the centre of many concerns about equity and justice in PES (see below and Dawson et al., this volume). Intermediaries, who facilitate interactions between 'buyers' and 'providers', play a fundamental role in PES project design and implementation. Participation of government actors in PES often comes in the form of an intermediary due to their role in assigning land rights allocation and in monitoring relationships between private sector 'buyers' and local citizen 'providers'. In some cases, government institutions act as the intermediary in negotiating the terms of contracts, while in others this role falls to civil society organisations. In all cases, effective and flexible institutions are important for PES implementation on the ground (Hejnowicz et al., 2015).

Given their role as facilitators and brokers, intermediaries are in a position of power in determining PES project design, objectives and who benefits. For example, in the 'Uganda Trees for Global Benefit' project, the project proponent (the intermediary) was a conservation organisation and chose indigenous tree species of lower market value than exotics thus improving environmental outcomes at the cost of local livelihood benefits (Schreckenberg et al., 2013). Vatn (2010) highlights that intermediaries are powerful in determining the conditions for participation in/benefit from PES, and Corbera et al. (2009) found that half of the payments linked to PES are going to intermediaries and verifiers.

Access to benefits from PES is often disproportionately accrued by households who are already better-off than the poorest households in a given community. Poudyal et al. (2016) found elite capture of resources in a REDD+ project in Madagascar, where local institutions were used to determine 'project-affected parties' who would/would not receive safeguards compensation as part of the establishment of a protected area linked to the REDD+ project. Similar challenges faced a project in Uganda, where poorer households were unable to participate in a tree-planting project due to lack of access to funds to cover upfront costs (Peskett et al., 2011).

For Ishihara et al. (2017) it is essential to analyse another layer of socio-ecological complexity: agency and power relations that arise from PES. Ecosystem service providers become 'institutional bricoleurs' who draw on social and cultural arrangements and institutional contexts to build new institutions that are adapted to their local contexts (Ishihara et al., 2017). Institutional bricolage thus challenges the view of actors as powerless victims of institutional change. Van Hecken et al. (2015) point to the flaws in the discourse that PES institutions can be 'designed to fit', given the complex power structures and social norms within which PES must operate. Locatelli et al. (2014) highlight the potential for PES to destabilise local institutions.

REDD+ has elicited concern regarding its impact on equity and power dynamics at both local and international scales, leading to worries over the potential for dispossession of both the lands and livelihoods of indigenous peoples (Mahanty and McDermott, 2013). The McDermott et al. (2013) equity framework has provided a useful lens to assess equity in REDD+, PES and other similar initiatives. Schreckenberg et al. (2013) applied the framework to a study of a carbon project in Uganda, and found a clear bias towards participation by better-off farmers in the project. Applying the framework to REDD+ in Indonesia, Ituarte-Lima et al. (2014) highlight the structural obstacles to participation of marginalised groups. Projects that require land ownership as a prerequisite for participation will exclude landless households, and consequently the poorest and most marginalised. In addition to being excluded from some projects, the landless poor can be impacted negatively if PES programmes restrict their access to rights or resources (Tacconi, 2012).

While some point to REDD+ safeguards as an example of best practice to mitigate some of these power imbalances and resulting inequity of the distribution of benefits, safeguards will not be enough to ensure that projects bring livelihood benefits to the poorest and most marginalised groups. Conceptualised as mechanisms that make sure projects 'do-no-harm', they do not require positive benefits per se (Sikor, 2013). As highlighted above, safeguard processes can be susceptible to elite capture and exclusion of marginalised groups (Poudyal et al., 2016). Mechanisms like FPIC (Free, Prior and Informed Consent) can help ensure consultations of local people and build on lessons from other initiatives/sectors (e.g. mining, certification), but are often carried out without the adequate time-frames, methodological flexibility and participatory learning that is needed (Mahanty and McDermott, 2013).

PES schemes are commonly developed from the top-down by governments, conservation agencies and NGOs, or developed with only partial involvement of a narrow range of stakeholders (Reed et al., 2017). However, bottom-up collaborative PES projects are increasingly promoted to address concerns about social justice, elite and/or regulatory capture and, particularly, for poverty alleviation (Vatn, 2010). Thus, a place-based approach is becoming particularly significant for PES.

Lessons learned: counterfactuals and local context as the way forward?

Our synthesis of three reviews of case studies evaluating different aspects of PES schemes such as social, environmental, economic and institutional dynamics

(Ezzine-de-Blas et al., 2016; Hejnowicz et al., 2014; Samii et al., 2014) revealed that none could find more than 55 papers that fit their criteria for inclusion. Several sets of scholars tried to run statistical models on PES impact evaluation results, but almost all of them recognised that their own strategies were severely impaired by the small sample size (ibid.). The heterogeneity of results outlined in earlier sections further complicates efforts to generalise. There is simply not enough empirical or counterfactual evidence to be able to glean solid generalised conclusions with relation to best PES theory and practice in order to have any standard procedures. Understanding empirical patterns emerging from the growing body of case studies worldwide (and indeed increasing the number of such reports) could be the best way forward to help us gain new insights for policies and best practices.

Although generalised conclusions about PES design and implementation are not possible at this point in time, some lessons have been learned that are relevant to achieving pro-poor and pro-environment PES:

Context matters

Many authors point to the importance of local context in design and implementation of PES schemes, and the effect of context (in all the forms discussed in this chapter) on PES outcomes (Poudyal, 2017; Rodríguez-Robayo and Merino-Perez, 2017). As Poudyal (2017) found in his review of ESPA's research on PES, locally adapted approaches are, to date, the most successful. Ezzine-de-Blas et al. (2016) highlight the importance of customised design of PES, and Börner et al. (2017) point to the importance of accounting for locally specific contextual dimensions (e.g. politics, institutions, pre-existing policies) in project design.

In order to understand how to create PES initiatives that provide win-wins, we need to recognise the trade-off between blueprints that can be implemented at a wider scale and the creation of efficient, effective and equitable PES models that are adapted to local contexts (Rodríguez-Robayo and Merino-Perez, 2017), and work with existing institutions in order to design PES but also recognise how existing power structures and social norms embedded within those institutions can influence pro-poor/equity outcomes (Van Hecken et al., 2015). The challenge lies in identifying the 'appropriate (hybrid, context-dependent and adaptive) institutional arrangements that can ensure optimal resource use, beneficial collective action and hence more equitable and ecologically sustainable governance' (Van Hecken et al., 2015: 119).

Language matters

The language of PES is important (Shelley, 2011). PES has been used as an umbrella term for many different types of interventions and project designs such that reviews of PES outcomes are clouded by their comparison of 'apples and oranges', which makes generalisations difficult and brings risks for social and environmental outcomes, particularly for the poorest and most marginalised. There has been a shift away from seeing PES as market-based payments towards more holistic rewards for stewardship. While there is variability, most PES/PES-like initiatives are voluntary and based on conditional rewards for changes in behaviour. The degree of conditionality and the type of reward/payment has impacts on both environmental and poverty/equity outcomes (Shelley, 2011). 'True-PES' may be an elusive beast without many real-world examples of its implementation but there are risks, particularly to the poorest and most marginalised, to lumping a wide range of interventions and projects designs under the 'PES-like' umbrella.

Equitable outcomes matter

PES has evolved to reward people who make livelihood-altering changes to how they manage the land for environmental stewardship. These stewards represent a wide range of actors with their own relationships with nature, and need to be rewarded (or incentivised) in ways that are appropriate to their context (social, cultural, economic, political) and provide just outcomes. Pro-poor and justice outcomes should not be a 'co-benefit' but instead a prerequisite. In order to achieve pro-poor/justice outcomes, interventions must be designed with pro-poor and equity-based objectives as central tenets from the outset. In particular, projects must address both direct and indirect impacts on the poorest and most marginalised households.

Power matters

Understanding existing power structures is essential to making pro-poor and equitable PES a reality. PES can increase long-term sustainability, local legitimacy and agency by emphasising local priorities and bottom-up project design which is adapted to local contexts. It also must recognise and explicitly address power dynamics and the roles of both informal and formal institutions and elite capture in influencing behaviours that affect ecosystem services, but also in determining access to ecosystem services and benefits from PES.

References

(ESPA outputs marked with '★')

Asquith N and Vargas MT. (2007) *Fair Deals for Watershed Services in Bolivia*. London: IIED.
Asquith NM, Vargas MT and Wunder S. (2008) Selling two environmental services: in-kind payments for bird habitat and watershed protection in Los Negros, Bolivia. *Ecological Economics* 65: 675–684.
★Bell A, Parkhurst G, Droppelmann K, et al. (2016) Scaling up pro-environmental agricultural practice using agglomeration payments: proof of concept from an agent-based model. *Ecological Economics* 126: 32–41.
Börner J, Baylis K, Corbera E, et al. (2017) The effectiveness of payments for environmental services. *World Development* 96: 359–374.

Börner J, Marinho E and Wunder S. (2015) Mixing carrots and sticks to conserve forests in the Brazilian Amazon: a spatial probabilistic modeling approach. *PLoS ONE* 10: p.e0116846.

Chhatre A, Lakhanpal S, Larson AM, et al. (2012) Social safeguards and co-benefits in REDD+: a review of the adjacent possible. *Current Opinion in Environmental Sustainability* 4: 654–660.

Clements T, John A, Nielsen K, et al. (2010) Payments for biodiversity conservation in the context of weak institutions: comparison of three programs from Cambodia. *Ecological Economics* 69: 1283–1291.

Corbera E. (2012) Problematizing REDD+ as an experiment in payments for ecosystem services. *Current Opinion in Environmental Sustainability* 4: 612–619.

Corbera E, Brown K and Adger WN. (2007) The equity and legitimacy of markets for ecosystem services. *Development and Change* 38: 587–613.

Corbera E, Soberanis CG and Brown K. (2009) Institutional dimensions of payments for ecosystem services: an analysis of Mexico's carbon forestry programme. *Ecological Economics* 68: 743–761.

★Daw T, Brown K, Rosendo S, et al. (2011) Applying the ecosystem services concept to poverty alleviation: the need to disaggregate human well-being. *Environmental Conservation* 38: 370–379.

Engel S. (2016) The Devil in the detail: a practical guide on designing payments for environmental services. *International Review of Environmental and Resource Economics* 9: 131–177.

Engel S, Pagiola S and Wunder S. (2008) Designing payments for environmental services in theory and practice: an overview of the issues. *Ecological Economics* 65: 663–674.

Ezzine-de-Blas D, Wunder S, Ruiz-Pérez M, et al. (2016) Global patterns in the implementation of payments for environmental services. *PLoS ONE* 11: e0149847.

Ferraro PJ. (2001) Global habitat protection: limitations of development interventions and a role for conservation performance payments. *Conservation Biology* 15: 990–1000.

★Fisher JA. (2013) Justice implications of conditionality in payments for ecosystem services: a case study from Uganda. In: Sikor T (ed.) *The Justices and Injustices of Ecosystem Services*. Abingdon, UK: Routledge, 21–45.

Government of Peru. (2014) Ley 30215. Ley de Mecanismos de Retribucion por Servicios Ecosistemicos.

★Hejnowicz AP, Kennedy H, Rudd MA, et al. (2015) Harnessing the climate mitigation, conservation and poverty alleviation potential of seagrasses: prospects for developing blue carbon initiatives and payment for ecosystem service programmes. *Frontiers in Marine Science* 2: 32.

Hejnowicz AP, Raffaelli DG, Rudd MA, et al. (2014) Evaluating the outcomes of payments for ecosystem services programmes using a capital asset framework. *Ecosystem Services* 9: 83–97.

Ishihara H, Pascual U and Hodge I. (2017) Dancing with storks: the role of power relations in payments for ecosystem services. *Ecological Economics* 139: 45–54.

★Ituarte-Lima C, McDermott CL and Mulyani M. (2014) Assessing equity in national legal frameworks for REDD plus: the case of Indonesia. *Environmental Science and Policy* 44: 291–300.

Jayachandran S, De Laat J, Lambin EF, et al. (2017) Cash for carbon: a randomized trial of payments for ecosystem services to reduce deforestation. *Science* 357: 267–273.

Jordan A, Wurzel RKW and Zito A. (2005) The rise of 'new' policy instruments in comparative perspective: has governance eclipsed government? *Political Studies* 53: 477–496.

Kaczan D, Pfaff A, Rodriguez L, et al. (2017) Increasing the impact of collective incentives in payments for ecosystem services. *Journal of Environmental Economics and Management* 86: 48–67.

*Keane A, Gurd H, Kaelo D, et al. (2016) Gender differentiated preferences for a community-based conservation initiative. *PLoS ONE* 11: e0152432.

Kerr JM, Vardhan M and Jindal R. (2014) Incentives, conditionality and collective action in payment for environmental services. *International Journal of the Commons* 8: 595–616.

Kosoy N and Corbera E. (2010) Payments for ecosystem services as commodity fetishism. *Ecological Economics* 69: 1228–1236.

Kosoy N, Martinez-Tuna M, Muradian R, et al. (2007) Payments for environmental services in watersheds: insights from a comparative study of three cases in Central America. *Ecological Economics* 61: 446–455.

*Kovacs EK, Kumar C, Agarwal C, et al. (2016) The politics of negotiation and implementation: a reciprocal water access agreement in the Himalayan foothills, India. *Ecology and Society* 21: 37.

Kumar P and Muradian R, eds. (2009) *Payment for Ecosystem Services (Ecological Economics and Human Well-Being)*. Oxford: Oxford University Press.

*Liu C, Lu J and Yin R. (2010) An estimation of the effects of China's priority forestry programs on farmers' income. *Environmental Management* 45: 526–540.

*Locatelli T, Binet T, Kairo JG, et al. (2014) Turning the tide: how blue carbon and payments for ecosystem services (PES) might help save mangrove forests. *Ambio* 43: 981–995.

*McDermott M, Mahanty S and Schreckenberg K. (2013) Examining equity: a multi-dimensional framework for assessing equity in payments for ecosystem services. *Environmental Science and Policy* 33: 416–427.

*Mahanty S and McDermott CL. (2013) How does Free, Prior and Informed Consent (FPIC) impact social equity? Lessons from mining and forestry and their implications for REDD+. *Land Use Policy* 35: 406–416.

*Muradian R, Arsel M, Pellegrini L, et al. (2013) Payments for ecosystem services and the fatal attraction of win-win solutions. *Conservation Letters* 6: 274–279.

Muradian R, Corbera E, Pascual U, et al. (2010) Reconciling theory and practice: an alternative conceptual framework for understanding payments for environmental services. *Ecological Economics* 69: 1202–1208.

Pagiola S, Arcenas A and Platais G. (2005) Can payments for environmental services help reduce poverty? An exploration of the issues and the evidence to date from Latin America. *World Development* 33: 237–253.

Pascual U, Phelps J, Garmendia E, et al. (2014) Social equity matters in payments for ecosystem services. *BioScience* 64: 1027–1036.

Peskett L, Huberman D, Bowen E, et al. (2008) Making REDD work for the poor. Poverty Environment Partnership.

Peskett L, Schreckenberg K and Brown J. (2011) Institutional approaches for carbon financing in the forest sector: learning lessons for REDD+ from forest carbon projects in Uganda. *Environmental Science and Policy* 14: 216–229.

Phelps J, Webb EL and Agrawal A. (2010) Does REDD+ threaten to recentralize forest governance? *Science* 328: 312–313.

Pokorny B, Scholz I and de Jong W. (2013) REDD plus for the poor or the poor for REDD plus? About the limitations of environmental policies in the Amazon and the potential of achieving environmental goals through pro-poor policies. *Ecology and Society* 18: 3.

Porras I, Barton DN, Miranda M, et al. (2013) Learning from 20 years of payments for ecosystem services in Costa Rica. London: International Institute for Environment and Development.

*Poudyal M. (2017) Ensuring participatory and pro-poor Payment for Ecosystem Services (PES) schemes: insights from ESPA research. *ESPA Policy and Practice Briefing*. Edinburgh, UK: Ecosystem Services for Poverty Alleviation (ESPA) Programme.

*Poudyal M, Ramamonjisoa B, Hockley N, et al. (2016) Can REDD+ social safeguards reach the 'right' people? Lessons from Madagascar. *Global Environmental Change* 37: 31–42.

Reed MS, Allen K, Attlee A, et al. (2017) A place-based approach to payments for ecosystem services. *Global Environmental Change* 43: 92–106.

Rodríguez-Robayo KJ and Merino-Perez L. (2017) Contextualizing context in the analysis of payment for ecosystem services. *Ecosystem Services* 23: 259–267.

Samii C, Lisiecki M, Kulkarni P, et al. (2014) Effects of Payment for Environmental Services (PES) on deforestation and poverty in low and middle income countries: a systematic review. *Campbell Systematic Reviews* 2014: 11.

*Schreckenberg K, Mwayafu D and Nyamutale R. (2013) Finding equity in carbon sequestration. A case study of the Trees for Global Benefits project, Uganda. Uganda Coalition for Sustainable Development.

Shelley BG. (2011) What should we call instruments commonly known as payments for environmental services? A review of the literature and a proposal. *Annals of the New York Academy of Sciences* 1219: 209–225.

*Sikor T, ed. (2013) *The Justices and Injustices of Ecosystem Services*. Abingdon, UK: Routledge.

Tacconi L. (2012) Redefining payments for environmental services. *Ecological Economics* 73: 29–36.

Van Hecken G, Bastiaensen J and Windey C. (2015) Towards a power-sensitive and socially-informed analysis of payments for ecosystem services (PES): addressing the gaps in the current debate. *Ecological Economics* 120: 117–125.

Vatn A. (2010) An institutional analysis of payments for environmental services. *Ecological Economics* 69: 1245–1252.

Viana VM. (2008) Bolsa Floresta: um instrumento inovador para a promoção da saúde em comunidades tradicionais na Amazônia. *Estudos Avançados* 22: 143–153.

*Vira B, Adams B, Agarwal C, et al. (2012) Negotiating trade-offs: choices about ecosystem services for poverty alleviation. *Economic and Political Weekly* 47: 67–75.

Visseren-Hamakers IJ, McDermott C, Vijge MJ, et al. (2012) Trade-offs, co-benefits and safeguards: current debates on the breadth of REDD+. *Current Opinion in Environmental Sustainability* 4: 646–653.

WCED. (1987) *Our Common Future: Report of the World Commission on Environment and Development (WCED)*. Oxford: Oxford University Press.

Wunder S. (2005) Payments for environmental services: some nuts and bolts. *Occasional Paper No. 42*. Bogor, Indonesia: CIFOR.

Wunder S. (2013) When payments for environmental services will work for conservation. *Conservation Letters* 6: 230–237.

Wunder S. (2015) Revisiting the concept of payments for environmental services. *Ecological Economics* 117: 234–243.

13
SCALING-UP CONDITIONAL TRANSFERS FOR ENVIRONMENTAL PROTECTION AND POVERTY ALLEVIATION

Ina Porras and Nigel Asquith

Introduction

In this chapter we assess the potential of conditional transfer (CT) schemes (including payments for ecosystem services (PES)) to support both poverty alleviation and environmental protection. We start with the observation that PES is not a stand-alone concept that was recently developed within the conservation movement. Rather, PES is a form of CT with a strong environmental component (Ma et al., 2017; Rodríguez et al., 2011) that in practice often operates alongside other policy instruments (Barton et al., 2017). We ground our arguments in the extensive global experiences in conditional transfers for social protection, and in particular the large-scale public works programmes that have already had important environmental impacts (Devereux, 2009; Kakwani et al., 2005; Koohi-Kamali, 2010; McCord, 2013).

The underlying questions that we seek to answer in this chapter are 'what shape are PES programmes taking in practice, and how can experiences from social protection inform poverty alleviation in PES?' To answer these questions, we draw lessons from conditional transfer schemes, both social and environmental, that have managed to achieve scale by moving beyond pilots or projects into established programmes. We thus use scale as an indicator of the potential to achieve important programmatic impacts for both people and the environment, not as an indicator of geographical reach. We first revisit the conceptual links between CT and PES, poverty alleviation and the conditions that enable these schemes to emerge and achieve scale. We then explore in more depth a series of programmes that have used conditionality to reach scale. Finally, we draw comparisons across the cases, highlighting lessons and identifying gaps where future research can support better decision making.

Conditional transfers and PES

CTs are social benefits used by governments to address welfare (Devereux, 2009). They are usually targeted to individuals economically at risk, chronically poor and/or socially vulnerable. Already in use for many years, they have also been widely evaluated. A wealth of knowledge has been produced on the way that conditionality affects outcomes (see for example, Abdoulayi et al., 2017; Rodríguez et al., 2011). CTs are designed to have short-term impacts on wellbeing (direct cash injection) and long-term impacts (improving health of people), and potential multiplier benefits across the economy such as pushing the demand for better education facilities (Kakwani et al., 2005).

As a relatively new policy instrument, PES schemes have attracted a lot of academic attention. PES has been defined in many different ways (Wunder, 2015; also see Menton and Bennett, this volume). However, few authors have focused on the profound conceptual similarities between CTs and PES (Ma et al., 2017), and the fact that in practice, PES is almost always a *de facto* subsidy paid as a conditional transfer.

Given their conceptual similarities, there is significant potential for cross-learning from CTs to PES. Indeed, some CTs, such as South Africa's Public Works Programme, have environmental conditions attached, such as removing invasive species in waterways, planting trees and engaging in watershed conservation. However, these CT programmes tend to be managed by social planning institutions, and so their environmental components are not always effective. In contrast, PES programmes tend to have built-in rural development objectives, but in practice often fail to effectively alleviate poverty (Börner et al., 2017). Notwithstanding these different foci, we argue that the only conceptual difference between CTs and PES is that the latter highlights the direct or indirect link between the recipients of the subsidy, and the payers of the transfer – i.e. the users who benefit from environmental services (e.g. hydroelectricity, water utilities, tourism) (Ma et al., 2017; Porras et al., 2016; Rodríguez et al., 2011), and thus incorporates the sense of an 'exchange' or 'market' into the otherwise non-market-based conditonal transfer model (Figure 13.1).

Might the conditionality of PES programmes hinder their ability to reduce poverty?

The conditions imposed by PES can, *de facto*, exclude poor and vulnerable people, or affect their access to natural resources (Sikor, 2013). Some requirements, notoriously land titles or minimum plot size, preclude or reduce the participation of many smallholders (Grillos, 2017). Other limitations are less tangible, such as access to inputs or know-how. For example, a woman-headed household without access to water nearby will struggle to carry enough water to plant and care for trees in a reforestation programme. The strict regulations of international carbon markets with regard to additionality and monitoring can be a burden to participants in these projects, who must constantly measure and manage trees (Fisher, 2013).

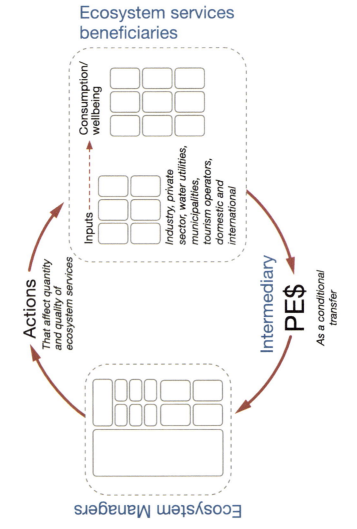

FIGURE 13.1 Conditionality, PES and Poverty Alleviation.

Technical and capacity limitations like these are equally common in social protection programmes, and much can be learned from their strategies in the design of realistic expectations. Importantly, conditions imposed on the 'ultra-poor' can actually have a negative effect and add to their burden, and it may be necessary to consider lifting some of the conditions attached to PES. An evaluation of the Malawi Social Cash Transfer Programme showed that unconditional transfers can be successful in helping very poor households improve their livelihoods (Abdoulayi et al., 2017). However, it is as yet unknown whether unconditional PES might be effective.

The conditionality element is what appears to make PES politically attractive. Conditionality offers a simple way to link policy (e.g. payment) to relatively simple outcomes (e.g. number of hectares of forest protected, number of jobs created). That said, linking conditionality to actual delivery of ecosystem services adds more complexity in terms of risk management and monitoring (discussed later in this chapter). However, while conditionality might not help affect behaviour of the ultra-poor, or the wealthy (who are able to comply with regulations without incentives), CTs appear to have great potential to change the behaviour of the medium-poor who have some access to and control of resources, and for whom the incentive levels may be a sufficient motivator (Rodríguez et al., 2011).

Selection of case studies

We looked at three types of schemes to evaluate how CT and PES programmes have managed to reach scale, and to assess whether lessons from CTs for social protection can help design programmes for the maintenance of ecosystem services:

Social conditional transfer programmes, such as the South African Environmental Public Works Programme. Although focused on social outcomes such as jobs and poverty alleviation, some programmes have had large-scale environmental impacts.

'Hybrid' CT/PES programmes, such as the Bolsa Floresta programme in Brazil, which combine protection of ecosystem services with social programmes targeting poor and vulnerable people.

PES programmes, both national top-down programmes such as the China Sloping Lands Conversion within the Eco Compensation Programme, and bottom-up initiatives such as payments for mangrove protection in Kenya.

Table 13.1 describes our key cases, which were selected because they are ongoing, have already achieved impacts at scale, and have both environmental and social objectives. Our selection includes projects at national/regional programmes (scale-up), as well as community projects that have expanded to other places (scale-out). Although we discuss all the cases in Table 13.1, we focus especially on the ongoing initiatives that have been studied under the ESPA programme (i.e. *Watershared*, and Community Carbon in Kenya, Uganda and Mexico). In addition, we incorporate relevant lessons from other cases such as the Mexican Payments for Hydrological Services Programme.

TABLE 13.1 List of case studies

Programme	Summary	Scale	References
Environmental Public Works Programme, South Africa (Social CT)	Provides jobs for vulnerable groups such as low-income workers, single-parent families and HIV/Aids-affected people. Alleviates poverty through provision of temporary work and skills development on watershed enhancement projects involving removal of invasive alien plants.	About US$33 million/year from central government's Social Responsibility and environmental portfolio. About 30,000 jobs/year, and 1 million hectares of invasive alien species cleared.	(Marais and Wannenburgh, 2008; Department of Environmental Affairs, 2016; Turpie et al., 2008)
Jatka conservation programme, Bangladesh (Hybrid CT/PES)	Combines prohibition (temporal fishing restriction) with in-kind (rice) payment to fisher families. An increased number of mature hilsa fish hatchlings and juveniles have been matched with noticeable impacts on supply chains.	US$23 million, funded by the government through the Vulnerable Group Feeding programme, with 223,000 families involved across 88 sub-districts in Bangladesh	(Islam et al., 2016; Porras et al., 2017b)
Bolsa Floresta programme, Brazil (Hybrid CT/PES)	Mix of cash and income-generating activities support; group associations and investment in social infrastructures. Combines multiple streams of funding from public and private sectors to make transfers at household and community level to conserve forests in Amazonas. Participants reduce deforestation and forest fires, and send their children to school.	Over US$1 million/year, or about US$70,000 for each of the 15 participating Amazon reserves. It involves over 30,000 people in remote areas, and has contributed to 12% reduction in deforestation relative to the beginning of the programme.	(Bakkegaard and Wunder, 2014; Sills et al., 2014)

Watershared in the Andes (Hybrid CT/PES)	In-kind conditional transfers as 'tokens of appreciation' that strengthen pro-conservation social norms. Grassroots-led, reciprocal agreements emerging from out-scaling successful scheme in Bolivia. Model focuses on publicly recognising individuals who contribute to the common good.	Fifty Bolivian municipalities have adopted *Watershared*, involving 5,635 upstream farmers and 245,000 water users transferring US$0.5 million/year. The model has been copied in Ecuador, Colombia and Peru.	(Asquith, 2013, 2016)
China Sloping Lands Conversion Programme (SLCP) (PES)	Combination of cash and in-kind payments throughout history of the programme. Innovative top-down and decentralised design to manage very large scales. The 'poverty' agenda is gaining importance.	Over US$69 billion and 32 million households since 1999	(Duan et al., 2015; Li et al., 2015; Liu and Lan, 2015)
Costa Rica (PES)	Direct cash transfers to private landowners for 5-year contracts for forest protection, reforestation, forest management and agroforestry. Relies on partnerships with local organisations for technical support.	US$30 million per year from central budget, mostly through earmarked revenues from fuel and water taxes. About 15,000 contracts signed by 2014.	(Porras et al., 2013; Rugtveit, 2012)
Trees for Global Benefits, (Uganda) Scolel-Te, (Mexico); Payments for mangrove protection (Kenya) (PES)	Cash payments from carbon sales support reforestation, agroforestry and conservation and rehabilitation of mangroves. Starting as single projects, many now seek to scale up by grouping smallholders to sell carbon offsets, and linking to the government and the national REDD+ strategies.	Uganda has issued over 1 million carbon offsets involving over 5300 farmers. Mexico's Scolel-Te project has issued almost 520,000 tonnes of carbon dioxide equivalent (TCO2e), working with 1,280 smallholders in 9 communities. The Kenya project generates about US$38,000/year.	(Rainforest Alliance, 2014; Locatelli et al., 2014; Wells et al., 2017)

Enabling conditions to scale up CTs to maintain ecosystem services

There are a considerable number of descriptions of how PES has been implemented in practice (e.g. Asquith and Wunder (2008), and more recently a practical guide by Engel (2016)). We combined these publications with the practical knowledge of CT/PES practitioners and researchers, brought together at an international workshop to share practical experience on the enabling conditions for PES (Porras et al., 2016, 2017a). We also draw on a series of key-informant interviews at two international conferences in China (the 5th and 6th International Eco-Compensation Conferences in Kunming (2016) and Chongqing (2017), respectively). In each case, we asked CT and PES practitioners to summarise the key conditions that helped their programmes emerge, be implemented and thrive.

Political support

Political support is a necessary condition to raise the profile of projects and, most importantly, to guarantee the budget allocation necessary for scaling-up to the programme level. The political window that often opens after natural disasters can open the space for PES to develop. Large floods in China, which claimed 4,150 lives in 29 provinces with damages estimated at US$25.5 billion, were catalytic in turning the attention of the government towards upstream watershed conservation and developing the Sloping Lands Conversion Programme (Li et al., 2015). Likewise, the impacts of Typhoon Haiyan in the Philippines prompted then President Aquino's commitment to coastal protection.

As large sections of the population become vulnerable to climate change, politicians may be more likely to take conservation action. For example, the fact that 60% of the Indian population practice rain-fed agriculture, and that climate change is driving increasing social problems like insecurity and migration, is used as an argument in the Mahatma Gandhi National Rural Employment Guarantee Act programme to ensure public resources to invest in rural actions (Tiwari et al., 2011; Government of India, 2014). Successful programmes have been able to rearrange their strategies to respond to national and international commitments, e.g. in relation to Sustainable Development Goals, Aichi targets and the Nationally Determined Contributions. Bolsa Floresta in Brazil has effectively grounded international issues in local agendas, and Costa Rica managed to develop its PES programme based on the pillars of sustainable development from Rio 1992 as a response to the structural adjustment plans of the 1990s.

While early proponents of PES highlighted the voluntary nature of the instrument, countries that have managed to integrate PES within their legal framework (e.g. Costa Rica, Mexico) have been more successful in establishing their programmes, leveraging political attention and budgetary allocations. It is also important that national and local laws related to environmental services and taxation are aligned (Corbera et al., 2011). This helps avoid contradictions in the allocation and transfer of property rights over ecosystems (e.g. land access and management) and ecosystem services (e.g. carbon offsets, water flows, biodiversity), and to guarantee the means to collect and allocate revenues such as water fees, and fines and taxes such as polluters' payments (Talla Takoukam and Morita, 2008). Moreover, firm and long-term commitments from municipal governments are key in achieving scale, as demonstrated in bottom-up initiatives like Bolivia's *Watershared*.

Sustainable finance from a combination of sources

Political support is important, but ultimately sustainable finance will determine whether a programme emerges and reaches sufficient scale. Making financing sustainable is critical if projects are to take the step from a one-off, usually donor-funded pilot to a programme with financial stability that allows for replication and scaling up. Grants and other forms of donor funding have helped to kick-start projects like *Watershared*, and to partially cover entry costs to international carbon markets (technical studies, registration fees, etc.). Nevertheless, it is important to have a clear strategy for ongoing revenues. Local governments and water users in Bolivia now provide 80% of *Watershared* payments (Asquith, 2016), and sales from carbon offsets generate important revenues in our Mexico, Uganda and Kenya cases.

For national programmes, pegging contributions to tax allocations can be a softer (and often more doable) form of earmarking. For example, in Costa Rica and Mexico, allocations are linked to fuel and water tax collection and are written into national law. Large countries like China, Mexico, India and Brazil use match contributions from national government with those from provincial/local budgets. This can help leverage funding from the private sector – almost 80% of Bolsa Floresta in Brazil is funded from private sources, including Coca-Cola, Samsung, Abril Media Group and Marriott International, through a REDD+ project selling carbon credits on the voluntary market (Viana et al., 2013). Costa Rica has also successfully combined revenues from taxes, voluntary contributions and donor funding. Useful innovations to manage these financial flows include developing secure finance management systems, such as creating independent trust funds, and diversifying the portfolio of economic instruments for capitalisation. The link to social protection can significantly increase the resources available for environmental management, as is the case in South Africa's Working for Water programme.

Lean institutional set-up

To operate at large scale, programmes need an efficient institutional set-up, which includes clear operational rules. Channels are required to coordinate across different government sectors, for example between social affairs and environmental departments. The institutional set-up can be a challenge in national programmes. For China's Sloping Lands Conversion Programme the challenge was to link a focus at scale – targeting 25 provinces that cover about 82% of the country – with an innovative, 'cascading' institutional design (Jin et al., 2017) (Figure 13.2).

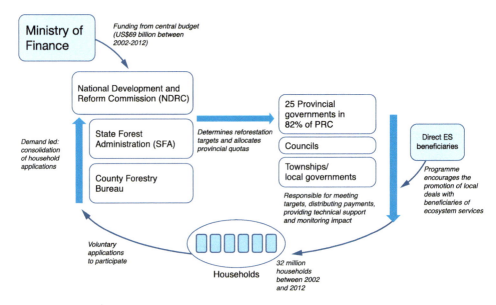

FIGURE 13.2 Institutions: linking top-down cascades with bottom-up demand in China's Sloping Lands Conversion Programme.

Payment delay is one of the most common complaints of programme beneficiaries – and this hits the poorest participants hardest. Innovations that lead to faster payments include the use of systems managed by recognised financial institutions, with project managers separate from funds disbursements. In Costa Rica, the PES programme switched from providing cheques to direct deposits. Direct payment to bank accounts has succeeded in Brazil and also in India, where it has reduced leakages and supports financial inclusion (Government of India, 2014). Mohammed and Uraguchi (2018) summarise useful experiences for financial products that can enable poor and disadvantaged women and men to access microcredit. Experiences like this can help shape the way PES resources are allocated and can have a maximum benefit for poor people.

Security of land tenure is an intrinsic predictor of the capacity of CT managers to enforce conditionality. However, in many parts of the world land tenure arrangements are often ill-defined. Formal PES schemes, especially government programmes such as those in Costa Rica and Ecuador, require land title for registration, meaning that the poorest landowners are sometimes unable to participate. Grassroots schemes are more able to manoeuvre around land tenure issues – for example, *Watershared* uses locally accepted definitions of who owns and controls, or grants access to, watershed forests (Asquith, 2016). Some schemes, such as the Uganda and Kenya carbon projects, are more open to other types of land tenure, such as customary land and ancestral land rights (Plan Vivo Foundation, 2008). This bespoke approach works well at the local level, but struggles to function at larger scales. Public works schemes in India and South Africa bypass the land tenure issue by providing jobs to vulnerable people, irrespective of land ownership.

Effective implementation

Programmes have different strategies to allocate their funds, and various characteristics appear to improve effectiveness (Table 13.2). It is not unusual to see targeting strategies evolving, either to respond to better information or political pressure. In Costa Rica the self-targeting approach of the first stages of the PES programme led to very low additionality. The prohibition to deforest effectively raised the competitiveness of the PES, which was then mostly appropriated by wealthier landowners who had land titles in place and ready access to technical support (Porras et al., 2013). Most programmes have therefore evolved a different approach. National PES programmes in Mexico and Costa Rica announce geographic (e.g. biological corridors, type of forest) or social (areas with low social development index) priorities each year. Applications are scored against criteria, and those with highest marks receive payments with additional funds allocated to non-priority areas.

South Africa has developed spatial frameworks for evaluating future investments through the Land User Incentive (LUI) programme with a stepwise approach to identification. Checklists are also important tools for targeting, and can offer practical guidance in projects such as *Watershared*. In its latest Phase IV, the Chinese SLCP is targeting only those who are poor, willing to convert and whose croplands are on a steep slope. Using models as a starting point can be very effective in increasing the efficiency of programmes, and can help identify the best ways to 'bundle' different objectives such as carbon, water and poverty (Wendland et al., 2010).

Many programmes we reviewed designed their activities in line with local needs and capacities, to ensure that participants are able to comply with conditions. Small-scale projects like *Watershared*, community carbon models and Bolsa Floresta provide technical assistance, which is important to increase local participation and support.

Government-led initiatives rely on more generic models for activities and often struggle to meet local needs. The hybrid CT/PES programme in Bangladesh promoted alternative income-generation training but achieved extremely low enrolment (Islam et al., 2016). Some, especially those with a focus on social protection, often lack the technical capacity to implement environmental activities at ground level.

Meaningful incentives to change behaviour, both cash and in-kind, are at the core of PES and CT programmes (see Table 13.3 for more detail). The types of incentives vary greatly, from cash payments by direct transfer to individuals to cover their opportunity cost of land conversion (Costa Rica), to delivery of community sanitation projects (Mikoko Pamoja, Kenya). Incentives can be allocated individually or at the community level, reflecting the fact that delivering ecosystem services requires group action and that wellbeing goes beyond individual household income

TABLE 13.2 Examples of targeting criteria

Strategy	Description
Self-targeting/ no targeting	By using low-level payments, the programmes try to target only those with the lowest opportunity costs – in theory the poorest. Some early-generation CT programmes, such as *Watershared*, used a 'first-come, first-served' approach, in which the programme publishes requisites and those who comply can apply. Although easier to manage and politically 'neutral', it can lead to financial resources allocated to areas with low risk of change and result in low additionality.
Economic targeting: benefit/cost targeting	Targeting resources that provide the highest environmental benefits per resource unit. Cost-targeting focuses on those least productive resources. Benefit-maximizing targeting looks at those areas that provide the largest environmental benefits for a given budget, which can be identified using models like InVEST, WaterWorld and Co$tingNature. Resources are then distributed through open bidding or auctions. This is most common in developed countries such as the USA, but has less traction in developing countries (Wünscher and Wunder, 2017).
Spatial targeting through models	Commonly used in national and subnational programmes such as REDD+ (Lin et al., 2014). Combinations of GIS-based models and multi-criteria decision analysis to identify potential areas of projects with highest potential for impact ('hot spots'). Often applies a stepwise approach, aiming first for *efficiency* (areas with high forest carbon content, high deforestation risk and low opportunity cost) and then for *co-benefits*: high biodiversity and high poverty rate. While this approach is useful as an initial step for geographic targeting, the heterogeneity of people on site will require further strategies to enable poorer people to participate or risk limiting their participation.
Stepwise approaches	Use some form of the previous strategies, usually: (1) identifying ecological focus areas; (2) using different application systems (e.g. bidding, auctions, fixed payments); (3) identifying pre-selected criteria to allocate applications.

Source: authors' own.

(see Coulthard et al., this volume). A common theme is that, to be effective in promoting changes in behaviour, incentives need to be 'meaningful'. However, what constitutes 'meaningful' varies, and will change over time. For example, incentives provided by the Philippines' Greening the Nation Programme appear sufficient for tree planting, but may be insufficient to ensure tree survival after 10 years (Lachica, 2014). The programme is studying the potential to use parallel incentives, such as capacity building and organization development support and mechanisms for long-term financing such as PES schemes, as well as addressing tenure issues in community forests.

TABLE 13.3 Examples of incentives under PES and CT programmes

Incentive	Description
Cash (as PES and as wages from work-schemes)	• Costa Rica and Mexico national PES make direct cash payments for activities. • South Africa makes cash payments in the form of a minimum wage equivalent in proportion to the infrastructure work required – to people doing environmental works. • Community carbon projects in Uganda and Mexico transfer part of the carbon revenues as individual payments, and a part is kept in a group fund. • These payments are often deposited directly in bank accounts.
In-kind	• Often used for community projects, where individual payments would be diluted if subdivided. Mikoko Pamoja (Kenya) spends 32% of its revenues to support community projects (chosen by the community): e.g. water and sanitation projects, improving local education and restoring mangroves. • *Watershared* in kind 'compensations' – beehives, barbed wire and fruit tree seedlings – are seen as tokens of appreciation or a behaviour change 'nudge', rather than economic transactions, and comprise much lower amounts than opportunity cost calculations would predict. • In Bangladesh, incentives (40 kg rice/family) are given to hilsa fishing households during ban periods. However, these incentives often do not compensate for the lost protein consumption during ban and few fishers engage with support for alternative income generating activities. There are also concerns regarding equity and political interference in the distribution of compensation, elite capture and high levels of inclusion and exclusion error (Haldar and Ali, 2014; Matin and Hulme, 2003; Rahman et al., 2012).
Mix	Bolsa Floresta uses a mix of incentives that include: • Bolsa Floresta Renda: community investments of about US$70 k/year/reserve to support income-generating activities in line with the protected area's management plan. Examples include value-adding on-farm processing activities, ecotourism and aquaculture. • Bolsa Floresta Social: an additional allocation of about US$30 k/year/reserve for improvements in education and community infrastructure. • Bolsa Floresta Associação: about US$10 k/year supporting associations of reserve dwellers. • Bolsa Floresta Familiar: approx. US$90 k/year/reserve distributed as monthly cash transfers of an average value of US$170 to the female spouse of the household.

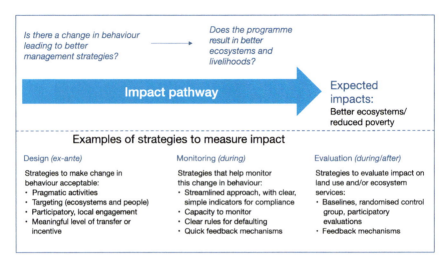

FIGURE 13.3 Clarity on the impact pathway helps to demonstrate programme impacts.

Demonstrating impact

Demonstrating impact is linked to two components: design, and monitoring and evaluation. Projects cannot have impact if they are not designed well, and their achievements cannot be demonstrated to policy makers without rigorous monitoring and evaluation (Figure 13.3).

Robust information that clearly demonstrates impact, in terms of healthier ecosystems and less poverty, is a major gap in almost all the programmes analysed. Few programmes had clear social or environmental baselines. There are few examples of rigorous project evaluations (e.g. Mexico and Costa Rica), but they tend to be site specific rather than at country level. Because of their long-term implementation, the community carbon programmes in Mexico and Uganda have also been the subject of multiple studies (e.g. Wells et al., 2017). The Bolivian *Watershared* programme has been evaluated through an ESPA-funded Randomized Control Trial (Grillos, 2017; Jack and Recalde, 2015).

At a smaller scale, monitoring is a very important condition for community carbon projects for private offset markets, and the systems must be clearly outlined before the projects are approved and certified. The project developer monitors communities and farmers in visits that often double as capacity building. Third parties conduct independent audits regularly to ensure transparency. While effective monitoring provides important reassurance on the impacts of the projects for offset buyers, these systems can be very expensive and difficult to scale up. A recent study of the Mexico and Uganda carbon community projects shows how combining models with a limited number of field visits can be important to provide robust carbon estimates, reassurance and inclusion to communities, and keep costs down (Wells et al., 2017).

Ex post payments for work completed, like those in South Africa, increase adherence to conditionality ('wages upon satisfactory work done'). However, understanding what constitutes 'satisfactory' for the environment can be a problem when technical capacity on the ground is limited. In Bangladesh, the Department of Fisheries lacks capacity at the sub-district level to implement the Jatka programme: the 'mobile court' used to enforce fishery regulations is hard to coordinate and the Bangladesh Fisheries Research Institute lacks resources to carry out its role as implementation partner.

Political engagement with CT/PES programmes is critical for initiation, and such engagement is usually gained when the programme has a tight link to a poverty-reduction agenda. However, such attention can be a problem when it comes to enforcing conditionality. Politicians do not want to see poor people losing programme benefits, even if they have not complied with the programme's environmental goals. Sanctions should be 'stiff' to ensure that programmes have an environmental impact, but it is sometimes not clear how this can be done in a politically acceptable way.

The cost effectiveness of a small-scale conservation intervention such as *Watershared* increases if there are only a few, motivated stakeholders, and such actors can play a critical role in monitoring. Most importantly, the geographical proximity of service users and providers can promote strong 'conditionality'. If a landowner cuts their forest, it will quickly be obvious to their downstream counterparts. Downstream authorities have a clear (and often fiduciary) responsibility to check whether the compensation mechanism (i.e. the development projects) has been implemented, and whether watershed conservation has occurred (Asquith, 2016).

Conclusions

CTs and PES have the same starting point: the assumption that direct, conditional incentives are the most effective way to change behaviour. However, although many PES schemes have rural development as an objective, they have struggled to implement mechanisms to engage the poor and alleviate poverty. In contrast, CTs have made great strides in promoting social protection and income stability, but their environmental impact has been limited. Table 13.4 highlights the differences between CTs and PES, but also suggests that there is significant scope for developing hybrid programmes that take advantage of model complementarities. Indeed, such hybrids are already being tested in the Bolsa Floresta, *Watershared* and Jatka conservation programmes.

Fulfilling commitments like the Sustainable Development Goals and the Aichi Targets will require a combination of the environmental protection and poverty alleviation agendas. There is a need to develop PES programmes that learn from the social protection programmes with environmental components, such as South Africa's Expanded Public Works Programme. For example, public funding might provide short-term investments – e.g. watershed works, removing invasive species or supporting changes to cleaner technologies, while revenues from PES

TABLE 13.4 Differences between conditional transfers and PES

Conditional social transfers tend to:	PES tend to:
Have a clear social objective and are able to focus on the poor and ultra-poor	Have rural development as a secondary objective, but often as an afterthought
Promote direct, one-off interventions with short-term impacts, which may not change long-term behaviour	Provide continuous low-level support that can change social norms and behaviour over the long term
Provide tangible benefits to the ultra-poor, including people without land	Support landowners and land managers, and so cannot effectively alleviate extreme poverty
Undertake environmental projects at large scale, but struggle to do so efficiently	Have environmental objectives as their primary goal

could encourage the long-term change in behaviour to prevent future ecosystem degradation.

PES practitioners need to recognise that focusing on poverty alleviation can catalyse important political support and new budget lines. However, the potential challenges of such an approach, such as high transaction costs and the risk of targeting sites with low environmental value, must be built into programmes to both protect the environment and enable transformative and sustainable livelihood improvements. An acknowledgement of the benefits and the trade-offs is a first step towards designing response actions.

There is also significant potential for cross-learning from social and environment CTs. Moreover, this can be a valid argument to promote greater integration across traditionally separate government departments (social and environment). New tools developed by academic research can help policy makers improve the efficiency and effectiveness of these programmes.

International support has often been instrumental in the emergence of local projects, funding studies that provide the evidence of pathways of impact and supporting dialogue inside countries, South–South collaborative learning and technological transfer for improved programme design, monitoring and evaluation. There is a clear value in identifying synergies between and lessons learned in both the CT and PES models.

Successful CT/PES schemes exhibit a series of enabling conditions: high-level political support, sustainable financing streams, lean institutional set-ups, tools and systems for effective implementation and a clear ability to demonstrate impact. Cross-learning from our cases has proved to be an effective way to build capacity, and to improve CT/PES programmes from the ground up. Capacity building, bringing in scientific advances in modelling, monitoring and understanding behaviour, should include mid-level technical government staff and not only universities. Research into the gaps and potential of including poor and vulnerable people into environmental policy needs to reach a wider audience that includes not just Environmental

Ministries and conservation professionals, but also mainstreaming into the agendas of ministries of finance, ministries of employment and the private sector.

References

(ESPA outputs marked with '★')

Abdoulayi S, Angeles G, Barrington C, et al. (2017) Evaluating the effectiveness of an unconditional social cash transfer programme for the ultra poor in Malawi. *Grantee Final Report*. New Delhi, India: 3ie: International Initiative for Impact Evaluation.

★Asquith N. (2013) Investing in Latin America's water factories: incentives and institutions for climate compatible development. *Revista: Harvard Review of Latin America* XII: 21–24.

Asquith N. (2016) Watershared: Adaptation, mitigation, watershed protection and economic development in Latin America. *Inside Stories on climate compatible development*. Climate & Development Knowledge Network (CDKN).

Asquith N and Wunder S. (2008) Payments for watershed services: the Bellagio conversations. IIED, Blue Moon Fund, CGIAR, DFID, EcoFund Foundation.

Bakkegaard RK and Wunder S. (2014) Chapter 2: Bolsa Floresta, Brazil. In: Sills EO, Atmadja SS, de Sassi C, Duchelle A, Kweka D, Aju Pradnja Resosudarmo I and Sunderlin W (eds) *REDD+ On the Ground. A Case Book of Subnational Initiatives Across the Globe*. CIFOR.

Barton DN, Benavides K, Chacon-Cascante A, et al. (2017) Payments for ecosystem services as a policy mix: demonstrating the institutional analysis and development framework on conservation policy instruments. *Environmental Policy and Governance* 27: 404–421.

Börner J, Baylis K, Corbera E, et al. (2017) The effectiveness of payments for environmental services. *World Development* 96: 359–374.

Corbera E, Estrada M, May P, et al. (2011) Rights to land, forests and carbon in REDD+: insights from Mexico, Brazil and Costa Rica. *Forests* 2: 301.

Department of Environmental Affairs. (2016) *Working for Water: Social Development*. Available at: www.environment.gov.za/projectsprogrammes/wfw

Devereux S. (2009) Social Protection Instruments: what's on the menu? *UNICEF Social Protection Training Course*. Brighton, UK: IDS.

Duan W, Lang Z and Wen Y. (2015) The effects of the Sloping Land Conversion Program on poverty alleviation in the Wuling mountainous area of China. *Small-Scale Forestry* 14: 331–350.

Engel S. (2016) The Devil in the detail: a practical guide on designing payments for environmental services. *International Review of Environmental and Resource Economics* 9: 131–177.

★Fisher JA. (2013) Justice implications of conditionality in payments for ecosystem services: a case study from Uganda. In: Sikor T (ed.) *The Justices and Injustices of Ecosystem Services*. Abingdon, UK: Routledge, 21–45.

Government of India. (2014) Report to the people: Mahatma Gandhi National Rural Employment Guarantee Act, 2005. New Delhi, India: Ministry of Rural Development, Department of Rural Development.

★Grillos T. (2017) Economic vs non-material incentives for participation in in-kind payments for ecosystem services program in Bolivia. *Ecological Economics* 131: 178–190.

Haldar GC and Ali L. (2014) The cost of compensation: transaction and administration costs of hilsa fish management in Bangladesh. *IIED Working Paper*. London: IIED.

Islam MM, Mohammed EY and Ali L. (2016) Economic incentives for sustainable hilsa fishing in Bangladesh: An analysis of the legal and institutional framework. *Marine Policy* 68: 8–22.

★Jack BK and Recalde MP. (2015) Leadership and the voluntary provision of public goods: field evidence from Bolivia. *Journal of Public Economics* 122: 80–93.

Jin L, Porras I, Lopez A, et al. (2017) Sloping Lands Conversion Programme, People's Republic of China. In: Porras I, Mohammed E and Steele P (eds) *Conditional Transfers, Poverty and Ecosystems: National Programmes Highlights*. London: IIED.

Kakwani N, Veras Soares F and Son HH. (2005) Conditional cash transfers in African countries, Working Paper No 9. Brazil: United Nations Development Programme, International Poverty Centre.

Koohi-Kamali F. (2010) Public works and social protection. European report on development. European University Institute.

Lachica A. (2014) Philippines: degraded forest rehabilitation and sustainable forest management in The Philippines. *Workshop on Degraded Forest Rehabilitation and Sustainable Forest Management*. Kunming, China: DENR – Forest Management Bureau.

Li H, Yao S, Yin R, et al. (2015) Assessing the decadal impact of China's sloping land conversion program on household income under enrollment and earning differentiation. *Forest Policy and Economics* 61: 95–103.

Lin L, Sills E and Cheshire H. (2014) Targeting areas for reducing emissions from deforestation and forest degradation (REDD+) projects in Tanzania. *Global Environmental Change* 24: 277–286.

Liu Z and Lan J. (2015) The Sloping Land Conversion Program in China: effect on the livelihood diversification of rural households. *World Development* 70: 147–161.

★Locatelli T, Binet T, Kairo JG, et al. (2014) Turning the tide: how blue carbon and payments for ecosystem services (PES) might help save mangrove forests. *Ambio* 43: 981–995.

Ma Z, Bauchet J, Steele D, et al. (2017) Comparison of direct transfers for human capital development and environmental conservation. *World Development* 99: 498–517.

McCord A. (2013) *Public Works and Social Protection in Sub-Saharan Africa: Do Public Works Work for the Poor?* London: ODI.

Marais C and Wannenburgh AM. (2008) Restoration of water resources (natural capital) through the clearing of invasive alien plants from riparian areas in South Africa – costs and water benefits. *South African Journal of Botany* 74: 526–537.

Matin I and Hulme D. (2003) Programs for the poorest: learning from the IGVGD program in Bangladesh. *World Development* 31: 647–665.

Mohammed EY and Uraguchi ZB, eds. (2018) *Financial Inclusion for Poverty Alleviation: Issues and Case Studies for Sustainable Development*. Abingdon, UK: Routledge.

Plan Vivo Foundation. (2008) The Plan Vivo Standards 2008. Plan Vivo Foundation.

Porras I, Barton DN, Miranda M, et al. (2013) Learning from 20 years of Payments for Ecosystem Services in Costa Rica. London: International Institute for Environment and Development.

Porras I, Mohammed E and Steele P. (2017a) *Policy Workshop: Conditional Transfers for Poverty Reduction and Ecosystem Management*. Cambridge, UK: IIED.

Porras I, Mohammed EY, Ali L, et al. (2017b) Power, profits and payments for ecosystem services in Hilsa fisheries in Bangladesh: a value chain analysis. *Marine Policy* 84: 60–68.

Porras I, Steele P and Mohammed EY. (2016) Upscaling solutions: the role of conditional transfers for poverty reduction and ecosystem management. London: IIED.

Rahman MA, Alam MA, Hasan SJ, et al. (2012) Hilsa fishery management in Bangladesh. *Status of Fishery and Potential for Aquaculture Regional Workshop*. Dhaka, Bangladesh: The WorldFish, Bangladesh and South Asia Office.

Rainforest Alliance. (2014) Verification assessment report for Trees for Global Benefits, ECOTRUST in Uganda. Richmond, VT: Rainforest Alliance Smartwood Program.

Rodríguez LC, Pascual U, Muradian R, et al. (2011) Towards a unified scheme for environmental and social protection: learning from PES and CCT experiences in developing countries. *Ecological Economics* 70: 2163–2174.

Rugtveit SV. (2012) Environmental effectiveness, economic effectiveness and equity: a case study of Payments for Environmental Services (PES) in Hojancha, Costa Rica. *CLTS Master Theses Series No. 5/2012*. Oslo, Norway: Department of Economics and Resource Management, Norwegian University of Life Sciences.

★Sikor T, ed. (2013) *The Justices and Injustices of Ecosystem Services*. Abingdon, UK: Routledge.

Sills EO, Atmadja S, de Sassi C, et al. (eds) (2014) *REDD+ On the Ground: A Case Book of Subnational Initiatives Across the Globe*. Bogor, Indonesia: Center for International Forestry Research (CIFOR).

Talla Takoukam P and Morita S. (2008) A Policy and Legal Framework Supporting Payments for Ecosystem Services. World Bank's Environment and International Law Unit.

Tiwari R, Somashekhar HI, Parama VRR, et al. (2011) MGNREGA for environmental service enhancement and vulnerability reduction: rapid appraisal in Chitradurga district, Karnataka. *Economic and Political Weekly* 46: 39–47.

Turpie JK, Marais C and Blignaut JN. (2008) The working for water programme: evolution of a payments for ecosystem services mechanism that addresses both poverty and ecosystem service delivery in South Africa. *Ecological Economics* 65: 788–798.

Viana V, Tezza J, Salviati V, et al. (2013) Programa Bolsa Floresta no estado do Amazonas. In: Pagiola S, von Glehn HC and Taffarello D (eds) *Experiências de Pagamentos por Serviços Ambientais no Brasil*. São Paulo, Brazil: Secretaria de Meio Ambiente.

★Wells G, Fisher JA, Porras I, et al. (2017) Rethinking monitoring in smallholder carbon payments for ecosystem service schemes: devolve monitoring, understand accuracy and identify co-benefits. *Ecological Economics* 139: 115–127.

Wendland KJ, Honzák M, Portela R, et al. (2010) Targeting and implementing payments for ecosystem services: opportunities for bundling biodiversity conservation with carbon and water services in Madagascar. *Ecological Economics* 69: 2093–2107.

Wunder S. (2015) Revisiting the concept of payments for environmental services. *Ecological Economics* 117: 234–243.

Wünscher T and Wunder S. (2017) Conservation tenders in low-income countries: opportunities and challenges. *Land Use Policy* 63: 672–678.

14
SOCIAL IMPACTS OF PROTECTED AREAS

Exploring evidence of trade-offs and synergies

Emily Woodhouse, Claire Bedelian, Neil Dawson and Paul Barnes

Introduction

Protected areas remain the cornerstone of efforts to conserve ecosystems and biodiversity globally. If the Aichi biodiversity targets of the Convention on Biological Diversity (CBD) are met, 17% of terrestrial biomes and 10% of coastal and marine areas will be protected by 2020, impacting the lives of people living in and around them. The relationship between protected areas and poverty forms a long-running and often polarised debate in academic and policy circles (Brockington and Wilkie, 2015). Protected areas certainly have the potential to play an important role in the delivery of crucial ecosystem services for poverty alleviation (Andam et al., 2010; Chan et al., 2006), but they remain in the spotlight for negative reasons too, with accusations of human rights violations against indigenous communities continuing to cause controversy (Matsuura, 2017). For both moral and instrumental reasons, international conservation policies and the approaches of many organisations are moving beyond the standard livelihoods approach to dealing with the social costs of conservation, to emphasise pro-poor strategies, human rights and equitable management with participation by local communities (Schreckenberg et al., 2016). Many protected areas are now established and managed based on the premise that there are synergistic relationships between social and ecological outcomes, or that social benefits related to protected areas can sufficiently compensate for any losses. However, efforts to balance ecological and social objectives remain challenging, and 'win-wins' are elusive.

Despite the increased presence of development goals within protected area objectives, guidance is lacking on how to identify, avoid or mitigate trade-offs, or even to realise win-win outcomes. This is in part because social dimensions of conservation have, until recently, been inadequately conceptualised. Integrated conservation and development programmes have proliferated since the 1980s, with limited success. A major weakness in these efforts was their restricted focus on material definitions of poverty and livelihoods, often embodying the perspectives of Western donors and NGOs about what appropriate development entails, and aggregated across social groups (Newmark and Hough, 2000). There is increasing acknowledgement that narrow economic indicators are inadequate for describing poverty and social wellbeing (Dawson, 2015; Coulthard et al., this volume). Indeed, it is partly the complexity, variety and distribution of impacts in different contexts that has fuelled controversy over protected areas. Protected areas are often established in regions of high biodiversity in the Global South where people are highly dependent on natural resources, and have historical and cultural relationships intertwined with nature. They represent discrete systems of governance with rules of access, management activities and a wide array of associated benefits and costs through different ecosystem services, disservices and elements of different people's wellbeing (Suich et al., 2015). Inspecting the various elements of these systems and complex relationships between social and ecological dimensions can elucidate processes and structures that best foster positive outcomes. However, income and assets remain the dominant indicators used to assess the social impacts of protected areas (de Lange et al., 2016). A growing number of papers using sophisticated scientific research designs, yet restricted to this material focus, simply conclude that protected areas have either no impact on local communities or make small positive contributions to poverty alleviation (Andam et al., 2010; Clements et al., 2014; Robalino and Villalobos, 2015). Broader reviews of the social impacts of protected areas (e.g. Oldekop et al., 2016; Pullin et al., 2013) are useful to map out and characterise the evidence base, but are less able to understand the relationships between and within social and ecological dimensions of protected area systems.

As studies increasingly apply more advanced conceptual framings to explore the social impacts of protected areas such as wellbeing, resilience, justice and equity, there is a growing acceptance that there are always winners and losers in the establishment and associated management activities, and trade-offs between different outcomes (Daw et al., 2015; McKinnon et al., 2016; Schreckenberg et al., 2016). The aim of this chapter is to inform both conservation science and practice by: (i) providing an overview of the state of knowledge on the impacts of protected areas on human wellbeing; (ii) characterising the nature of trade-offs and synergies within and between social and ecological outcomes; and (iii) reflecting on the implications for protected area governance and management. In line with the emerging approach of international conservation organisations (IUCN and WCPA, 2016) and the growing diversity of protected areas, we define protected areas to be any area-based conservation measure for which the primary or explicit objective is conservation, including sustainable use.

The social impacts of protected areas

Protected areas can impact people's lives in a multitude of ways. Using the lens of multi-dimensional wellbeing allows insights into the range of, and interconnections between, social impacts on aspects of people's lives which they value (Woodhouse et al., 2015). Definitions of wellbeing have coalesced around a conceptualisation that encompasses three dimensions: (i) objective material circumstances; (ii) subjective evaluation and experiences, and the meaning and values ascribed to the processes and outcomes, including socio-cultural values; and (iii) a relational component focusing on how people engage with others to meet their needs and achieve their goals (Coulthard et al., this volume). Impact evaluations of external interventions have tended to privilege objective material wellbeing (including income and assets), overlooking the non-material social and cultural aspects which are vital to people's sense of wellbeing. Research within the ESPA programme has particularly embraced the subjective dimensions of wellbeing and involved in-depth analyses of what it means to live well in a local context, according to the values, preferences and perceptions of people themselves (Abunge et al., 2013; Dawson and Martin, 2015; Gross-Camp, 2017). People act upon how they feel, so that understanding and supporting subjective wellbeing is crucial for local legitimacy and engagement. Subjective experiences may contradict objective outcomes – for example, perceived wellbeing can decline despite increases in asset-based wealth due to inequitable distribution of benefits, conflict and unmet expectations (Gurney et al., 2014). Wellbeing analysis also provides a crucial foundation for justice research (see Dawson et al., this volume) that looks beyond the distribution of costs and benefits to perceptions of procedural justice and recognition of cultural values, aspects which have been shown to be important in the local legitimacy of protected areas.

We can consider three related processes through which the establishment of protected areas impacts both positively and negatively on human wellbeing across the three interlinked dimensions (Figure 14.1). First, protected area management always involves a level of resource control, which can protect and increase the flow of regulating and supporting ecosystem services to people (Chan et al., 2006). However, protected areas that successfully protect or enhance wildlife populations can also result in 'ecosystem disservices', most notably in the form of 'human wildlife conflict', which can have visible impacts such as injury and livestock predation, but also hidden effects such as on mental health (Barua et al., 2013). Exclusionary approaches, which have dominated conservation historically, have resulted in displacement through: physical removal; economic exclusion from the pursuit of a livelihood; and cultural exclusion of people from landscapes which have historical and symbolic meaning (Lele et al., 2010). Alternatively, the establishment of protected areas can secure resource rights and improve sustainable management, leading to improved access to ecosystem services important for wellbeing (Clements et al., 2014).

Second, how protected areas are governed will determine not only what management decisions are taken and therefore access to ecosystem services, but

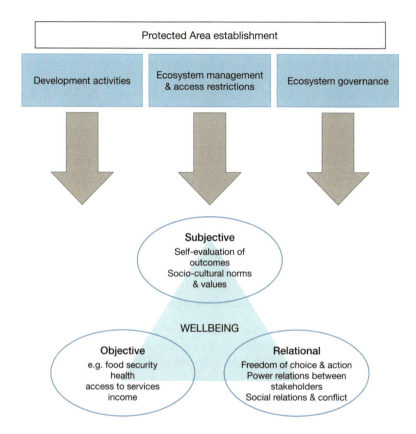

FIGURE 14.1 Conceptual framework showing the processes by which protected areas impact on the three dimensions of human wellbeing.

also affect the relational and subjective aspects of wellbeing. Governance refers to the processes and structures whereby decisions are made and implemented (Nunan et al., this volume), and different regimes will vary in institutional arrangements, levels of participation, accountability and responsibilities by different actors. Protected areas are fundamentally social and political processes that can transform institutional arrangements and power relationships affecting social relations and cultural practices, and ultimately the sustainability of the intervention (Brechin et al., 2002). Anthropological research has highlighted how, through a process of territorialisation, protected areas can transform landscapes into partitioned units, imposing the European nature–culture dichotomy to the exclusion of local knowledge and associated management institutions (Bluwstein and Lund, 2018; Goldman, 2003). Imposed institutions can undermine freedom of choice and action (Abunge et al., 2013) and create feelings of insecurity as rules change (Baird et al., 2009), but where interventions improve natural resource governance and local stakeholders have meaningful influence over decisions, they can increase feelings of empowerment (Gurney et al., 2014) and a sense of pride and ownership (Mahajan and Daw, 2016).

Last, protected areas are rarely implemented or managed as isolated interventions and will typically exist in conjunction with other development initiatives, such as tourism, alternative livelihoods, infrastructure and education. These projects may form part of 'community-based conservation' initiatives, or development may be attracted to the area in a more uncoordinated and opportunistic manner, increasing interactions between communities and a range of external organisations (Baird, 2014). A variety of actors at different scales can play a role in resource management institutions, provide economic opportunities and constraints, and shape communities' perceptions of a project – affecting all three dimensions of wellbeing and ecological success (Mahajan and Daw, 2016). Interventions associated with protected areas and aimed at improving livelihoods and economic wellbeing overall tend to distribute fortune unevenly (see below), which can exacerbate social inequity and lead to conflict affecting the relational dimensions of wellbeing.

Synergies between social and ecological outcomes

Protected areas are often purported to support positive relationships between social and ecological processes and outcomes. In a review of research on 165 protected areas, Oldekop et al. (2016) provide convincing evidence that positive ecological outcomes are linked to positive socio-economic outcomes, which in turn are more likely where co-management arrangements exist. Likewise, a review of community-based projects shows that synergies exist between economic and ecological success (Brooks et al., 2012). These reviews suggest that positive synergies are possible, especially where governance arrangements allow for local involvement, capacity building, secure tenure rights and equitable distribution of benefits. However, by not capturing the full range of wellbeing impacts, or how these affect groups of people in different ways, many studies may fail to acknowledge trade-offs that ultimately affect conservation success and justice. For example, many conservation and development initiatives focus on creating alternative livelihoods, such as commodity-driven agriculture, to enhance local incomes and reduce dependence on resources within protected areas. Yet, such promoted and incentivised changes may inhibit subsistence production causing short-term and seasonal food insecurity, create land and resource tenure insecurity (especially for those reliant on customary or informal access) and disrupt local trade, social protection systems, customary interactions and knowledge exchange. Focusing on win-wins to the exclusion of trade-offs can ultimately back-fire, and lead to disappointment and negative effects on long-term community support (Chaigneau and Brown, 2016). Overall, there is a lack of studies that combine social and ecological measures of success, and the processes by which these outcomes occur, to fully assess whether and how synergies are produced.

Protected area trade-offs and implications for conservation success

A wide range of literature suggests that trade-offs are typical in protected area conservation. We have identified that trade-offs can occur between (i) social and ecological outcomes; (ii) different social outcomes; and (iii) different social groups, and all these trade-offs vary across spatial and temporal scales (Table 14.1).

Trade-offs between social and ecological outcomes

Creating stricter rules on access and greater enforcement can mean that biodiversity, habitats and ecosystems are better protected but at the cost of human wellbeing. This trade-off is most evident where restriction of resource use leads to a loss of access to provisioning services, such as forest or fisheries resources, and the associated cultural significance of these livelihoods and land or seascapes. The static nature of conventional protected areas can be particularly problematic for mobile groups such as pastoralists who rely on temporally and spatially dynamic resource use (Reid et al., 2014). These trade-offs can play out differently at different scales due to zoning, where some areas have more restrictions limiting farming but offer no benefits to compensate (Dawson et al., 2017b). Although regulating and supporting ecosystem services may be enhanced through protected areas, these may primarily accrue to non-local users who do not experience the direct costs – for

TABLE 14.1 Summary of key trade-offs in protected areas and variations at scale

Type of trade-off	Across local scales	Across national and global scales	Across temporal scales
Between social and ecological outcomes: restriction of provisioning and cultural ecosystem services due to loss of access	Different restriction zones result in different trade-offs	Regulating and supporting ecosystem services accrue at larger scales	Time lags in ecological outcomes and ecosystem service benefits to wellbeing
Between social outcomes: Gains in some aspects of wellbeing not commensurate with costs to others	Inequitable compensation	Tourism income, tax and infrastructure benefits greater nearer to urban centres and at national level	Benefits are delayed, or tail off when funding stops
Between social groups: The poorest and most marginalised lose out	Accessible elites gain most benefits	Gains for distant populations through carbon sequestration and conservation of charismatic species	Greatest benefits to future generations

example, watershed protection leads to better water provision downstream from the protected area (Sikor, 2013). Whereas costs and benefits to material wellbeing from conservation are more immediate, it can take time for synergies to emerge as ecosystem processes are restored, although future perceived benefits may be enough to generate collective action within communities to enforce protected area rules (Chaigneau and Brown, 2016).

Trade-offs between different social outcomes

Protected areas can produce both gains and losses across different aspects of wellbeing. Positive impacts on the flow of regulating ecosystem services can come at the expense of other social outcomes, by preventing access to material resources or undermining a sense of freedom (Box 14.1). Compensation provided through, for example, revenue sharing from tourism may increase wealth for some, but is often not commensurate with losses to other aspects of wellbeing – for example, the ability to maintain traditional practices and related social interactions through access to medicinal plants or subsistence hunting (Martin et al., 2016). Remoteness can be a key variable at play in social trade-offs at the local scale. For example, Poudyal et al. (2016) found systematic spatial bias in the social safeguarding assessment process for REDD+ in Madagascar, with inaccessible households less likely to be identified as eligible for compensation. Economic benefits tend to accrue in urban centres or at a national level – for example, in Tanzania wildlife is prioritised over local community livelihoods due to the vast amounts of revenue that tourism brings to the national economy (Homewood et al., 2009). Impacts are not static, and benefits from associated development activities such as livelihood interventions can take time to emerge (Box 14.1). Conversely, as in the case of an integrated Marine Protected Area (MPA) in Indonesia, positive wellbeing impacts which occurred during the implementation period did not continue after external funds and expertise were withdrawn (Gurney et al., 2014).

BOX 14.1 TRADE-OFFS IN THE BIODIVERSITY OFFSET OF THE AMBATOVY MINE IN MADAGASCAR

Bidaud et al. (2017) investigated the social impacts of a biodiversity offset project used to compensate for the impacts of the development of a major nickel mine on biodiversity. The offset project restricted forest activities and extraction, but also provided micro-development projects (training, agricultural assets and equipment) to compensate people for the costs of stopping their forest-related activities. Using key informant interviews, focus group discussions and a household survey, the authors found both positive and negative social impacts of the protected area on human wellbeing, and a number of trade-offs:

- Trade-offs between social outcomes: the offset project was perceived to have both positive and negative impacts on material wellbeing. There were the potential benefits of forest protection on water availability and thus agricultural productivity, and the increased training and material donations from development projects. However, the offset simultaneously restricted people's ability to access the forest, thus reducing the opportunity for agricultural expansion and collecting resources. People experienced negative impacts on relational wellbeing as the project introduced new social tensions surrounding the reporting of illegal activities, and conflicts arose around the distribution of development project activities.
- Trade-offs between different social groups: members of forest management associations, or those with better social and family connections, were more likely to receive benefits from development projects.
- Trade-offs at different spatial scales: at the local scale, those who felt they suffered the costs of conservation restrictions were not those who benefited from the development projects. Residents living in the village centres reported material benefits, whereas those more likely to experience the costs of fines for breaking conservation restrictions lived closer to the forest. Respondents also perceived trade-offs between household and national scales. At the household level they perceived negative impacts, inadequate benefits and an inequitable sharing of costs and benefits, yet they perceived the offset to have a positive impact on Madagascar as a whole. Forest protection was seen as positive in its own right, and also for the provision of fresh water and the future use of the forest.
- Trade-offs between different temporal scales: there was a mismatch in timing between the costs of the immediate forest restrictions and the delay in benefits from the associated development projects.

The authors argue that although the development project activities provided by the offset have the potential to deliver benefits to the wellbeing of local people, this is weakened by the mismatch between costs and benefits at different spatial and temporal scales. More consideration of these trade-offs is critical in the development of offset projects if they are to be sustainable in the long term.

Trade-offs between different social groups

The most common and significant trade-offs found in the literature are between different social groups resulting in distributive inequity. Social differentiation and disaggregated analyses on values held and outcomes are crucial in providing insights into the impacts on and between different groups (Daw et al., 2011; Fisher et al., 2014). Even well-meaning interventions can unintentionally disadvantage some groups relative to others, unless attention is paid to the social and political composition of communities. Trade-offs occur across a range of different social groupings according to wealth (Dawson et al., 2017b), gender (Daw et al., 2015; Brown and Fortnam, this volume), age (Keane et al., 2016), ethnic group (Dawson and Martin, 2015) and livelihood group (Clements et al., 2014). The common pattern across scales is that benefits tend to accrue to those in the position of greater power, whereas the costs fall on the poorest and most marginalised. Impacts and opportunity costs of protected areas tend to be borne at the local scale, while benefits from ecosystem services, intrinsic and bequest values are enjoyed by distant wealthy beneficiaries (Balmford and Whitten, 2003).

Implications of trade-offs for conservation success

Trade-offs can have important implications for conservation success through social feedbacks. Negative social impacts can result in reduced local support for

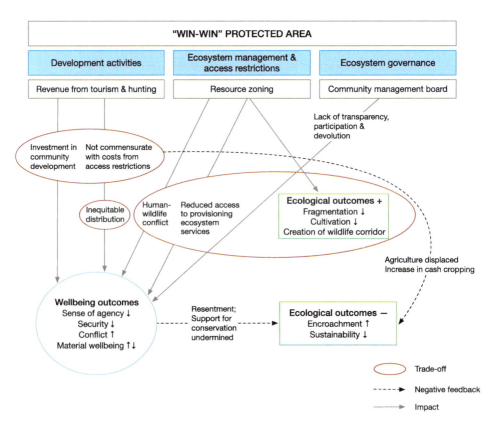

FIGURE 14.2 Illustration of impacts, trade-offs and negative feedbacks resulting from a protected area. Example of Wildlife Management Areas in Tanzania.

Source: Based on Bluwstein et al., 2016; Homewood et al., 2015; Moyo et al., 2016.

conservation and cause spill-overs and unintended consequences that ultimately and often negatively impact conservation objectives through negative feedbacks (Milner-Gulland, 2012). There is growing evidence that distributive inequity (in wellbeing outcomes across social groups), alongside broader procedural injustice and lack of recognition, can affect the legitimacy and effectiveness of protected areas (Dawson et al., 2017a). Figure 14.2 illustrates the variety of impacts, trade-offs and negative feedbacks that can occur, with the example of Wildlife Management Areas (WMAs) in Tanzania. Although WMAs provide tourism revenue and indirect economic benefits through protecting rangelands against fragmentation, inequity in distribution and a lack of transparency, downward accountability and community participation have undermined support for conservation and led to violent confrontation (Homewood et al., 2015). Restrictions on resource use and insufficient compensation from tourism revenue increased the desire to rent farmland and graze livestock elsewhere (Bluwstein et al., 2016). Moreover, increased maize damage by elephants due to the presence of the WMA encouraged the growth of a cash crop, sesame, as a less risky alternative. This in turn increased the overall demand for agricultural land, as most who farm sesame also rent land elsewhere to grow maize (Moyo et al., 2016).

Managing trade-offs and creating synergies in protected area conservation

Given the ubiquity of trade-offs in protected areas, how can they be managed to improve the balance between different outcomes? Referring back to Figure 14.1, we first examine the factors that affect the relationships between ecosystem services and wellbeing, how the current evidence suggests these mediate the extent and distribution of trade-offs and the potential for creating synergies. We then look at the common strategy of providing compensation to offset trade-offs and its potential pitfalls. Last, we explore how analysing and negotiating trade-offs may be the most effective way to foster synergies.

Factors determining trade-offs and synergies

Ecosystem management to balance multiple stakeholders' priorities alongside biodiversity conservation

Protected areas vary in the levels of access and use permitted, ranging from strictly protected units, in which resource use and even physical access are forbidden, and sustainable use areas that allow for controlled resource extraction, and in some instances land use change and human settlements. Strict protection is often deemed necessary where pressure on resources is high, but this view is countered with evidence that sustainable use can leverage local support and the enforcement of protective regulations (Porter-Bolland et al., 2012), and that indigenous managed areas are particularly successful where pressures are high (Nolte et al.,

2013). Stricter protection does not always align with improved ecological outcomes because social conflicts that result can affect support for, and undermine, conservation (Ferraro et al., 2013). Overall, extreme protectionism is unlikely to meet the needs and rights of impoverished local populations, unless compensation is deemed sufficient to account for losses by these groups or substitute ecosystem services that meet people's needs are available in the wider landscape (Dawson and Martin, 2015).

Quality of participatory governance

IUCN and the CBD recognise four broad types of governance of protected areas: (i) by government; (ii) shared (by various rights holders and stakeholders); (iii) by private organisations and individuals; and (iv) by indigenous peoples or local communities (Borrini-Feyerabend et al., 2013). The ways in which protected areas are governed on the ground are far more variable than this categorisation implies, and it is not only the type but the quality of governance that is important in producing social and ecological synergies. Whether local or state authority is more effective in generating positive ecological and social outcomes remains a key debate in protected area conservation (Brockington and Wilkie, 2015). Devolved governance, such as in community-based forestry management, has potential to provide a sense of agency and encourage voluntary compliance (Gross-Camp, 2017)

BOX 14.2 DOES GOVERNANCE TYPE IN PROTECTED AREAS MATTER FOR POVERTY? A RAPID ASSESSMENT OF THE EVIDENCE FROM SUB-SAHARAN AFRICA

Contributed by: Yvonne Erasmus and Laurenz Langer (2017), Africa Centre for Evidence, University of Johannesburg

How governance structures and processes are set up has a direct impact on how protected areas are managed, and consequently on conservation and social outcomes.

Following the identification of an evidence synthesis gap, we conducted a Rapid Evidence Assessment aimed at answering the following research question: What is the impact of different governance structures in protected areas on ecosystem services and multi-dimensional poverty alleviation in sub-Saharan Africa?

We distinguished the four types of governance identified by IUCN: government, shared, private and community (Borrini-Feyerabend et al., 2013). Following the screening of 9,493 search hits identified by a systematic search, we included 26 studies in our assessment, 20 of which were used in the synthesis of results following critical appraisal of studies' trustworthiness.

The 26 studies were conducted in 10 countries concentrated in Southern (*n* = 11) and Eastern Africa (*n* = 11). In terms of individual countries, Tanzania (*n* = 7) and Namibia (*n* = 5) had the highest number of studies. The most prominent type of governance featured was governance by local communities (*n* = 14); with fewer studies focusing on governance by government (*n* = 6); comparison of different types of governance (*n* = 4); and shared governance (*n* = 2). We identified no studies assessing the effects of privately governed protected areas.

The included studies cover 36 different protected areas in sub-Saharan Africa, 33 of which are terrestrial. The majority assessed the effects of different types of governance structures on SDG 1: poverty reduction (*n* = 18).

Impacts on socio-economic outcomes

The different governance types in protected areas do not seem to result in the alleviation of poverty in any form, but findings suggest that there is increased livelihood insecurity among affected communities. Alternative livelihood activities in protected areas governed by government are not sufficient compensation for livelihood loss, and community structures in community-governed protected areas cannot be seen as proxies for community benefit. There is evidence of equity concerns and conflict, especially around livelihood loss (alternatives are inadequate, unevenly distributed and evidence of elite capture exists). When governance types are considered independently of one another, there are few differences in outcomes by type.

Impacts on environmental outcomes

The evidence base contains little information on conservation rates measured, or on aspects of sustainable use. As a result, there is an absence of evidence on the impact of different governance structures on environmental outcomes, although there are examples of tensions between conservation and development objectives around protected areas. A weakness of the included evidence base is that these environmental outcomes are not assessed empirically, which makes it difficult to investigate the links and synergies between ecosystem services and conservation activities and poverty reduction.

Impacts on governance processes

There is similarity across governance types in the barriers to effective governance structures. In protected areas governed by government and by communities, participation by communities in the governance structures is insufficient and unequal and communication between governance structures and communities is inadequate, while there is evidence of elite capture of governance structures.

leading to positive ecological outcomes (Persha et al., 2011). There are numerous examples showing that, in practice, devolved power is rife with tensions and difficulties due to the variety of actors involved, the tendency for elites to dominate the process, inhibitive costs of participation, and vulnerability to external perturbations (Agrawal and Gibson, 1999). Co-management arrangements may serve to buffer communities against the risks of full devolution, strengthen formal recognition of tenure rights and promote equitable distribution of benefits (Oldekop et al., 2016). Overall, the evidence suggests that no single governance blueprint can guarantee the production of synergies (Box 14.2), but instead regimes should be tailored to the ecological, historical, political and cultural context. Therefore, rather than advocating a standard governance model, focus has intensified on embedding 'good governance' principles in protected areas (such as strategic direction, giving a voice to stakeholders, accountability and rights), across regime types, as a primary means of influencing effectiveness, equity and social outcomes (Borrini-Feyerabend et al., 2013).

Power relations at inception and beyond

Attention to governance processes and how they impact on the relational dimension of wellbeing suggests the importance of understanding power relations in protected areas. Differences in power between stakeholder groups at multiple scales can influence whose perspectives and values influence ecosystem governance, the negotiation of trade-offs, and consequently the distribution of benefits and burdens across social groups. Marginalised groups, who have limited agency and a weak ability to negotiate and participate in decision-making processes alongside powerful state actors and non-governmental organisations, may be particularly disadvantaged (Dawson and Martin, 2015). Recent research has highlighted the importance of the starting point in a given context – 'step zero' – and in particular the power dynamics and political systems existing prior to inception of a protected area as factors influencing the perceived incremental impacts and therefore social and ecological success (Mahajan and Daw, 2016).

Cultural values and preferences

People value ecosystem services and conceptualise wellbeing in different ways, and so the experience of protected area impacts is mediated by cultural values, social roles and livelihoods (Abunge et al., 2013). The notion that all aspects of wellbeing are constituted through the lens of culture is well evidenced, and highlights the relative importance of the subjective and relational wellbeing dimensions. However, such understanding is often excluded from discussions surrounding strategies to enhance social outcomes associated with conservation.

The problems with a compensation model for mitigating trade-offs

Compensation is commonly offered to local people identified as suffering negative impacts from the establishment of protected areas, implicitly acknowledging the existence of a trade-off relationship (McShane et al., 2011). Mechanisms to distribute compensation are diverse, as are the form in which compensation is given including micro-development projects for biodiversity offsets (Box 14.1), direct payments for losses from human–wildlife conflict, alternative livelihoods and Payment for Ecosystem Service schemes. Three distinct issues make it challenging to address trade-offs through compensation. First, who to compensate and how to identify those affected. Questions of who the true rights holders are can be contentious, and place some legitimate claimants who do not fit an identity profile at a disadvantage (Brockington and Wilkie, 2015; Poudyal et al., 2016). Second, how to distribute revenues equitably. In the case of Burunge WMA in Tanzania, revenues were distributed equally between villages on the assumption that this was fair, but some villages were experiencing more costs from human–wildlife conflict than others, resulting in feelings of resentment and conflict (Moyo et al., 2016). Third, ensuring that compensation is commensurate with any loss as felt by those affected by the protected area. Simplistic compensation strategies assuming that material payments are commensurate with non-material losses fail to recognise the importance of relational and subjective wellbeing. For example, 'sacred values' such as dignity or cultural heritage cannot simply be traded-off against secular items such as money (Daw et al., 2015), and to try to do so results in injustice. Alternative livelihoods may not match the aspirations, traditional knowledge and cultural identity of families, again emphasising the need to understand local conceptions of wellbeing through the lens of cultural values. For example, although cash conservancy payments are assumed to encourage people to move away from livestock grazing in the Mara (Bedelian and Ogutu, 2017), there is a strong preference for livestock even at the risk of getting fined (Keane et al., 2016).

Confronting and negotiating trade-offs

Rather than compensating for assumed costs from an external perspective, there needs to be better acknowledgement and recognition among stakeholders that hard choices are the norm in natural resource management (McShane et al., 2011). Explicit recognition by policy makers and practitioners of the range of trade-offs across different aspects of wellbeing, social groups and at different scales, and the distributional implications of different management and policy choices, are likely to improve the chance of success in both conservation and human wellbeing objectives, reducing the likelihood of unrealised expectations and conflict. Trade-off analysis can be used at the inception of a protected area to provide lessons for conservation practice. The use of a 'trade-off lens' can systematically take into account the wellbeing of marginalised groups in decision making, e.g. improving opportunities for those doing ecologically destructive activities to benefit from other jobs (Daw et al., 2015). Participatory modelling was used as a tool for co-producing knowledge with stakeholders to collectively explore trade-offs and novel solutions that maximise wellbeing in a fishery in Kenya. This approach allowed not only deliberation over 'hard choices', but the development of ideas of how to transform the dynamics of the system that would eliminate the need for trade-offs in the first place – for example, to allow women to access fish that support their livelihoods (Galafassi et al., 2017). Too narrow a focus on livelihood benefits or ecosystem services not only ignores the broader set of trade-offs that are important to people affected, but also the potential ways in which protected areas can lead to wellbeing improvements that can be maintained over longer periods and have wider reach. For example, Chaigneau and Brown (2016) show the importance of looking beyond emphasising the direct economic benefits of an MPA, in the form of increased fish catches, to more collective values, such as the existence value of the MPA, both for current and future generations. This can ensure longevity through increased local support for the protected area, especially if direct economic benefits fall away.

Conclusions

We have highlighted the need to take a broader perspective that engages with social complexity, spatial and temporal dynamics and context when examining the effects of protected areas on local communities – both in terms of the processes by which impacts occur and in how impacts are conceived. Protected areas are not simply technical instruments for resource management, but must be understood as social and political processes that involve a variety of actors and development activities to affect institutions, social relations and cultural norms. Research that takes a people-centred approach using a wellbeing lens is enabling us to gain a more sophisticated picture of the social dimensions of protected areas, with better potential to integrate social and ecological goals into decision making. We have highlighted the centrality of relational and subjective dimensions of wellbeing in people's experiences of and engagement with these interventions. Studies that exclude these aspects of wellbeing risk ignoring the variety of trade-offs that not only create inequity but can result in negative feedbacks, ultimately undermining the success of protected areas in conserving biodiversity. Trade-offs are typical in protected area conservation, so that attempts to promote synergies that balance social and ecological outcomes through mitigation or compensation measures must engage with and confront these trade-offs at the inception stage. This kind of trade-off analysis can form an element of governance that embeds democratic processes, transparency and allows local voices to be heard. However, wellbeing should be considered a process rather than a state, and people's priorities and conceptions will change in the context of dynamic social-ecological systems that influence their livelihood choices, aspirations and demand for ecosystem services. Such dynamism and social complexity suggests that analysis of trade-offs should not be a one-off event, but a process of continued dialogue within adaptive governance systems.

As described in this chapter, contemporary research into social dimensions of protected areas has uncovered the importance of social and cultural difference in influencing experienced and perceived impacts. Traditional ecological knowledge and relational values of the environment, as well as gendered analyses of protected area governance and impacts, continue to receive inadequate attention. Additionally, the mechanisms linking changes in wellbeing or equity to specific behavioural responses affecting conservation effectiveness remain poorly elaborated and evidenced. Future research should seek to go beyond linear, outcome-focused impact evaluations to capture these processes, and be grounded in in-depth qualitative research that allows subjective understandings of wellbeing impacts to come through, and captures the way in which dynamic social, political and ecological factors shape how outcomes are experienced.

References

(ESPA outputs marked with '*')

*Abunge C, Coulthard S and Daw TM. (2013) Connecting marine ecosystem services to human well-being: insights from participatory well-being assessment in Kenya. *Ambio* 42: 1010–1021.

Agrawal A and Gibson CC. (1999) Enchantment and disenchantment: the role of community in natural resource conservation. *World Development* 27: 629–649.

Andam KS, Ferraro PJ, Sims KRE, et al. (2010) Protected areas reduced poverty in Costa Rica and Thailand. *Proceedings of the National Academy of Sciences* 107: 9996–10001.

Baird TD. (2014) Conservation and unscripted development: proximity to park associated with development and financial diversity. *Ecology and Society* 19: 4.

Baird TD, Leslie PW and McCabe JT. (2009) The effect of wildlife conservation on local perceptions of risk and behavioral response. *Human Ecology* 37: 463–474.

Balmford A and Whitten T. (2003) Who should pay for tropical conservation, and how could the costs be met? *Oryx* 37: 238–250.

Barua M, Bhagwat SA and Jadhav S. (2013) The hidden dimensions of human–wildlife conflict: health impacts, opportunity and transaction costs. *Biological Conservation* 157: 309–316.

Bedelian C and Ogutu JO. (2017) Trade-offs for climate-resilient pastoral livelihoods in wildlife conservancies in the Mara ecosystem, Kenya. *Pastoralism* 7: 10.

*Bidaud C, Schreckenberg K, Rabeharison M, et al. (2017) The sweet and the bitter: intertwined positive and negative social impacts of a biodiversity offset. *Conservation and Society* 15: 1–13.

*Bluwstein J and Lund JF. (2018) Territoriality by conservation in the Selous–Niassa Corridor in Tanzania. *World Development* 101: 453–465.

*Bluwstein J, Moyo F and Kicheleri RP. (2016) Austere conservation: understanding conflicts over resource governance in tanzanian wildlife management areas. *Conservation and Society* 14: 218–231.

Borrini-Feyerabend G, Dudley N, Jaeger T, et al. (2013) *Governance of Protected Areas: From Understanding to Action. Best Practice Protected Area Guidelines Series No. 20*. Gland, Switzerland: IUCN.

Brechin SR, Wilshusen PR, Fortwangler CL, et al. (2002) Beyond the square wheel: toward a more comprehensive understanding of biodiversity conservation as social and political process. *Society and Natural Resources* 15: 41–64.

Brockington D and Wilkie D. (2015) Protected areas and poverty. *Philosophical Transactions of the Royal Society B: Biological Sciences* 370: 20140271.

Brooks JS, Waylen KA and Borgerhoff Mulder M. (2012) How national context, project design, and local community characteristics influence success in community-based conservation projects. *Proceedings of the National Academy of Sciences* 109: 21265–21270.

★Chaigneau T and Brown K. (2016) Challenging the win-win discourse on conservation and development: analyzing support for marine protected areas. *Ecology and Society* 21: 36.

Chan KMA, Shaw MR, Cameron DR, et al. (2006) Conservation planning for ecosystem services. *PLoS Biology* 4: e379.

Clements T, Suon S, Wilkie DS, et al. (2014) Impacts of protected areas on local livelihoods in Cambodia. *World Development* 64: S125-S134.

★Daw T, Brown K, Rosendo S, et al. (2011) Applying the ecosystem services concept to poverty alleviation: the need to disaggregate human well-being. *Environmental Conservation* 38: 370–379.

★Daw TM, Coulthard S, Cheung WWL, et al. (2015) Evaluating taboo trade-offs in ecosystems services and human well-being. *Proceedings of the National Academy of Sciences* 112: 6949–6954.

★Dawson N. (2015) Bringing context to poverty in rural Rwanda: added value and challenges of mixed methods approaches. In: Roelen K and Camfield L (eds) *Mixed Methods Research in Poverty and Vulnerability: Sharing Ideas and Learning Lessons*. London: Palgrave Macmillan, 61–86.

★Dawson N, Grogan K, Martin A, et al. (2017a) Environmental justice research shows the importance of social feedbacks in ecosystem service trade-offs. *Ecology and Society* 22: 12.

★Dawson N and Martin A. (2015) Assessing the contribution of ecosystem services to human wellbeing: a disaggregated study in western Rwanda. *Ecological Economics* 117: 62–72.

★Dawson N, Martin A and Danielsen F. (2017b) Assessing equity in protected area governance: approaches to promote just and effective conservation. *Conservation Letters*.

de Lange E, Woodhouse E and Milner-Gulland EJ. (2016) Approaches used to evaluate the social impacts of protected areas. *Conservation Letters* 9: 327–333.

★Erasmus Y and Langer L. (2017) *Does governance type in protected areas matter for poverty? A Rapid Assessment of the Evidence from Sub-Saharan Africa*. Johannesburg, South Africa: Africa Centre for Evidence.

Ferraro PJ, Hanauer MM, Miteva DA, et al. (2013) More strictly protected areas are not necessarily more protective: evidence from Bolivia, Costa Rica, Indonesia, and Thailand. *Environmental Research Letters* 8: 025011.

★Fisher JA, Patenaude G, Giri K, et al. (2014) Understanding the relationships between ecosystem services and poverty alleviation: a conceptual framework. *Ecosystem Services* 7: 34–45.

★Galafassi D, Daw TM, Munyi L, et al. (2017) Learning about social-ecological trade-offs. *Ecology and Society* 22: 2.

Goldman M. (2003) Partitioned nature, privileged knowledge: community-based conservation in Tanzania. *Development and Change* 34: 833–862.

★Gross-Camp N. (2017) Tanzania's community forests: their impact on human well-being and persistence in spite of the lack of benefit. *Ecology and Society* 22: 37.

Gurney GG, Cinner J, Ban NC, et al. (2014) Poverty and protected areas: an evaluation of a marine integrated conservation and development project in Indonesia. *Global Environmental Change* 26: 98–107.

★Homewood K, Bluwstein J, Lund JF, et al. (2015) The economic and social viability of Tanzanian wildlife management areas. *Policy Briefs (Copenhagen Centre for Development*

Research), No. 04/2015. Department of Food and Resource Economics, University of Copenhagen, Denmark.

Homewood K, Kristjanson P and Trench P. (2009) Staying Maasai? Livelihoods, conservation and development in East African rangelands. New York: Springer.

IUCN and World Commission on Protected Areas (WCPA). (2016) *IUCN Green List of Protected and Conserved Areas: User Manual, Version 1.0*. Gland, Switzerland: IUCN.

★Keane A, Gurd H, Kaelo D, et al. (2016) Gender differentiated preferences for a community-based conservation initiative. *PLoS ONE* 11: e0152432.

Lele S, Wilshusen P, Brockington D, et al. (2010) Beyond exclusion: alternative approaches to biodiversity conservation in the developing tropics. *Current Opinion in Environmental Sustainability* 2: 94–100.

McKinnon MC, Cheng SH, Dupre S, et al. (2016) What are the effects of nature conservation on human well-being? A systematic map of empirical evidence from developing countries. *Environmental Evidence* 5: 8.

McShane TO, Hirsch PD, Trung TC, et al. (2011) Hard choices: making trade-offs between biodiversity conservation and human well-being. *Biological Conservation* 144: 966–972.

Mahajan SL and Daw T. (2016) Perceptions of ecosystem services and benefits to human well-being from community-based marine protected areas in Kenya. *Marine Policy* 74: 108–119.

★Martin A, Coolsaet B, Corbera E, et al. (2016) Justice and conservation: the need to incorporate recognition. *Biological Conservation* 197: 254–261.

Matsuura N. (2017) Humanitarian assistance from the viewpoint of hunter–gatherer studies: cases of Central African forest foragers. *African Study Monographs* Suppl. 53: 117–129.

Milner-Gulland EJ. (2012) Interactions between human behaviour and ecological systems. *Philosophical Transactions of the Royal Society B: Biological Sciences* 367: 270–278.

★Moyo F, Ijumba J and Lund JF. (2016) Failure by design? Revisiting Tanzania's flagship wildlife management area Burunge. *Conservation and Society* 14: 232–242.

Newmark WD and Hough JL. (2000) Conserving wildlife in Africa: integrated conservation and development projects and beyond. *BioScience* 50: 585–592.

Nolte C, Agrawal A, Silvius KM, et al. (2013) Governance regime and location influence avoided deforestation success of protected areas in the Brazilian Amazon. *Proceedings of the National Academy of Sciences* 110: 4956–4961.

Oldekop JA, Holmes G, Harris WE, et al. (2016) A global assessment of the social and conservation outcomes of protected areas. *Conservation Biology* 30: 133–141.

Persha L, Agrawal A and Chhatre A. (2011) Social and ecological synergy: local rulemaking, forest livelihoods, and biodiversity conservation. *Science* 331: 1606–1608.

Porter-Bolland L, Ellis EA, Guariguata MR, et al. (2012) Community managed forests and forest protected areas: an assessment of their conservation effectiveness across the tropics. *Forest Ecology and Management* 268: 6–17.

★Poudyal M, Ramamonjisoa B, Hockley N, et al. (2016) Can REDD+ social safeguards reach the 'right' people? Lessons from Madagascar. *Global Environmental Change* 37: 31–42.

Pullin AS, Bangpan M, Dalrymple S, et al. (2013) Human well-being impacts of terrestrial protected areas. *Environmental Evidence* 2: 1–41.

Reid RS, Fernández-Giménez ME and Galvin KA. (2014) Dynamics and resilience of rangelands and pastoral peoples around the globe. *Annual Review of Environment and Resources* 39: 217–242.

Robalino J and Villalobos L. (2015) Protected areas and economic welfare: an impact evaluation of national parks on local workers' wages in Costa Rica. *Environment and Development Economics* 20: 283–310.

★Schreckenberg K, Franks P, Martin A, et al. (2016) Unpacking equity for protected area conservation. *Parks* 22: 11–26.
★Sikor T, ed. (2013) *The Justices and Injustices of Ecosystem Services*. Abingdon, UK: Routledge.
★Suich H, Howe C and Mace G. (2015) Ecosystem services and poverty alleviation: a review of the empirical links. *Ecosystem Services* 12: 137–147.
Woodhouse E, Homewood KM, Beauchamp E, et al. (2015) Guiding principles for evaluating the impacts of conservation interventions on human well-being. *Philosophical Transactions of the Royal Society B: Biological Sciences* 370: 20150103.

PART IV
Achieving sustainable wellbeing

While the ESPA programme started by questioning how ecosystem services could contribute to poverty alleviation, the research reported in this section focuses on wellbeing. Coulthard and colleagues (Chapter 15) discuss how the shift from a poverty framing towards one of wellbeing provides a more well-rounded interpretation of a person's life and assigns poor people greater agency, avoiding the risk of labelling them as 'hapless victims'. Considering wellbeing in all its dimensions (material, relational and subjective) also allows for a different perspective on what constitutes progress in poverty reduction. By understanding environmental degradation as the result of the varied wellbeing aspirations of different people, we can avoid the risk of unfairly blaming poorer (and often more local) people when actions of wealthy (and more distant) people may be more significant drivers. Brown and Fortnam (Chapter 16) take forward the idea of disaggregation, highlighting the particular need to reveal women's often hidden uses and experiences of ecosystems. The fact that these are often cultural and regulatory services with no cash value increases their invisibility relative to provisioning services that are more typically the subject of cost–benefit analyses. The dearth of research into women's ecosystem service preferences constitutes a serious 'blind spot', suggesting that ecosystem service approaches are in danger of reinforcing gender biases previously noted in other environmental interventions. The intersection of gender with factors like age, caste and ethnicity can further reduce the inability of women to make their voices heard.

In Chapter 17, Szaboova and colleagues examine the complex interactions between wellbeing and resilience. They address the fact that natural resources may be exploited in the short term despite the known longer-term negative impacts that may result. A key reason for this is that such trade-offs are often the product of competing preferences and needs of different stakeholder groups, compounded by power asymmetries between them. These can lead to winners and losers across different spatial and temporal scales. An example of this is provided by Diz and Morgera (Chapter 18), who explore the relationship between wellbeing and sustainability through the lens of small-scale fisheries. Many small-scale fishers are affected by decisions taken at national and international level about fishing rights for large-scale operators. At the same time, these large-scale operators may benefit from actions by small-scale fishers to conserve coastal spawning grounds. Determining an appropriate ecosystem scale for assessing sustainable fish catch can be particularly challenging in data-poor contexts but, increasingly, methods that draw on global data and models are able to provide adequate information for marine spatial planning at regional, national and local levels. However, this chapter reinforces the need expressed in preceding chapters for disaggregated social data, especially regarding gender and marginalised groups, to support planning that takes account of varied uses of the ecosystem. All four chapters in this section reaffirm the need for transparent and inclusive processes to involve local stakeholders in the design and implementation of environmental interventions to address and minimise potential trade-offs.

15
MULTIPLE DIMENSIONS OF WELLBEING IN PRACTICE

Sarah Coulthard, J Allister McGregor and Carole White

Introduction

In 2005 the Millennium Ecosystem Assessment (MA) placed the relationship between human wellbeing and ecosystems firmly at the centre of the agenda for academics and policy makers concerned with sustainable development for the following decades (MA, 2005). The decision to use the concept of human wellbeing was relatively novel and ambitious at the time. Four years later, that decision was decisively underlined by the Commission on the Measurement of Economic Performance (Stiglitz et al., 2009), commissioned by the then French President Nicolas Sarkozy and chaired by Joe Stiglitz, Amartya Sen and Jean-Paul Fitoussi. This report made a comprehensive case that if we are to achieve sustainable and inclusive development in our societies, then it is necessary to reform our major systems of statistical data collection from being focused on measuring progress in terms of production and consumption, to measuring it in terms of human wellbeing. Since that report there has been an explosion of initiatives to conceptualise and measure human wellbeing, and to put it into practice in academia and policy (Bache and Reardon, 2016; Helliwell et al., 2017).

Many different wellbeing frameworks have been advanced, but there is considerable consensus in the literature concerned with its application in public policy that the concept of wellbeing should be multi-dimensional (Stiglitz et al., 2009). It should take account of the objective condition of people and their subjective assessments of their lives (Adler and Seligman, 2016). Most frameworks also increasingly and explicitly recognise a relational dimension, arguing that aside from the objective and subjective condition of the person, it is also necessary to take account of their social relationships and how these shape the terms whereby they are able to participate in society (Gough et al., 2007; White, 2017). These three dimensions were present in the wellbeing model that was originally used in the MA – for example, material conditions and health (objective), security and social relations (relational) and freedom defined in terms of what an 'individual *values* doing and being' (subjective) (MA, 2005), but they have been significantly elaborated in the broader wellbeing literature since then (Boarini et al., 2014).

Since the MA, there has been considerable development of the concept of wellbeing in respect of its application to studying the relationship between people and the natural environment (Helne and Hirvilammi, 2015; McGregor, 2014; Woodhouse et al., 2015). There is also a strong historical root to the current wellbeing and Quality of Life literatures in the field of health (see Schmidt and Bullinger, 2007 for an overview), which has been drawn upon in ecosystem services research to demonstrate the connections between health and the natural environment (Sandifer et al., 2015). However, it is worth noting here that the commonly used phrase 'health and wellbeing' speaks largely to an expanded concept of health, but in doing so gives health a separate status (returning to a uni-dimensional model of the human), or gives health a higher (and expertly imposed) prioritisation. The multi-dimensional concept of wellbeing reviewed in this chapter takes health as being one of many wellbeing domains ('health in wellbeing'), to align with the MA framework.

This chapter reviews the ways that research in the Ecosystem Services for Poverty Alleviation (ESPA) programme has taken up the multi-dimensional notion of wellbeing, and explores how this work provides new insights into the relationship between poverty and ecosystem services. We draw on a desk-based synthesis of ESPA-funded academic publications that use multi-dimensional conceptual frameworks or methodologies to study poverty or wellbeing, and discuss these in the context of the broader wellbeing and environment literature. The chapter is organised as follows. First, we clarify the relationship between multi-dimensional wellbeing and contemporary thinking about poverty and poverty alleviation, emphasising the significance of moving from multi-dimensional poverty to multi-dimensional wellbeing framings. We then provide an overview of three key contributions of 'ESPA wellbeing research' to wider debates on ecosystem services and poverty reduction. These are: (i) recognising the need for social differentiation; (ii) identifying and tackling trade-offs (between different ecosystem services and dimensions of wellbeing); and (iii) highlighting inequality and injustices around how ecosystem services are distributed. These contributions are closely related, and could be viewed as a logical set of queries to unpack any ecosystem service and wellbeing relationship: first, how people are different in terms of their wellbeing needs and strategies; second, how ecosystem services contribute to people's wellbeing in different ways, and what factors underpin who benefits and who does not; and third, the uneven distribution of ecosystem services to wellbeing, and the extent to which this is perceived as fair or unjust. Each contribution is supported by empirical examples from ESPA research, and the broader literature. Collectively, these examples demonstrate the value of adopting multi-dimensionality in their assessment of wellbeing, in particular subjective and relational dimensions, which generate new insights and opportunities for poverty reduction. The chapter concludes by summarising how these insights might contribute to improving the sustainable management of ecosystems in ways that contribute to poverty reduction.

Poverty and wellbeing: from income to multi-dimensionality

We start by clarifying the relationship between poverty and human wellbeing. Given the emergence of a sophisticated multi-dimensional poverty literature (Alkire and Santos, 2013; van Staveren et al., 2014), the relationship between the concept of wellbeing and how we understand poverty has become blurred. This has been evident in the ESPA programme, where the focus on making a difference in terms of poverty alleviation has encouraged many researchers towards more of a poverty frameworks approach (Suich et al., 2015). Furthermore, the terms wellbeing and poverty are frequently used interchangeably, often as the antonym of one another (Roe et al., 2014). This lack of distinction retains many of the drawbacks of the poverty approach but also loses much of the positive value offered by framing the analysis in terms of a broader conception of wellbeing.

Anyone who lives or works with poor people in any part of the world soon realises that there is more to their lives than their poverty. Poverty may be oppressive and relentless, but it does not drive out other aspects of the humanity of these men, women and children. The recognition of the rounded humanity of people living in poverty is what has stimulated the rise of multi-dimensional approaches to understanding poverty, and ultimately the shift towards wellbeing. Important contributions include Amartya Sen's capabilities framework, which has underpinned a campaign for thinking about poverty in terms of 'human development' and as being about more than just income (Nussbaum and Sen, 1993). He argues that judgements of a quality of life should focus on what people are able to achieve, rather than solely on what they have or what they lack. Around the same time, the emergence of 'participatory' approaches to development (Chambers, 1983) argued that, to understand poverty fully we must hear from the people who are themselves experiencing it. The World Bank's Voices of the Poor (VoP) study (Narayan et al., 2000) formally introduced the voice of people living in poverty to the poverty policy arena, and affirmed that there are other dimensions of being poor that are important to consider. Most significantly however, it underlined that peoples' subjective perceptions of what they need to participate in society or to live a decent life are important to consider in any deliberation about poverty alleviation. These developments have shifted the poverty debate from a narrow focus on objective dimensions of poverty (and mainly income poverty) to a broader discussion about wellbeing – about what people need to be able to have, to be able to do and be able to feel in order to be well in society (Gough et al., 2007). These developments were clearly evident in the MA framework, which thus helped stimulate a departure from common singular, income-based notions of poverty (Pinho et al., 2014).

From the extensive literature we can distil three key reasons that have both moral and scientific aspects, why it is considered important to shift from a poverty frame of analysis to a wellbeing framing (see Box 15.1). The first is that poor people cannot be defined by their poverty alone and, even in dire circumstances, they are still actively engaged in the pursuit of what they perceive of as wellbeing for

> **BOX 15.1 Three reasons for shifting to a wellbeing framing**
>
> - Poverty analyses can miss crucial wellbeing strategies which underpin the relationship between ecosystem services and human wellbeing.
> - Wellbeing is a well-rounded interpretation of a person's life, which avoids labelling poor people as hapless victims.
> - Wellbeing provides a holistic, person-centred analysis incorporating social and subjective assessments of life.

themselves and their families (Gough et al., 2007). Poverty framings shape the focus of analysis to emphasise what people lack, and they do not sufficiently focus on what they have, how innovative they are with what they have, and what they are trying to achieve. In doing this they delimit analysis in ways that can miss important attributes of people's lives, which can often influence the ways that their wellbeing considerations drive their relationships with ecosystem services (Coulthard et al., 2011). The poverty framing also means that the research focus is likely to be inadequate in its consideration of non-poor populations, overlooking those living on the margins of poverty and those doing well – analysis of both groups can reveal important insights into poverty dynamics (Krishna, 2011). The second is that defining people only in terms of their poverty denies the fundamental humanity of poor people, tending to categorise them as hapless victims rather than active agents capable of change. A positive focus on wellbeing enables analysis to avoid the labelling and stigmatisation of 'the poor', the process of 'othering' that is often present in policy and practice (White, 2010). The third is that wellbeing provides a holistic outlook that rejects compartmentalisation of people's lives (as per *homo economicus*), but focuses on the person (Douglas and Ney, 1998; McGregor and Pouw, 2017). This more holistic ontology demands a more socially informed analysis of people's lives and their relationships with others, which in turn provides a more substantial insight into the production and reproduction of poverty and how their engagement with the environment relates to this (McGregor, 2014; White, 2010).

Key contributions of multi-dimensional wellbeing research

The importance of social differentiation and the need for disaggregated assessment of how ecosystem services can contribute to wellbeing

The MA stimulated international recognition of the universal dependence of human wellbeing on ecosystem services. A major contribution of ESPA research has been to detail this dependence across a breadth of different ecosystem services spanning contexts as diverse as small-scale fishers in coastal Bangladesh (Hossain et al., 2016) to pastoralists in sub-Saharan Africa (Homewood et al., 2018). This detailing has highlighted the importance of understanding social complexity, as an important first step towards understanding ecosystem services–wellbeing relationships (Abunge et al., 2013; Dawson and Martin, 2015; Dearing et al., 2014). Different people have different ideas about what is important for their wellbeing and about how they should seek to achieve wellbeing; they also have different dependencies upon ecosystem services. For example, poor people are usually more directly and immediately dependent for their livelihoods on the exploitation of the natural environment than are others (such as middle- and upper-class city dwellers or wealthier people residing in rural areas) in their societies (Bidaud et al., 2017; Trivedi, 2009).

Drawing from examples across coastal ecosystem services, Daw et al. (2011) argue the importance of disaggregating wellbeing in such a way that focuses on who derives which benefits from ecosystems, and how such benefits contribute to the wellbeing of the poor:

> First, different groups derive wellbeing benefits from different ES [ecosystem services], creating winners and losers as ecosystem services change. Second, dynamic mechanisms of access determine who can benefit. Third, individuals' contexts and needs determine how ES contribute to wellbeing. Fourth, aggregated analyses may neglect crucial poverty alleviation mechanisms...
> (Daw et al., 2011: 370)

For the design and implementation of interventions in ecosystems, it is important to understand what wellbeing differences exist in the population. These lines of social difference may be wealth orientated, but others (e.g. caste, religion, gender) may also be significant. In their study of conflict surrounding the designation of the Gulf of Mannar National Park and Biosphere Reserve, India's largest marine protected area, Bavinck and Vivekanandan (2011) start by recognising the diverse social makeup of the coastal community, which includes diverse castes and religions, both of which influence livelihood traditions. They argue that conflicts between individuals or groups derive from their various and sometimes contrasting wellbeing goals. In the study, conflicts occur between different users of the marine resource, in particular small-scale fishermen and trawler fishermen who operate over the same fishing grounds, with the former blaming the latter for damage to fish stocks and small-scale gears. Conflict also occurs between park managers and fishers, the former harbouring aspirations for strong marine conservation within the park, which is heralded as a biodiversity hotspot of global value. Fishers' aspirations, however, are often more integrated with concerns of social justice, conflict avoidance and the fairness with which conservation regulations are implemented. In particular, small-scale fishers lament weak consultation with the park authorities, and feel that conservation efforts would be better served by controlling destructive fishing practices such as trawling, through stronger implementation of existing legislation. The authors argue that park authorities need to be aware of the variations that exist in the wellbeing aspirations of coastal populations, and that such variety can only be suitably addressed through a diverse governance approach and through political participation. They argue that the development of governance partnerships could contribute to more balanced decision making and a greater appreciation among the target population of the 'fairness' of MPA policy, in order to improve the legitimacy of the park's rulings.

Dawson and Martin (2015) problematise the inadequate recognition of social complexity in ecosystem services research (see Box 15.2), using the term 'socio-ecological reductionism'. They further argue that a multi-dimensional wellbeing framing can enable a fuller exploration of linkages between ecosystem services and human wellbeing. This is demonstrated in Dawson et al. (2016), who apply multi-dimensional wellbeing to critically analyse the wellbeing impacts of 'Green Revolution' agricultural modernisation policies in rural Rwanda, such as the adoption of modern seed varieties and credit systems to increase yields of specific

---

BOX 15.2 COMMON INSTANCES OF SOCIO-ECOLOGICAL REDUCTIONISM

1. Failure to consider different types of values: different people may value an ecosystem service differently based on how it contributes to their wellbeing, and thus may react differently to changes in how that service is managed.

2. Aggregation of people and preferences: over-simplification of population characteristics (e.g. by using average statistics) means that winners and losers resulting from a particular change are unrecognised.

3. Failure to understand power relations and politics: these determine who controls, or benefits, from ecosystem services, and who does not.

4. A focus on single land-use types: an overly narrow focus neglects multiple uses of the wider landscape, and risks missing synergies and trade-offs.

5. Lack of attention to changes and their drivers at multiple scales: the relationship between ecosystem services and wellbeing is affected by environmental, social, demographic, political, economic and technological changes, which operate at different spatial and temporal scales. People's wellbeing may be influenced by microsocial processes, or global economic change; some changes may be gradual, whilst others may be rapid shocks.

Source: Dawson and Martin (2015)

marketable crops. While policies have been deemed successful in raising yields and reducing poverty levels (as measured through conventional means), the authors found that this national-level image of success diverged significantly from local experience. By considering what farming households value and aspire to achieve, and assessing the progress towards these self-determined goals, a different view of how agricultural policy reform was contributing to poverty alleviation emerges. This assessment highlights negative impacts for particular groups of people, exacerbating landlessness and inequality for some of the poorest, and finds that only a relatively wealthy minority have been able to take up the imposed modernisation schemes. The authors conclude that policies promoting a Green Revolution in sub-Saharan Africa cannot automatically be considered to be pro-poor.

Identification and tackling of trade-offs between the environment and human wellbeing

The conditions of poverty, combined with critical dependence on ecosystems, can produce circumstances in which poor people, and resource governors, must face hard choices. These choices may involve people having to make difficult trade-offs either in terms of which aspects of their own wellbeing they will prioritise (for example income or dignity), or whether they will prioritise some aspect of their wellbeing over the health of the ecosystem. At their most extreme, these trade-offs can be emotive and charged with moral challenge: they may be between their children eating today or taking actions that may be to the detriment of the environment on which they depend (Dearing et al., 2014). As the examples discussed thus far have illuminated, social disaggregation reveals how different people are dependent upon ecosystem services in different ways, resulting in a plurality of different values attached to ecosystem services (Bavinck and Vivekanandan, 2011). Just as important are the power relations and politics, which mediate access to ecosystem service benefits (Dawson and Martin, 2015) and influence trade-offs resulting from different resource governance decisions.

Daw et al. (2015) detail trade-offs (defined as 'when gains for one ecosystem service or group of people results in losses for others' (p. 6949)), which became apparent through an innovative interdisciplinary method applied in the context of Kenyan coastal fisheries. This combines ecological simulation of marine ecosystem services, participatory assessment of social-ecological system structure and qualitative research into subjective wellbeing of five different stakeholder groups dependent on the fishery, differentiated by livelihood and gender. These three data types were integrated into a simplified 'toy model' that illustrates the dynamics of the system and how it delivers benefits to different user groups. Despite an apparent win–win between conservation and profitability at the aggregate scale (McClanahan, 2010), food production, employment and wellbeing of different actors are differentially influenced by management decisions leading to trade-offs. The ecological model of the fishery suggests a win–win between system-level goals of conservation (through reducing environmentally damaging beach seining) and profitability (greater landings of high value fish), a management rationale that is promoted throughout Kenyan fisheries and in other parts of the world (McConney and Baldeo, 2007). However, model outputs suggest that the potential conservation–profit win-win comes at the expense of local food production, which declines because of reduced fishing effort with beach seine, which land high volumes of cheap 'trash fish' (McClanahan, 2010). Disaggregating different stakeholders revealed a range of potential trade-offs and win-wins in different groups' wellbeing, with particular disadvantages for those dependent upon beach seine for employment, and women traders who rely on beach seine landings for affordable fish, which is fried and sold locally. Not only do these groups represent some of the poorest and most vulnerable in the society (Béné and Merten, 2008), but trash fish is also an important source of protein-rich food security for the wider coastal population (see also Daw et al., 2016). As the authors conclude:

> Environmental management inevitably involves trade-offs among different objectives, values, and stakeholders. Most evaluations of such trade-offs involve monetary valuation or calculation of aggregate production of ecosystem services, which can mask individual winners and losers. . .Such trade-offs are often ignored because losers are marginalized or not represented by quantification . . .
>
> (Daw et al., 2015: 6949)

Inequalities in ecosystem service distribution

A third area of research relates to the extent to which inequalities are inherent in ecosystem service distribution, and how this can lead to injustice (see also Dawson et al., this volume). As the MA recognised, there is a fundamental inequality in the ways in which ecosystem services are accessed and transformed into wellbeing outcomes (Fisher et al., 2013). While the exploitation of ecosystem services has enabled huge growth in wellbeing for some, others have experienced little benefit, while the negative effects of environmental degradation, and the management interventions designed to reduce degradation, often fall disproportionately on poor people (Coulthard et al., 2011; McDermott et al., 2013; Satyal et al., 2017). Examples can be found in many different contexts. Lakerveld et al. (2015) describe how the inadequate establishment of access rights to forest resources after independence in India led to widespread state appropriation, which ruptured and disabled prior community-based institutions. The Forest Department, with limited institutional capacity and political pressures to favour commercial interests, was unable to prevent large-scale deforestation, and a return to a depleted open-access resource has impacted both environmental health and the ability of forest dwellers to locate sufficient wood for their daily needs. Similarly, Dearing et al. (2014) describe the deterioration of water quality in catchment areas in China (Yunnan Province and Shucheng County) as being predominantly driven by economic development, particularly agricultural intensification and increased fertilizer use and local fossil fuel-based industries. They cite the 'huge challenges' facing local government to harness the momentum of economic growth to reduce poverty, while reconciling growth with the need to restore badly damaged ecosystems and ecological processes.

The more direct relationship that poor people have with the natural environment has often led to the poorest people being blamed for ecosystem degradation. ESPA research has been a critical commentator of the over-simplification of Malthusian arguments that brush over questions of how ecosystem services are distributed (Coulthard et al., 2011), and the displaced impacts of higher consumption lifestyles (Fisher et al., 2013). ESPA research has also helped recognise that, perhaps because of the visibility of poor people and their dependence on the environment, some conservation and environmental management regimes can and have been particularly punitive for the poorest people. For instance, Pinho et al. (2014) detail that in Latin America, Payments for Ecosystem Services Schemes (PES) are often touted as a pro-poor natural resource management option, despite evidence that the poor still face discrimination, with very limited real benefits on the ground (see Menton and Bennett, this volume). As Sikor (2013) remarks, different types of ecosystem services result in justices and injustices for different people so that any ecosystem management needs to consider a socially and spatially differentiated assessment of its impacts on people. In his book *Just Conservation*, Adrian Martin (2017) brings together wellbeing and social justice to directly challenge some of the injustices that resound in current conservation approaches:

> Some problems are presented as being so urgent that they require states to operate outside of everyday norms of fairness – to act in the wider interest of a nation, or the planet, even if this rides roughshod over the rights of a few. There is a danger that conservation is thought of in this way: that its need for action is so exceptional that almost any activity to save biodiversity is morally justified...However, it is flawed thinking to conclude that effective responses to this crisis will necessarily run into conflict with norms of social justice.
>
> (Martin, 2017: 19)

Bidaud et al. (2017) use a multi-dimensional wellbeing framing to illuminate some of the social impacts, and subsequent injustices, resulting from a biodiversity offsetting project established by the Ambatovy mine, a major nickel and cobalt mine in Madagascar, a country that has large numbers of poor people living alongside some of the world's most valued biodiversity. The study is particularly relevant for its effective use of multi-dimensional wellbeing that reveals 'hidden' social impacts that mono-dimensional approaches are likely to miss, and has clear relevance for similar offsetting projects worldwide. The research details local people's perceived impacts of introduced biodiversity offset projects on wellbeing. First, results show that the offset projects were implemented in sites where people are very poor, and have high dependence on the forest for everyday necessities (illustrating impacts on poorer sectors of society). Second, local people perceived that the biodiversity offset project had highly differentiated impacts on wellbeing. In particular, development benefits (such as donated chickens and agricultural equipment) were seen as benefitting some, but also erosive to social relations (conflicts had arisen around the distribution of development benefits), a good example of a trade-off between material and relational wellbeing. Furthermore, in some sites the conservation restrictions were enforced by locally employed people who were expected to report on their neighbours, which introduced new social tensions. An even bigger source of social tension relates to pressure on land among villages with growing populations in the conservation areas.

The research highlights an injustice in the ways that development benefits are distributed, which clearly illustrates the role of power and social position in determining ecosystem service access. Data reveal that the most important predictors of a household receiving donations or training is not the extent of forest dependence (indicated by distance to forest, or collection of forest products), or poverty, but rather being a member of a forest management association. While the offset project has both positive and negative impacts on wellbeing for different groups of people, overall, local perceptions highlight a negative impact, through restricted land use and declining social relations. In a similar vein to earlier examples, the authors point to a lack of social differentiation of communities at the local scale as being particularly problematic: 'There remains a mismatch between who benefits from the development activities and who bears the cost of the conservation restrictions' (Bidaud et al., 2017: 11).

Conclusions

Our review of ESPA research which has adopted a multi-dimensional framing of wellbeing in its approach, illuminates the value of multi-dimensionality and its capacity to unpack differences between people and their ecosystem service–wellbeing relationships. The importance of acknowledging social complexity and disaggregating how ecosystem services translate into wellbeing outcomes is highlighted in all the empirical examples above, as a necessary precursor to the adequate evaluation of how ecosystem change and policy interventions affect people's lives. Considering the material, relational and subjective dimensions of wellbeing underpins a much more detailed analysis and understanding than mono-dimensional approaches, and can paint a very different picture of progress in poverty reduction – as demonstrated particularly well by Dawson et al. (2016) and their critique of agricultural reform in Rwanda. Ignoring social difference in any assessment of ecosystem service–wellbeing relationships is therefore clearly problematic and leads to inadequate assessment of interventions and failure to spot injustice, especially for marginalised and poor men, women and children.

This has implications for sustainability narratives at the global level. The recently arrived notion of 'the Anthropocene' tends to be deployed in global debates in ways that blame 'people' generally and in an undifferentiated way for their misuse of the natural environment resulting in profound changes in the world in which we live. However, when we look at particular situations of environmental degradation we find a good deal of evidence across ESPA research and beyond that suggests that it is often more wealthy actors that are the more significant drivers of ecosystem degradation (Dearing et al., 2014; Klein, 2015; Szabo et al., 2016). In this sense we can understand that processes of environmental degradation and of unsustainable development are driven by a desire for wellbeing in some form or another but, as ESPA research underlines, this is not enough to conceive ecosystem damage and decline as being poverty driven. At a systemic level it is the wellbeing aspirations and demands of people at all places in nation states and in a global system that drive ecosystem pressures. Compared with the level of damage that is driven by the wellbeing aspirations of poor people, the level of damage that is driven by demand in highly integrated globalised markets and that articulates metropolitan cities and remote rural communities is massive.

Given the stated goal of the ESPA programme to find ways of aligning sustainable management of ecosystems and poverty alleviation, the notion of the Anthropocene appears to be inadequate in its specification. It introduces the potential for an anti-poor bias into sustainability policy thinking, and in that sense the label 'Capitalocene' would appear to be more sensitive to the social justice issues that are involved (Moore, 2015; see also Holmes et al., 2017). Rather than separating thinking about ecosystems from thinking about people and how societies and economies are organised, as single-disciplinary science does, it appears to be more fruitful to conceive of people as agents who are part of these ecosystems and who are making decisions at all levels based on their wellbeing aspirations and motivations. It is this aspect of the ESPA programme, with its stimulation of interdisciplinary research across natural and social sciences, which has enabled a much greater incorporation of multi-dimensional wellbeing analysis in ecosystem services research. As some have argued, the future success of the global sustainability agenda depends on the absorption of significant and sophisticated conceptions of wellbeing into its analysis (Helne and Hirvilammi, 2015; McGregor, 2014), and the application of multi-dimensional wellbeing in ESPA research is an important contribution.

References

(ESPA outputs marked with '★')

★Abunge C, Coulthard S and Daw TM. (2013) Connecting marine ecosystem services to human well-being: insights from participatory well-being assessment in Kenya. *Ambio* 42: 1010–1021.

Adler A and Seligman MEP. (2016) Using wellbeing for public policy: theory, measurement, and recommendations. *International Journal of Wellbeing* 6: 1–35.

Alkire S and Santos ME. (2013) A multidimensional approach: poverty measurement & beyond. *Social Indicators Research* 112: 239–257.

Bache I and Reardon L. (2016) *The Politics and Policy of Wellbeing: Understanding the Rise and Significance of a New Agenda.* Cheltenham, UK: Edward Elgar.

★Bavinck M and Vivekanandan V. (2011) Conservation, conflict and the governance of fisher wellbeing: analysis of the establishment of the Gulf of Mannar National Park and Biosphere Reserve. *Environmental Management* 47: 593–602.

Béné C and Merten S. (2008) Women and fish-for-sex: transactional sex, HIV/AIDS and gender in African fisheries. *World Development* 36: 875–899.

★Bidaud C, Schreckenberg K, Rabeharison M, et al. (2017) The sweet and the bitter: intertwined positive and negative social impacts of a biodiversity offset. *Conservation and Society* 15: 1–13.

Boarini R, Kolev A and McGregor JA. (2014) Measuring well-being and progress in countries at different stages of development: towards a more universal conceptual framework. *OECD Development Center Working Papers* 325: 1–59.

Chambers R. (1983) *Rural Development: Putting the Last First*. Colchester, UK: Longman.

★Coulthard S, Johnson D and McGregor JA. (2011) Poverty, sustainability and human wellbeing: a social wellbeing approach to the global fisheries crisis. *Global Environmental Change* 21: 453–463.

★Daw T, Brown K, Rosendo S, et al. (2011) Applying the ecosystem services concept to poverty alleviation: the need to disaggregate human well-being. *Environmental Conservation* 38: 370–379.

★Daw TM, Coulthard S, Cheung WWL, et al. (2015) Evaluating taboo trade-offs in ecosystems services and human well-being. *Proceedings of the National Academy of Sciences* 112: 6949–6954.

★Daw TM, Hicks CC, Brown K, et al. (2016) Elasticity in ecosystem services: exploring the variable relationship between ecosystems and human well-being. *Ecology and Society* 21: 11.

★Dawson N and Martin A. (2015) Assessing the contribution of ecosystem services to human wellbeing: a disaggregated study in western Rwanda. *Ecological Economics* 117: 62–72.

★Dawson N, Martin A and Sikor T. (2016) Green revolution in sub-Saharan Africa: implications of imposed innovation for the wellbeing of rural smallholders. *World Development* 78: 204–218.

★Dearing JA, Wang R, Zhang K, et al. (2014) Safe and just operating spaces for regional social-ecological systems. *Global Environmental Change* 28: 227–238.

Douglas M and Ney S. (1998) *Missing Persons: A Critique of the Personhood in the Social Sciences*. Berkeley, CA: University of California Press.

★Fisher JA, Patenaude G, Meir P, et al. (2013) Strengthening conceptual foundations: Analysing frameworks for ecosystem services and poverty alleviation research. *Global Environmental Change* 23: 1098–1111.

Gough I, McGregor JA and Camfield L. (2007) Theorizing wellbeing in international development In: Gough I and McGregor JA (eds) *Wellbeing in Developing Countries: From Theory to Research*. Cambridge, UK: Cambridge University Press.

Helliwell J, Layard R and Sachs J. (2017) World Happiness Report 2017. New York: Sustainable Development Solutions Network.

Helne T and Hirvilammi T. (2015) Wellbeing and sustainability: a relational approach. *Sustainable Development* 23: 167–175.

★Holmes G, Sandbrook C and Fisher JA. (2017) Understanding conservationists' perspectives on the new-conservation debate. *Conservation Biology* 31: 353–363.

★Homewood K, Keane A, Rowcliffe M, et al. (2018) Pastoralism, conservation and resilience: causes and consequences of pastoralist household decision-making. In: Gardner S, Ramsden S and Hails S (eds) *Agricultural Resilience: Perspectives from Ecology and Economics*. London: British Ecological Society.

*Hossain MS, Dearing JA, Rahman MM, et al. (2016) Recent changes in ecosystem services and human well-being in the Bangladesh coastal zone. *Regional Environmental Change* 16: 429–443.

Klein N. (2015) *This Changes Everything: Capitalism vs. the Climate*. New York: Simon and Schuster.

Krishna A. (2011) *One Illness Away: Why People Become Poor and How They Escape Poverty*. Oxford: Oxford University Press.

Lakerveld RP, Lele S, Crane TA, et al. (2015) The social distribution of provisioning forest ecosystem services: evidence and insights from Odisha, India. *Ecosystem Services* 14: 56–66.

MA. (2005) *Millennium Ecosystem Assessment, 2005. Ecosystems and Human Well-Being: Synthesis*. Washington, DC: Island Press.

McClanahan TR. (2010) Effects of fisheries closures and gear restrictions on fishing income in a Kenyan coral reef. *Conservation Biology* 24: 1519–1528.

McConney P and Baldeo R. (2007) Lessons in co-management from beach seine and lobster fisheries in Grenada. *Fisheries Research* 87: 77–85.

*McDermott M, Mahanty S and Schreckenberg K. (2013) Examining equity: a multidimensional framework for assessing equity in payments for ecosystem services. *Environmental Science and Policy* 33: 416–427.

McGregor JA. (2014) Poverty, wellbeing, and sustainability. In: Atkinson G, Dietz S, Neumayer E, et al. (eds) *Handbook of Sustainable Development*. Cheltenham, UK: Edward Elgar.

McGregor JA and Pouw N. (2017) Towards an economics of well-being. *Cambridge Journal of Economics* 41: 1123–1142.

*Martin A. (2017) *Just Conservation: Biodiversity, Wellbeing and Sustainability*. Abingdon, UK: Routledge.

Moore JW. (2015) *Capitalism in the Web of Life: Ecology and the Accumulation of Capital*. London: Verso.

Narayan D, Patel R, Schafft K, et al. (2000) *Voices of the Poor: Can Anyone Hear Us?* New York: Oxford University Press (for the World Bank).

Nussbaum M and Sen A, eds. (1993) *The Quality of Life*. Oxford: Oxford University Press.

*Pinho PF, Patenaude G, Ometto JP, et al. (2014) Ecosystem protection and poverty alleviation in the tropics: perspective from a historical evolution of policy-making in the Brazilian Amazon. *Ecosystem Services* 8: 97–109.

*Roe D, Fancourt M, Sandbrook C, et al. (2014) Which components or attributes of biodiversity influence which dimensions of poverty? *Environmental Evidence* 3: 3.

Sandifer PA, Sutton-Grier AE and Ward BP. (2015) Exploring connections among nature, biodiversity, ecosystem services, and human health and well-being: opportunities to enhance health and biodiversity conservation. *Ecosystem Services* 12: 1–15.

*Satyal P, Shrestha K, Ojha H, et al. (2017) A new Himalayan crisis? Exploring transformative resilience pathways. *Environmental Development* 23: 47–56.

Schmidt S and Bullinger M. (2007) Cross-cultural quality of life assessment approaches and experiences from the health care field. In: Gough I and McGregor JA (eds) *Wellbeing in Developing Countries: From Theory to Research*. Cambridge, UK: Cambridge University Press.

*Sikor T, ed. (2013) *The Justices and Injustices of Ecosystem Services*. Abingdon, UK: Routledge.

Stiglitz JE, Sen A and Fitoussi J-P. (2009) Report by the Commission on the Measurement of Economic Performance and Social Progress. 1–292.

*Suich H, Howe C and Mace G. (2015) Ecosystem services and poverty alleviation: a review of the empirical links. *Ecosystem Services* 12: 137–147.

★Szabo S, Brondizio E, Renaud FG, et al. (2016) Population dynamics, delta vulnerability and environmental change: comparison of the Mekong, Ganges–Brahmaputra and Amazon delta regions. *Sustainability Science* 11: 539–554.
★Trivedi MR, Mitchell AW, Mardas N, Parker C, Watson JE and Nobre AD (2009) REDD and PINC: a new policy framework to fund tropical forests as global 'eco-utilities'. *IOP Conference Series: Earth and Environmental Science* 8: 012005.
van Staveren I, Webbink E, de Haan A, et al. (2014) The last mile in analyzing wellbeing and poverty: indices of social development. *Forum for Social Economics* 43: 8–26.
White SC. (2010) Analysing wellbeing: a framework for development practice. *Development in Practice* 20: 158–172.
White SC. (2017) Relational wellbeing: re-centring the politics of happiness, policy and the self. *Policy and Politics* 45: 121–136.
Woodhouse E, Homewood KM, Beauchamp E, et al. (2015) Guiding principles for evaluating the impacts of conservation interventions on human well-being. *Philosophical Transactions of the Royal Society B: Biological Sciences* 370: 20150103.

16

GENDER AND ECOSYSTEM SERVICES

A blind spot

Katrina Brown and Matt Fortnam

Introduction

In the field of international development, gender has emerged as a major focus in research, policy and practice over the past three or more decades. Gender issues have not received the same attention in natural resource management and environmental conservation, but are a major consideration in research and, increasingly, in international conservation organisations. As Meinzen Dick et al.'s review (2014) asserts, gender and sustainability have been highly prominent on the development agenda since the 1980s, but are rarely considered together in any systematic way. Gender remains a critical gap in ecosystem services literature; Cruz-Garcia et al.'s (2017) systematic review of 462 papers on ecosystem services and wellbeing identified only five from 49 case studies that focused on gender – they identify gender as a 'blind spot' in ecosystem services research. But why does this omission matter? In the context of managing ecosystem services for poverty alleviation, it matters on two key fronts. First, gender is likely to be a critical determinant of how people differentially benefit from ecosystems, and the absence of the perspective makes ecosystem service frameworks weakly aligned with the central concerns of global development around equity, justice, knowledge and voice. Second, it matters because the policy imperative of the global community, articulated through Agenda 2030 and operationalised in the Sustainable Development Goals (SDGs), seeks to 'leave no-one behind'. In other words, inclusive and sustainable development cannot be achieved without detailed consideration of social difference and, in particular, gender.

Researchers have grappled with understanding the systematic gender biases and the complex relationships between gender, environment and development. Early work, dating from the 1980s, emphasised women's socially defined roles as users and managers of natural resources, and as carers within households and

TABLE 16.1 Gender and ecosystem services: key literatures and approaches

Approach	Assertions	Implications for gender and ecosystem services
Eco-feminism	Women have greater inherent connection to nature – it makes essentialist and (almost) universal arguments	Women are more directly dependent on ecosystem services than men; women recognise and value ecosystem services, and are more affected by changes in flows of ecosystem services than men
Gender and development	Women and men have different roles and responsibilities, and this results in gendered divisions of labour	Women's relationships with ecosystem services are predicated on their roles and responsibilities in terms of provision of food, fuel, water and care for children and the elderly
Household bargaining	Within households, different members have different power in negotiating strategies and roles	Decision making on the allocation of household resources, including labour, reflects men's priorities – for example, in the adoption of new technology for land and water management
Feminist political ecology	Gender dimensions of relations with the environment are shaped by gendered knowledge; rights and responsibilities; politics and grassroots action. Gender intersects with different axes of identity (e.g. class, caste, race, age)	Ecosystem services are gendered because of the social and political relations of access, ownership and control. The relationship between individuals and ecosystems is shaped by their distinct identities, part of which is gender
Natural resource management	Women's participation in decision making and collective action is limited; women have different interests and motives compared to men	Women are more motivated by social than private benefits than men, emphasising security over profit and perhaps subsistence over cash benefits from ecosystem services
Social vulnerability	Women (and children) may be more vulnerable to environmental change – including climate change – and to extreme events than men	Women may be more sensitive to changes to supporting and regulating services than men

Sources: Leach et al. (1995); Meinzen Dick et al. (2014); Ravera et al. (2016).

communities, conferring special status on women as having a close affinity with the environment (Leach et al., 1995). While this perspective continues to be reflected in the rhetoric of some campaigning organisations, scholars have challenged and dismissed its essentialist assumptions. Themes emerged that understand women's relationship to the environment within the context of gender divisions of labour, property rights and institutions, knowledge and power, and the wider political economy. The literature on gender, environment and development is rich and diverse, informed by a number of development and feminist theoretical perspectives (see Table 16.1).

How does the field of ecosystem services learn from or inform these views? The Millennium Ecosystem Assessment (MA, 2005) did not have a specific focus on gender, but its findings do support some of the common assumptions of the literature on gender and environment. For example, the MA highlights that significant differences between the roles and rights of men and women in many societies lead to women's increased vulnerability to changes in ecosystem services. Rural women in developing countries are the main producers of staple crops like rice, wheat and maize. Because the gendered division of labour within many societies places responsibility for the routine care of the household on women, even when women also play important roles in agriculture, the degradation of ecosystem services such as water quality or quantity, fuelwood, agricultural or rangeland productivity often results in increased labour demands on women. This can affect the household by diverting time from food preparation, childcare, education of children and other beneficial activities. Yet gender bias persists in agricultural policies in many countries, and rural women involved in agriculture tend to be the last to benefit from – or in some cases are negatively affected by – development policies and new technologies. Therefore, one immediate inference is that ecosystem services approaches need to be inclusive and understand the gender biases of earlier approaches to international development and environmental conservation.

Here we analyse how research undertaken in the Ecosystem Services for Poverty Alleviation (ESPA) programme informs these important issues of gender and ecosystem services. We have undertaken a review of ESPA literature, and consider this within the context of a broader emerging literature on ecosystem services and development. Reflecting the absence of gender in wider ecosystem service research, our literature search only found seven ESPA papers that identified with 'gender' or 'women' in title or abstract, although there are likely to be gender-related data generated by ESPA projects that have not yet been analysed or published.

Engendering ecosystem services

Research on how ecosystems contribute to the wellbeing and poverty alleviation of different individuals and social groups remains limited (Daw et al., 2011, 2015). To date, much of the literature has assumed that ecosystem services confer aggregate benefits to society as a whole, following economic models (Fisher et al., 2013). In this respect, much of the work on ecosystem services is 'gender blind', yet ecosystem services and their role in alleviating poverty are predicated on a set of social relations that are inherently gendered. An emerging literature has shown that men and women have divergent socio-cultural perceptions, values and preferences for ecosystem services. They also use, experience and benefit from ecosystem services differently.

Some empirical studies report that women are more likely to perceive and value ecosystem services than men (Calvet-Mir et al., 2016; Martín López et al., 2012; Shen et al., 2015), while others report the opposite (Hartter, 2010; Orenstein and Groner, 2014; Rönnbäck et al., 2007; Warren-Rhodes et al., 2011). These contrasting findings are likely to be due to gender intersecting with contextual and other forms of identity, such as age, wealth, education, cultural traditions and access to information and decision-making processes (Costanza, 2000; Daily, 1997; Daw et al., 2011; Muhamad et al., 2014; Plieninger et al., 2013). Indeed, the ability to secure benefits from and access ecosystem services is often strongly linked to gender and wealth (Rönnbäck et al., 2007). Some studies have also identified a preference among men for provisioning services and a preference among women for regulating services (Kalaba et al., 2013; Martín López et al., 2012; Oteros-Rozas et al., 2014). The contrasting conclusions on the relationship between ecosystem services and gender show that it is important not to make universal or 'essentialist' assumptions about gender roles based on empirical evidence from contextually specific cases.

These studies are predominantly undertaken in developed countries, and so they offer limited insights on how the relationship between ecosystem services and poverty alleviation is gendered for poor communities in developing countries. Importantly, they do not explain why these gendered differences exist. To understand this, we need to combine literature on gender, environment and development, and empirical insights. For example, the ESPA SPACES project (Fortnam et al., 2018) shows that gendered social processes in East Africa, such as behavioural expectations, knowledge systems, formal institutions and the patriarchal society, make ecosystem services gendered. It found that specific coastal ecosystem services in East Africa are strongly associated with male and female roles and responsibilities, and that physical spaces are highly gendered, with men exploiting marine ecosystem services while women tend to exploit ecosystem services accessible from land. Male activities also focus on provisioning services such as fish and mangrove poles, and high-value activities, such as large-scale fish trading or tourism-based activities (e.g. boat operators). In contrast, women use or experience a larger variety of ecosystem services, which tend to be non-monetised and often regulatory or cultural services. This finding resonates with literature on gender and forests. Agarwal (2000) showed that men prefer trees with high timber productivity, while women prefer trees that offer a wide range of services that support wellbeing more broadly, such as the provision of fuel, fodder and shade.

These less visible ecosystem services valued by women play an important role in supporting household livelihoods. Porter et al. (2008) show in Tanzania that the male-dominated fishery never completely supports households, with coastal livelihoods comprising a variety of economic activities, including livestock

BOX 16.1 A DISAGGREGATED ANALYSIS OF GENDERED VALUES ASSOCIATED WITH ECOSYSTEM SERVICES

Women value mangroves more than men, for their contribution to a wider variety of wellbeing domains, but men value mangroves for physical security more than women, linked to their use of mangrove poles for self-defence weapons. The figures show that men and women value ecosystem services differently, often because of their culturally defined gendered roles and responsibilities.

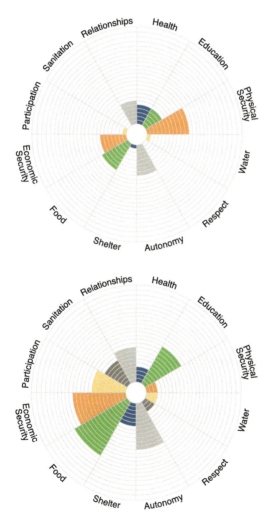

FIGURE 16.1 Showing how men (top) and women (bottom) value mangroves for several wellbeing domains (further elaborated in Fortnam et al., 2018).

husbandry, seaweed farming and agriculture. Women play a pivotal role in these subsidiary activities.

Hamann et al. (2015) mapped social-ecological systems based on how households directly use ecosystem services in South Africa. The gender of the household head was a key factor, in addition to land tenure and household income, for determining low, medium and high levels of ecosystem service use. The authors link this finding to gender differences in resource dependence, with women, especially those with a low income, relying most on natural resources. Female-headed households located in communal areas faced major challenges in accessing ecosystem services due to their insecure land tenure, linked to South African customary law. That female household heads have greater dependence on, but less access to, ecosystem services has important implications for poverty alleviation and ecosystem services strategies and trade-offs, discussed below.

These findings are supported by past research on the relationship between gender and the environment (Leach, 2007; Rocheleau and Edmunds, 1997). This has shown that women often have strong dependencies on environmental resources, particularly common property or open-access resources in, for example, forests, grasslands and savanna. They also have primary responsibility in most of the developing world for collection of water and fuelwood, and for providing meals for the family. Hence, the convergence of domestic and productive tasks and the differentiated roles and responsibilities of women in households, families and communities are observed in many contexts. However, women often lack control of or access to land and its associated resources, and are therefore discriminated against in using or benefitting from ecosystem services. Labour, roles and responsibilities are often divided by gender, but they are culturally defined and vary from context to context. Furthermore, because of these differences, women and men have different perceptions and preferences for the use and management of ecosystems.

Box 16.1 shows a rare example of a gender-disaggregated analysis of preferences for ecosystem services undertaken by the ESPA SPACES project. While gendered social relations may be barriers to women accessing ecosystem services, they may also render women particularly vulnerable to changes in ecosystems services (e.g. Adams et al., 2013). They may also expose them to risk – for example, women in Sierra Leone are more likely to contract Lassa fever because their role in agriculture brings them into contact with the rats transmitting the disease (Dzingirai et al., 2017).

Gendered trade-offs

Changes to ecosystems create 'winners' and 'losers' (to put it crudely), since individuals and social groups value and benefit from ecosystem services differently. While such trade-offs are often unavoidable, conservation and development policies and practices often fail to consider them and, instead, focus on socially acceptable win-win opportunities (McShane et al., 2011). Given the differences in how men and women use, experience and benefit from ecosystem services, it is likely that some trade-offs will be gendered. Furthermore, socio-cultural preferences and values related to gender, as well as other factors such as education and age, underpin what people are willing to trade off and what is sacred and non-tradeable (Daw et al., 2015; Martín López et al., 2012). Yet, a systematic literature review by Howe et al. (2014) found that out of 92 reviewed case study reports of where ecosystem services had been used for human wellbeing, no studies analysed trade-offs between men and women.

Trade-offs can be overlooked or obscured if marginalised groups are excluded from assessment and decision-making processes (Daw et al., 2015). While trade-offs between landscape-scale ecosystem services are being researched, such as between grazing for food production and wetlands for floodwater storage, there has been little research on trade-offs between the wellbeing of different social groups, including between men and women. The ESPA P-mowtick project illustrates the existence of 'hidden' trade-offs that may affect the wellbeing of poor or vulnerable groups of women (Box 16.2). Often the services used and experienced by women are not marketable, but instead provide direct subsistence to households. They are, therefore, not accountable in conventional cost–benefit analyses. All this implies that ecosystem services work, while being gender-blind, might also be biased because of the invisibility of women's activities and views, and the focus on particular ecosystem services.

Ecosystem management decision-making processes are often biased towards men, which results in a tendency to favour provisioning services and a focus on single ecosystem services. Thus, it might be that implicit trade-offs are made between provisioning services that men exploit and a broader set of non-monetary ecosystem services that benefit the roles and responsibilities of women. The exclusion of women, or assuming men represent a community, risks excluding important ecosystem services from decision-making processes. In marine and coastal social-ecological systems, women and men, as the P-mowtick project demonstrated, fish in different ways and target different species. Therefore, the design of marine protected areas and other measures should consider a wide range of habitats and species including those targeted by women (Kleiber et al., 2015).

Ecosystem interventions tend to be designed with the assumption that a community is homogenous and has shared interests, or that overall gains to society offset any disadvantages (Pascual et al., 2014). Without prior consideration, this can generate unintended trade-offs across sub-groups of individuals that hold variable preferences, opportunities and constraints. Because of gendered roles and responsibilities, and asymmetrical power relations, in the household and community, interventions that alter ecosystem service provision or access can differentially affect men and women. As illustrated in Box 16.3, a failure to engage with social diversity may unintentionally create winners and losers, and therefore sources of resistance and support.

In other instances, because of culturally defined roles and responsibilities, women disengage with a project as it becomes irrelevant to them. For example, Corbera et al. (2007) found that women's participation in a carbon project in Yalum was high

BOX 16.2 GENDERED TRADE-OFFS IN A SMALL-SCALE FISHERY IN MOMBASA, KENYA

In Nyali, near Mombasa on the Kenya coast, the small-scale fishery connects various primary stakeholders through their use of and impacts on the coral reef and seagrass system. Most of the stakeholders are poor, but they are differentiated by, for example, gender, the different species and parts of the social-ecological systems they exploit, and by their use and access to ecosystem services.

The ESPA 'P-mowtick' project examined how five of the primary stakeholders in the social-ecological system benefitted from ecosystem services associated with the fishery:

- captains of illegal but widely used large beach seine nets;
- labourers used in teams to pull beach seine nets;
- independent fishers using other gears, such as small gill nets and spears;
- male traders, who specialise in large fish for high-value markets; and
- female traders, who buy smaller and cheaper fish, typical of beach seine catches, and fry them to sell to local communities.

The project developed a 'toy model' to represent how management and social drivers affect fishing effort and the resultant effects on ecological dynamics, catches and earning opportunities for each primary stakeholder group. Secondary stakeholders – including resource managers and decision makers in government and NGOs – played with the model in a facilitated workshop to explore the trade-offs associated with different management options for the fishery.

One trade-off that emerged from the analysis was that changes in fishing effort resulted in ecological responses that altered the composition of catches and the distribution of wellbeing benefits among the stakeholders. Reduced fishing effort would likely increase catches of large, high-value fish, which would benefit male fishers and male large-scale traders while disadvantaging female traders, who depend on and only have access to smaller fish.

The case shows that well-meaning conservation programmes that aim to reduce fishing effort and increase profitability can unintentionally affect marginalised groups. Because of gendered access mechanisms, there was a trade-off between female traders' interests and either profit or conservation. Furthermore, many stakeholders judged that interventions that made already vulnerable groups, such as women traders, worse off, were morally wrong.

Source: Daw et al. (2015)

> **BOX 16.3 GENDERED PREFERENCES IN COMMUNITY-BASED CONSERVATION IN KENYA**
>
> In the Maasai Mara, in Kenya, a form of payment for ecosystem services exists: households lease plots of their privately owned land to nature conservancies to be used for ecotourism instead of using it for grazing or cultivation. Keane et al. (2016) analysed the gendered preferences of local community members towards livelihoods and the conservancy.
>
> They found that women value membership of the conservancy more than men, and value waged income, cultivation and access to conservancy land for grazing less than men. The authors attribute this difference to the amount of control women have over waged income compared with conservancy payments. Wages are earned by men and are often not spent on the household; conservancy payments in contrast are paid monthly directly into household bank accounts, use of which women may be able to influence. In some parts of Kenya, the payments are strategically made to maximise household benefits – for example, to coincide with the dates when school fees are due. The authors also highlight, however, how the loss of grazing land to conservancies may shift livelihoods away from livestock to waged labour, from which women are less able to access benefits for themselves and their family.
>
> Source: Keane et al. (2016)

when it was focused on community development in the earlier years, such as planting fruit trees in home gardens, but declined when the project narrowed its focus to extensive tree planting in agricultural lands and pastures – an activity that women are not involved in. The project had failed to address the causes of gender exclusion in forest management, a finding also uncovered by Boyd (2002) in Bolivia and Fisher (2013) in Uganda. Earlier feminist political ecology analyses point to the gendered social relations underpinning forest access, management and practice (Rocheleau and Edmunds, 1997).

Market-based approaches to managing ecosystem services are popular in international policy, including payments for ecosystem services (PES), such as biodiversity conservation and carbon sequestration (see Menton and Bennett; Porras and Asquith, both this volume). Social equity has increasingly become a key concern in PES discourse, especially related to Reduced Deforestation and Forest Degradation (REDD+) schemes, which can have substantial gender implications.

Men and women use and experience forests differently, so REDD+ policies that alter how forests are used differentially affect men and women. In some cases, REDD+ may limit women's access to forest ecosystem services (Brown, 2011).

TABLE 16.2 Gender dimensions of ecosystem services interventions

Aspect of intervention	Gender dimensions	Possible implications if gender dimension is ignored
Outcomes	Wellbeing is socially constructed; men and women value different aspects and have different needs	Aspects of wellbeing valued by women (e.g. social relations above private profit) may be undermined
Access and property rights	Costs and benefits are determined by how people access resources, technology and knowledge, and how this is shaped by formal and informal property rights – all are very strongly gendered	Women are barred from accessing key resources because of technology (e.g. fishing gears, boats) or from managing assets (e.g. trees) because of informal and formal rights
Decision-making and voice	Formal and informal institutions at all scales are dominated by men; women's voices and views are excluded	Women are under-represented in forest, water and fisheries user groups and management associations; women are sidelined into women-only groups
Priorities and interests	Masculine values and interests dominate	Emphasis on cash rather than subsistence production; timber over fuelwood
Framing and power	Ecosystem services are framed in limited ways, emphasising economic and financial values	'Women's priorities' are hidden

In other cases, the banning of logging in order to sequester carbon has resulted in the development of non-timber products that are often collected by women. This places additional labour burdens on women without providing any social safeguards (Arora-Jonsson, 2014). Brown (2011) studied the gender implications of a REDD+ programme in the Congo Basin. As in many parts of the world, women and men are both highly dependent on forest ecosystem services, but women are disadvantaged by having insecure access and property rights to forests, forest resources and land. The REDD+ process has done little to address these gender issues, with women participating very little in the decision-making and policy processes on REDD+ in the riparian nations of Cameroon, Central African Republic and Democratic Republic of Congo. In Nepal, the participation of women in REDD+ projects is a key criterion for receiving payments for forest carbon sequestration, but Khadka et al. (2014) argue that this was insufficient to achieve gender-equitable benefits since it did not address the deeply gendered power relations and socio-cultural institutions of Nepalese society.

PES is often implemented through common property rights, which create further institutional barriers to delivering gender-equitable PES initiatives. Development agencies face the dilemma of whether to operate through locally defined and often gendered institutions or challenge them to establish more inclusive and fair property rights (Corbera et al., 2007). The latter is likely to be met with stronger resistance and make project implementation costlier in terms of time and investment.

Table 16.2 summarises some of the gender dimensions which are often overlooked in designing ecosystem services interventions, and moves beyond distribution of costs and benefits to consider who shapes the agenda and what social and institutional mechanisms actually determine the outcomes for different actors, the likelihood that interventions will be considered fair or unfair, and in turn whether they are likely to be supported or resisted (see also Daw et al., 2015; Pascual et al., 2014; and Dawson et al., this volume).

Identifying interventions that work for gender equality and ecosystem services

Gender is increasingly mainstreamed into ecosystem management interventions and, as a result, participation of women has become a requirement of most donor-driven environmental projects. However, requiring participation of women in a process does not necessarily give them voice or the capacity to influence the process, as the Nepal REDD+ example suggests, since it does not address the power relations that disadvantage women and reduce the masculine bias in policies and interventions. To give women true agency in decision making, they need to have sufficient capacity to make decisions and influence the decisions of others. Rather than a project add-on or deliverable, this is a long-term, complex process that seeks to transform cultural norms and practices and entrenched gendered power relations. When considering the perceptions, values and uses of ecosystem services by women, they should not be treated as a homogenous group but instead considered in terms of class, racial, cultural and ethnic difference too. This points to the need to give agency to all marginalised stakeholders in ecosystem management processes, not just women, and to do more than simply avoiding the negative impacts on women. It begs the question, are there ecosystem services interventions that are likely to contribute towards women's wellbeing and empowerment?

International development has amassed a large body of experience in the field of advancing women's status and empowering women through development interventions, so there are important lessons here. There is a large literature about the potential pitfalls and perils of 'gender mainstreaming' (Cornwall et al., 2007), but this approach is widely adopted in development and biodiversity conservation programmes. However, few interventions on ecosystem services take rights-based approaches to transform the structures by which women are inhibited from benefiting from ecosystems. There are many examples of widening participation and providing incentives for women to be involved in management and decision making, especially in forestry and conservation. For instance, Agarwal (2010) found the gender composition of executive committees to be a reasonable proxy for women's 'effective' participation in community forestry in India – with 30% of women on the executive committee being a critical threshold. Increasing women's participation can start to chip away at some of the institutional constraints to women's full and meaningful participation in strategising and decision making around ecosystem services, and to gain a fairer share of benefits.

One example of how ecosystem services might support women's empowerment comes from Kenya, where a mangrove boardwalk was built and run by the women's group on Wasini Island. The boardwalk, located on the periphery of the mangrove system, weaves into the mangroves near an open area called the coral garden. Tourists pay a small fee to visit the mangroves, after a tour of the coral reef and dinner at a hotel on the island. The small income generated by the boardwalk enables women to keep their children in school. In interviews carried out as part of the SPACES project (Fortnam et al., 2018), women explained how this meant they could invest in their daughters' education in a culture where boys' education is generally prioritised over girls':

> For me, if there would not have been many of these developments, I would not have been able to have attended secondary level of education. The group assisted me in achieving, and many other more, as we were many who were assisted. For me, if there was not the women group, I would have not been able to reach the level.
>
> (Wasini Women Group member)

International agencies have suggested a research agenda to address current bias in ecosystem services work. Box 16.4 presents a synthesis of key issues identified for further research from CGIAR's Water, Land and Environment Programme and OpenNESS, an international collaborative research programme. Gender trade-offs need to be more fully understood and assessed, and gender dimensions should be embedded in all ecosystem assessment processes. This might change some practices but will not necessarily address structural inequalities as needed to meet the objectives of SDG 5 (gender equality), and to ensure that development 'leaves no-one behind'.

Conclusion: towards inclusive and just ecosystem services

Ecosystem services frameworks have the potential to highlight rather than exacerbate gender inequalities in ecosystem management. By shedding light on the multiple services provided by ecosystems, they could reveal often hidden uses and experiences of ecosystems linked to the roles and responsibilities of women. These tend to be non-monetised cultural and regulatory services, which are invisible in cost–benefit analyses that focus on provisioning services such as timber and fish. They have the potential to reconfigure policy-making away from giving primacy to those services that are valued by and benefit men to better account for a wider variety of services, including those that are valued by and benefiting women. To date, however, women's knowledge and views have not been given a true voice.

BOX 16.4 PROPOSED RESEARCH QUESTIONS ON GENDER AND ECOSYSTEM SERVICES

- What are the different ways in which women and men depend on ecosystem services for their livelihoods?
- How can ecosystem service trade-offs and synergies be managed, so that they are more equitable for poor women and men? What kind of policies, services and information can help women address the loss of ecosystem services?
- How do the gendered human–nature relationships influence preferences for ecosystem services? Are there ecosystem services particularly valued by women, and how do we ensure their conservation and/or restoration? How can institutions and decisions build on these preferences or priorities?
- What is the role of gender in improving environmental quality and ecosystem services, including the relationship between women's reproductive rights, population growth and conservation, and the types of institutions (markets, community organisations, cooperatives, networks) that women interact with?
- How do social/gender relations (e.g. norms, perceptions, attitudes and behaviours) and gender roles determine women's and men's participation in incentive systems for environmental services, such as the certification for social, environmental or nutritional benefits of commodity systems, PES and command and control?

Source: CGIAR (2014); Kelemen et al. (2016).

The findings presented here demonstrate that there is a danger that ecosystem services approaches may reinforce gender biases evident in past and existing natural resource management, conservation and development interventions. Research needs to interrogate assumptions about ecosystem services and disservices – and how they relate to gendered social processes and outcomes. The research questions summarised in Box 16.4 would go some way towards uncovering the differences in ecosystem services and who benefits and how, and serve to illuminate the distributional aspects of benefits and responsibilities among people and their links to ecosystems, and also describe the ways in which people can participate in decision making and priority setting. We argue there is also a need to address underlying issues of knowledge, value and governance, and to understand how gender intersects with other dimensions of identity, such as sexuality, age, caste and ethnicity. Socially just approaches to ecosystem services must engage with these underlying issues, which underpin the social processes that produce and re-produce gendered patterns of use, access, benefits and costs associated with ecosystem services.

References

(ESPA outputs marked with '★')

★Adams H, Adger WN, Huq H, et al. (2013) Wellbeing-ecosystem service links: mechanisms and dynamics in the southwest coastal zone of Bangladesh. *ESPA Deltas Working Paper #2.* 56 pp.

Agarwal B. (2000) Conceptualising environmental collective action: why gender matters. *Cambridge Journal of Economics* 24: 283–310.

Agarwal B. (2010) Does women's proportional strength affect their participation? Governing local forests in South Asia. *World Development* 38: 98–112.

Arora-Jonsson S. (2014) Forty years of gender research and environmental policy: where do we stand? *Women's Studies International Forum* 47: 295–308.

Boyd E. (2002) The Noel Kempff project in Bolivia: gender, power, and decision-making in climate mitigation. *Gender and Development* 10: 70–77.

Brown HCP. (2011) Gender, climate change and REDD+ in the Congo Basin forests of Central Africa. *International Forestry Review* 13: 163–176.

Calvet-Mir L, March H, Corbacho-Monné D, et al. (2016) Home garden ecosystem services valuation through a gender lens: a case study in the Catalan Pyrenees. *Sustainability* 8: 718.

CGIAR. (2014) Gender strategy. Colombo, Sri Lanka: CGIAR Research Program on Water, Land and Ecosystems (WLE), International Water Management Institute (IWMI). 27.

Corbera E, Brown K and Adger WN. (2007) The equity and legitimacy of markets for ecosystem services. *Development and Change* 38: 587–613.

Cornwall A, Harrison E and Whitehead A, eds (2007) *Feminisms in Development: Contradictions, Contestations and Challenges.* London: Zed Books.

Costanza R. (2000) Social goals and the valuation of ecosystem services. *Ecosystems* 3: 4–10.

Cruz-Garcia GS, Sachet E, Blundo-Canto G, et al. (2017) To what extent have the links between ecosystem services and human well-being been researched in Africa, Asia, and Latin America? *Ecosystem Services* 25: 201–212.

Daily G. (1997) *Nature's Services: Societal Dependence on Natural Ecosystems.* Washington, DC: Island Press.

★Daw T, Brown K, Rosendo S, et al. (2011) Applying the ecosystem services concept to poverty alleviation: the need to disaggregate human well-being. *Environmental Conservation* 38: 370–379.

★Daw TM, Coulthard S, Cheung WWL, et al. (2015) Evaluating taboo trade-offs in ecosystems services and human well-being. *Proceedings of the National Academy of Sciences* 112: 6949–6954.

★Dzingirai V, Bett B, Bukachi S, et al. (2017) Zoonotic diseases: who gets sick, and why? Explorations from Africa. *Critical Public Health* 27: 97–110.

★Fisher JA. (2013) Justice implications of conditionality in payments for ecosystem services: a case study from Uganda. In: Sikor T (ed.) *The Justices and Injustices of Ecosystem Services.* Abingdon, UK: Routledge, 21–45.

★Fisher JA, Patenaude G, Meir P, et al. (2013) Strengthening conceptual foundations: analysing frameworks for ecosystem services and poverty alleviation research. *Global Environmental Change* 23: 1098–1111.

★Fortnam M, Brown K, Chaigneau T, et al. (2018) The gendered nature of ecosystem services. ESPA SPACES (Sustainable Poverty Alleviation from Coastal Ecosystem Services) Working Paper No.9, March 2018.

★Hamann M, Biggs R and Reyers B. (2015) Mapping social-ecological systems: identifying 'green-loop' and 'red-loop' dynamics based on characteristic bundles of ecosystem service use. *Global Environmental Change* 34: 218–226.

Hartter J. (2010) Resource use and ecosystem services in a forest park landscape. *Society and Natural Resources* 23: 207–223.

★Howe C, Suich H, Vira B, et al. (2014) Creating win-wins from trade-offs? Ecosystem services for human well-being: a meta-analysis of ecosystem service trade-offs and synergies in the real world. *Global Environmental Change* 28: 263–275.

Kalaba FK, Quinn CH and Dougill AJ. (2013) The role of forest provisioning ecosystem services in coping with household stresses and shocks in Miombo woodlands, Zambia. *Ecosystem Services* 5: 143–148.

★Keane A, Gurd H, Kaelo D, et al. (2016) Gender differentiated preferences for a community-based conservation initiative. *PLoS ONE* 11: e0152432.

Kelemen E, Potschin M, Martín-López B, et al. (2016) Ecosystem services: a gender perspective. *OpenNESS Ecosystem Services Reference Book*. EC FP7 Grant Agreement no. 308428.

Khadka M, Karki S, Karky BS, et al. (2014) Gender equality challenges to the REDD+ initiative in Nepal. *Mountain Research and Development* 34: 197–207.

Kleiber D, Harris LM and Vincent AC. (2015) Gender and small-scale fisheries: a case for counting women and beyond. *Fish and Fisheries* 16: 547–562.

Leach M. (2007) Earth mother myths and other ecofeminist fables: how a strategic notion rose and fell. *Development and change* 38: 67–85.

Leach M, Joeks S and Green C. (1995) Gender relations and environmental change. *IDS Bulletin* 26: 1–8.

MA. (2005) *Millennium Ecosystem Assessment, 2005. Ecosystems and Human Well-Being: Synthesis*. Washington, DC: Island Press.

McShane TO, Hirsch PD, Trung TC, et al. (2011) Hard choices: making trade-offs between biodiversity conservation and human well-being. *Biological Conservation* 144: 966–972.

Martín López B, Iniesta Arandia I, Garca-Llorente M, et al. (2012) Uncovering ecosystem service bundles through social preferences. *PLoS ONE* 7: e38970.

Meinzen Dick R, Kovarik C and Quisumbing A. (2014) Gender and sustainability. *Annual Review of Environment and Resources* 39: 29–55.

Muhamad D, Okubo S, Harashina K, et al. (2014) Living close to forests enhances people's perception of ecosystem services in a forest – agricultural landscape of West Java, Indonesia. *Ecosystem Services* 8: 197–206.

Orenstein DE and Groner E. (2014) In the eye of the stakeholder: changes in perceptions of ecosystem services across an international border. *Ecosystem Services* 8: 185–196.

Oteros-Rozas E, Martín-López B, González JA, et al. (2014) Socio-cultural valuation of ecosystem services in a transhumance social-ecological network. *Regional Environmental Change* 14: 1269–1289.

Pascual U, Phelps J, Garmendia E, et al. (2014) Social equity matters in payments for ecosystem services. *BioScience* 64: 1027–1036.

Plieninger T, Dijks S, Oteros-Rozas E, et al. (2013) Assessing, mapping, and quantifying cultural ecosystem services at community level. *Land Use Policy* 33: 118–129.

Porter M, Mwaipopo R, Faustine R, et al. (2008) Globalization and women in coastal communities in Tanzania. *Development* 51: 193–198.

Ravera F, Iniesta-Arandia I, Martín-López B, et al. (2016) Gender perspectives in resilience, vulnerability and adaptation to global environmental change. *Ambio* 45: 235–247.

Rocheleau D and Edmunds D. (1997) Women, men and trees: gender, power and property in forest and agrarian landscapes. *World Development* 25: 1351–1371.

Rönnbäck P, Crona B and Ingwall L. (2007) The return of ecosystem goods and services in replanted mangrove forests: perspectives from local communities in Kenya. *Environmental Conservation* 34: 313–324.

Shen Z, Wakita K, Oishi T, et al. (2015) Willingness to pay for ecosystem services of open oceans by choice-based conjoint analysis: a case study of Japanese residents. *Ocean and Coastal Management* 103: 1–8.

Warren-Rhodes K, Schwarz A-M, Boyle LN, et al. (2011) Mangrove ecosystem services and the potential for carbon revenue programmes in Solomon Islands. *Environmental Conservation* 38: 485–496.

17
RESILIENCE AND WELLBEING FOR SUSTAINABILITY

Lucy Szaboova, Katrina Brown, Tomas Chaigneau, Sarah Coulthard, Tim M Daw and Thomas James

Introduction

Wellbeing and resilience are already central to debates on how to achieve sustainable development alongside the eradication of poverty (Brown, 2016), and are evident in the articulation of the UN's Agenda 2030 and the Sustainable Development Goals (SDGs). Therefore, they could become instrumental in developing approaches and interventions to implement the SDGs, as they represent language that is already familiar to key actors and audiences. For example, they are embedded in the sustainable development discourses and programming of international agencies such as FAO and the World Bank, bilateral aid organisations such as DFID and USAID, major NGOs (International Red Cross, World Food Programme), as well as many philanthropic organisations.

Wellbeing concepts (see Coulthard et al., this volume) can give insights into individuals' choices and behaviour (Armitage et al., 2012). As behaviour can be understood as the pursuit of wellbeing (Coulthard, 2012), wellbeing should not be conceived only as an outcome, but must also be understood as a process (Gough et al., 2007). Yet more dynamic approaches to wellbeing have only recently started to emerge in the literature (e.g. Coulthard, 2011; White, 2010). Resilience – broadly defined as the ability to successfully deal with change – brings insights from complex systems and provides a way of understanding change as non-linear, across scales, and in multiple dimensions (Brown, 2016). A resilience perspective on social-ecological systems (Reyers and Selomane, this volume) elicits an integrated systems-based view of how human society is linked with ecosystem change, and how change occurs within that linked system. However, resilience has been critiqued for its insufficient engagement with aspects of the social system, such as agency, that shape people's ability to respond to these changes (Brown and Westaway, 2011).

Although wellbeing and resilience approaches are rooted in quite distinct disciplinary traditions, they may complement each other, because resilience brings a

TABLE 17.1 Key resilience concepts

Resilience concept	Definition
Resilience	The ability to successfully deal with change. It is a characteristic that can be applied to individuals, communities, states, ecosystems or linked social-ecological systems (Brown, 2016: 2)
Persistence	Absorbing disturbance and maintaining a status quo. Persistence involves 'conserving what you have and recovering to what you were' (Folke et al., 2010: 1)
Adaptation	Adjusting to responses to changing external drivers and internal processes and thereby allowing for development along a current trajectory (Folke et al., 2010: 6)
Transformation	Profound 'shifts in perception and meaning, social network configurations, patterns of interactions among actors including leadership and political and power relations, and associated organisational and institutional arrangements' (Folke et al., 2010: 5)
Feedback loops	Closed sequences of causes and effects (Richardson and Pugh, 1981: 4)
Tipping points and thresholds	The point at which one relatively stable state or regime gives way to another (Kinzig et al., 2006: 20)

dynamic view of complex systems and can thus enhance emerging notions of wellbeing as process, while the social theories underpinning wellbeing work can assist the better integration of social concepts (e.g. agency) into resilience thinking. Resilience scholars draw on concepts from systems science to unpack how society and the environment might respond to change (Table 17.1), which can occur suddenly or gradually and can be environmental, social, economic or political in nature. These concepts can be instrumental for a more dynamic understanding of how such changes shape poor people's wellbeing over time, their ability to benefit from ecosystem services and their capacity for resilience.

This chapter explores the application of resilience and wellbeing concepts in research funded within the Ecosystem Services for Poverty Alleviation (ESPA) programme, and situates it within the wider literature to ascertain how these concepts might inform the future sustainable development agenda. Our analysis elucidates four themes that inform and illustrate some of the existing challenges around ecosystem services and poverty alleviation, and provides important insights for the contemporary sustainability agenda. The analysis highlights the following: politics, power and representation; multiple values attributed to ecosystem services and wellbeing and how they are often shaped by external factors; complex interaction and reciprocity between human and natural systems; and the scale at which these interactions unfold. These are all critical if we are to find sustainable development solutions that leave no one behind.

Power, politics and representation

Fisher et al.'s (2013) synthesis of frameworks for ecosystem services and poverty alleviation proposes that resilience approaches rarely address issues of politics and agency at collective and individual scales. This gap in understanding is empirically probed by studies that explore how resilience concepts of persistence, adaptation and transformation interact with issues of agency, capability, freedom and power over change in ecosystem services. For example, Coulthard (2011) suggests that the resilience of social and ecological systems depends on the power of multiple interests to participate in changing the institutions that influence how ecosystem services are managed. Adams et al.'s (2013a) analysis shows how transformation of land use in Bangladesh, for food security and generation of foreign currency, transfers the benefits of ecosystem services to powerful groups, rather than those living in poverty. This highlights how outside interests can shift a system into less desirable states for those who lack power to shape decision making yet critically depend on appropriated ecosystem services for their wellbeing.

Due to these complex and multi-layered mechanisms at play, it is essential to disaggregate the benefits of ecosystem services with regard to different groups of society who share them unevenly (Daw et al., 2011). Disaggregation is perceptive of change (environmental, social, economic, etc.), social difference and power asymmetries that mediate access to ecosystem services. For example, although the aggregate availability of a service may be unchanged, the processes, mechanisms and institutions governing access to and use of these services may change and, in turn, alter the distribution of benefits, creating winners and losers. Porter and colleagues (2008) illustrate this by highlighting how global demand for octopus has led to the commodification of this service and a consequent shift in local access dynamics, whereby men displaced women from performing the traditional livelihood activity of tapping octopus in inshore waters. Women, constrained by cultural codes of conduct, were no longer able to maintain access to the fishery, although the total availability of octopus remained unchanged. Access is thus mediated by a variety of mechanisms, including customary tenure regimes (Coulthard et al., 2011) and social relationships (Adams et al., 2013b). Traditional and customary access rights of the poor, however, are challenged by legalised formal claims of more powerful, often external, actors towards previously common land or resources as a result of their monetisation or conversion into more lucrative uses (Humphreys Bebbington, 2013), leading to the dispossession of the poor and their exclusion from ecosystem benefits.

Analysis of trade-offs across multiple scales generates important insights into the disaggregated distributional impacts of interventions in ecosystem services management (Dawson and Martin, 2015; Vira et al., 2012). For example, Dawson and Martin (2015) use the example of the suffering of indigenous Twa, caused by the deforestation of the Gishwati Forest, Rwanda, to analyse the ways in which social differentiation and power influence how trade-offs occur at local scales. These insights tell us that analysis of trade-offs at finer scales can enhance the potential for interventions to better address the needs and wants of specific groups towards the ecosystem services on which they depend. While conservation and development initiatives claim to enhance wellbeing, evidence from research points to impacts contrary to this ethos. Conservation and agricultural policies that disregard existing local social and political dynamics are shown to have negative repercussions for poor people's access to land, leading to the criminalisation of traditional livelihoods and loss of vital resources (e.g. non-timber forest products) (Adams et al., 2013b; Bavinck and Vivekanandan, 2011; Broegaard et al., 2017; von Maltitz et al., 2016), creating winners and losers.

Hence, evidence from research questions the effectiveness of current approaches to devising and implementing conservation and development programmes that fail to integrate the knowledge, needs and preferences of local stakeholders who are most affected by them (e.g. Abunge et al., 2013; Adams et al., 2013b; Bavinck and Vivekanandan, 2011). This, in turn, relinquishes the poor of what Sen refers to as 'procedural control' (Sen, 1985) and has important implications for the success of such interventions (Abunge et al., 2013), as well as for procedural justice (Dawson and Martin, 2015). Participation in decision making determines the distribution

---

BOX 17.1 GAS EXTRACTION, POWER ASYMMETRIES AND TRANSFORMING ACCESS RIGHTS IN THE BOLIVIAN CHACO

In the Bolivian Chaco, indigenous communities face a series of challenges caused by hydrocarbon extraction, which saw the arrival of multi-national corporations welcomed by the central state. The global valuation of natural gas stands in contrast to local values and uses attached to indigenous land within the Chaco. Existing social disparities and power asymmetries between various local populations in the Chaco (such as the Weenhayek and the Guaraní), and between local and central actors within Bolivia, have deepened as a result of top-down ecosystem service governance driven by the state and hydrocarbon corporations. While compensation schemes have been put in place, these did not acknowledge existing power asymmetries or local values and meanings attached to the land in question, thus exacerbating existing inequalities and creating new divisions. As a result, the governance process designed to facilitate gas extraction gave rise to a series of procedural inequities: the property rights of hydrocarbon companies were honoured over the claims of indigenous people over land and territory, while indigenous people have not had access to important economic information. These inequities have thwarted the ability of these populations to advance their territorial claims and exercise effective control over their territories, reducing their access to vital ecosystem services, especially those linked to water.

Source: Humphreys Bebbington (2013)

of benefits, which are reflective of existing power relations. Thus failing to integrate the poor and marginalised into decision making acts to strengthen and reproduce already existing disparities and disadvantage (Daw et al., 2016; Dawson and Martin, 2015; Box 17.1; also see Dawson et al., this volume).

Multiple dimensions of ecosystem services and wellbeing

Ecosystem services research increasingly acknowledges the multi-dimensional nature of ecosystem services, which contribute to multiple aspects of wellbeing by means of multiple mechanisms (e.g. Ramirez-Gomez et al., 2015; Roe, 2014), as well as the multi-dimensional nature of poverty and wellbeing, which encompass material as well as non-material dimensions (Abunge et al., 2013; Adams et al., 2013b; Dawson et al., 2016; Roe, 2014; also see Coulthard et al., this volume). Fisher et al. (2013) also draw our attention to the role of non-ecosystem service sources. Findings from the ESPA Deltas project indeed showcase the role of remittances and off-farm labour in wellbeing creation (Adams et al., 2013b; Szabo et al., 2016).

Recent debates in ecosystem services research have recognised that ecosystem services are socially constructed and valued differently at different scales and by different groups of society (e.g. Chan et al., 2012; Dawson and Martin, 2015). Therefore, the assumption that there is a positive relationship between ecosystem services and wellbeing is overly simplistic, because dependence on ecosystem services can also act as a poverty trap (Adams et al., 2013b), and may exacerbate households' vulnerability (Suich et al., 2015). In this vein, ESPA research has identified a variety of ecosystem disservices that may hinder or harm wellbeing. Examples include conflict between humans and wildlife (Roe, 2014), zoonosis and human health (Wood et al., 2012) and agricultural intensification and access (see Martin et al., this volume). These essentially represent trade-offs between the provision of certain ecosystem services and human wellbeing, which may benefit some stakeholders (e.g. in the case of agricultural intensification) while negatively affecting others who may lose access to land (e.g. to give way for agricultural land or wildlife). A growing emphasis on the indirect benefits of many services is also evident. For example, Daw et al. (2011) critique the Millennium Ecosystem Assessment (MA) for neglecting income and employment, and call for more focus on these. Indeed, livelihoods and material wellbeing (i.e. income and employment) emerge as dominant themes within ESPA research. It is suggested that income is closely linked to other aspects of wellbeing, especially food security. As such, rising incomes should act as a buffer against the loss of traditional livelihood sources (e.g. subsistence agriculture, grazing, non-timber forest products), but evidence to support this claim remains inconclusive. Broegaard et al. (2017) and Dawson et al. (2016) use empirical evidence to demonstrate that income alone is not sufficient for food security, as a multitude of other factors (e.g. access to markets, culture and attitudes) mediate rural households' nutritional outcomes. However, Gasparatos et al. (2012) find that increased incomes do enhance food security, even when households abandon food production in favour of cash crops. Suich et al. (2015) propose that focusing only on income could hinder our understanding of the multiple links and causal relationships between ecosystem services and wellbeing/poverty. Taking a multi-dimensional approach to the food security/income dilemma reveals the less obvious, contextual meanings attached to food production and consumption. Dawson et al. (2016) show that the poor value the traditional uses of land and livestock, as well as their pragmatic contribution to food security, and thus raising livestock also contributes to non-material aspects of wellbeing (Box 17.2). There

---

BOX 17.2 RAISING LIVESTOCK MEANS MORE THAN FOOD AND INCOME IN RURAL RWANDA

In recent years, rural Rwanda has seen the emergence of policies seeking to mimic the success of the Green Revolution in Asia, manifest in a top-down orchestration of technocratic solutions designed to eliminate poverty. However, Dawson and colleagues' analysis of the impact of such policies on the ground shows that agricultural intensification and a shift away from subsistence activities towards cash crops does not produce uniform outcomes for western Rwandans. They highlight that local conceptions of wellbeing differ from national-level development indicators, including material as well as non-material aspects. Data collected during interviews also revealed that ecosystem services are interlinked. For example, cultural and provisioning services go hand in hand in the context of food production, because the traditional practices involved in livestock rearing or working the land are just as important for wellbeing as the income or food obtained as a result. Thus subsistence livelihoods contribute to material and non-material dimensions of wellbeing. However, a forced shift from subsistence to cash crops means the loss of these traditions and the associated benefits. Moreover, the study demonstrates that these policies in their current form are not truly pro-poor, as they favour the less poor or slightly wealthier members of the community who are able to capitalise on existing assets, while the poor are pushed into landlessness, casual labour and struggle to adapt to the new system. The assumption that increased income leads to increased food security is challenged by this research, which shows that the poorest members of society get trapped in the vicious cycle of landlessness, inability to produce their own food, income insecurity and rising food prices. The authors conclude that caution is to be exercised in branding Green Revolution policies pro-poor, because if they do not take into account local values, priorities and aspirations, they can become as much a poverty trap for some as they are a way out of poverty for others.

Source: Dawson et al. (2016)

appears to be an interesting tension between emphasising the importance and centrality of income, cash and material wealth, while also acknowledging and highlighting the importance of non-monetary benefits and the risk of appropriation and capture of more commercialised ecosystem services by more powerful groups, to the dis-benefit of poorer groups within society.

Feedbacks between natural and human systems

Feedbacks and conditionality between ecosystem services and wellbeing have important implications for future sustainable development. Feedback dynamics provide a window to the non-linear linkages within and between ecosystem services and multiple dimensions of wellbeing. For example, von Maltitz et al.'s (2014) resilience assessment of jatropha projects in Malawi and Mozambique describes how feedback dynamics drive the collapse of the projects. While jatropha projects promised a unique opportunity to capitalise on global demands for biofuels, many have failed to deliver on initial promises of success due to feedbacks between global, national and local driving factors. These included a decline in oil prices, time lags in production due to a lengthy process of land acquisition, weak national institutions and lack of biofuel policies, as well as the lack of support for developing a local market. The concept of tipping points is also used to explain how transformation at system scales (e.g. land transformation) can manifest as economic or welfare tipping points at livelihoods scales (e.g. loss of traditional livelihoods), with either desirable or undesirable effects (Coulthard, 2012; Howard, 2013; Tanner et al., 2014). For example, Howard (2013) suggests that passing biodiversity tipping points in the Amazon, which entail the loss of species, ecosystems and ecosystem services, might cause human population collapse, forced migration and conflict. Yet, a lack of empirical evidence substantiating the cause–effect relationships inherent to feedbacks is symptomatic of limitations in the broader ecosystem service and poverty alleviation literature (Suich et al., 2015).

Food security is perhaps the greatest driver of human/ecosystem feedbacks. As Poppy et al. (2014) point out, ecosystems are vital for food production, however, food production is one of the main drivers of ecosystem degradation. Several studies highlight the complex linkages between social and ecological systems, as well as between the ecological functions that underpin the delivery of ecosystem services (e.g. Adams et al., 2013a; Amoako Johnson et al., 2016; Sjögersten et al., 2013; Zhang et al., 2015). Adams and colleagues (2013a), for example, discuss the interconnectivity between provisioning, supporting and regulating services. While agriculture seeks to maximise certain provisioning services, at the same time it disrupts vital supporting and regulating functions that underpin these, and has negative repercussions for future agricultural production and human wellbeing (Adams et al., 2013a). While these feedback loops clearly determine the future delivery of ecosystem services, the dominance of linear approaches to wellbeing/poverty and ecosystem services in research and policy continues to prevail, posing a key challenge for sustainable resource management and development.

Importantly, our analysis highlights the negative social impacts of some types of resource use and management. Pursuing economic growth through intensive forms of production or the introduction of cash crops brings a series of challenges that redefine the *modus operandi* of poor rural societies. Among other things, they challenge existing institutions of ownership and access, as well as disrupting local social and cultural norms and the moral economy (e.g. reciprocity, non-materialistic cultures, meanings attached to traditional practices) (Adams et al., 2013b; Amoako Johnson et al., 2016; Dawson et al., 2016; von Maltitz et al., 2016), thus potentially compromising social sustainability.

For example, human practices, such as agricultural intensification, driven by local and international demand for food, have hindered rural people's livelihood options (see Martin et al., this volume). Diminished livelihood diversity compromises the adaptive capacity of the poor and their resilience to global environmental change (Adams et al., 2013a; Broegaard et al., 2017). However, the impacts of human resource use may not be evident in the short term, as they unfold along different temporal (Dearing et al., 2014; Hejnowicz et al., 2015) and spatial scales (Hejnowicz et al., 2015; Howe et al., 2013). Climate change is a good example of delayed human impact (Watts et al., 2015), which poses a complex challenge for sustainability, presenting a justice dilemma (especially intergenerational) as well as a development one.

Importance of scale and change in ecosystem services for poverty alleviation

While the environment's contribution to poor people's wellbeing has been extensively addressed within and beyond ESPA research, there remains a dearth of understanding about how ecosystem services contribute to and are affected by change (e.g. of livelihoods, biodiversity), including the consequent wellbeing implications of such changes (Kent and Dorward, 2012; Roe, 2014). ESPA research addresses this by developing a better understanding of the mechanisms linking ecosystem services and wellbeing. ESPA scholars focus on two main types of mechanisms: direct use (e.g. through consumption) and exchange (e.g. through market or other trade), which are facilitated by a range of linked mechanisms – market mechanisms underpin trade and exchange, while access mechanisms mediate direct use (Abunge et al., 2013) and access to markets (Broegaard et al., 2017; van der Horst et al., 2012).

Alongside change, scale is another important factor, as decisions regarding resource management are often driven by the values and priorities of removed or external stakeholders. Humphreys Bebbington (2013) exemplifies how national state interests can place indigenous populations at a disadvantage (see Box 17.1). External factors, such as economic trends (e.g. prices, demand), can also influence locally held values of ecosystem services and penetrate local decisions about ecosystem management, transforming livelihood practices and the pathways of benefit derived from ecosystem services (i.e. from direct to exchange). For example, the increased demand for certain crops (e.g. cash crops) or high-value resources (e.g. shrimp), combined with high prices, have led to a shift from traditional/subsistence agriculture towards more intensive forms of production (Islam et al., 2015; Szabo et al., 2016). Ecosystem services that were previously directly consumed are now traded for income (Daw et al., 2011).

Importantly, ESPA research draws attention to the interaction between scale and change in ecosystem services for poverty alleviation, and emphasizes the temporal and spatial dimensions of change. For example, Buytaert et al. (2016) find that change in local water services is difficult to determine unless weather patterns and water uses can be understood across local and regional spatial scales. These complexities can be compounded by misalignment between the temporal and spatial scales of political decision making and water basin boundaries. Elsewhere, Dearing et al. (2014) emphasise intergenerational ecosystem service issues by highlighting that decision making commonly focuses on near-term decisions rather than longer-term decisions that might support sustainability of ecosystem services. These researchers thus make an important contribution towards understanding the cross-scale dynamics of change that shape people's relationships with ecosystem services.

Resilience and wellbeing can help unpack ecosystem services for poverty alleviation

Our review demonstrates how ecosystem services for poverty alleviation research engage with concepts from the fields of resilience and wellbeing, to explain linkages and unpack non-linearities between ecosystem services and poverty alleviation. Insights from the analysis presented in this chapter clearly demonstrate the contribution of this research to critical debates around wellbeing and resilience, and showcase potential opportunities for convergence between the two frameworks. These findings suggest that although wellbeing and resilience approaches are rooted in quite distinct disciplinary traditions, they could complement each other and thereby potentially reframe how we understand the ecosystem services, wellbeing and poverty relationship.

From a static to a dynamic notion of wellbeing

Existing conceptualisations of the ecosystem services and wellbeing relationship (e.g. MA framework (MA, 2005) or the 'cascade model' (Potschin and Haines-Young, 2011)) have been widely critiqued for oversimplifying these links by presenting them in a linear fashion (Daw et al., 2011; Lele et al., 2013). Arguably, this can, in part, be attributed to static notions of wellbeing, as a state or outcome to be achieved (e.g. good health, happiness), which create fertile ground for one-directional thinking that views wellbeing as a normative end that can be achieved by means of ecosystem services. However, ecosystem services research begins to recognise the complex linkages between wellbeing and ecosystem services, and emphasises the role of feedbacks between human and natural systems. This is also manifest in discussions of the various mechanisms by which ecosystem services can contribute to wellbeing or poverty alleviation (e.g. trade/exchange, or direct use) (Abunge et al., 2013; Broegaard et al., 2017). There is an evident departure within the ESPA programme from a linear framing of the ecosystem services and poverty alleviation relationship, by acknowledging that wellbeing is not derived from a single ecosystem service in isolation, but is rather a result of complex interactions between several services that together produce wellbeing (Fisher et al., 2013).

Thus, recent research on ecosystem services and wellbeing and poverty alleviation progresses beyond normative calls for dynamic systems perspectives, and draws on resilience theory to conceptually and empirically investigate links between ecosystem services and poverty alleviation in a much more sophisticated way. While ESPA engages with the resilience approach, this engagement does not extend to explicit resilience analyses of social-ecological systems, but instead involves the use of resilience concepts for exploring the ecosystem services and poverty alleviation relationship through a more dynamic lens. Specifically, applying concepts of shock and gradual change enabled ESPA research to gain a broader sense of the social and environmental drivers of change in ecosystem services and wellbeing (Galafassi et al., 2017). Furthermore, the concept of feedbacks has helped ESPA researchers to describe how feedback dynamics might shape the future trajectory of sustainable poverty alleviation (Gasparatos et al., 2015; Kafumbata et al., 2014). The emphasis of scale, including cross-scale power dynamics, relationships and influences, further elaborates the complex nature of interlinked human-natural systems (Daw et al., 2015; Suich et al., 2015; Villa et al., 2014). These advances indicate that integrating resilience concepts into existing ecosystem services–wellbeing frameworks could support a much-needed transition towards a more dynamic approach that conceptualises wellbeing as a process (Coulthard et al., 2011; Gough et al., 2007), rather than merely a 'static' normative goal.

Bringing social theories into resilience

Resilience thinking has developed beyond its ecological foundations to embrace a social perspective on change. The merits and pitfalls of marrying ecological and social resilience are well documented (Adger, 2000). Yet, despite recent strides to socialise resilience, resilience research is critiqued for being apolitical, for struggling to address issues of agency and for rarely acknowledging social difference (Brown, 2014; Brown and Westaway, 2011). ESPA research makes an important contribution to these unfolding debates. Coulthard (2012) applies the concept of agency to investigate how individuals pursue wellbeing preferences while simultaneously remaining resilient to environmental change. ESPA research also demonstrates the role of power in processes of ecosystems management. Powerful groups have greater opportunity to appropriate benefits from ecosystem services (Daw et al., 2011; Fisher et al., 2013). We also learn that the ability of some groups to exert more power than others over the outcomes of decision-making processes can result in the rejection of such processes and thereby transform ecological systems to alternative, undesirable states (Adams et al., 2013b). These advances demonstrate a broadening of resilience research to acknowledge dimensions of social difference, and indicate a shift towards integrating a contextual understanding of wellbeing into the systems perspective that typically characterises resilience research.

A key principle for resilience practice is the broadening of participation in decision-making processes. Sensitive approaches that engage a diverse and representative set of stakeholders offer the potential to develop social capital for enhanced management of ecosystem services (Leitch et al., 2015). ESPA research has made important steps towards developing and applying participatory and inclusive approaches to understanding trade-offs in the ecosystem services and wellbeing relationship. As demonstrated by Daw et al. (2015) and Galafassi et al. (2017), ESPA research presents approaches that start to probe different and at times conflicting priorities, and provide a platform for marginalised views to be better incorporated into decision-making processes. Such approaches offer promising potential for the science of resilience, as they emphasise how social difference shapes resilience at specific scales. These features also establish practical ways of integrating diverse needs, wants and assumptions into decision-making processes for sustainable development.

Conclusions

Poverty and the direct dependence of the poor on ecosystem services may drive the over-exploitation of many resources in developing countries. At times exploitation takes place despite the recognition of negative impacts resulting from the activity. This raises important questions about trade-offs between ecosystem services and wellbeing, and suggests that these are bound together in a web of complex and intertwined social and ecological processes and factors that shape decisions regarding resource use and management. However, much existing empirical work tends to take a piecemeal approach, failing to fully address this complexity.

Insights from our review of ecosystem services for poverty alleviation research make important strides towards remedying this shortcoming, and unpacking the drivers and implications of a series of trade-offs in ecosystem services and wellbeing. First, we highlight that trade-offs between ecosystem services and between different wellbeing domains are driven by multiple and often competing values, preferences and needs of local and removed stakeholders, which can affect the underlying ecosystem functions and processes, and thus the system's ability to deliver a breadth of diverse services in the future, posing interesting implications for sustainability. Second, we show that trade-offs between beneficiaries are largely driven by power asymmetries that create winners and losers as a result of the unequal distribution of ecosystem benefits in favour of more powerful and better-endowed groups. These trade-offs are intimately linked to resource governance and access dynamics, and often unfold across different spatial and temporal scales. As such, they pose a complex challenge for sustainable development and poverty alleviation initiatives, and create a justice dilemma concerning representation and participation in decisions regarding the management and use of land and resources. Thus future policy and action would benefit from an understanding of existing local practices and the integration of the needs, values and preferences of the rural poor into decision making, as an effective solution for addressing and minimising trade-offs from conservation, resource management and government policies.

Acknowledgement

We would like to thank participants at the Bickleigh Workshop in September 2017 who have contributed to our thinking on this topic.

References

(ESPA outputs marked with '★')

★Abunge C, Coulthard S and Daw TM. (2013) Connecting marine ecosystem services to human well-being: insights from participatory well-being assessment in Kenya. *Ambio* 42: 1010–1021.

★Adams H, Adger NW, Huq H, et al. (2013a) Transformations in land use in the southwest coastal zone of Bangladesh: resilience and reversibility under environmental change. *Proceedings of Transformation in a Changing Climate*. International Conference. Oslo, Norway: University of Oslo, 160–168.

★Adams H, Adger WN, Huq H, et al. (2013b) Wellbeing-ecosystem service links: mechanisms and dynamics in the southwest coastal zone of Bangladesh. *ESPA Deltas Working Paper #2*. 56 pp.

Adger WN. (2000) Social and ecological resilience: are they related? *Progress in Human Geography* 24: 347–364.

★Amoako Johnson F, Hutton CW, Hornby D, et al. (2016) Is shrimp farming a successful adaptation to salinity intrusion? A geospatial associative analysis of poverty in the populous Ganges–Brahmaputra–Meghna Delta of Bangladesh. *Sustainability Science* 11: 423–439.

Armitage D, Béné C, Charles AT, et al. (2012) The interplay of well-being and resilience in applying a social-ecological perspective. *Ecology and Society* 17: 15.

Bavinck M and Vivekanandan V. (2011) Conservation, conflict and the governance of fisher wellbeing: analysis of the establishment of the Gulf of Mannar National Park and Biosphere Reserve. *Environmental Management* 47: 593–602.

★Broegaard RB, Rasmussen LV, Dawson N, et al. (2017) Wild food collection and nutrition under commercial agriculture expansion in agriculture-forest landscapes. *Forest Policy and Economics* 84: 92–101.

Brown K. (2014) Global environmental change I: a social turn for resilience? *Progress in Human Geography* 38: 107–117.

Brown K. (2016) *Resilience, Development and Global Change*. London: Routledge.

Brown K and Westaway E. (2011) Agency, capacity, and resilience to environmental change: Lessons from human development, well-being, and disasters. *Annual Review of Environment and Resources* 36: 321–342.

★Buytaert W, Dewulf A, De Bièvre B, et al. (2016) Citizen science for water resources management: toward polycentric monitoring and governance? *Journal of Water Resources Planning and Management* 142: 01816002.

Chan KMA, Guerry AD, Balvanera P, et al. (2012) Where are cultural and social in ecosystem services? A framework for constructive engagement. *Bioscience* 62: 744–756.

★Coulthard S. (2011) More than just access to fish: the pros and cons of fisher participation in a customary marine tenure (Padu) system under pressure. *Marine Policy* 35: 405–412.

★Coulthard S. (2012) Can we be both resilient and well, and what choices do people have? Incorporating agency into the resilience debate from a fisheries perspective. *Ecology and Society* 17: 4.

★Coulthard S, Johnson D and McGregor JA. (2011) Poverty, sustainability and human wellbeing: a social wellbeing approach to the global fisheries crisis. *Global Environmental Change* 21: 453–463.

★Daw T, Brown K, Rosendo S, et al. (2011) Applying the ecosystem services concept to poverty alleviation: the need to disaggregate human well-being. *Environmental Conservation* 38: 370–379.

★Daw TM, Coulthard S, Cheung WWL, et al. (2015) Evaluating taboo trade-offs in ecosystems services and human well-being. *Proceedings of the National Academy of Sciences* 112: 6949–6954.

★Daw TM, Hicks CC, Brown K, et al. (2016) Elasticity in ecosystem services: exploring the variable relationship between ecosystems and human well-being. *Ecology and Society* 21: 11.

★Dawson N and Martin A. (2015) Assessing the contribution of ecosystem services to human wellbeing: a disaggregated study in western Rwanda. *Ecological Economics* 117: 62–72.

★Dawson N, Martin A and Sikor T. (2016) Green revolution in sub-Saharan Africa: implications of imposed innovation for the wellbeing of rural smallholders. *World Development* 78: 204–218.

★Dearing JA, Wang R, Zhang K, et al. (2014) Safe and just operating spaces for regional social-ecological systems. *Global Environmental Change* 28: 227–238.

★Fisher JA, Patenaude G, Meir P, et al. (2013) Strengthening conceptual foundations: analysing frameworks for ecosystem services and poverty alleviation research. *Global Environmental Change* 23: 1098–1111.

Folke C, Carpenter S, Walker B, et al. (2010) Resilience thinking: integrating resilience, adaptability and transformability. *Ecology and Society* 15: 20.

★Galafassi D, Daw TM, Munyi L, et al. (2017) Learning about social-ecological trade-offs. *Ecology and Society* 22: 2.

★Gasparatos A, Lee LY, von Maltitz GP, et al. (2012) Biofuels in Africa: impacts on ecosystem services, biodiversity and human well-being. *UNU-IAS Policy Report*. United Nations University-Institute of Advanced Studies, 116.

★Gasparatos A, von Maltitz GP, Johnson FX, et al. (2015) Biofuels in sub-Sahara Africa: drivers, impacts and priority policy areas. *Renewable and Sustainable Energy Reviews* 45: 879–901.

Gough I, McGregor IA and Camfield L. (2007) Theorizing wellbeing in international development. In: Gough I and McGregor JA (eds) *Wellbeing in Developing Countries: From Theory to Research*. Cambridge, UK: Cambridge University Press.

★Hejnowicz AP, Kennedy H, Rudd MA, et al. (2015) Harnessing the climate mitigation, conservation and poverty alleviation potential of seagrasses: prospects for developing blue carbon initiatives and payment for ecosystem service programmes. *Frontiers in Marine Science* 2: 32.

★Howard P. (2013) Human resilience in the face of biodiversity tipping points at local and regional scales. In: O'Riordan T and Lenton T (eds) *Addressing Tipping Points for a Precarious Future*. Oxford: British Academy, 104–126.

★Howe C, Suich H, van Gardingen P, et al. (2013) Elucidating the pathways between climate change, ecosystem services and poverty alleviation. *Current Opinion in Environmental Sustainability* 5: 102–107.

★Humphreys Bebbington D. (2013) Extraction, inequality and indigenous peoples: insights from Bolivia. *Environmental Science and Policy* 33: 438–446.

★Islam GT, Islam AS, Shopan AA, et al. (2015) Implications of agricultural land use change to ecosystem services in the Ganges delta. *Journal of Environmental Management* 161: 443–452.

★Kafumbata D, Jamu D and Chiotha S. (2014) Riparian ecosystem resilience and livelihood strategies under test: lessons from Lake Chilwa in Malawi and other lakes in Africa. *Philosophical Transactions of the Royal Society B: Biological Sciences* 369: 20130052–20130052.

★Kent R and Dorward A. (2012) Biodiversity change and livelihood responses: ecosystem asset functions in southern India. *CeDEP Working Paper September 2012*. London: SOAS, University of London.

Kinzig A, Ryan P, Etienne M, et al. (2006) Resilience and regime shifts: assessing cascading effects. *Ecology and Society* 11: 20.

Leitch AM, Cundill G, Schultz L, et al. (2015) Broaden participation. In: Biggs R, Schlüter M and Schoon ML (eds) *Principles for Building Resilience: Sustaining Ecosystem Services in Social-Ecological systems.* Cambridge, UK: Cambridge University Press, 201.

★Lele S, Springate-Baginski O, Lakerveld R, et al. (2013) Ecosystem services: origins, contributions, pitfalls, and alternatives. *Conservation and Society* 11: 343.

MA. (2005) *Millennium Ecosystem Assessment, 2005. Ecosystems and Human Well-Being: Synthesis.* Washington, DC: Island Press.

★Poppy GM, Chiotha S, Eigenbrod F, et al. (2014) Food security in a perfect storm: using the ecosystem services framework to increase understanding. *Philosophical Transactions of the Royal Society B: Biological Sciences* 369.

Porter M, Mwaipopo R, Faustine R, et al. (2008) Globalization and women in coastal communities in Tanzania. *Development* 51: 193–198.

Potschin MB and Haines-Young RH. (2011) Ecosystem services: exploring a geographical perspective. *Progress in Physical Geography* 35: 575–594.

★Ramirez-Gomez SOI, Torres-Vitolas CA, Schreckenberg K, et al. (2015) Analysis of ecosystem services provision in the Colombian Amazon using participatory research and mapping techniques. *Ecosystem Services* 13: 93–107.

Richardson GP and Pugh A. (1981) *Introduction to System Dynamics Modeling with DYNAMO.* Cambridge, MA: MIT Press.

★Roe D. (2014) Poverty and biodiversity: evidence about nature and the nature of evidence. *IIED Briefing Papers, March 2014.* London: IIED.

Sen A. (1985) Well-being, agency and freedom: the Dewey lectures 1984. *Journal of Philosophy* 82: 169–221.

★Sjögersten S, Atkin C, Clarke ML, et al. (2013) Responses to climate change and farming policies by rural communities in northern China: a report on field observation and farmers' perception in dryland north Shaanxi and Ningxia. *Land Use Policy* 32: 125–133.

★Suich H, Howe C and Mace G. (2015) Ecosystem services and poverty alleviation: a review of the empirical links. *Ecosystem Services* 12: 137–147.

★Szabo S, Hossain MS, Adger WN, et al. (2016) Soil salinity, household wealth and food insecurity in tropical deltas: evidence from south-west coast of Bangladesh. *Sustainability Science* 11: 411–421.

Tanner T, Lewis D, Wrathall D, et al. (2014) Livelihood resilience in the face of climate change. *Nature Climate Change* 5: 23–26.

★van der Horst D, Chibwe TK and Vermeylen S. (2012) Soap security: African home economics after the biofuel hype. *The Solutions Journal* 3: 23–27.
★Villa F, Voigt B and Erickson JD. (2014) New perspectives in ecosystem services science as instruments to understand environmental securities. *Philosophical Transactions of the Royal Society B: Biological Sciences* 369.
★Vira B, Adams B, Agarwal C, et al. (2012) Negotiating trade-offs: choices about ecosystem services for poverty alleviation. *Economic and Political Weekly* 47: 67–75.
★von Maltitz G, Gasparatos A and Fabricius C. (2014) The rise, fall and potential resilience benefits of Jatropha in Southern Africa. *Sustainability* 6: 3615–3643.
★von Maltitz GP, Gasparatos A, Fabricius C, et al. (2016) Jatropha cultivation in Malawi and Mozambique: impact on ecosystem services, local human well-being, and poverty alleviation. *Ecology and Society* 21: 3.
Watts N, Adger WN, Agnolucci P, et al. (2015) Health and climate change: policy responses to protect public health. *The Lancet* 386: 1861–1914.
White SC. (2010) Analysing wellbeing: a framework for development practice. *Development in Practice* 20: 158–172.
★Wood JLN, Leach M, Waldman L, et al. (2012) A framework for the study of zoonotic disease emergence and its drivers: spillover of bat pathogens as a case study. *Philosophical Transactions of the Royal Society B: Biological Sciences* 367: 2881–2892.
★Zhang K, Dearing JA, Dawson TP, et al. (2015) Poverty alleviation strategies in eastern China lead to critical ecological dynamics. *Science of the Total Environment* 506–507: 164–181.

18

INSIGHTS FOR SUSTAINABLE SMALL-SCALE FISHERIES

Daniela Diz and Elisa Morgera

Introduction

Fish comprises 17% of all protein consumed around the world, and is of particular nutritional importance for consumers in developing countries (FAO, 2016). Increasing demand has contributed to 31.4% of fish stocks being fished at unsustainable levels, while 58.1% of fish stocks are estimated to be fully fished (FAO, 2016). Rebuilding overfished stocks and recovery of depleted marine ecosystems could increase production by 16.5 million tonnes and annual rent by US$32 billion (Ye et al., 2013). The sustainable management of fisheries requires taking into account and mitigating other anthropogenic effects, particularly from climate change, as these can have significant negative impacts on the productive capacity of ecosystems (FAO, 2016). Rebuilding fish stocks requires a series of conservation and management measures, including measures to conserve areas important for supporting and regulating ecosystem services such as marine and coastal habitats (e.g. mangroves, seagrass meadows, coral reefs, deep water corals and sponges) (FAO, 1995).

If recovery of fish stocks is achieved, a critical question is: who would benefit the most from rebuilt stocks and ecosystems? Current governance regimes tend to favour the large-scale fishing sector, despite the important role of small-scale fisheries for national economies, food security, livelihoods, nutrition and poverty reduction, as well as cultural and social wellbeing (Béné et al., 2010; Coulthard et al., 2011). It has been estimated that the small-scale sector contributes to roughly half of the global fish catches (HLPE, 2014) and employs about 90% of wild-capture fish workers. Furthermore, fish, as a source of protein and essential micronutrients, has been considered an important dietary component for coastal communities, especially women and young children (FAO, 2016).

In this chapter we explore research findings related to the contribution of the ecosystem services framework and associated tools to sustainable fisheries management and poverty alleviation in small-scale fishing communities. The chapter is organised around three areas in which we find the ecosystem services framework can make important contributions to fisheries management, namely: (a) data availability; (b) conservation and management measures; and (c) integrated oceans governance, including the assessment of trade-offs for more equitable decision-making outcomes.

Data availability for fisheries management

There is international policy consensus that conservation and management measures related to fisheries should be based on the best scientific evidence available. This requires collecting data to improve scientific knowledge of fisheries, including their interaction with the ecosystem, as well as integrating communities' traditional knowledge of the resources and their habitat, and relevant environmental, economic and social factors (FAO, 1995). Developing countries often have limited ability to collect or analyse data (e.g. biological, oceanographic and catch data) or to run sophisticated models. Furthermore, data (e.g. catch, employment, value) on small-scale fisheries are often incomplete, which leads to inaccurate assessments of fishing pressure and an underestimation of the sector's economic importance at global and national levels (Pauly and Zeller, 2016). This section demonstrates that the use (and proper recalibration) of global models and data (e.g. satellite data) can support assessments at regional, national and local levels, including in these data-poor contexts.

A key component of science-based fisheries management is to define ecologically meaningful boundaries based on biogeography, capturing the core of a functional ecosystem for management purposes (Kenny et al., 2017). The identification of these units is also important for assessing the ecosystem services flows across different scales, to identify winners and losers within and across these units as well as appropriate management interventions (CBD, 2004). Ecosystem service flows are also better understood within appropriate biogeographical scales complemented by multi-scalar considerations. Poppy et al. (2014) underscore the need to consider biophysical processes in conjunction with institutional processes that may operate at distinct spatial and temporal scales. Such an approach can enable the understanding of the biophysical limits of what can be extracted from an ecosystem in a sustainable manner over time (Poppy et al., 2014). Understanding these multi-scalar considerations can contribute to the determination of safe ecological limits for fisheries' impacts on ecosystems and can inform the design of equitable interventions between different actors.

Kenny et al. (2017) discuss methods suited to data-poor situations, such as use of satellite imagery to assess primary production, to define these functional units in terms of their productivity and diversity. Defining these units is important for determining productivity-based total catch ceilings at the ecosystem level (Kenny et al., 2017). For each biogeographic unit, multi-species models should normally be developed to complement single-species assessments (Garcia et al., 2003).

Usually, these models require intense data parameterisation. However, less intensive methods have been developed. For instance, size-spectra analysis, which requires fairly simple data collection techniques (Kerr and Dickie, 2001), can be used for measuring communities' size composition as a means for assessing fisheries exploitation responses (Kenny et al., 2017).

Cochrane et al. (2011) identify several data-poor management frameworks for small-scale fisheries, such as rapid rural appraisals and application of reference directions instead of reference points. They suggest that at a minimum, the emphasis in data-poor small-scale fisheries contexts where poverty is prevalent should be on avoiding disaster situations, such as collapse of fish stocks. Fernandes et al. (2016) use a combination of size-spectrum and multi-species models that use biological and general knowledge to provide projections with sparse data under climate and socio-economic scenarios in Bangladesh.

Marine ecosystems are subject to multiple anthropogenic pressures, not only from the fisheries sector, but also increasingly from climate change-induced temperature rises and ocean acidification effects. Cumulative impacts, including the effects of climate change on fisheries and communities, thus need to be accounted for when developing management measures. For instance, Fernandes et al. (2016) project that fish production in the Bangladesh exclusive economic zone is likely to decrease by up to 10% by 2060 under climate change scenario A1B of the Intergovernmental Panel on Climate Change. The production decrease is more severe for two major commercial species: Hilsa shad (*Tenualosa ilisha*) and Bombay duck (*Harpadon nehereus*). Hilsa shad is the largest catch species in Bangladesh, employing approximately 460,000 fishers and 2.5 million people in the wider sector (trading, processing, among others), while Bombay duck constitutes the second largest catch species (Fernandes et al., 2016).

The authors also project that over-fishing, combined with climate change effects (increased sea-surface temperatures by 2–3 °C), could reduce Hilsa catches by up to 95% by 2060. Different management scenarios (business-as-usual, over-fishing and maximum sustainable yield (MSY)) will result in different outcomes for fishery productivity and associated livelihoods. Hilsa decline would stabilise and be able to support current production under MSY (at 175,000 t) by 2035, while under business-as-usual and further overfishing scenarios it collapses around the same period (Fernandes et al., 2016). For Bombay duck, a decline of roughly 35% is predicted due to climate change under all management scenarios, but to different degrees: if managed under MSY, catch potential by the 2020s is predicted to produce over 20% more fish than in the business-as-usual scenario; however, if business-as-usual catch levels are kept until the end of the century, a 40% decline is predicted (ibid.). These results could contribute to the redesign of existing conservation and management measures. These entail spatial/temporal closures accompanied by small in-kind (rice) payments to fishers which are, however, criticised for being insufficient to compensate for loss of revenue and household protein (Porras et al., 2017). Better modelling of catch projections under different management and climate scenarios would also add value to current conservation interventions by incorporating climate-resilient measures.

An example of how global models can be used to support integrated vulnerability assessment and adaptation planning for coastal communities is provided by Cochrane et al. (2017). The authors adapted global models to regional and local contexts off the coast of Madagascar and the Mozambique channel by working with local experts to develop regional climate change indicators (e.g. coral bleaching index) to complement generic indicators (long-term sea-surface temperature trend).

The integration of traditional knowledge of indigenous peoples and local communities, such as small-scale fishers, in these assessments is essential because it complements natural sciences while also providing the opportunity for these communities to engage in the design of subsequent fisheries management measures. More integrated, multi-disciplinary and participatory assessments are increasingly being implemented (Garcia and Rosenberg, 2010; see also Buytaert et al., this volume), and could also benefit from methodologies for stock assessments adapted to data-poor contexts (Kenny et al., 2017).

Conservation of marine and coastal ecosystems

Conservation and management measures to ensure the long-term sustainability of fish stocks constitute a fundamental international obligation for states under the UN Convention on the Law of the Sea. This section demonstrates that, when well-designed, conservation measures can benefit the poor and contribute to enhanced wellbeing. However, there is growing international recognition that conservation measures should be complemented by broader social safety nets and policies that enable more equitable outcomes, particularly for vulnerable groups, while also contributing to the long-term sustainability of the marine ecosystems in question (FAO, 2015). This approach can contribute to the achievement of the Sustainable Development Goals (SDGs) in a holistic manner.

The loss of biodiversity poses threats to ecosystem structure and function and therefore the system's resilience (McCauley et al., 2015). The need to conserve diversity to avoid ecological changes for fisheries has been highlighted in the literature since the 1970s (Longhurst, 2010). Marine species' decline can result in severe consequences for marine ecosystems and their services. Roman et al. (2014) identify important ecosystem services played by great whales, including in nutrient and carbon cycles. Other species groups also play a key role in ecosystem structure and function through regulating mechanisms. For instance, key ecosystem services provided by coral reefs, mangroves and seagrass meadows for coastal resilience, fisheries productivity and quality of life have been identified in the literature (Githaiga et al., 2017; Januchowski-Hartley et al., 2017; see also Box 18.1).

Against this background, the conservation of areas important for biodiversity and ecosystem services has been the object of global attention (CBD, 2010). However, the notion of conservation and management measures contributing to poverty

> **BOX 18.1 THE ROLE OF PES IN COASTAL CONSERVATION AND POVERTY ALLEVIATION**
>
> The CESEA project has estimated carbon sinks in seagrass meadows in Gazi Bay, Kenya. This study fulfils a research gap in understanding carbon sink processes in seagrass meadows in the region, beyond well-studied areas such as the Mediterranean and Australia (Githaiga et al., 2017). The authors recommend bundling seagrass ecosystem services with those of mangroves, given the ecological connectivity of the two systems. The Gazi Bay area already hosts a pioneering community-based carbon offset project, Mikoko Pamoja (see Wylie et al., 2016).
>
> In considering the role of voluntary carbon markets, Locatelli et al. (2014) assess how a carbon sequestration and storage-related PES scheme in mangrove forests in Gazi Bay has led to increased conservation, restoration and sustainable use, which has in turn contributed to other mangrove ecosystem services (e.g. provision of fisheries) and the wellbeing of local communities. Locatelli et al. (2014) suggest further exploring PES in the form of fisheries licensing fees, noting that 'the commercial exploitation of offshore fisheries of species that spend part of their life cycle in mangroves is more likely to be a source of PES' (p. 985), rather than for fisheries occurring solely in mangrove areas which contribute significantly to local communities' subsistence. Furthermore, given the multiple ecosystem services provided by mangrove forests, the authors note the potential for marketing of 'bundled' ecosystem services, while also cautioning that this approach may be limited by trade-offs among services. To ensure success, Hejnowicz et al. (2015) argue such a PES scheme must be inclusive, with effective (probably locally devolved) institutions and clearly defined tenure and property rights. The latter is particularly important, as '[w]here clear, formal recognition of customary or group rights is lacking, evidence from East Africa suggests that prospects of increased value through carbon sequestration may prompt land seizure by powerful local elites' (Locatelli et al., 2014: 991).

alleviation is still contested (see Woodhouse et al., this volume). In analysing the socio-economic outcomes of marine resource management in sub-Saharan Africa, van Rooyen and Tannous (2017) note the tenuous links between biodiversity conservation and poverty reduction (see Box 18.2). However, the UN Special Rapporteur on Human Rights and the Environment underscored in 2017 that 'The loss of biodiversity-dependent ecosystem services is likely to accentuate inequality and marginalisation of the most vulnerable (. . .) by decreasing their access to basic materials for a healthy life and by reducing their freedom of choice and action' (Knox,

BOX 18.2 MARINE RESOURCE MANAGEMENT: IMPACTS ON MULTI-DIMENSIONAL POVERTY IN SUB-SAHARAN AFRICA

Contributed by: Carina van Rooyen and Natalie Tannous (2017), Africa Centre for Evidence, University of Johannesburg

Protecting marine ecosystems is on the agendas of international bodies such as the United Nations (UN), with one of the Sustainable Development Goals, SDG 14, being to 'conserve and sustainably use oceans, seas and marine resources' (UN, 2015). An evidence synthesis gap exists of literature that focuses on marine resources management, human outcomes and sub-Saharan Africa. With this gap in mind, we conducted a rapid evidence assessment aimed at answering the following research question: what is the impact of marine resources management on multi-dimensional poverty in sub-Saharan Africa?

Our search threw up 9,699 records, which were whittled down to an evidence base of just 21 studies by applying exclusion criteria.

For the impact of different marine resources management interventions on socio-economic outcomes, we categorised management interventions according to the aim of the intervention. In the evidence base we found studies dealing with protection of marine resources through marine protected areas, and the administering of marine resources conservation through fisheries management restrictions.

Our evidence base included marine protected areas of various kinds, but only one had a positive impact on income (measured as fish sales). All others had either neutral or negative perceived impacts on socio-economic outcomes. Gender, geographical location and socio-economic factors (such as fisheries livelihood) all influenced the experience of impact for all types of marine protected area. Specifically for the two community-based protected areas in the set, the extent of involvement in the protected area, as well as the extent of external support, hinted at differential impacts.

Whereas the socio-economic impacts of no-take zones were found to be positive for livelihoods and food security, the impacts of this intervention included a sense of displacement and despair for communities, and the perception that benefits accrue to government more than to self and communities. The overall direction of impact on wellbeing was not positive. Gear restriction was perceived to have a positive impact on income, and it was also the preferred fisheries management intervention for local fishers, although this is from a small evidence base. Our evidence base on other fisheries restrictions (e.g. seasonal closure, minimum size fish and species restriction) is too limited to draw conclusions. Any socio-economic impacts of fisheries management

> restrictions are differential for geographical location and socio-economic groupings.
>
> We also considered whether there were differential impacts for marine resource management interventions that have as a goal the achievement of both biodiversity conservation and poverty reduction, versus those that were more protection-focused. From a small evidence base for especially protection-focused interventions, we hesitantly take note that whether an intervention is protection-focused or aims for both biodiversity conservation and poverty reduction, it seemingly makes no significant difference to the socio-economic outcomes. In both cases, the distribution of socio-economic impacts was unequal based on location and socio-economic conditions.

2017: para 24). Conversely, the need for inclusive participation in decision making of local communities, especially the most marginalised groups, is essential for conservation and the achievement of global conservation targets (Milner-Gulland et al., 2014). In a detailed assessment of three marine protected areas in the Philippines, Chaigneau and Brown (2016) highlight the importance of not overstating the potential benefits of protected areas, as this can lead to reduced community support if expected benefits do not materialise, or fluctuate over time. They also find that a focus on community goals, such as maintaining fish stocks for the future, rather than economic benefits for individual households, can provide a more solid foundation for long-term conservation success.

Diz et al. (2017a) discuss the establishment of locally managed marine areas with conservation, poverty reduction and enhanced wellbeing objectives in northern Mozambique, highlighting the need for integrated efforts towards different SDGs when implementing SDG 14 ('to conserve and sustainably use the oceans, seas and marine resources'), especially those addressing social safety nets and capacity building, to ensure the long-term sustainability of the conservation measure in question and of the benefits it provides to livelihoods. van Rooyen and Tannous (2017) suggest coupling inclusive and participatory marine resource management interventions with external elements such as reproductive health. In a similar vein, Hossain et al. (2015) show that improved access to electricity, sanitation, drinking water and primary education, general health and income from small-scale fishing in the south-west coastal region of Bangladesh has contributed to the five dimensions of human wellbeing emphasised in the MA (2005), namely, health, material, security, freedom and social relations. However, the salinity increase due to shrimp farming in the region has reduced crop production, creating unemployment for farmers because of the low labour demand in shrimp farming compared with crop production (Hossain et al., 2015). This suggests a need for a holistic consideration of trade-offs, which can be facilitated by integrated management processes (see below).

Integrated ocean governance across sectors and scales

In this section we discuss the role of integration across sectors and levels of governance in addressing multiple dimensions of poverty, with a particular emphasis on trade-offs. Integrated management can help address a range of anthropogenic pressures on important areas for ecosystem services. For instance, although Payo et al. (2016) focus on the potential impact of sea-level rise and erosion on the Sundarban mangroves in Bangladesh, they acknowledge the need to consider anthropogenic causes of mangrove losses, such as oil spills from ships passing through the Sundarbans, suggesting the need for integrated (watershed, coastal and marine) management. In northern Mozambique, conflicts between large- and small-scale fisheries and other sectors (e.g. oil and gas) would benefit from an integrated approach (Diz et al., 2017a).

There is international policy consensus that integrated management should be achieved through a decentralised, social process to factor in societal choices, as well as the rights and interests of indigenous peoples and local communities, and intrinsic as well as tangible and intangible values attached to biodiversity, in order to balance local interests and the wider public interest (CBD, 2004). The need to integrate local fishers and their traditional knowledge in the design, planning and implementation of fisheries management, including marine protected areas, through participatory processes such as co-management, has been underscored in the context of the right to food as an essential component of wellbeing and poverty alleviation (De Schutter, 2012), and by the FAO (2015) Voluntary Guidelines for Securing Sustainable Small-Scale Fisheries (SSF Guidelines). The SSF Guidelines have also called for the equitable sharing of benefits from sustainable fisheries with small-scale fishing communities (FAO, 2015: para 5.15; see also Mahajan and Daw, 2016). Fair and equitable benefit-sharing to reward traditional knowledge holders and ecosystem stewards is linked to procedural guarantees for meaningful participation in decision making and management planning (Morgera, 2016).

Against this background, the identification of ecosystem services flows among different members of the community under different policy and management scenarios can contribute to more meaningful participatory processes and outcomes. Marine spatial planning can provide a tool for integration, transparency, conflict resolution and consensus building regarding marine conservation and sustainable use (Ehler and Douvere, 2009). It can also facilitate the identification of important ecosystem services trade-offs at appropriate scales (Ntona and Morgera, 2017). Daw et al. (2011) have analysed trade-offs within and across groups involved in small-scale fisheries, shedding light on often overlooked wellbeing aspects of marginalised or under-represented groups (e.g. women) in the sector.

Understanding trade-offs to inform societal choices

Ecosystem services methodologies can contribute to the identification of ecosystem services flows in space and time while identifying beneficiaries and losers at appropriate scales – at inter- and intra-state levels of governance. The interface between inter- and intra-state levels is highlighted by Poppy et al. (2014: 4), who note that 'for ecosystem services of global concern, such as biodiversity conservation and carbon sequestration, it is also important to determine how the needs of global beneficiaries interact with or affect the ability of local people to obtain the ecosystem services they need to support their livelihoods'. Conflicts between large- and small-scale fisheries require intra-state regulations to protect the access rights of traditional fishing communities from industrial fishing, including through the introduction of exclusive artisanal fishing zones and exclusive user rights for small-scale fisheries (De Schutter, 2012: para 61; FAO, 2015: para 5.7). But they also require inter-state interventions, such as increased regulation of industrial fishing operations by their state of origin vis-à-vis the state in whose waters these large-scale vessels operate, and more equitable agreements between these two states (De Schutter, 2012: para 62(b); Diz et al., 2017b). This is important, because local food supplies can be reduced by inter-state bilateral fishing access agreements providing fishing licences to foreign fleets if these are not properly designed. These agreements must also draw on accurate catch data information to determine sustainable catch levels, as unsustainable catch levels by large-scale fisheries can impact small-scale fishing communities (Diz et al., 2017b).

The disaggregation of ecosystem services beneficiaries is a key component of the ecosystem services framework, which allows social injustices or inequities within communities to be identified and addressed (Poppy et al., 2014). Such disaggregated data can provide important information for selecting equitable conservation and management measures. Milner-Gulland et al. (2014), for example, have pointed to conservation initiatives that can contribute to wellbeing of men to the detriment of women's. Disaggregated data, however, are often lacking, especially on gender (see Brown and Fortnam, this volume). Photovoice methods have been suggested as a promising method for revealing the different roles and priorities of men and women in small-scale fisheries (Simmance et al., 2016).

Disaggregated data, including regarding the wellbeing of marginalised groups within communities, are also important to inform decision makers about often-overlooked trade-offs that can be perceived at first as win-win situations, such as those related to conservation and fisheries profitability (Daw et al., 2015). Highlighting the need for spatial and temporal considerations in assessing trade-offs, Daw et al. (2015: 6949) note that '[a] key challenge is to understand and deal with trade-offs, in which gains for one ecosystem service or group of people results in losses for others'.

Another key issue is the fact that the wellbeing contribution of small-scale fisheries is underestimated by aggregate economic assessments that do not account for: who the beneficiaries are; how equitably these benefits are shared; and how the benefits actually help to meet the needs of particular beneficiaries (Daw et al., 2011). For instance, issues related to the marginal utility of income (money earned by the poor has more 'value' than if earned by the rich), and the provision of nutrition to those who most depend on this source of protein, rather than producing fish for high-value markets, are not part of aggregate economic assessments, thus undermining the contribution of small-scale fisheries to poverty alleviation (Daw et al., 2011). Thus connecting an octopus fishery to international markets in Tanzania led to the displacement of women, who traditionally had exclusive access to the fishery, by men attracted by the higher prices (Porter et al., 2008). Although the net value of the ecosystem services benefits of male fishers was enhanced, the already marginalised poor women were left behind even more (Daw et al., 2011). For this reason, valuation approaches that integrate a pluralistic way of valuing (beyond the mere economic value) should be promoted (Pascual et al., 2017a).

At the inter-state level, participatory exercises for assessing trade-offs (see Daw et al., 2015) could also inform new practices, such as fisheries impact assessments prior to giving access to foreign, large-scale fisheries. Such assessments should consider the right to food and other poverty dimensions of concern to small-scale fishing communities (De Schutter, 2012) and contribute to a more comprehensive understanding of transboundary trade-offs (Diz et al., 2017b). On this basis, industrial fishing activities that could affect the ecosystem services upon which small-fishing communities depend could trigger an impact assessment, which could integrate guidance adopted under the Convention on Biological Diversity, including on the identification of ecosystem services impacts (CBD, 2012).

Incorporating consideration of ecosystem services into comprehensive and integrated impact assessments for the fisheries sector and marine spatial plans is important to move the ecosystem approach to fisheries beyond place-based assessments. Better accounting for cross-scale ecosystems and governance interactions is essential for sustainability – for example, to avoid management decisions in one fishery creating an 'off-stage ecosystem burden' by displacing fishing effort to a less well-regulated area (Pascual et al., 2017b). This is particularly important in the context of marine ecosystems. Given the interconnectedness of ecosystems and processes that ultimately affect the ecosystem capacity to produce ecosystem services that contribute to the livelihoods of fishing communities, addressing governance issues from a multi-scalar perspective – from global to local – is essential (Diz et al., 2017b). For instance, current UN negotiations on a new treaty on the conservation and sustainable use of marine biodiversity in areas beyond national jurisdiction (ABNJ) could incorporate such considerations when setting a new governance regime, since cumulative effects of anthropogenic pressures on marine ecosystems in ABNJ can affect species upon which local communities depend, as noted in the case of the Sargasso Sea (Diz et al., 2017b; Pendleton et al., 2014; Sumaila et al., 2013).

Conclusions

To enhance the sustainability of fisheries and related ecosystem services in a way that recognises their importance for poverty alleviation, we find that there has been insufficient cross-fertilisation between ecosystem services and fisheries management literature, but that both fields can benefit from each other's knowledge base. A key area concerns methodologies for defining appropriate ecosystem scales for assessing fisheries productivity, even in data-poor contexts, including in light of climate change and in combination with methods for assessing sustainable catch levels accounting for major climate-induced changes in highly important targeted species. Furthermore, a wide range of biodiversity values in policy and decision making can be integrated through transparent and inclusive processes involving stakeholders from the start (at planning and design phases), and with disaggregated data, especially regarding gender and marginalised groups. Disaggregated data can also contribute to a better understanding of intra-state and intra-community trade-offs, with a view to developing appropriate social safety nets that protect the most vulnerable groups in society and address multiple dimensions of poverty. Understanding these trade-offs is also relevant for resolving use conflicts through marine spatial planning and integrated impact assessments of (foreign) large-scale fishing activities and other anthropogenic impacts on marine ecosystems and ecosystem services upon which local communities depend.

With respect to outstanding research needs, it is important to note that ecosystem services tools to date have tended to focus on more localised contexts, although literature on transboundary ecosystems, where regional and global-level beneficiaries have been identified, has started to emerge (Armstrong et al., 2014; Pendleton et al., 2014; Sumaila et al., 2013). This means that most of the ecosystem services literature is helpful in exploring intra-state dimensions of equity and fairness in the context of fisheries, but only little research is available to contextualise ecosystem services from an inter-state dimension. This imbalance also makes it difficult at this stage to rely on ecosystem services literature to better understand ecosystem services flows from the local to the global level, and vice versa, which appears an essential task in fully implementing an ecosystem approach to fisheries (Diz et al., 2017b; also see Pascual et al., 2017b). Finally, ecosystem services science alone may not be sufficient to address small-scale fishing poverty traps, as social measures and social safety nets outside the sector need to be implemented accordingly. This reinforces the notion that for SDG 14 to be achieved, related SDGs on poverty, hunger, health, education and institutional capacity, among others, need be implemented concurrently. In turn, ignoring the impacts on marine and coastal biodiversity and broader ecosystems can risk surpassing ecological thresholds, making the poor even more vulnerable.

References

(ESPA outputs marked with '★')

Armstrong CW, Foley NS, Kahui V, et al. (2014) Cold water coral reef management from an ecosystem service perspective. *Marine Policy* 50: 126–134.

Béné C, Hersoug B and Allison EH. (2010) Not by rent alone: analysing the pro-poor functions of small-scale fisheries in developing countries. *Development Policy Review* 28: 325–358.

CBD. (2004) Convention on Biological Diversity (CBD) Decision VII/11. Ecosystem approach. Kuala Lumpur, Malaysia: Convention on Biological Diversity.

CBD. (2010) Convention on Biological Diversity (CBD) Decision X/2. The Strategic Plan for Biodiversity 2011–2020 and the Aichi Biodiversity Targets Nagoya, Japan: Convention on Biological Diversity.

CBD. (2012) Revised Voluntary Guidelines for the Consideration of Biodiversity in Environmental Impact Assessments and Strategic Environmental Assessments in Marine and Coastal Areas, Doc. UNEP/CBD/COP/11/23. Hyderabad, India: Convention on Biological Diversity.

★Chaigneau T and Brown K. (2016) Challenging the win-win discourse on conservation and development: analyzing support for marine protected areas. *Ecology and Society* 21: 36.

Cochrane KL, Andrew NL and Parma AM. (2011) Primary fisheries management: a minimum requirement for provision of sustainable human benefits in small-scale fisheries. *Fish and Fisheries* 12: 275–288.

★Cochrane KL, Rakotondrazafy H, Aswani S, et al. (2017) Report of the GLORIA Workshop, Antananarivo, Madagascar, 14–16 June 2016. 78 pp.

★Coulthard S, Johnson D and McGregor JA. (2011) Poverty, sustainability and human wellbeing: a social wellbeing approach to the global fisheries crisis. *Global Environmental Change* 21: 453–463.

★Daw T, Brown K, Rosendo S, et al. (2011) Applying the ecosystem services concept to poverty alleviation: the need to disaggregate human well-being. *Environmental Conservation* 38: 370–379.

★Daw TM, Coulthard S, Cheung WWL, et al. (2015) Evaluating taboo trade-offs in ecosystems services and human well-being. *Proceedings of the National Academy of Sciences* 112: 6949–6954.

De Schutter O. (2012) The right to food, Interim report of the Special Rapporteur on the right to food, UN Doc. A/67/268.

★Diz D, Johnson D, Riddell M, et al. (2017a) Mainstreaming marine biodiversity into the SDGs: the role of other effective area-based conservation measures (SDG 14.5). *Marine Policy* [in press].

★Diz D, Morgera E and Wilson M. (2017b) Sharing the benefits of sustainable fisheries: from global to local legal approaches to marine ecosystem services for poverty alleviation. *Science Policy Working Paper No. 7*. Strathclyde Centre for Environmental Law and Governance (SCELG), University of Strathclyde, UK.

Ehler C and Douvere F. (2009) Marine Spatial Planning: a step-by-step approach toward ecosystem-based management. IOC Manual and Guides No. 53, ICAM Dossier No. 6. Paris, France: Intergovernmental Oceanographic Commission and Man and the Biosphere Programme.

FAO. (1995) *Code of Conduct for Responsible Fisheries*. Rome, Italy: FAO.

FAO. (2015) *Voluntary Guidelines for Securing Sustainable Small-Scale Fisheries in the Context of Food Security and Poverty Eradication*. Rome, Italy: FAO.

FAO. (2016) *The State of World Fisheries and Aquaculture 2016. Contributing to Food Security and Nutrition for All*. Rome, Italy: FAO.

Fernandes JA, Kay S, Hossain MAR, et al. (2016) Projecting marine fish production and catch potential in Bangladesh in the 21st century under long-term environmental change and management scenarios. *ICES Journal of Marine Science* 73: 1357–1369.

Garcia SM and Rosenberg AA. (2010) Food security and marine capture fisheries: characteristics, trends, drivers and future perspectives. *Philosophical Transactions of the Royal Society B: Biological Sciences* 365: 2869–2880.

Garcia SM, Zerbi A, Aliaume C, et al. (2003) The ecosystem approach to fisheries: issues, terminology, principles, institutional foundations, implementation and outlook. *FAO Fisheries Technical Paper. No. 443*. Rome, Italy: FAO, 71 pp.

*Githaiga MN, Kairo JG, Gilpin L, et al. (2017) Carbon storage in the seagrass meadows of Gazi Bay, Kenya. *PLoS ONE* 12: e0177001.

*Hejnowicz AP, Kennedy H, Rudd MA, et al. (2015) Harnessing the climate mitigation, conservation and poverty alleviation potential of seagrasses: prospects for developing blue carbon initiatives and payment for ecosystem service programmes. *Frontiers in Marine Science* 2: 32.

HLPE. (2014) Sustainable Fisheries and Aquaculture for Food Security and Nutrition: A Report by the High Level Panel of Experts on Food Security and Nutrition of the Committee on World Food Security. Rome, Italy: FAO.

*Hossain MS, Johnson FA, Dearing JA, et al. (2015) Recent trends of human wellbeing in the Bangladesh delta. *Environmental Development* 17: 21–32.

*Januchowski-Hartley FA, Graham NAJ, Wilson SK, et al. (2017) Drivers and predictions of coral reef carbonate budget trajectories. *Proceedings of the Royal Society B: Biological Sciences* 284.

*Kenny AJ, Campbell N, Koen-Alonso M, et al. (2017) Delivering sustainable fisheries through adoption of a risk-based framework as part of an ecosystem approach to fisheries management. *Marine Policy* [in press].

Kerr SR and Dickie LM. (2001) *The Biomass Spectrum: A Predator–Prey Theory of Aquatic Production*. New York: Columbia University Press.

Knox J. (2017) Report of the Special Rapporteur on the issue of human rights obligations relating to the enjoyment of a safe, clean, healthy and sustainable environment. Doc. A/HRC/34/49. 22 pp.

*Locatelli T, Binet T, Kairo JG, et al. (2014) Turning the tide: how blue carbon and payments for ecosystem services (PES) might help save mangrove forests. *Ambio* 43: 981–995.

Longhurst A. (2010) *Mismanagement of Marine Fisheries*. Cambridge, UK: Cambridge University Press.

MA. (2005) *Millennium Ecosystem Assessment, 2005. Ecosystems and Human Well-Being: Synthesis*. Washington, DC: Island Press.

McCauley DJ, Pinsky ML, Palumbi SR, et al. (2015) Marine defaunation: animal loss in the global ocean. *Science* 347: 1255641.

Mahajan SL and Daw T. (2016) Perceptions of ecosystem services and benefits to human well-being from community-based marine protected areas in Kenya. *Marine Policy* 74: 108–119.

Milner-Gulland EJ, Mcgregor JA, Agarwala M, et al. (2014) Accounting for the impact of conservation on human well-being. *Conservation Biology* 28: 1160–1166.

Morgera E. (2016) The need for an international legal concept of fair and equitable benefit sharing. *European Journal of International Law* 27: 353–383.

*Ntona M and Morgera E. (2017) Connecting SDG 14 with the other Sustainable Development Goals through marine spatial planning. *Marine Policy* [in press].

Pascual U, Balvanera P, Díaz S, et al. (2017a) Valuing nature's contributions to people: the IPBES approach. *Current Opinion in Environmental Sustainability* 26–27: 7–16.

*Pascual U, Palomo I, Adams WM, et al. (2017b) Off-stage ecosystem service burdens: a blind spot for global sustainability. *Environmental Research Letters* 12: 075001.

Pauly D and Zeller D. (2016) Catch reconstructions reveal that global marine fisheries catches are higher than reported and declining. *Nature Communications* 7: 10244.

*Payo A, Mukhopadhyay A, Hazra S, et al. (2016) Projected changes in area of the Sundarban mangrove forest in Bangladesh due to SLR by 2100. *Climatic Change* 139: 279–291.

Pendleton L, Krowicki F, Strosser P, et al. (2014) *Assessing the Economic Contribution of Marine and Coastal Ecosystem Services in the Sargasso Sea*. NI R 14–05. Durham, NC: Duke University.

*Poppy GM, Chiotha S, Eigenbrod F, et al. (2014) Food security in a perfect storm: using the ecosystem services framework to increase understanding. *Philosophical Transactions of the Royal Society B: Biological Sciences* 369.

Porras I, Mohammed EY, Ali L, et al. (2017) Power, profits and payments for ecosystem services in Hilsa fisheries in Bangladesh: a value chain analysis. *Marine Policy* 84: 60–68.

Porter M, Mwaipopo R, Faustine R, et al. (2008) Globalization and women in coastal communities in Tanzania. *Development* 51: 193–198.

Roman J, Estes JA, Morissette L, et al. (2014) Whales as marine ecosystem engineers. *Frontiers in Ecology and the Environment* 12: 377–385.

*Simmance A, Simmance F, Kolding J, et al. (2016) In the frame: modifying Photovoice for improving understanding of gender in fisheries and aquaculture. In: Taylor WW, Bartley DM, Goddard CI, et al. (eds) *Global Conference on Inland Fisheries, UNFAO*. Food and Agriculture Organization of the United Nations; Michigan State University; American Fisheries Society, 77–89.

Sumaila UR, Vats V and Swartz W. (2013) Values from the Resources of the Sargasso Sea. Sargasso Sea Alliance Science Report Series, No 12. 24 pp.

UN. (2015) *Goal 14: Conserve and Sustainably Use the Oceans, Seas and Marine Resources*. Available at: www.un.org/sustainabledevelopment/oceans/

*van Rooyen C and Tannous N. (2017) What is the impact of marine resources management on multi-dimensional poverty in sub-Saharan Africa? A rapid evidence assessment report. Johannesburg, South Africa: Africa Centre for Evidence.

Wylie L, Sutton-Grier AE and Moore A. (2016) Keys to successful blue carbon projects: Lessons learned from global case studies. *Marine Policy* 65: 76–84.

Ye Y, Cochrane K, Bianchi G, et al. (2013) Rebuilding global fisheries: the World Summit Goal, costs and benefits. *Fish and Fisheries* 14: 174–185.

PART V
Concluding thoughts

19
ECOSYSTEM SERVICES FOR HUMAN WELLBEING

Trade-offs and governance

Georgina Mace, Kate Schreckenberg and Mahesh Poudyal

Introduction

Following the publication of the Millennium Ecosystem Assessment in 2005, the ESPA research programme was developed to address outstanding research and policy questions concerning how ecosystem services could contribute to sustainable poverty alleviation. The research programme landed on fertile ground because many researchers and policy-makers were deeply interested in and committed to finding synergies between environmental management and sustainable development. However, this interface between environment and development had traditionally been rather narrow, largely based in development science and with tensions of many kinds between addressing the needs of people, especially the poorest and most vulnerable, and addressing pressing conservation problems in biodiversity rich areas of the world. While some of the on-the-ground tensions between environmental conservation and poverty alleviation were well exposed, if not resolved, others highlighted continuing differences between the relevant research and policy communities. For example, how should environmental goods and services be prioritised in development, and how could they contribute to sustainable growth in developing countries and emerging economies? Does the commodification of nature benefit the poorest through trickle-down effects from economic growth? How do intensively and extensively managed landscapes affect the wellbeing of the poor? Are there local and regional biophysical limits and thresholds that cannot be avoided and how might they be identified? These, and a series of related questions at the intersection of the relevant environment and development science disciplines, have been the focus of much recent research including significant contributions from the ESPA programme. They have informed, and in turn have been informed by, other initiatives in science and policy, and been influenced also by events in the wider world. In this chapter we provide an overview of this body of work, drawing extensively on the chapters in this volume. We synthesise key messages and highlight research gaps.

At the outset, it is useful to reaffirm some central ideas that have stood the test of time and are widely accepted in research and in practice. Most fundamental is the understanding that people everywhere depend ultimately upon ecosystems. Ecosystem functions and processes directly and indirectly underpin people's health and wellbeing (MA, 2005), and are called ecosystem services. However, they are not inevitable; ecosystems need to be managed for these services to be secured, shared and sustainable. Over the course of human history, the relationship between people and ecosystems has mostly been exploitative, based around food, materials and energy, but there has been increasing concern about maintaining the regulatory processes of ecosystems (for example, mitigating the impacts of climate change and natural hazards, or maintaining ecosystem functions in soils and oceans). There are also significant cultural values associated with ecosystems, which are not easily generalised across places and cultures and which are easily overlooked in dominant framings for natural resources and ecosystem service management (Chan et al., 2012; Díaz et al., 2018).

Nowadays, dominant land and sea use continue to drive the intensification of food production and wider urbanisation, and do not take account of the impact this has on the people now most directly dependent on ecosystem services (many local, poor and powerless), nor on future generations whose options will thereby be limited. At the same time, growing pressures from an ever-expanding consumer class (Putt del Pino et al., 2017), with increasing demands and global connections, place new strains on ecosystems everywhere. The trend towards urbanisation continues, with over half the world's population now living in cities, including many of the poorest and most vulnerable (UN, 2014). While in the past there was usually the option to move or seek resources elsewhere when they became limiting locally, now there are global-scale markets, pressures, and flows of materials and people that overwhelm local resource management practices and plans (Burger et al., 2012).

Recent decades have, however, seen some successes. Largely as a result of ecosystem transformation, the adoption and use of new technologies, advances in public health and global economic growth, significant improvements have been achieved and overall levels of poverty have been reduced. Nevertheless, many people still lack access to adequate food, clean drinking water and sanitation and while economic growth in countries like China and India has lifted millions out of poverty, progress has been uneven. Women are more likely to live in poverty than men due to unequal access to paid work, education and property (UN, 2015) and inequality is increasing. South Asia and sub-Saharan Africa now account for 80% of those defined as being in extreme poverty. New threats brought on by climate change, conflict and food insecurity mean that different and greater efforts will be needed to sustain and build upon recent successes, especially as ecosystem degradation and deterioration affect the poorest and most vulnerable first.

The development and environment agendas have also shifted and evolved, most notably with the agreement on the UN SDGs that apply across developed and developing countries, and are a shared commitment for societies, economy and the environment. Considerations of the many linkages involved have highlighted the overall complexity across scales of both ecosystems and relevant governance systems (Carpenter et al., 2009), interdependencies and complex interactions between people and ecosystems (Geijzendorffer et al., 2017; Reyers et al., 2013) and the significant governance challenges that are implicit in the SDG framework (Waage et al., 2015). Over recent decades, two strong trends have converged. On the one hand, earth system scientists have highlighted the risks from transgressing 'safe operating spaces' for major systems such as climate, water and the biosphere (Steffen et al., 2015). On the other, the global environmental justice movement has developed and highlighted a suite of concepts and persistent issues including the environmentalism of the poor, climate justice, food sovereignty, land-grabs and water justice (Martinez-Alier, 2002). There are many ways in which these concepts of environmental boundaries, environmental justice and ecosystem services converge, especially considering the priorities for development and environment in the global South (Lele et al., 2013; Raworth, 2012; Sikor, 2013a).

This is the context for the research relating to ecosystem services and wellbeing which we consider here. Referring back to the original ESPA framework (Figure 0.1 in the Preface), it is clear that while much work has focused on unpacking the central core of 'wellbeing', relatively little dealt with the surrounding 'ecosystems' circle. By far the largest component tackled the outer 'enabling conditions' circle, highlighting the overriding importance of external drivers, the political economy and governance systems in determining how ecosystem services contribute to human wellbeing.

Key findings

The complexity of the social-ecological system

Links between ecosystem services and poverty are just one element of the social-ecological system. This is a complex system with multiple interactions across scales of space and time. It is difficult, or even impossible, to predict the consequences of actions across scales and sectors (DeFries and Nagendra, 2017). The complex system is characterised by feedback loops, non-linearities and alternative states, which means that apparently straightforward interventions nearly always have unintended consequences (Dearing; Reyers and Selomane, both this volume). Specifically, in many contexts, there is clear evidence that even well-intentioned and well-designed interventions for ecosystem services can fail the poorest, most vulnerable and powerless (Adger and Fortnam; Dawson et al.; Marshall et al.; Martin et al.; Whittaker et al., all this volume), leading to a bad situation persisting or worsening. Poverty traps are one consequence.

A related conclusion applies to protected areas. These are potentially a significant tool for securing biodiversity and they may have many potential benefits for enhancing ecosystem services. Protected areas are a major focus of intergovernmental environmental commitments such as the CBD. However, there are continuing tensions when restrictive practices conflict with the rights and livelihoods of local communities (Woodhouse et al., this volume). Similarly, there are few quick and easy fixes to ecosystem degradation; restoration is difficult, costly and time-consuming, and may not simply reverse the loss of ecosystem services or the associated wellbeing outcomes (Cameron, this volume).

The cross-scale, cross-system features of the social-ecological system enhance the likelihood of unanticipated outcomes and are likely to be a persistent feature, making ecosystem management a wicked problem. But this is no justification for inaction or adopting only simple policies and interventions. Embracing the complexity and working with it will not only limit unforeseen consequences but may also suggest useful new approaches (DeFries and Nagendra, 2017; Reyers and Selomane, this volume).

Trade-offs

In fact, we find that trade-offs are a ubiquitous outcome affecting many different parts of the system. Trade-offs should not be a surprise – they are inevitable. Preparing and planning for trade-offs is necessary and not just a way to avoid undesirable outcomes; exploring trade-offs, especially with respect to poverty and environmental resources, can reveal many potential opportunities.

Trade-offs of many kinds are evident in theory and in practice. At a fundamental level there are trade-offs within ecosystems whereby the ecological processes enhanced by one kind of management necessarily place constraints on what can be delivered overall (Dearing, this volume). Among other consequences, enhancement of one kind of ecosystem service will have consequences for others that were not the object of management. For example, actions to enhance or improve productivity usually do provide improved yields in agricultural landscapes, fisheries and peri-urban areas, but almost always to the detriment of regulating services such as air, water and soil quality, climate regulation and biodiversity conservation (Dearing; Marshall et al.; Martin et al., all this volume). The detrimental effects may quickly become evident, but may also accumulate only slowly over time (for example, biodiversity losses in harvested areas; Cameron; Diz and Morgera, both this volume), lead to abrupt shifts or even be experienced in other places or by future generations (Dearing; Reyers and Selomane, both this volume). These offsite impacts of ecosystem services management plans are both pervasive and poorly understood (Pascual et al., 2017).

A more recent realisation that is especially relevant to the management of ecosystem services for poverty alleviation concerns the trade-offs among different groups of people, even within the same ecosystem and concerning the same proposed benefits. A particular problem is that it is the poor and the powerless who tend to be the losers, even when there seemed to be good reasons to believe that they would benefit, and examples are many. Within communities there are some people who benefit, while others lose out (Brown and Fortnam; Coulthard et al.; Dawson et al.; Marshall et al.; Woodhouse et al., all this volume). Even within a household, men, women and children vary in how they access and benefit from different ecosystem services and are affected by ecosystem management (Daw et al., 2011). Finally there are trade-offs as well as important synergies among different wellbeing components (Coulthard et al., this volume), and these multi-dimensional interactions across wellbeing components and groups of people mean that aggregate estimates may be especially misleading (Daw et al., 2011, 2015).

Exploring the likely consequences of interventions and policies for ecosystem services can expose the winners and losers, but needs to be done carefully, using participatory approaches that ensure that all stakeholders really are explicitly considered. One of the ways to reveal trade-offs (hidden or otherwise) and perceptions about trade-offs among different actors could be the use of knowledge co-production processes, by bringing together scientists with governance actors and local stakeholders, to explore and understand complex social-ecological dynamics and potential outcomes of different management actions (Galafassi et al., 2017). Due consideration, however, must be given to individuals and groups that are likely to be marginalised or lack representation in such participatory processes, as recognition of such groups and their proper participation in the process are crucial in ensuring just outcomes.

Environmental justice

Concerns over environmental justice first arose primarily over rights to natural resources, especially forestry, minerals and water (Martinez-Alier, 2002), and relate to how differences in power, wealth, identity or status can limit people's just claims over environmental resources. This is a broad issue in the political economy, but has a central role in ecosystem services debates (Sikor, 2013b) and is a significant factor in the face of the inevitable trade-offs just described (Brown and Fortnam; Coulthard et al.; Pascual and Howe; Szaboova et al., all this volume). In practice, a consequence of the existence of trade-offs and the way in which decisions are negotiated and agreed is that decisions will almost inevitably be inequitable and often unsustainable (Whittaker et al., this volume), and are likely to benefit the powerful at a cost to the poor and powerless. There is an inescapable link between environmental degradation and considerations of equity and justice that requires the 'justice gap' to be closed if environmental resources are to be sustainably managed to benefit the poor (Dawson et al., this volume). A first step is to recognise this issue in order to put in place mechanisms and processes to ensure that decisions are just and equitable. Dawson and colleagues (this volume) describe three broad areas of concern that dominate theories of social justice: recognition, procedure and distribution. Exploring the environmental policy literature shows that while each of these dimensions may sometimes at least be referenced in environmental policy, it is never the case that all are included. In practice, the implementation is weak – and mostly with inadequate inputs from the groups of people concerned. Bridging this justice gap is not only important for moral reasons; there is also increasing acknowledgement and evidence to suggest that equitable governance is instrumental to achieving environmental policy goals, rather than contrary to them (Dawson et al.; Nunan et al., both this volume). More explicit framings of justice or equity will be needed, such as those outlined by McDermott et al. (2013) for Payments for Ecosystem Services and that by Schreckenberg et al. (2016) for protected area conservation, which could be adapted for wider ecosystem management.

Wellbeing

A further important perspective related to trade-offs concerns the measurement of poverty, and highlights the many benefits of moving away from one-dimensional poverty, as measured by an absence of wealth or material goods, and towards the assessment of multi-dimensional wellbeing (Coulthard et al.; Szaboova et al., both this volume). Coulthard et al. (this volume) summarise many of the developing ideas to conceptualise wellbeing, and they point to the hazards of assuming that poverty and wellbeing are simply opposite ends of a single spectrum. Measures of poverty, especially if they are limited to income or material wealth, fail to recognise the multi-dimensional, relative and relational aspects of wellbeing and so may miss many people's needs and desires. This risks stigmatising the poor as 'hapless victims', whereas wellbeing recognises them as active agents capable of change. Wellbeing is a broader concept that can be developed in context and with metrics that are sensitive to local needs, customs and demands. Disaggregation of wellbeing metrics according to income or societal status, gender, age-class is also necessary as aggregate or average values can obscure groups that are being failed or excluded, or whose needs are different, and hide the gaps that keep the poor and marginalised away from benefits (Brown and Fortnam; Coulthard et al.; Szaboova et al., all this volume). Wellbeing has many advantages as a concept and as a means to frame significant factors in development other than wealth, including the emerging priorities for increased resilience. Resilience implies that wellbeing is a process and not simply an outcome, and poor people's wellbeing over time will be governed by their dynamic responses to changes in society and the environment (Szaboova et al., this volume).

Pitfalls with payments

Payments and compensation schemes hold obvious attraction. The simple idea is that ecosystem services have a value (by definition) and therefore a buyer can compensate or reward an environmental manager for specific ecosystem services. In practice it is not so simple, and there is a complex history of efforts to formalise a system of Payments for Ecosystem Services (PES). As Menton and Bennett (this volume) describe, this led initially to a focus on determining the monetary value of ecosystem services and the opportunity costs of stewardship, in order to guide compensation payments. Over time, the focus has shifted increasingly towards social issues beyond monetary value and markets, but there are many ways that they fail and in doing so it is the poor, landless and powerless that suffer most (McDermott et al., 2013).

Many examples show that payments for ecosystem services or compensation schemes rarely work to reduce poverty sustainably or for multiple ecosystem services. In certain cases they further disbenefit the poor especially where the benefits can be captured by others (e.g. Menton and Bennett, this volume), where payments are conditional on environmental conditions that are difficult to measure or to achieve reliably (Porras and Asquith; Whittaker et al., both this volume), and where the 'valued' services are at odds with local needs and demands (Whittaker et al., this volume). PES is better considered not as a conditional agreement based around payments, which can often be imposed externally, but rather as a reward for environmental stewardship. It is important to include the modes and institutional arrangements (formal and informal) for negotiating the agreements, noting that lasting and effective motivations may be culturally driven.

Two approaches are promising: first, unconditional payments whereby custodians of ecosystem services or those disproportionately affected by conservation restrictions are paid using secure sustained financing, in a way that is analogous to social protection schemes (see Porras and Asquith, this volume). Second, negotiated agreements between beneficiaries of ecosystem services and those conserving or altering their land-use behaviour to protect the ecosystems, based in reciprocity and consensus rather than markets, and often mediated informally, have been shown to have longer-lasting benefits (Asquith, 2016). In both cases it is necessary that both social (i.e. pro-poor) and environmental outcomes are considered in the payments (cash or in-kind), even if they are not explicitly linked (Porras and Asquith; Whittaker et al., both this volume).

On occasion, local peoples' motivations for conservation might be crowded out by PES schemes (Muradian et al., 2013), or cash payments for environmental goods and services that are supposed to be 'public goods' may not be politically palatable. So, while valuation of ecosystem services might be considered useful in designing PES schemes, designing effective and equitable schemes for incentivising environmental stewardship requires an understanding of local social-ecological system dynamics, including potential winners and losers, trade-offs and existing institutional arrangements and governance.

Governance and institutions for ecosystem services

The relationships between ecosystem services and wellbeing, including payments, are ultimately mediated by governance systems and relevant institutions that determine how decisions are taken over what issues and by whom. The centrality of governance is fundamental to enhancing wellbeing through ecosystem services as is increasingly recognised in the evolving frameworks (Pascual and Howe, this volume), and indeed it is central in the IPBES conceptual framework that now serves as the organising basis for the forthcoming global synthesis on ecosystem services and nature's contributions to people (Díaz et al., 2015, 2018).

Nunan et al. (this volume) highlight the gaps and frailties of existing governance systems for ecosystem services as they relate to poverty alleviation and wellbeing. Existing systems tend to be organised sectorally (e.g. food, water, timber) and be dominated by certain powerful groups, especially landowners, and be regularly subject to political pressures. Participatory approaches have had only limited success and have weak representation from poor and marginalised groups. While governance for enhanced wellbeing from ecosystem services fundamentally implies multi-sector, multi-scale governance, these barely exist and are extremely difficult to establish (Diz and Morgera; Nunan et al., both this volume).

Local-level governance of ecosystem services is also increasingly affected by external drivers from globalisation, especially international flows of materials, capital and investments (Nunan et al., this volume). This, in part, mirrors the impacts of globalisation on land use change, particularly in the Global South. A consequence is that local, regional and national-scale governance for ecosystem services must consider the impacts of these global drivers alongside specific and place-based factors (Meyfroidt et al., 2013; Nunan et al., this volume).

Governance also determines access to data and information and the potential flows of knowledge and information necessary for evidence-based decision making. Potentially transformational advances in technology and the advent of big data and machine learning tools hold huge promise for better monitoring, management and improved wellbeing from ecosystems highlighting the needs of locally dependent, poor communities (Buytaert et al., this volume). Nevertheless, such advances are easily captured by technically competent and well-connected elites and can simply become a source of power and influence that marginalises most people, but especially the poor (Pascual and Howe, this volume). This is not inevitable however, and Buytaert et al. (this volume) demonstrate that ICT advances offer the potential for polycentric governance based on open and transparent data that can be enabling and inclusive if designed with that in mind.

Lessons for the SDGs

The findings here have several implications for global ambitions to achieve the 17 SDGs. First, although the goals are stand-alone objectives it is clear that there are many interconnections between them that may suggest hopes for synergies and easy wins; but there are also many possibilities for perverse and unintended outcomes from pursuing single goals without considering the overall system of which they are a part (Stafford-Smith et al., 2017). Even in the context of ecosystem services and wellbeing, it is clear that the complexity of the system and the extent of interconnectedness means that simple and directed solutions rarely work as planned.

We recommend instead embracing the complexities, working with established and emerging participatory approaches to ensure that all stakeholders are involved, and using systems approaches to define just and safe outcomes for environmental conditions.

Second, a significant feature of the SDGs is that both developed and developing countries are included and the goals relating to poverty and wellbeing therefore apply everywhere. This raises a tension between objective (absolute) and relative approaches to measuring poverty and other components of wellbeing. However, this is well resolved by taking a capability approach which focuses on the kind of life that people have 'reason to value' (Sen, 1999) and on what people are able to achieve, rather than solely on what they have or what they lack (Coulthard et al., this volume).

Third, equitable and just outcomes for sustainable wellbeing will not be achieved by processes that fail to consider the different dimensions of justice (recognition, procedure, distribution) as well as the complexity of the social-ecological system. This finding has significant implications for actions designed to achieve the SDGs, and the goal of 'leaving no one behind'.

Ecosystem service management can make an important contribution to achieving the SDG agenda (Wood et al., 2018). Doing so by 2030 requires rapid action. A clear conclusion is that, complexity notwithstanding, we have enough knowledge and understanding to design and implement environmental policies and interventions that are 'good enough'. By embedding decisions in adaptive governance processes, these policies can be adjusted as our understanding deepens and unexpected outcomes become evident. Nevertheless, there are areas in which more research could accelerate progress towards enhancing wellbeing in an environmentally sustainable manner, such as: how can governance at local, national and international levels be better connected vertically and across sectors to ensure that decision making in one place doesn't inadvertently close down options or impose costs on others? Can more be done to ensure accountability of current decision makers (often overly focused on short-term political cycles) to future generations? What combination of regulatory and market-based approaches is most effective in different contexts? In particular, how do we govern the commons (from our global atmosphere to trans-boundary fisheries and local pastures) and limit creeping privatisation and elite capture? To what extent can ecosystem service-based approaches be combined with more conventional technological and socio-institutional innovations? Where restoration is necessary, how do we ensure it meets the requirements of multiple stakeholders and is achieved rapidly and at scale? How do we harness the forces of globalisation and, especially, the opportunities provided by increasingly widespread information and communication technologies, as a positive factor supporting more effective and just decision making? None of these questions can easily be pigeon-holed as the domain of a single discipline. Indeed, the chapters in this book highlight the need for more co-produced and interdisciplinary research to more effectively provide implementation-ready solutions to policy-makers' questions.

Conclusions

It is impossible to read the chapters in this book and not detect a collective sense of frustration at the injustices that are still suffered by large segments of the population, often in the name of well-intentioned projects intended to achieve some undefined vision of 'progress' or mitigate against some of its negative impacts. The idea that beneficial outcomes for people can be achieved simply by managing ecosystems for ecosystem services turns out to have many pitfalls in practice, and especially so as a means for the poor to move sustainably out of poverty. Over even quite short periods the system becomes dominated by certain easy-to-achieve and profitable ecosystem services, which can readily be captured and sequestered by the most powerful sectors/elites. Privatisation of what were once public goods is increasing, especially in relation to freshwater and fisheries, but even for wildlife conservation and tourism. Provisioning services tend to dominate ecosystem decisions, commonly driven by markets that are not accessible to local communities. Regulating services tend to suffer, with more serious and lasting consequences for local communities and future generations. With the poorest and most vulnerable also being most dependent on local ecosystem goods and services, and in the absence of any effective trickle-down of wealth, simple interventions often fail the poorest and many are in any case unsustainable.

Moving away from a linear model, conceived to somehow provide a causal link between ecosystem services and wellbeing, and instead recognising the complexity of the social-ecological system provides a more realistic basis for design and planning of interventions. This approach forces a more inclusive approach and means that the feedbacks, non-linearities and threshold responses that are likely do not come as a surprise and can be built into the design. This approach is obviously more complicated, but by making the real risks, co-benefits and opportunities more obvious, and by forcing an explicit understanding of the potential winners and losers, decisions can become both more transparent and more realistic.

Ecosystem services are important – directly and indirectly – for the wellbeing of all people. Yet it is the wellbeing of the poor – the focus of this book – that is most directly dependent upon the natural environment through cultural, subsistence and income-generating activities. However, their justified aspirations for a decent life encounter externally driven obstacles and threats that are beyond the capacity of local people to tackle; their options are constrained by decisions taken elsewhere. Recognising trade-offs as conflicts between the varied wellbeing aspirations of different groups of people highlights the political nature of the associated value judgements. Taking an environmental justice approach to ecosystem governance can help resolve trade-offs by recognising the rights of the poor, women and other marginalised groups to have a voice, establishing the procedures for them to use that voice and ensuring fair distribution of benefits. Accountable and adaptive governance systems will be necessary to connect people across local to global scales, recognising joint responsibility for environmental stewardship and global wellbeing outcomes for all.

References

(ESPA outputs marked with '★')

Asquith N. (2016) Watershared: adaptation, mitigation, watershed protection and economic development in Latin America. *Inside Stories on Climate Compatible Development*. Climate & Development Knowledge Network (CDKN).

Burger JR, Allen CD, Brown JH, et al. (2012) The macroecology of sustainability. *PLoS Biology* 10: e1001345.

Carpenter SR, Mooney HA, Agard J, et al. (2009) Science for managing ecosystem services: beyond the Millennium Ecosystem Assessment. *Proceedings of the National Academy of Sciences* 106: 1305–1312.

Chan KM, Guerry AD, Balvanera P, et al. (2012) Where are cultural and social in ecosystem services? A framework for constructive engagement. *BioScience* 62: 744–756.

★Daw T, Brown K, Rosendo S, et al. (2011) Applying the ecosystem services concept to poverty alleviation: the need to disaggregate human well-being. *Environmental Conservation* 38: 370–379.

★Daw TM, Coulthard S, Cheung WWL, et al. (2015) Evaluating taboo trade-offs in ecosystems services and human well-being. *Proceedings of the National Academy of Sciences* 112: 6949–6954.

DeFries R and Nagendra H. (2017) Ecosystem management as a wicked problem. *Science* 356: 265–270.

★Díaz S, Demissew S, Carabias J, et al. (2015) The IPBES conceptual framework – connecting nature and people. *Current Opinion in Environmental Sustainability* 14: 1–16.

Díaz S, Pascual U, Stenseke M, et al. (2018) Assessing nature's contributions to people. *Science* 359: 270–272.

★Galafassi D, Daw TM, Munyi L, et al. (2017) Learning about social-ecological trade-offs. *Ecology and Society* 22: 2.

Geijzendorffer IR, Cohen-Shacham E, Cord AF, et al. (2017) Ecosystem services in global sustainability policies. *Environmental Science & Policy* 74: 40–48.

★Lele S, Springate-Baginski O, Lakerveld R, et al. (2013) Ecosystem services: origins, contributions, pitfalls, and alternatives. *Conservation and Society* 11: 343.

MA. (2005) *Millennium Ecosystem Assessment, 2005. Ecosystems and Human Well-Being: Synthesis*. Washington, DC: Island Press.

★McDermott M, Mahanty S and Schreckenberg K. (2013) Examining equity: a multidimensional framework for assessing equity in payments for ecosystem services. *Environmental Science and Policy* 33: 416–427.

Martinez-Alier J. (2002) *The Environmentalism of the Poor*. Cheltenham, UK: Edward Elgar.

Meyfroidt P, Lambin EF, Erb K-H, et al. (2013) Globalization of land use: distant drivers of land change and geographic displacement of land use. *Current Opinion in Environmental Sustainability* 5: 438–444.

★Muradian R, Arsel M, Pellegrini L, et al. (2013) Payments for ecosystem services and the fatal attraction of win-win solutions. *Conservation Letters* 6: 274–279.

★Pascual U, Palomo I, Adams WM, et al. (2017) Off-stage ecosystem service burdens: a blind spot for global sustainability. *Environmental Research Letters* 12: 075001.

Putt del Pino S, Metzger E, Drew D, et al. (2017) The Elephant in the Boardroom: Why Unchecked Consumption Is Not an Option in Tomorrow's Markets. *WRI Working Paper, March 2017*. Washington, DC: World Resources Institute.

Raworth K. (2012) A safe and just space for humanity: can we live within the doughnut? *Oxfam Policy and Practice: Climate Change and Resilience* 8: 1–26.

Reyers B, Biggs R, Cumming GS, et al. (2013) Getting the measure of ecosystem services: a social-ecological approach. *Frontiers in Ecology and the Environment* 11: 268–273.

★Schreckenberg K, Franks P, Martin A, et al. (2016) Unpacking equity for protected area conservation. *Parks* 22: 11–26.

Sen A. (1999) *Development as Freedom*. Oxford: Oxford University Press.

★Sikor T. (2013a) Introduction: linking ecosystem services with environmental justice. In Sikor T (ed.) *The Justices and Injustices of Ecosystem Services*. Abingdon, UK: Routledge.

★Sikor T, ed. (2013b) *The Justices and Injustices of Ecosystem Services*. Abingdon, UK: Routledge.

Stafford-Smith M, Griggs D, Gaffney O, et al. (2017) Integration: the key to implementing the Sustainable Development Goals. *Sustainability Science* 12: 911–919.

★Steffen W, Richardson K, Rockström J, et al. (2015) Planetary boundaries: guiding human development on a changing planet. *Science* 347: 1259855.

UN. (2014) *World Urbanization Prospects: The 2014 Revision*. New York: United Nations, Department of Economic and Social Affairs, Population Division.

UN. (2015) *The World's Women 2015: Trends and Statistics*. New York: United Nations, Department of Economic and Social Affairs, Statistics Division.

Waage J, Yap C, Bell S, et al. (2015) Governing the UN Sustainable Development Goals: interactions, infrastructures, and institutions. *Lancet Global Health* 3: E251–E252.

Wood SLR, Jones SK, Johnson JA, et al. (2018) Distilling the role of ecosystem services in the Sustainable Development Goals. *Ecosystem Services* 29: 70–82.

INDEX

Page numbers in *italics* indicate an illustration, **bold** a table or box

Adams, Helen 84, 275, 279
Adger, W Neil 83
Agarwal, Bina 260, 267
agroforestry restoration 150
Aichi Target 11 27; and ecosystem restoration **143**, 222
Amazon: frontier migrants and ecosystem services 84, 85; indigenous knowledge, value of 34; rotational migration 79

Bangladesh: climate mitigation project 44; ecosystem services and seasonal poverty 78; fish production and climate change effects 290; integrated ecosystem governance 295; Jatka conservation programme **208**, 213, **215**, 217; land use intensification and trade-offs 101, 106, 131, 294; livelihood mobility 86; mobile phones and migration pattern data *181*; operating space analysis, coastal zone 65, 67–68
Bavinck, Maarten 247–248
Bell, Andrew 195
Belmont Forum DELTAS project 65, *66*
Berkes, Fikret **40**, 81, 82
Bidaud, Cécile **228–229**, 251
biodiversity: Aichi targets for 2020 222; ecosystem condition and safe boundaries 58; ecosystem restoration 147–148, 196; ecosystem service framing 9, 11–12, 22; household size pressures 88; marine protected area, stakeholder conflicts 247–248; offsetting programme inequalities 149, 161, 197, **228–229**, 251–252; poverty reduction impact 148, 291–294
biofuel production: cross-scale dynamics 44, 279; service trade-offs 43
Bluwstein, Jevgeniy 165–166, **170**
Bolivia: power dynamics and access inequalities **276**; reciprocal water agreements (RWAs) 136, 137; *Watershared* in the Andes projects **209**, 211, 212, 213, 216; water supply and power dynamics 131, 137
Börner, Jan 196, 198
Brazil: Bolsa Floresta programme **208**, 210, 211, 212, 213, **215**
Broegaard, Rikke **104**, 277
Brown, HCP 266
Brown, Katrina 85, 236, 294
Burgdorfer, Jason 84, 88
Buytaert, Wouter 129, **170**, 281, 312

Call, Maia A 86
Cambodia 196
Campese, Jessica 159–160
CGIAR 268, **269**
Chaigneau, Tomas 236, 294
China: frontier migrants and forestry 85; land use intensification and trade-offs **102**, 250–251; lower Yangtze basin, system transition 63, *64*, 66; migration and remittance flows 83; operating space

analysis, lake catchments 60, *61*, 65–66; Sloping Land Conversion Program (SLCP) 150–152, 196, **209**, 210, 211, *212*, 213; water management perspectives 32
citizen science 178, 180, 183, *183*
Cleaver, Frances 167
climate change: conditional transfer programmes 210; ecosystem restoration funding **143**; effects on migration 86, **181**; forest–water relationships 129; impact prediction and planning 280, 290–291, 298, 306; safe operating space exceedance 58, 60, 307
Cochrane, Kevern 290, 291
Collaborative Partnership on Forests 126
Collins, Kevin 183–184
Colombia 183, **209**
Commission on the Measurement of Economic Performance 243
complex adaptive systems (CAS) **40**, 55
conditional transfers: aims and target groups 205; conditional limitations of PES schemes 205, 207, 217–218; hybrid CT/PES programmes 207, **208–209**, 218–219; PES programmes 207, **209**; PES scheme similarities and differences 193, 205, *206*, **218**; social conditional transfer programmes 207, **208**
conditional transfers, scaling-up conditions: impact, demonstration of 216–217, *216*; implementation and incentives 213–214, **215**, 216; institutional set-up 211–213, *212*; political support 210–211; sustainable finance 211
Congo Basin 266
Convention on Biological Diversity (CBD): Aichi Target 11 27; Aichi Targets and ecosystem restoration 143, 222; Nagoya Protocol **28**; protected areas governance 232
Cooper, Gregory 68–69, *68*
Corbera, Esteve 191, 193, 197, 263–264
Costa Rica: Pago por Servicios Ambientales programme 135, 137, **194**, **209**; PES project, key conditions 210, 211, 213, **215**, 216
Coulthard, Sarah 275, 282, 310
cross-scale dynamics 42, 44, *45*, 50–51, 281

Cruz-Garcia, Gisella 46, 257

Daily, Gretchen 5
Daw, Tim M: EcoSim fisheries model, trade off analysis 67; elasticity in ecosystem services 63, 65; social-ecological 'toy model', Kenyan fisheries **182**, 182–183, 249–250, 295; wellbeing differences 247, 277, 296
Dawson, Neil: food security/income issues 277, **278**, 278; indigenous stakeholder inequalities 26, 275, 309–310; protected areas and stakeholders 31–32; socio-ecological reductionism **248**, 248–249, 252
Dearing, John A: cross-scale dynamics 44, 281; land use intensification and trade-offs **102**, 250–251; non-linearities 47; safe and just operating space 60, *61*
decision support systems 177–178, 184, **185**
Delang, Claudio O 151–152
Department for International Development (DFID) xviii
de Sherbinin, Alex 86, 89
DIVERSITAS 6
diversity and multidimensional services 44, 46–47, *46*, 50
Diz, Daniela 294
Dorward, Andrew 48
'doughnut' model 50, 60
Drivers-Pressures-States-Impacts-Responses (DPSIR) 6, 7
Dublin Statement on Water and Sustainable Development (1992) 27

East Africa: ecosystem services and gendered roles 260; Lake Victoria, fisheries-based livelihoods 79, 81
ecoSERVICES 6
ecosystem governance: cultural/local practice not recognised 23, 26, 29; decision procedure, stakeholder equity 23, 31–32, 33; distribution and service access 23, 33–34; environmental justice and equity dimensions **24**; equity and justice concerns 22–23, 25–29, *26*, **28**, 161–163; financial mechanism limitations 23, 26, 27, 34; governance principles, best practices 168–169, **170**; institutions, functions and influences 167–168; integrated ocean governance 295–297; justice and equity integration studies 29, **30**, 31–32, 34–35; mobile systems and livelihood challenges 81–82; multi-level and multi-actor perspectives 166–167, 312, 313; participatory and decentralised approaches 163–166, **164**, 180–184, **182**, 186; polycentric governance 176–177, 312; power dynamics and justice gap 32–34, *33*,

312; regulatory and market-based approaches 160–161, **163**; rights-based approaches 161–163; social foundation, just spaces 60, 62

ecosystem restoration: active and passive interventions 145–146, 152–153; definitions **144**; drivers of degradation 146–147; ecosystem functioning and goals 147–148, 152; goal setting and ecosystem services 144–145, 153; policy and funding initiatives **143**; poverty alleviation, impact analysis 148–150; research and funding bias 143–144; Sahel region, re-greening project 150; Sloping Land Conversion Program (SLCP), China 150–152, 210

ecosystem service frameworks: biodiversity and poverty linkages 9, 11–12, 22; co-production of services 13; core and satellite framework evolution 5–9, *8*, 16–18; epistemic communities' influence 3–4, 9, *11*, 16–17; key conceptual attributes **10**; payments for ecosystem services (PES), influence on 15–16; poverty alleviation, conceptual linkage *41*; social-ecological systems (SES) 4–5, 12; social power relations 13–14; valuation, changing approaches 14–15, 22

ecosystem services, concept 5, 306

Ecosystem Services for Poverty Alleviation (ESPA): conceptual framework development 5, 6, 7, 8–9, 12, 16; contribution to worldwide initiatives xix–xxi; DELTAS project 65, 131, 277; ESPA framework *xx*; P-mowtick project 263, **264**; SPACES project 260, 262, 268

formation and objectives xvii–xviii, 56; future challenges xxi–xxii; non-linearities research 47–48, 50; resilience research 48; simulation models, development and use 67; social-ecological systems (SES) approaches 43, 47–51; wellbeing focus 12

ecosystem service trade-offs: distribution and access inequalities 250–251, 275–276, 280–281, 283–284, 296–297, 308–309; ecosystem governance and social justice 22–23, 25–26, *26*; equity and justice, operational integration 29, **30**, 31–32, 34–35; forest–water relationships 129, 131, **132–133**, 133–134; framework re-evaluation 22; gendered roles and responsibilities 262–263, **264–266**, 265–267; land use intensification **101**, 101–103, **102**, **103**, 306; normative and implementation deficiencies 32–34, *33*, 308; PES financed projects 195–197; protected areas and human wellbeing **227**, 227–230, **228–229**; social-ecological policies, equity and justice 26–29, **28**, 306–307, 309–310; stimulation modelling, Kenyan fishery 67

ecosystem service valuation 14–15, 22

Ecuador: migration and remittance flows 83; seasonal fishing practices 79; water funds 135

Engel, Stefanie 190

'environmentalist's paradox' 99, **102**, 149

environmental justice and equity: ecosystem degradation, blame injustices 251, 252–253; ecosystem governance 25–26, *26*; ecosystem service trade-offs 29, **30**, 31–32, 306–307, 309–310; power dynamics 33; social-ecological policies 26–29, **28**; three dimensions **24**; water sector 27

Erasmus, Y **232–233**

ESPA DELTAS project 65, 131, 277

ESPA P-mowtick project 263, **264**

ESPA SPACES project 260, 262, 268

Ezzine-de-Blas, Driss 199

Fernandes, Jose A 290

fertility rates and poverty 88–89

Fisher, Janet A *41*, 42, 136, 193, 265, 275

fisheries management: conservation and human wellbeing **293–294**, *294*; data collection, multi-scalar approaches 289–291, 298; global fish stocks 288; integrated ocean governance 295–297, 298

fishing communities: fishing regulation, stakeholder equity 23, 81, 165, 296; gendered activities and roles 260, 262, **264**, 275, 297; lagoon fishery, safe space modelling *68*, 68–69; seasonal practices and mobility 79, *80*; social-ecological systems 46, *46*; trade-offs, coastal fishery 67, **182**, 236, 249–250, 294; trade-offs, threat to poor 101, 296–297; wellbeing differences, marine protected area 247–248, **293–294**

'flickering' 47, 65

Folke, Carl **40**, 51

Food and Agricultural Organization (FAO): ecosystem degradation 142;

fisheries management 288, 295; Forests and Water Action Plan 126
food security: challenges and strategies 94–95; human/ecosystem feedback 279; income and wellbeing 277–279, **278**; land use intensification 102, **104**, 106; peri-urban agriculture, urbanisation impacts **113–114**
forest management: carbon PES project 150, 196, 197, 198; community-based governance 163–164, **164**; gendered activities and roles 260; hydrological cycle, impacts on 127–129; migration flows and ecosystem pressures 84–85; poverty alleviation, equity issues 205; stakeholder and power dynamics 23, 33, **115**, 118, 197, 250
forest–water relationships: forests and water quality, yield and flows 127–129; global policy initiatives 126; key drivers and impacts 129, *130*; negotiated water management 134–135; payments for ecosystem services (PES) 135–136, 137; poverty alleviation, equity issues 136–137; reciprocal water agreements (RWAs) **115**, **133**, 134, 136, 137; trade-offs with ecosystem services 129, 131, **132–133**, 133–134; water-sensitive forest management 137–138
Fraser, Nancy **24**
Free, Prior and Informed Consent (FPIC) 162, 167, 198

Galafassi, Diego 182–183
Garrett, Rachael D 85
Gasparatos, Alexandros 43, 277–278
Geist, Helmut 129
gender and ecosystem services: gendered trade-offs 262–263, **264–266**, 265–267, 297; gender equality, potential interventions 267–268, **269**; key literatures and approaches **258**; socio-cultural perceptions and roles 14, 259–260, **261**, 262, 275, 296
governance of protected areas 232
Grillos, Tara 137
Gross-Camp, Nicole 165

Hajra, Rituparna 133–134
Hamann, Maike 47, 262
Hejnowicz, Adam P **292**
Holling, Crawford S 55
Hossain, Md Sarwar 67
Hossain, Mostafa AR 294
Howard, Patricia 279

Howe, Caroline 44, 149, 263
Humphreys Bebbington, Denise **276**, 280
hysteresis 56, **57**, 58, 60, *61*

India: conditional transfer programmes 210, 212; ecosystem services, reduction in 133–134, 250; gender equality interventions 267; lagoonal fishery, safe space modelling *68*, 68–69; livelihood mobility 79; peri-urban agriculture, urbanisation impacts **113–114**, 117–118; rural–urban reciprocal water agreement **115**, 118, **170**; water supply and urbanisation **132–133**; wellbeing differences, marine protected area 247–248
indigenous peoples: Free, Prior and Informed Consent (FPIC) 162, 167, 198; knowledge co-generation 183; land tenure and access 168, **276**; land use change and wellbeing inequalities 25, 105, 106, 248–249, 275–276, 280–281; stakeholder inequalities 309–310
Indonesia 198, 228
Intergovernmental Science-Policy Platform on Biodiversity and Ecosystem Services (IPBES) 234; conceptual framework 7–8, 11, 13, **28**; ecosystem restoration initiatives **143**; MA initiative 4; Nature's Contributions to People (NCP) approach 4–5, 6, 12
International Union for the Conservation of Nature (IUCN) **28**, 232
Ishihara, Hiroe 197–198

Jones, Julia PG 85

Kaczan, David 195
Kafumbata, Dalitso 43, 48
Kai, Zhang 85
Kairu, Anne **170**
Karpouzoglou, Timothy 33
Keane, Aidan 195
Kenny, Andrew 289–290
Kent, Rebecca 48
Kenya: carbon offset and mangrove protection **209**, 211, 212, **215**, **292**; conservation offset, gendered preferences **265**; fishing regulation, stakeholder equity 23, 165; forest management **170**; gendered trade-offs, coastal fishery 263, **264**; mangrove loss 129; Mikoko Pamoja, community

project 213, **215**, **292**; trade-offs, coastal fishery 67, **182**, 236, 249–250; women's empowerment 268
knowledge co-generation, ecosystem services: citizen science 180, 183, *183*; conceptual framework 178, *179*; data processing, participatory approaches 180–184, **182**, 186; decision making, access and capabilities 175–176, 312; ICT, data collection and networking 177–178; knowledge dissemination and interaction 184, **185**; mobile phones and networking 180, **181**; polycentric approach 176–177; satellite imagery 179, 289
Kosoy, Nicolás 193
Kovacs, Eszter K **115**, **170**
Kyrgyzstan 168

Lakerveld, Roan P 134, 250
Lambin, Eric 129
land use intensification: activity categories 95–96; definition 95; disaggregated wellbeing outcomes 103, **104**, 105; ecological trade-offs 101, **101**, 102; food security strategy 94–95; human wellbeing outcomes and trade-offs 101–102, **103**, 131, 280, 294; multidimensional outcomes, research evaluation 97–99, *98–99*, **100**, 102; process, pathways and policy 96–97, *96*; research and practice development 106–107; social-ecological outcome pathways 105–106; social-ecological trade-offs 103, 250–251, 306
Langer, L **232–233**
Laos: land use intensification and food security issues 102, **104**, 106; protected areas and stakeholders 31–32
Leisher, Craig 148
Lewis, Kristina **164**, 168, **170**
limits and thresholds: elasticity in ecosystem services 63, 65, 69–70; planetary boundaries 56, **56–57**, 58, *59*, 60; research development 69–70; safe operating spaces 56, 58, 60, *61*, 62; simulation models, development and use 67–69, *68*; stakeholder education 70; system path, SES approaches 62–63, 69; temporal dynamics, case studies evaluated 63, *64*, 65–66, *66*, 69
Limits to Growth (Meadows) 55
Liu, Can 196
Liu, Jianguo 88–89
Liu, Zhen 151

livelihood mobility 78–79, *80*, 86
Locatelli, T 198, **292**
López, Erna 84
López-Carr, David 84, 88
Lu, Xin **181**
Lund, Jens Friis **170**

McClanahan, Tim R **182**
McDermott, Constance L 162
McDermott, Melanie 150, 165, 198
Mace, Georgina M 58
MacKinnon, James **163**
Madagascar: biodiversity offsetting inequalities 149, 161, **163**, 197, 228, **228–229**, 251–252; community forest management 164–165; Corridor Ankeniheny-Zahamena (CAZ) protected area **163**; fisheries management 291; migrants and forestry 85
Malawi: cross-scale dynamics 44, *45*; jatropha project failures 44, 279; Social Cash Transfer Programme 207
mangrove forests: gendered values **261**; loss through urbanism 129; natural hazard protection 85, 86, 128; PES scheme, potential role **292**; viability and economic impacts 78, 79, 83
Mapping and Assessment of Ecosystem Services (MAES) 4
marine and coastal ecosystems: conservation and social safety nets 291–294, 298; integrated ocean governance 295–297; resource management and wellbeing impacts **293–294**, 296–297; UN protection goal **293**
Marine Protected Area (MPA) 228, 236, 247–248
Martin, Adrian: indigenous stakeholder inequalities 25, 168, 275; social justice and wellbeing 31, 251; socio-ecological reductionism **248**
May, Robert M 55
Meinzen Dick, Ruth 257
Mexico: Payment for Hydrological Environmental Services 135, 137; PES project, key conditions 211, 213, **215**, 217; Scolel-Te project **209**
Meyfroidt, Patrick 85
migration and population dynamics: circular migration 79, *80*, 83; demographic factors and ecosystem provisioning 88–89; loss of ecosystem services 85–86, **87**, 88; migration and

remittance flows 83; migration patterns 79; mobile ecosystems, governance challenges 81–82; multifaceted social system 82–83; place and cultural ecosystem influences 84, 89; pressures on frontier ecosystems 84–85, 129; rotational migration 79; seasonal variability and livelihood mobility 78–79, *80*, 89–90; urban ecosystem services 89

Millennium Development Goals (MDGs) xvii

Millennium Ecosystem Assessment (MA): core ecosystem service framework 5–6, 7–8, 13; developmental damage xvii; economic valuation 14–15; ecosystem restoration 147; ESPA, UK initiative xvii–xviii; gender and ecosystem services 259; human wellbeing elements 12, 243–244, 277; initiative promotion 4, 56

Milner-Gulland, EJ 296

mobile phones and networking 177–178, 180

models for ecosystem services: 'doughnut' model 50, 60; ESPA DELTAS project 65, 131, 277; ESPA P-mowtick project 263, **264**; ESPA SPACES project 260, 262, 268; planetary boundaries 56, **56–57**, 58, *59*, 60; social-ecological 'toy model' 46, *46*, 67, **182**, 182–183, 249–250, 263, **264**

Mohammed, Essam 212

Mozambique: fisheries management 291, 294, 295; jatropha project failures 279; land use intensification and multi-dimensional wellbeing **100**, 102, 106

Muchagata, Marcia 85

multi-level governance 82, 167, 297

Multi-dimensional Poverty Index **100**, **104**

multidimensional wellbeing: ecosystem degradation, unequal impacts 252–253; ecosystem services, distribution inequalities 250–252; food security/income issues 277–279, **278**; framing approaches 43, 46–47, 224, 243–244, 310; land use intensification, impact study **100**, 102, 106; poverty analysis developments 245–246, **246**; protected areas, social impact analysis 224–226, *225*; social complexity, ecosystem service impacts 246–249, **248**, 252, 277; socio-ecological reductionism **248**, 248–249; trade-offs,

environment and stakeholder groups 249–250

Muradian, Roldan 193, 197

natural capital 6–7
natural disasters and displacement 85
natural resource governance: definition 159–160; multi-level and multi-actor perspectives 166–167; participatory and decentralised approaches 163–166, **164**; *see also* ecosystem governance

Nepal: gender inequalities 266; water supply and urbanisation **132–133**

non-linearities: 'doughnut' model 50, 60; identifying system transitions 47–48, 50; tipping points 47, 50, 56, 58

Nunan, Fiona 167–168

Oldekop, JA 164, 226
Ostrom, Elinor 167, 176–177
Otsuki, K 166

Pagiola, Stefano 195
Palomo, Ignacio 13
participatory geographic information systems (PGIS) 183
participatory modelling 181–183, **182**, 186, 236
Pascual, Unai 196
pastoral systems: ecosystem governance constraint 81–82, 168, 227; mobility variations 79–80, *80*
Patenaude, Genevieve **164**, 168, **170**
payments for ecosystem services (PES): conditionality on actions/outcomes 193–194, **194**, 205, *206*, 207, 311; definitions and implementation developments 190–193, *191*, **191**, 310–311; framing influences 15–16; gender issues 266–267; hydrological services and forests 135–136, 137; local justice failures 34; payment/reward distribution 194; power dynamics and inequalities 161, 196, 197–198, 251; project development, important criteria 198–200, **292**, 311; pro-poor vs pro-environment centred 195–197; Sloping Land Conversion Program (SLCP), China 151–152, 210
Payo, Andres 295
peri-urban ecosystems: environment characteristics 113; governance ambiguity 116; industrial-led changes and impacts 113, **113–114**, 121; integration complexities 118–119,

121–122; poverty links 117–118; resource management and trade-offs 113, **115**, 116, 117–118; transformations and poverty alleviation, analysis framework 119–121, *120*
Persha, Lauren 163–164
Peru **185**, 192
Philippines 214, 216
Pinho, Patricia 251
planetary boundaries: biodiversity and ecosystem condition 58; concept 56, 58; ecosystem services and poverty alleviation relationship **56–57**; global functioning, risk evaluation 58, *59*, 60; non-linearities research 47, 50; social foundation 60
Pokorny, Benno 196
Poppy, Guy 43, 279, 289, 296
population dynamics *see* migration and population dynamics
Porras, Ina **194**
Porter, Marilyn 260, 262, 275
Poudyal, Mahesh 149, **163**, 197, 198, 228
poverty alleviation: biodiversity, framing of linkage 9, 11–12; ecosystem restoration, impact analysis 148–150; poverty analysis, income to wellbeing dimensions 245–246, **246**
protected areas: Aichi Target 11 proposals 27; Aichi targets for 2020 222; co-management to negative exclusions 226; compensation issues 235; conservation inequalities 160, 224, 230–231; cultural/local practice not recognised 234, 235; ecosystem governance principles 31; managing priorities 231–232, 294, 308; mobile ecosystems, governance challenges 81–82; participatory governance and power dynamics 232, **232–233**, 234, 263, 295; payments for ecosystem services (PES) 15–16; social impacts, wellbeing analysis research 224–226, *225*, 236–237; trade-offs, conservation and human wellbeing 227–230, **227–229**, 247–248, **293–294**; trade-offs, conservation implications 230–231, *230*, 235–236

Qin, Hua 83

Rakotonarivo, O Sarobidy **163**
Ramirez-Gomez, Sara OI 183
Rasolofoson, Ranaivo 164–165
Raworth, Kate 60

reciprocal water agreements (RWAs) **115**, **133**, 134, 136, 137
Redman, Charles 70
Reducing Emissions from Deforestation and Forest Degradation (REDD+): gender issues 265–266; local justice failures 34, 228; multi-level governance 167; payments for ecosystem services (PES) **191**, 196; project 'safeguards' and inequalities 149, 161, **163**, 197, 198
Reed, James 166–167
resilience: analytical approach 51; concept 42, 273–274, **274**; decline and 'flickering' 65, 70; as ecosystem service 15; improvement in, through ecosystem restoration 147–148
resilience: analytical approach 51; concept 42, 273–274, **274**; decline and 'flickering' 65, 70; as ecosystem service 15; gendered activities and perspectives **258**, 259–260, 262; improvement in, through ecosystem restoration 147–148; livelihood mobility 78–79, 80, 86; marine and coastal ecosystems; 291; peri-urban integration issues 121–122; research advances, SES approach 48, 49, 50; social ecological diversity 44–45; system theories 55
resilience and wellbeing: concepts and applications 273–274, **274**; ecosystem services, resilience approach 281–282; human/ecosystem feedbacks 279–280; power dynamics and inequalities 275–277, **276**, 283–284; scale and change in ecosystem services 280–281; social theories and resilience thinking 282–283
resilience research 48
resource-dependent households: biodiversity offsetting inequalities 149, 161, **163**; ecosystem services, reduced access and poverty 131, 133–134, 149; ecosystem service variability and poverty links 78, 86; land use intensification and wellbeing outcomes **100**, 102, **104**, 105, 249–250; livelihood insecurity and fertility choice 88–89; peri-urban agriculture, benefits and risks **114**, 117–118
Rey-Benayas, José M 147–148
Reyers, Belinda: ecosystem service co-production 13, 50; SES framework 41
Rideout, Alasdair 129

Rockström, Johan 56, 58, 62
Roe, Dilys 148
Roman, Joe 291
Rwanda: farming/forestry rights 25, 106, 248–249, 275

safe operating spaces: concept 56; and 'doughnut' model 60; regional safe and just spaces 60, *61*, 62; safe, cautionary and dangerous 57, 58; social foundation 60, 62
Samii, Cyrus 196
satellite imagery 179
Schlosberg, David **24**
Schreckenberg, Kate 31, 165, 198
Sen, Amartya 245, 276
Shelley, BG 194
Sikor, Thomas 31, 161, 196, 251
social-ecological systems (SES): concepts and definitions **40**; cross-scale dynamics 42, 44, *45*, 50–51, 308; diversity and multidimensional services 44, 46–47, *46*, 50; ecosystem restoration, research asset 152–153; ESPA research and evaluations 43, 47–51; interactions and feedback 43, 50, 307; limits and thresholds, defining metrics 62–63, *64*, 65–70, *66*, *68*; non-linearities 47–48, 50; polycentric governance 176–177; poverty alleviation, conceptual linkage *41*; principal elements 40, 42; research and practice development 4–5, 12, 51–52; resilience 48, 51
social-ecological 'toy model': fisheries management 46, *46*; gendered trade-offs, coastal fishery 263, **264**; trade-offs, coastal fishery 67, **182**, 182–183, 249–250
socio-ecological reductionism **248**, 248–249
South Africa: Environmental Public Works Programme 207, **208**, 211; gender and ecosystem service use 262; Land User Incentive (LUI) 213; migration and remittance flows 83; operating space analysis 60, 62
stakeholders: community-based governance 163–166, **164**; cross-scale dynamics 44; decision making, equity issues 23, 33; education challenges 70; environmental policy, justice gaps 27–29; financial mechanism limitations 27, 31–32; fishing regulation and equity 23, 81, 165, 296; forest management and power dynamics 23, 33, **115**, 118, 197, 250;

indigenous peoples' inequalities 25, 275, 309–310; land use intensification and food security issues 102, **104**, 105, 106, 131; local communities undervalued 23, 25, 29, 248–249; peri-urban agriculture, urbanisation impacts **114**; PES projects and inequalities 197–198; protected areas, guidance principles 31; protected areas, trade-offs and governance **227–229**, 227–232, **232–233**, 234–236, 247–248; resources and governance issues **115**, 118; trade-offs, modelling of 67
Steffen, Will 58
sub-Saharan Africa: ecosystem service maps 184; multidimensional wellbeing 248–249; protected areas, trade-offs and governance **232–233**; Sahel region, re-greening project 150; trade-offs, conservation and human wellbeing 292, **293–294**
Suich, Helen 44, 65, 278
Sustainable Development Goals (SDGs): governance challenges xxi–xxii; 307, 312–313; inclusivity policy 257; land use intensification, role in 95, 107; marine sustainability (SDG 14) 291, **293**, 294, 298; resilience and wellbeing 273
Sustainable Livelihoods Framework 6–7
systems theories 55
Szaboova, Lucy 48

Tannous, Natalie 292, **293–294**, 294
Tanzania: coastal livelihoods 260, 262; forest management, stakeholder equity 23, 164, **164**, 165, 180; wildlife management areas (WMAs) 165–166, **170**, 228, *230*, 231, 235
The Economics of Ecosystems and Biodiversity (TEEB) 4, 6, 7, *41*
Thom, René 55
tipping points: identifying system transitions 43, 47–48, 50, 58, 279; regional ecosystems 63, 65, 279
trade-offs *see* ecosystem service trade-offs

Uganda 86, **87**; Trees for Global Benefit project 150, 197, 198, **209**, 212, **215**, 217
UN Convention to Combat Deforestation (UNCCD) **143**
UN Framework Convention for Climate Change (UNFCCC) **143**, 167

United Kingdom National Ecosystem Assessment (UK NEA) 4, 6, 11
United Nations (UN): Agenda 2030 51, 257, 273; ecosystem restoration initiatives **143**; environmental policy development 55–56; marine ecosystem protection **293**, 294, 297; Special Rapporteur on Human Rights and the Environment 292
Uraguchi, Zenebe 212
urban ecosystems and services: ecosystem service and poverty alleviation, analysis framework 119–121, *120*; migration and provisioning challenges 89; peri-urban ecosystems and poverty links 117–118; peri-urban governance issues 116; peri-urban integration issues 118–119, 121–122; peri-urban transformations 113, **113–115**, 116; population dynamics 111; research and policy developments 111–113
US Environmental Protection Agency **25**

Van Hecken, Gert 198
van Rooyen, Carina 292, **293–294**, 294
Vatn, Arild 197
Verburg, Peter H 67
Vietnam 83, 85
Visseren-Hamakers, Ingrid 196
Vivekanandan, Vriddagiri 247–248
von Maltitz, Graham 279–280

Wang, Rong 44, 47, 60, *61*
water management: citizen science applications 180; cross-scale dynamics 44, 281; forests, impact on hydrological cycle 127–129; local community involvement 32, 134–135; non-linearities research 46; payments for ecosystem services (PES) 135–136, 137; peri-urban transformation impacts **114**; power dynamics and supply issues 131, 137–138; reciprocal water agreements (RWAs) **115**, **133**, 134, 136, 137; safe and just operating space 60, *61*; system transition and water equality 63, *64*; transboundary issues 33; universal access 27; wastewater issues 32, 33, **114**
Wei, Yongping 32, 183–184
wellbeing *see* multidimensional wellbeing; resilience and wellbeing
Willcock, Simon 47–48, 184
World Bank: Biocarbon Fund **143**; Voices of the Poor (VoP) study 12, 245
Wunder, Sven 190, 192, 195

Yuan, Zhen 151–152

Zeitoun, Mark 33
Zhang, Ke 44, 48, **102**
Zimmer, Anna 33
Zoomers, EB 166
Zulkafli, Zed 47, 184, **185**